REEL TRACKS

Australian Feature Film Music and Cultural Identities

Edited by
Rebecca Coyle

John Libbey
JL
LONDON · PARIS · ROME · SYDNEY
perfect
beat
publications

Cataloguing in Publication Data

Reel Tracks: Australian Feature Film Music and Cultural Identities

Bibliography.
Includes index.

1. Australian Cinema   2. Film Music.   I. Coyle, Rebecca (1956–).

ISBN: 0 86196 658 9 (Paperback)

Design and Setting by John Libbey Publishing
Front Cover: Image from Japanese Story *courtesy of Sue Maslin*

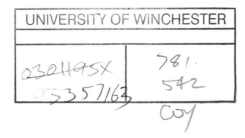
Published by
John Libbey Publishing, Box 276, Eastleigh SO50 5YS, UK
e-mail: john.libbey@libertysurf.fr; web site: www.johnlibbey.com

Orders: **Book Representation & Distribution Ltd**. info@bookreps.com

Distributed in North America by **Indiana University Press**, 601 North Morton St,
Bloomington, IN 47404, USA. www.iupress.indiana.edu

Distributed in Australasia by **Elsevier Australia**, 30–52 Smidmore Street,
Marrickville NSW 2204, Australia. www.elsevier.com.au

Distributed in Japan by **United Publishers Services Ltd**,
1-32-5 Higashi-shinagawa, Shinagawa-ku, Tokyo 140-0002, Japan. info@ups.co.jp

Printed in Malaysia by Vivar Printing Sdn. Bhd., 48000 Rawang,
Selangor.

Contents

Acknowledgements

This anthology would not have been completed without assistance from many people. Thanks first of all to those authors who agreed to prepare chapters and undertake extensive research for their contributions. Thanks also to those filmmakers, composers, sound personnel, producers, and film distributors who assisted in many various ways with research. Specific names are listed at the end of several chapters and thanks to those cited as interviewees. Thanks to librarians at Southern Cross University and Macquarie University, and Sarah Sanderson in the AFI Library in Melbourne. Thanks also to my colleagues in the School of Arts, Southern Cross University for various assistances in research, technical advice and moral support. I wish to thank others for their help: Perfect Beat Publications and John Libbey for enthusiasm for the project, John Whiteoak for initial tips on approaching publishers, Jerome Madulid for research, the Coyle clan for general support, Ruth and Roy Hayward for childcare support and refreshments, Philip Hayward for innumerable assistances throughout the project, and Rosa and Amy for those gorgeous cuddles after long periods on screen.

ILLUSTRATIONS

Thanks to the following for provision of illustrative material: Robert Connolly for *The Boys* image; Sue Maslin for *Japanese Story* images; and Tait Brady and Rachel Pemberton for *Lantana* images (courtesy of Jan Chapman).

Introduction

FILM MUSIC MNEMONICS: Australian Cinema Scores in the 1990s and 2000s

REBECCA COYLE

Reel Tracks consolidates and expands on the studies provided in an earlier anthology titled *Screen Scores* (Coyle, 1998) that offered models for analysis of film music in Australian features. This approach has been extended in *Reel Tracks* and applied to feature films released in the millennial transition period. *Reel Tracks* specifically deals with studies of Australian films released in the 1990s and early 2000s, concentrating on aspects of their music, and examining how the music tracks speak for notions of contemporary cultural identities. The chapters in this book indicate changes that have occurred in film and film music production in Australia and also in film music analysis. Most obviously, the use of 'reel' in the title refers to the original film production artefact while also indirectly referring to the manner in which both this and the earlier anthology have made a case for the significance of film music to be realised in film and music analysis. While the music cannot be 'seen' as such (even when performers appear onscreen), its impact on and contribution to the audio-visual text – the 'reel' – is decidedly 'real'.

In relation to how the music is interpreted in an audio-visual work, most chapters do not offer musicological studies of film music but examinations of the musical operations within a complex set of practices and aesthetics. Many of the chapters address sounds and sound design as integral to and informing the music track, for instance, Melissa Iocco's and Anna Hickey-Moody's chapter on *Bad Boy Bubby* (dir: Rolf de Heer, 1993), Mark Evans's discussion of Frank Lipson's sound design for *Chopper* (dir: Andrew Dominik, 2000), and my interview with Andrew Plain, supervising sound designer for *Lantana* (dir: Ray Lawrence, 2001).

As with *Screen Scores*, this book addresses Australian films, an identifying element that requires some explication. The categorisation of a film (or, indeed, any other cultural artefact) as 'Australian' goes beyond the nationality or self-identification of the central production personnel, the film funding sources, location of the screenplay or other empirical elements. It also raises issues of cultural perception of images and sounds as being able to stand for 'Australia'. There is a sequential argument here, building from the relationship of music to Australian film, of film to national identities, and (therefore) of film music to national identities.

Midway through the last decade, a major event enabled a set of strongly stated signifiers of Australian identity/ies to be made available globally. Most importantly, this event – the Olympic Games held in Sydney in 2000 – drew markedly on Australian films and film music to make such statements. Subsequently, vexed issues of national identity and identification resurfaced after momentous events threatening security in different countries occurred in the early 2000s. These events at once highlighted those characteristics that bring 'us' together (in an inclusive model of nation) as well as spotlighted differentiating elements (whether religious, ideological, linguistic or broadly cultural). Furthermore, these events revised and strengthened international allegiances, for example, the association of Australia with the USA, UK and other countries in the Gulf conflicts. Inevitably, war and its after effects – including movements of people from one place to another – invigorate disputes over national boundaries, whether geographic or symbolic. At the same time, the 2004 Free Trade Agreement between Australia and the USA, while largely a negotiated deal on agricultural and industrial arrangements, is touted to have major implications for Australian culture by restricting or weakening Australia's control over media content that operates via production quotas and subsidies[1]. Such concerns[2] speak to the etymology of 'identity' where its definition includes both those aspects that are points of "sameness or likeness" (Delbridge et al, 2001: 944) as well as marking out individuality – "condition, character or distinguishing features of persons or things" (ibid).

Engaging with and reflecting this emphasis on identity/ies, this anthology focuses on the ways in which Australian feature film music draws upon similar identifying elements, as well as on those points where distinct divergences occur. While, in some cases, the chapters illustrate common approaches to music (for example, due to the same composers working on a number of scores, or similarity of compositional approach), at the same time, they represent a period in which markedly divergent approaches are also apparent. In addition, the similarities in approach seem to be informed more by industry factors affecting composers (and other music personnel such as music supervisors) than by developments in a unique Australian 'sound' or identifiable musical style.

In this introduction, I will discuss identifying markers in Australian cinema as they are informed by film music, then refer to film music analytical methods. I will start with a brief discussion of terms and terminology adopted for this anthology.

I: Terms and terminology

Despite the growth in film music analysis in the last twenty years, film sound has only recently developed a set of terms specific to it, rather than borrowed from film studies or music. But even these terms are not necessarily widely used and/or accepted. Furthermore, terms used in film music analysis tend to be informed by and reflective of specific research methods and approaches. In his *Sound Theory, Sound Practice* (1992), Rick Altman noted this situation and showed how specific musical terms are often inappropriate for discussing film sound. He proposed that future film sound studies devise a "new vocabulary, more attuned to the way in which film sound makes, rather than merely possesses, meaning" (1992: 249) and the neologisms offered by Michel Chion (1994) also offer a seminal contribution to this project. For this anthology, it is necessary to define interpretations of terminology used, ones that derive from reactions to some 'standard' – often problematic – applications of various relevant film sound and music concepts.

The term 'soundtrack' itself requires definition. 'Soundtrack' is commonly used to mean two different elements of a film, namely, the film's sound (especially the music) track, and its related soundtrack album. The loose use of 'soundtrack' in conjunction with a 'soundtrack album' encompasses a misperception about the nature of an album product that uses sound items from a film in an audio-only format. The manner in which items are selected for this medium, the remixes accomplished for the album's items and their relationship to the actual film music track and narrative, inform a different production outcome. Mark Evans refers to this phenomenon in relation to the music track and soundtrack CD for *Chopper*. Another use of the term 'soundtrack' mistakenly assumes that it specifically refers to the film's music – although the music is highly mediated by other film sounds such as various forms of the voice (dialogue, voice-over, etc), sound effects and atmosphere, as well as by the (various post-production) mix(es). Such usage generalises the music into a continuous, coherent whole (despite the fact that film music is not always consumed as such) and also marginalises the other sound components of the film.

A distinction between soundtrack albums and the sound elements of a film in this volume is indicated by the use of 'soundtrack' to indicate album and 'sound track' (with a space) to indicate film sound accompanying an image track. Overall this book uses specific interpretations of 'sound track' to mean the entire sound mix of the film, and 'soundtrack album' to mean the audio package distributed via music suppliers. Furthermore, 'music track' distinguishes the musical component of the sound track from other sounds.

A further loosely-used term is that of the film 'score'. This can literally mean the notated musical cues drawn up by the composer and/or arranger/orchestrator to guide musicians in their performance for the film music. Such scores are less commonly available as composers write, record, edit and mix their cues using computer software packages. More generally, the term 'score' is used to mean the recorded cues composed and produced by the *original music* composer, and thus does not include *songs* or other musical items included in the film music track that were not composed specifically for the film or by its 'original music' composer. This suggests that the composer's role does not encompass re-arranging, remixing, re-recording or composing variations of songs. In fact, as Jude Magee's chapter shows in the case of Ross Edwards's music for *Paradise Road* (dir: Bruce

3

Beresford, 1997), the composer's task can be much more than devising original music cues that may only amount to a few minutes of actual screen time. Consequently, in this volume, the term 'score' generally means *all* of the musics created for or included in the film sound track where the film composer has had some input to it, whether re-arranged existing songs or original music. Songs are distinguished from other cues by using the term 'songs' where they (or, as is more usually the case, excerpts of songs) operate as distinct items.

The term 'source music' is one of several used to describe musical items not originally written or recorded by the film composer. Indeed, like 'needledrop tracks', 'source music' usually indicates songs or musical items inserted into a music track with no composer intervention. Given that it is sometimes difficult to determine how a composer had input to the source music[3], the term is used more generally in this anthology to indicate items where little observable intervention has been made to the pre-recorded track. An awareness of the operation of source music is pertinent to an understanding of recent Australian cinema, as well as marketing strategies and the use of films as cultural 'ambassadors' for 'Australia'.

II: Sounding Australia

In September 2000, Australia's largest city, Sydney, hosted the Olympic Games. The marketing, promotion and spectacular Opening and Closing ceremonies of the Games offered vivid evocations of Australia as both a location and a 'nation'. In addition, signifiers of popular Australian films were highlighted in segments in both the Opening and Closing ceremonies. These effectively linked national identity with both recent film successes *and* their representational strategies. Furthermore, both Opening and Closing ceremonies used musical or musically based extracts to represent the particular films. This highlighted the significance of the film scores in their narrative constructions. As a pan-national event, the Olympic Games ceremonies are significant for their reference to the Australian social imaginary.

The ceremonies most obviously operated on dual levels. The Opening ceremony, in particular, utilised distinctly Australian imagery most accessible to a national audience. The Closing ceremony, by contrast, featured references to Australian international hit films and celebrities that promoted Australian global successes, offering internationally recognisable signifiers of Australia specifically via these filmic representations and public personnae.

The Sydney 2000 Olympics Opening ceremony, staged at the Homebush Stadium, incorporated a segment of orchestral music by Bruce Rowland originally composed for the film *The Man From Snowy River* (dir: George Miller, 1982). This accompanied a large group of horse riders dressed in Australian bush gear – such as akubra hats, drizabone coats and RM Williams boots. The riders suggested the central theme of the film. While based on the Banjo Paterson ballad about the capture of a runaway colt, the film concentrates on the coming-of-age of a young horseman. This can be understood as a metaphor for Australian colonialism and frontiership in settler history. For Australian audiences, this filmic reference significantly acknowledges the 'Revival' period in Australian cinema, after a lull in production from the 1930s to the 1960s. In terms of the music, the film stands for a period of Australian film music composition that emphasised through-composed and orchestral scores rather than popular pre-recorded songs frequently used in 1990s films.

The Olympics Closing ceremony reprised this celebration of Australian cinema in a more obvious manner. There were obligatory speeches, the Olympic flag hand-over from Sydney to Greece, and various anthems and musical performances (including Christine Anu's version of *My Island Home* [1995] evoking the Australian continent as a homogenous 'island'[4] and Savage Garden's euphoric *Affirmation* [1999]). Then two Australian films of the early 1990s, *Strictly Ballroom* (dir: Baz Luhrmann, 1992) and *The Adventures of Priscilla, Queen of the Desert* (dir: Stephan Elliott, 1994) were specifically eulogised. Ballroom dancing champions Jason Gilgerson and Peta Robie ran onto the central podium and commenced dancing to a simple duple metre beat that transformed into introductory instrumental samba music. Ballroom dancing couples of various ages and in different 'Latin' outfits streamed onto the racetrack. They were interspersed with dancers holding huge footprint placards and arrows above their heads, suggesting the type of footwork illustrations found in dance instruction manuals. In addition, floats with gigantic kewpie dolls in brightly coloured dresses moved around with the dancers. The television host announced "a night of celebration and a parade of all things uniquely Australian" by way of introducing John Paul Young[5]. Dressed in a silver suit, Young rose from a trapdoor in the podium and commenced singing a version of his hit song from the 1992 *Strictly Ballroom* film, *Love is in the Air* (originally written by Vanda/Young in 1976). Variously emphasising the duple metre, then the samba rhythm, the song incorporated three instrumental breaks that allowed dancers to demonstrate Samba, Waltz and a Voguing-style dance drawing upon Paso Doble and Tango movements.

This extended segment was followed by several musical performances by well-known Australian rock bands, including INXS, Midnight Oil and Yothu Yindi. It led into a dramatic entrance for pop diva Kylie Minogue, perched on a giant thong[6] float that was pulled by men dressed in old-fashioned body hugging swimsuits, reminiscent of early Bondi Beach lifesavers' outfits[7]. Accompanied by surf guitar music, Minogue transferred to a surfboard and 'swam' to the podium. Her outfit then changed from a Nikki Webster style beach dress[8] to a Las Vegas style showgirl outfit. Surrounded by stylishly suited male dancers, she sang Abba's *Dancing Queen* (1976), a song that was re-popularised in Australia through its connection to the central protagonist in the successful Australian feature film, *Muriel's Wedding* (dir: PJ Hogan, 1994). This segment moved into the introduction to several floats for so-called Australian 'living legends and icons', that is, Australians who have become internationally famous (especially in the USA). They included: golfer Greg Norman (known as 'The Shark' and hence the musical accompaniment of John Williams's theme for the film *Jaws* [dir: Steven Spielberg, 1975]); Elle Macpherson (known as 'The Body') atop a gigantic camera zoom lens; and Paul Hogan riding on a giant slouch hat

5

float and dressed in a 'Crocodile Dundee' outfit first presented in Peter Faiman's *Crocodile Dundee* (1986). These celebrities all gained their international reputations through audio-visual representations and are recognisable figures to USA and European audiences[9]. For example, Macpherson trades on her 'clean cut' Australian image, while Hogan exploits the laconic, outback adventurer image of Australian masculinity. These gender-informed performances then gave way to a sequence referring to a film featuring transsexual and cross-dressing characters, *The Adventures of Priscilla, Queen of the Desert* (henceforth *Priscilla*).

Individuals floats were followed by a lavender-painted bus similar to that used for the *Priscilla* film, bedecked with a huge pink wig and eyelashes. Figures in extravagant drag outfits walked beside the bus and carried a huge mascara brush and a powder puff. A silver gowned figure, with long silver drape floating upwards in the breeze, sat on a giant silver stiletto sandal mounted on the bus top. This was a direct reference to a core image used in the *Priscilla* film and in its promotional material. However, rather than miming to the extract of Verdi's *La Traviata* opera aria heard in two film scenes, this segment of the ceremony played CeCe Peniston's *Finally* (1991), the song used in the film for the climactic Alice Springs performance by the three central protagonists. This 'celebrities and film' segment of the Closing Ceremony concluded with Minogue, this time dressed in a long shimmering gown and accompanied by pink-suited male dancers (reminiscent of Madonna's music video for *Material Girl* [1985]), singing *On a Night Like This* (2000) while floats continued to circulate. The entire segment suggested a camp approach to the celebrities it acknowledged, and it gave a self-reflexive slant to what could have become a jingoistic nationalism literally embodied in a handful of individuals who had 'made it' in a particular prescribed manner, that is, in USA or European markets[10].

The segment's reliance on film references, particularly film *music* references, to carry its celebratory message suggested a curious situation. The filmic constructions of Australia presented in the fictional diegeses of the films were, in this context, allowed to stand for or seemingly represent (as in re-present) 'Australia'. Yet, inevitably, such film references do not so much represent 'the nation' but rather signal a set of filmic explorations of culture and place. The use of these film references for such public, internationally televised events enables a further examination of two main arguments: first, the relationship between Australian film music and national identities; and second, the particular role of source music (especially popular song) as specifically signifying both Australian film and Australian 'culture' per se.

This book explores the role of original music score in its own right in addition to its operation with source music. Several films studied in the following chapters centre upon different genres of popular music, for example, *Blackrock* (dir: Steven Vidler, 1997) draws largely upon popular grunge rock songs; *Paradise Road* focuses on popular classics; *Lantana* (dir: Ray Lawrence, 2001) features Cuban salsa tracks; and *One Night The Moon* (dir: Rachel Perkins, 2001) explores folk-style ballads. These song items are used to underline each film's preoccupation with broader concepts and their relations to Australian culture. For example, in *Lantana*, the dance tracks are used to highlight the development of relationships and intimacy in the central protagonists (a topic explored in Bruce Johnson's and Gaye Poole's chapter surveying musical elements used for sexuality and sexual encounters). The analyses demonstrate how the creation of original music in addition to the incorporation of source songs and other music tracks around these broad themes was a central concern for the film composers.

The chapters in this volume explore the vexatious relationship between musics derived from 'classical' music styles and those whose roots derive from popular song. Individual authors examine the work of these musics in five ways: as they operate separately; as they work in conjunction with each other; how they tie to image track and narrative; how they variously operate within film and music industrial and production contexts; and how they engage with broader social and cultural discourses. In doing so, their analyses challenge cinema and film analytical dualisms between: image and sound; classical music and popular song; 'underscore' and source music; original and pre-recorded music; and so on.

The investigation of relationships between component parts of film music tracks is a tantalising analytical project, especially given the dearth of material dealing with a holistic approach. Even in seminal film composing manuals like Fred Karlin and Rayburn Wright's *On The Track: A Guide to Contemporary Film Scoring* (1989), little direction is offered for how to deal with source songs. Their discussion of film scoring and source music (whether pre-recorded or remixed) is limited to a short entry covering just a few pages (in a volume of almost 600 pages). What has been missing from film sound and music analysis until recently is an in-depth discussion of the kinds of film music tracks detailed in several chapters in this volume, where the composer has little input to source songs but must variously work with and around them. Even Karlin and Wright largely assume that composers are working directly with songs that are being written specifically for the film (see Chapter 26: 524-545), rather than with existing recordings. Furthermore, there is little discussion of the kinds of reworking that composers must do on pre-recorded songs or musical items, ranging from creating new resolutions to entirely re-mixing the item.

In addition to case studying specific films, the chapters in this volume indicate the current state of play in film composition, that is, ranging from virtually entirely through-composed (for example, Alan John's score for *The Bank* [dir: Robert Connolly, 2001] discussed in Michael Hannan's chapter) to largely source songs (for example, in *Blackrock*). Australian composers are rarely required to actually write compositions that might function as theme songs or as hit songs from the film in their own right (see, for example, Smith's 1998 discussion of Henry Mancini's *Moon River* used in *Breakfast at Tiffany's* [dir: Blake Edwards, 1961]). Also few Australian composers are known for their skills in this regard, apart from Peter Best[11] and a handful of others. But an existing song (or songs) can become integral to narrative, as Philip Hayward observes in the use of Scott Walker's version of Bob Dylan's *I Threw It All Away* (1969) in his chapter discussing *To have and to hold* (dir: John Hillcoat, 1996). Australian composers are often expected to compose and arrange around pre-recorded songs. This in turn affects the manner by which film music tracks and their songs are analysed.

III: Analysing Popular Source Songs As Film Music

The issue of popular source music (especially songs) in Australian feature films continues to be contentious amongst composers, filmmakers, critics and consumers (both film audiences and soundtrack fans). The number and styles of popular music songs used in each film dictates the approach and contribution by the composers, often to the extent of marginalising their work (and even, in some cases, equating them with music editors). While the analyses included here indicate the value of composer input, they are not intended to offer a directive to future Australian feature filmmakers as to the necessity of original music incorporation into local films. Successful films can be made with little input from composers. However, having a composer involved in a film's music track can result in a more sophisticated sonic experience, as Tony Mitchell has outlined in his chapter on Clara Laws's collaborations with composers, and as Kate Winchester observes in her study of the music-informed creative process for *One Night The Moon*.

Increasingly, Australian filmmakers are calling upon the services of a music supervisor to assist in the popular music input of their productions. A music supervisor's role, according to researcher Jeff Smith in relation to the Hollywood industry, can include such tasks as:

> *the creation of a music budget, the supervision of various licensing arrangements, the negotiation of deals with composers and songwriters, and the safeguarding of the production company's publishing interests.* (1998: 209)

In Australia, however, well-respected music supervisor Christine Woodruff (interviewed in the course of research for my chapter on *Lantana*) argues that the role tends to be more "multi-functional" than it is in the USA, involving a great deal of licensing negotiations, as well as liaising with director, producer, composer, sound department, arranging recording sessions, budgeting, researching and suggesting songs for particular scenes, and negotiating soundtrack album deals.

A music supervisor can also determine who is chosen for film composer, as David Bell notes in labeling the music supervisor "a sort of musical casting director" (cited in Smith, 1998: 210). The input of such a music supervisor is considered of dubious value by many composers in the Australian film industry, who believe that music budgets for original composed and produced cues have been reduced due to the fees allocated to music supervision and song clearances[12].

In devoting so much discussion to analysis of popular music and source songs, I am attempting to *value* filmic emphases on source music rather than support arguments that the increasing use of source music represents a demise in 'genuine', that is, purely through-composed (especially so-called 'symphonic' or 'orchestral') film scores. At the same time, this is not to diminish the value and significance of through-composed scores, as Catherine Summerhayes's and Roger Hillman's chapter establishes with regard to Carl Vine's score for *beDevil* (dir: Tracey Moffatt, 1993). Rather, these analyses of film music tracks show how film music is complicated by popular songs used as source, offering a peculiarly multifaceted text for analyst and listener/viewer alike, as well as composer and other film production personnel. Although Rick Altman (1999) argues that early film exhibition practices show that film musical directors and composers have plundered various musical sources for film musical accompaniment (not merely European-inspired light classical music)[13], contemporary uses of source songs in film music tracks take this argument into another dimension. The difference between scores that are through-composed – however much based on 'source' music – and those relying on pre-recorded songs in the style of a 'compiled' score, is in the overall impression of the (musical) work. In a through-composition, the same kinds of rhythms, instrumentation, arrangements and/or orchestrations (in addition to compositional style) can be used to tie source music of different genres together with the film, and this sort of musical composition practice is explored by Michael Atherton in discussing David Hirschfelder's score for *Strictly Ballroom*. But in 'compiled' scores, pre-recorded songs can operate as stand-alone musical elements that relate only peripherally (if that) to original music cues[14], as evident in *Lantana*'s dance music tracks that are distinctly different to the improvisatory original music cues but have a specific function in the narrative.

In the sense referred to above, the overall 'sound' of film music, particularly from the perspective of the film viewer who leaves the cinema humming a popular song, is diverted from the composer. It is associated instead with the director whose individual tastes and background the film reflects, or the producer and/or music supervisor whose interests often lie in the business of the film production rather than its aesthetics[15]. Attention may also be directed to lyrical content of songs rather than performative and musical expression. This argument acknowledges the role of music more generally in informing director/producer inputs, that is, allowing for the specific musical interests of the director and/or producer/s in determining music choices. As such it may be regarded as an auteur approach to film analysis, criticism and reception/perception rather than recognising the collaborative team reality of film production[16]. As a consequence, films may become associated with songs and artist/band names, and with directors' musical tastes, rather than composers. Popular perception of PJ Hogan's *Muriel's Wedding* (1994) is a case in point here, as critic Lawrence Zion, in his argument that the film is Australia's greatest, acknowledges:

> [Muriel's Wedding's] *big comic moments are hysterically funny, especially when embracing music. Even non-ABBA fans known to this writer have willingly succumbed to Muriel and Rhonda's inspired lip-synching to ABBA's* Waterloo *video clip – now easily the most commonly referenced scene from the film.* (Zion, 2004: R4)

Yet, however much the director/producer and/or music supervisor intervene or dictate the music cues (whether 'overscore' or 'underscore', source or original music), the film music cannot entirely reflect their input. The contribution of a composer will always affect a set of images, modifying and manipulating their emotive impact. This phenomenon is noted by composer Elizabeth Drake in relation to resolving music chords used in *Japanese Story* (dir: Sue Brooks, 2003) that were criticised by screenwriter Alison Tilson as pre-emptive of the on-screen action (discussed in Johnson's and Poole's chapter). Musical impact is partly due to the musical medium that, of course, speaks to an entirely different sensual experience. In addition, the composer's contribution relates to the nature of that particular artist's work. So film music reflects both another medium and another individual's (or musical team's) 'take' on the story and emotions of the film.

Apart from the challenges that popular source songs offer to production practices, songs in Australian feature film music also question methodological approaches used for their analysis. If popular music is not necessarily well served by musicology as a methodological approach (as argued by McClary and Walser, 1990, and others), then film music that incorporates a significant amount of popular music may not greatly benefit from a detailed note-based musicological analysis. Popular music items require their own analytical approaches to production sound and mixing, vocal performance and rendition, and so on. In addition, the nature of film music's relation to the image and narrative means that the culture, history and literature of both music and film are brought into play in any film sound or music track analysis (as Helen O'Shea demonstrates in her discussion of the 'neo'-Celtic music in Gregor Jordan's 2001 *Ned Kelly*). Furthermore, film music analysis must refer to two sets of primary media industries: those connected with music and those with film, industries that are increasingly interconnected and thereby require interdisciplinary research and analysis. On an additional, broader level, developments in media industries influence each other; for example, the use of music video to promote soundtrack albums creates an obvious link with film (despite differences in form) while musicians are also perceived as being influenced in their style and musical imagery by film.

The analyses in this book cumulatively outline an approach to interpreting feature film music that is inclusive, and examine how various styles of music operate in *composite* film music tracks. The anthology is structured around three sections: 'Musical Identities' examining the cultural contextualisation of the music tracks and their constructions; 'Musical Sounds' exploring the interweaving of music with sound to create musical sound tracks; and 'Musicscapes' in which authors identify the specific operations of particular scores and composers. In her 2002 literature review of film music, Robynn Stilwell proposes to

> build theories from the ground up rather than from the top down. Rather than postulating how film works, we might investigate how individual films work. (2004: 47).

Along these lines, in *Reel Tracks*, each section includes one chapter that offers an overview approach to several films, followed by a number of chapters that case study one or two films.

The overlap of practice with critical theory is a contentious area of film studies analysis, and flows into the analysis of music tracks in these chapters. Robynn Stilwell opines: "[p]erhaps the greatest challenge to the study of film music is finding a balance between technical analysis and meaningful interpretation" (2002: 47-48). The three sections in *Reel Tracks* are prefaced with summaries of their chapters, and show how analytic and research methods for film music are as multifarious as the music tracks they signpost. Furthermore, the analyses show how the music can be read within discussions of cultural identity. When a film is perceived to somehow stand for a national culture, film songs from international sources complicate and/or question the nature of that culture. As Brian McFarlane notes, in relation to films adapted from Australian novels:

> *Art forms do not exist in a vacuum; they emerge from a particular state of culture, reflect and/or criticize aspects of the ideology of that culture, and they exist in relation to each other.* (1983: 17)

IV: The State of the (Australian Film Music) Nation

The role of source songs in Australian film music is connected to debates around local industry paternalism and national identity. There is a conflation of the argument for protection of local cultural products and industries (in the context of globalisation) with expectations for a set of national sounds, images and coherent 'identity', particularly in the most recent era of free trade negotiations. But preserving media industries in a local context does not mean that local artists can be assumed to bear the responsibility for a particular set of myths and meanings related to a generalised idea of 'Australia'. After all, ultimately these artists are operating as individuals in the context of a commercial industry. Nevertheless, filmmakers are not 'culture-free', and cannot escape a culturally-informed perspective. Even so, this does not commit them to carrying what Gill Branston terms the "burden of representation" (2000: 171), meaning that their films must "stand in for" (ibid) or represent certain perceived realities of specific or national groups.

Arguments about source songs reflect the ambivalence about the value of homegrown product experienced by settler Australians since virtually the earliest days of colonial settlement. The idea of 'value' and 'worth' immediately raises problems of how such judgments can be measured. Australians do not seem to have a problem with measuring national value via sporting achievements, for instance, but cultural products offer a less–easily measured set of artefacts. The media euphoria experienced after Australian sportspeople won 58 medals in the Sydney 2000 Olympics[17] reached new heights when International Olympics Committee President, Juan Antonio Samaranch, proclaimed the Sydney 2000 event to be "the best Olympic Games ever"[18]. This was interpreted as approval for the cultural and social product being offered by Sydney as host city for the Games. Australian cultural artefacts tend to be measured either according to international recognition (for instance, for Australian film, by international box office figures) or according to assumptions as to what is an "authentic" Australian product – and they can be found to be lacking either way.

This sort of confusion is apparent in comments made by Michael Gudinski, then Head of Australia's largest music company Mushroom Records, at a forum on globalisation held in 1999[19]. Gudinski noted that artists like Kylie Minogue and Savage Garden are not distinctively Australian but rather successful "in today's world, generally" (1999: 305). Furthermore, he continued, "The Australian public knows whether our artists are measuring up. There's an international standard" (ibid). In relation to the issue as to whether there is a special 'flavour' to Australian music, Gudinski acknowledged:

> Outside of Australia's indigenous artists... there really has never been a homegrown sound, a musical groundswell that is distinctively Australian, easily recognised the world over. From Johnny O'Keefe to silverchair, our popular music has been massively derived from the American and British artists we have been listening to and looking at. (ibid)

Like Gudinski, journalist Bruce Elder interprets Australian music from the perspective of rock and roll and finds it lacking, arguing:

> The story of Australian rock 'n' roll is a unique tale of cover versions and imitative styles propped up and sustained by that ugliest of Australian impulses: the insistence that if something is Australian it should not be criticised. (2001: 5)

Nevertheless, Gudinski also observed "there are musical acts that only make sense in their homeland" (1999: 317). This could equally well apply to film music where certain connotations interpreted within the texts will be accessible to Australia-raised viewers more than to those with minimal cultural connection to Australia, even though the musical texts do not originate in Australia.

Beyond the actual films discussed, this volume asks to what extent identity is determined by nationalist constructions, what part geographies (real and/or imagined) play in it, and how such geographically-informed identities are reflected in music. At its most basic, music is informed by the cultural history that results from musical institutions operating with inter-related public and industrial support. Music is affected by formal and informal education (and pedagogical orientations), and the work of musical institutions can be traced in musics arising from that culture. The media plays a role in the circulation and promotion of particular musics, reflecting and informing and contributing to musical operations. This was most evident in the Sydney 2000 Olympics ceremonies where the films represent cultural identity largely through *musical* items that signify key themes from the films. This is where the notion of place comes into the argument.

Cultural geographer Jeff Hopkins argues that a geography *in* film refers to geographical descriptions of the images on the screen, while a geography *of* film is bound up with the meanings produced from the representation of space and the implications of this in film. Furthermore, Hopkins contends:

> The meanings constituted through film do not simply reflect or report on space, place and society, but actively participate in the production and consumption of larger cultural systems of which they are a part. (1994: 50)

This anthology is not only premised on place (specifically *Australian* films) but also examines place on broader levels: in terms of actual geography and location; in relation to pre-ordained 'positions' in society imposed by various means; and a self-constructed cultural badging. The musics in the selected films have variously carved out political/social cultures, identity politics and environmental cultures. It is not irrelevant which cultures and locations are shown in a film, given that place and geography are inter-woven with culture (see Kress, 1988). Geography informs population movements, just as environment informs agriculture, and the constitution of a population inevitably affects its musical expression and cultural life. A nation's geography tailors the human behaviour within it and in turn results in what Catherine Simpson terms "place identity" (2000: 9). This 'place identity' provides a lens through which both filmmakers construct and consumers interpret or participate in film. Film sound and music are critical to the development of such a (metaphorical) lens – not for their literal representative nature (after all, film sound mixes are highly mediated and manipulated elements) but for the cultural connotations they carry with them. Just as definitions of nation carry information about who is *not* included as much as who *is* included in a national populace (as Jon Stratton argues in this volume), so film sound and music carry information about selective associations of sounds with particular locations.

Simpson cites filmmaker and critic Ross Gibson, arguing that, "particu-lar locations are charged with particular stories which ... arrange ideas, fears, aspirations, pleasures and pains spiritually in geographical patterns and temporally in narrative rhythms that can be experienced and re-expe-rienced" (ibid: 11). Just as knowledge of local (national) identity is formed by stories, and by filmmaking as a form of storytelling, so too do songs and music contribute to identity with their own stories. These are at once locating and dislocating, fixed to a time and place of origin, and speaking for universal impressions and ideas. Furthermore, a film that uses various musical resources, including popular music songs, draws upon a "virtual geography" (1994: 225) in McKenzie Wark's term, where cultural identity and value appear subject to flux. The music and songs are variously 'fixed' to the fictional time and place of the film story – or at least to each interpretation of the film text – rather than to literal specifics. As Marj Kibby observes, in *Rabbit-Proof Fence* (dir: Phillip Noyce, 2002), the non-specific musics and sounds used by Peter Gabriel with Andrew Skeoch and Sarah Koschak for the environmental recording team, Listening Earth, suggest floating signifiers of generalised 'world' music rather than specifics of Australia the continent or specific locations within Australia. They speak for the universal themes of longing, familial connection and injustice exposed in the narrative.

The films studied in this anthology highlight the various ways in which film music can identify 'Australia' as a geographic location and a set of sentiments, cultural imaginings and discourses. The film music establishes that 'nation' is only one force operating on the individual and, in fact, interwoven identities (around, for example, gender, sexuality and culture) cross national boundaries. The inflection on Australian sexuality that is supported and informed by musical explorations of and for sexual encoun-ters in recent Australian cinema is examined in Bruce Johnson's and Gaye Poole's chapter.

In terms of national identification, the films discussed in this volume draw upon both visual images and sound/music to address various ideas around what constitutes Australia as a place and people. For many settler Australians (especially those of Anglo/Irish origin), the millennium celebrations and Centenary of Federation events that followed the Sydney 2000 Olympic Games led to self-conscious analyses of national identity. Around this period, issues of ethnicity and multiculturalism were explored in a spate of (highly regarded) films such as *Looking for Alibrandi* (dir: Kate Woods, 1998), *Head On* (dir: Ana Kokkinos, 1998) and *The Wog Boy* (dir: Aleksi Vellis, 1999)[20] and this is discussed in Jon Stratton's chapter in relation to the films' (mainly popular source) music.

In any film, there is a (variously achieved) balance between specifically local and universal human experience. The literal specifics of geography as represented on-screen cannot be ignored and affect all aspects of the film (even to the point of the quality of light portrayed and the acoustics of spaces), just as specifics of the film (and music) industries from which the film derives are partial determinants of its content. National identity is therefore defined by occupation of a space as much as by community feelings and social imaginary. This line of argument about the association of representation with 'reality' can be applied to Australian cinema. Tom O'Regan contends:

> *Australian cinema will be always something more and something less than the representations critics make of it. Film-making is necessarily a mundane, ambiguous, multivalent, rhetorically strong assemblage within which the same resources permit and even encourage widely divergent uptakes by audiences, critics and film-makers. Film-makers pursue aesthetic concerns and social problematizations, not those currently in fashion in cultural criticism and government policy but of interest to diverse audiences.* (1996: 353)

The film references used in the Olympics ceremonies operate as aggregations of elements about national cinema rather than as cinema 'reflecting' nation. So while cinema requires 'nation' to operate within, nevertheless there is a relative autonomy between the two concepts. Yet this autonomous relationship between nation and filmic constructions was not recognised in the Sydney 2000 Olympic ceremonies. Instead, the ceremonies highlighted a definition of 'nation' that centres on its people's cultural imaginings (and desire for a particular kind of internationally-acclaimed success) over the political and economical 'nation-state'[21]. This use of the film references elides the fact that they primarily refer to (international) film culture, techniques, production practices and industries as much as they do to an Australian national imaginary. Furthermore, these aspects and concepts are integrally tied into the music.

The global identity sought by the Sydney 2000 Olympic Games' ceremonies presents a kind of oxymoron, asking how Australia can be both globally identifying and yet specifically – nationally – unique. This is played out in the specifics of the music in the films analysed in this anthology, offering models for film music in future Australian cinema. Stratton argues that, in order for Australian films to genuinely tackle multiple cultures in Australia, music tracks must come to terms with musical genres and styles, such as hip hop, that have been little used in film scores to this point. Of course, by choosing to concentrate on mainstream feature films, the book is necessarily skewed towards hegemonic discourses as well as mainstream industry practices[22]. A further project would examine 'arthouse', alternative, documentary, animation and short films, asking to what extent the musics and musical uses challenge mainstream practices.

Nevertheless, several films discussed in this volume were made on limited budgets that constrained decisions relating to the music track. Modest production budgets result in two main outcomes: first, as Jude Magee (1996) argues, musical scores (particularly in more recent films) are recorded by small to medium sized ensembles. Second, the absence of technical training facilities, music team structures, and readily available and purpose-built film orchestra and recording stages in Australia has meant that a set of common practices has not developed within the industry. This has led to what Magee terms "a distinctive individualism rather than a homogenous style" (1996: 150) that she sees as industry-driven rather than reflective of an Australian film music compositional 'school' as such. It is notable that several of the composers who feature in the films discussed in the following chapters have moved into film composition after experience in popular music performance or songwriting, for example, David Bridie, Paul Kelly and Mick Harvey. The analyses of their music scores suggest that these composers use a different approach to composition and conceptualising the music tracks, and represent a 'new generation' of film composer. In one example, the improvisatory approach to cue construction for *Lantana*, undertaken by regular collaborators, Paul Kelly, Shane O'Mara, Bruce Haymes, Steve Hadley and Peter Luscombe, was quite different to the notated orchestral score approach associated with Hollywood studio productions. Atherton's chapter includes discussion of Peter Weir's use of three composers for his Hollywood production, *Master and Commander: The Far Side of the World* (2003), offering another challenge to more commonly accepted approaches, especially for a production undertaken in Los Angeles. One of the composers, Iva Davies, argues that his background in popular music informed his approach to the task of composing the score:

> the city of LA is full of film school writers whose entire raison d'etre is to write film music – and their lives are measured by those soundtrack albums – so they've got an agenda which can be quite contrary to how well the music supports the film. They want to end up like Leonard Bernstein or whoever, creating concert pieces. But that's nothing like my approach. Right from the beginning there wasn't any question of what my job was. My job was to give the Director what he required, for better or for worse. I had no agenda. That was the job and it was a luxury for me because I've got other stuff that I do which exists outside this world – other projects that are 100 percent about the music. (in Stewart, 2003: 45)

Debates around national identification have been revisited in recent times, taking into account current factors relating to free trade negotiations, as well as border protection and national security. While the film industry is increasingly driven to co-productions and several Australian directors use

15

Australian production crew and facilities for Hollywood film productions, these question the nature of 'local' productions. At the same time, Brian Rosen, appointed Chief Executive of the Film Finance Corporation in 2004 after twenty years as a film producer, argues that this crucial funding agency for Australian cinema should focus larger budgets on fewer films and directors with track record, rather than distribute more small amounts largely to first-time directors (see Urban, 2004). This questions the effect of such a policy on music budgets for Australian features. While the paucity of (original) music budgets for Australian films is frequently decried by Australian film composers (see Tyson-Chew, 2003; and Michael Atherton's chapter in this volume), bigger budgets do not necessarily mean more funding for Australian composers. In fact, the funding may well end up in the hands of music supervisors to cover music clearance costs for international tracks, or be directed to well-known international composers. In this case, it is worth continuing to debate the relation of home-grown compositional style and practices to Australian film. If there is some way in which the sound of Australian film correlates with composer background, then this continues to be a critical line of argument. At the most obvious level as well, funding for Australian composers ensures their livelihoods in this competitive field of creative endeavour and continued Australian musical input to Australian stories[23].

The multifaceted nature of music in the Australian feature films in this volume is analogous with key debates in representation studies (see Branston, 2000; and Barker, 2000). Such studies present the problem of how to acknowledge difference and hybridity while at the same time recognising the socially shared aspects of cultures, that is, aspects that unite people across gender, race and cultural identifications, as well as class and social divisions. Given that film music serves as both a bonding agent across scenes and edited moments, locations and characters, *in addition to* a pointer to difference via individual themes, motifs and aesthetics, then film music engages in such a debate. In other words, film music in such contemporary uses speaks for characters and filmmakers, and to audiences and social groups, with a complex set of ideas at once centred on *shared* pleasures, memories and the familiar as well as on *unique* stories and idiosyncrasies. In this sense, film music enables interpretations of identity as fluid. Film music – sometimes problematically – proposes sets of identities that can change according to time, place and circumstance. Such changes are inevitably chameleon-like and linked to social situations so that, rather than individual identity standing in opposition to social awareness, they interrelate. Perhaps, paradoxically, it is the interrelation of musics from various genres and national cultures (as well as production and compositional approaches) that forms the most fertile ground for constructing and understanding Australian identity in national cinema. With these tunes, motifs and arrangements in our ears, we may well proceed more confidently into the future.

Thanks to Bruce Johnson for research tips and to Philip Hayward for comments on an early draft.

Notes

1. This system is increasingly challenged by co-productions, as evidenced by the Australian local claims for Green Card (dir: Peter Weir, 1990).

2. Represented in the 'free2baustralian.org.au' website, http://www.alliance.org.au/free2baustralian

3. For example, while several popular music source songs are used in a memorable way in *Priscilla*, the composer Guy Gross had input to the tracks by writing and recording resolving endings. See Chapter 5: '"Drag Queens in the Outback": Nation, Gender and Performance in *Priscilla*'s music', in Coyle, R (2003: 214–284).

4. Somewhat ironically for an Australian of Torres Strait Islander descent. While *My Island Home* is now irrevocably associated with Anu's release of a cover version in 1995, the song was originally written by Neil Murray for the Central Australian Aboriginal Warumpi Band in the late 1980s. Creswell and Fabinyi claim this song to be "a defacto national anthem" (2000: 186).

5. It is notable that, while Olympics ceremonies director Ric Birch wanted to showcase Australian artists, many of those who performed were born overseas. This reflects the heterogeneous nature of Australian society. Guiffre (2000) explores the popular press response to the artists chosen that debated definitions of 'Australian' and nationalist essentialism.

6. Sometimes known as a 'flip-flop'; a cheap informal plastic sandal worn by Australians, mainly at the beach.

7. The references to gay and camp culture in Minogue's act, for a 'show' located in Sydney, are worthy of examination elsewhere, along with her self-reflexive reference to her own image and career transformations. (Bondi Beach is a popular tourist destination in Sydney.)

8. 14-year old Webster was used in the Opening Ceremony, dressed in a beach dress, and representing the relative youth of European settlement in Australia.

9. *Sirens* (dir: John Duigan, 1994) starring Macpherson and *Crocodile Dundee* (dir: Peter Faiman, 1986) are both regularly screened on US cable television.

10. After another musical performance segment by various well known musicians (including Men At Work performing their tongue-in-cheek 1980 hit song *Down Under*) the Closing ceremony culminated in the late popular country singer Slim Dusty performing *Waltzing Matilda* (a song self-consciously referred to in several Australian films).

11. Best wrote songs for several significant Australian films including the Barry McKenzie films from the 1970s, the 1995 version of the classic Australian tale *On Our Selection* with two tracks sung by country folk balladeer John Williamson, and also for Chris Kennedy's *Doing Time for Patsy Cline* (2001). See two forthcoming works: Coyle, R (forthcoming 2005) 'Nashville And Back – Country Music And Film Representation In *Doing Time For Patsy Cline* 'in Evans, M and Walden, G (eds); and Coyle, R and Hannan, M (2004) 'Bazza's Bawdy Ballads... And Other Aspects of the Barry McKenzie Film Musics', conference paper for Credits Rolling! 12th Biennial Conference of the Film and History Association of Australia and New Zealand.

12. The grievance relates to the budgetary allocations. Australian films do not necessarily have smaller music allocations in film budgets to equivalent film industries elsewhere but more of the music budgets appears to be spent on music clearance and supervision and less directed to the original music composer. Analysing why this is so would make a useful industry study.

13. Diane Napthali notes the frequent use of "previously composed music" in early Australian (sound era) cinema (1999: 333). Noting how film music was "disregarded by critics and the public", she argues:

    The perception was that locally composed film music was an art form outside the existing musical heritage of Australia. That it did not arouse interest suggests it may have been

17

dismissed as unimaginative or lacking originality or verve, with the inference that it was neither technically accomplished nor artistic enough to flourish. (ibid)

Furthermore, Napthali pursues this argument in relation to recent films, arguing that, "[t]he practice of including previously composed (and well-known) music in scores to underpin plot developments has continued" (ibid: 334). Napthali's analysis offers two important points relevant to this chapter. First, it examines the object of analysis by looking from the outside in, hearing Australian film music primarily from a global perspective. This means that the work of the Australian musicians and composers of this period is not considered significant in its own right. For example, despite the fact that cues were provided from external sources, the performance of pre-composed cues *in specific Australian contexts* must have created a particular cinematic/musical event relevant to Australia. Second, the details of the composer's or performer's work emphasises the supposed 'derivative' nature of it without due emphasis given to specific local content. While it is not relevant in this chapter to tackle such arguments about earlier cinema, they establish research questions pertaining to the contemporary era and relevant to this set of arguments.

14. A further problem associated with an over-emphasis on source music and its negative effects is the manner in which the analysis of popular songs can overshadow discussion of other sounds in the film sound track. This subject merits further examination elsewhere.

15. It may also be associated with the actor-performer of the song, for instance, in the case of Baz Luhrmann's *Moulin Rouge* (2001), Ewan McGregor singing *Your Song* (Elton John/Bernie Taupin, 1970) and Nicole Kidman, *One Day I'll Fly Away* (Will Jennings/Joe Sample, 1980) and jointly singing *Come What May* (David Baerwald, 1957) and other popular songs.

16. This issue is discussed in relation to Peter Weir's approach to source music, often at the expense of original music cues, in Johnson and Poole (1998).

17. Taken further in the media coverage of the medal tally after the Athens 2004 Olympics where Australian sportspeople achieved 49 medals and gained 3rd place in the medals tally when measured according to medals per population (see Australian Bureau of Statistics Media Release [30/08/2004] 'ABS medal tally: Australia finishes third', http://www.abs.gov.au/abs).

18. In his speech at the Closing Ceremony.

19. From *The Age*, July 15, 1999, cited in Terrill (2000).

20. Also, in the early 21st century, media-driven current affairs dealing with so-called 'boat people' and asylum seekers in detention have triggered (often poorly informed) reflections of multicultural social policies, immigration and Australian cultural identity.

21. Although the Closing Ceremony included politically-charged 'statements' by Midnight Oil performing their 1988 hit song *Beds Are Burning* followed by Yothu Yindi performing their land rights song *Treaty* (1999). The television coverage featured cuts to camera close-ups of Prime Minister John Howard's unexpressive response to the performances.

22. However, this is a relative construction, given that the anthology does not feature some of the films that attracted the highest box office returns (such as *Strictly Ballroom*, *Priscilla* or Baz Lurhmann's 2001 Hollywood-produced film, *Moulin Rouge*).

23. Interest in work in Hollywood productions is evident in the tone and approach of several articles in the special issue of *Sounds Australian* journal n61, 2003, titled 'Australian Screen Music: The Art and Craft of Composing to Moving Image', edited by AGSC chair, Art Phillips with Yantra de Vilder.

Section I:
MUSICAL IDENTITIES

These chapters associate the film music in specific case studies with cultural and social contexts informing their narratives and musical approaches. Film music in these chapters is shown to reflect and also to inform cultural interests and concerns. The chapters range from: specific working class cultures in the east coast city of Newcastle; generalised 'Celtic' traits informing settler identity; expatriate European exploits in the Pacific; and Chinese-Australian and migrant Chinese experiences; to an overview of multiculturalist ideologies explored in a handful of recent Australian feature films.

Exploring specifics of place identity, Shane Homan argues that the film music tracks in *Blackrock* (dir: Steven Vidler, 1997) and *Bootmen* (dir: Dein Perry, 2000) contribute significantly – although differently – to an imagined "post-rust belt" identity for Novocastrians[1]. Addressing the 'compiled score' approach used in these films, Homan discusses the use of Oz Rock source songs to explore youth values, masculinity and class.

In Chapter Two, Helen O'Shea considers changes in Australian identifications with the Irish-Australian collective imaginary by comparing musical uses in two film versions of the Ned Kelly story – Tony Richardson's release in 1970 and Gregor Jordan's in 2003. In the 30 or so years between these productions, contemporary attitudes to diasporic Irish cultural representation have changed to the point where O'Shea argues that Jordan offers a "new-age Ned" in his recent film. Furthermore, O'Shea observes that the music presents an identification with an internationalised Celtic cultural sensibility rather than a specifically Australian or Irish-Australian perspective.

In his discussion of John Hillcoat's *To have and to hold* (1996) and Bill Bennett's *In a Savage Land* (1998), Philip Hayward explores representations of white angst in Papua New Guinea. Hayward argues that the films follow a representational trajectory of "fantasy, anxiety and nostalgia" by Europeans and Australians towards PNG. Both films involved composers from

19

experimental music backgrounds: Nick Cave, Mick Harvey and Blixa Bargeld for the former, and David Bridie (well known for his collaborations with PNG musicians through Melbourne band Not Drowning, Waving) for Bennett's production. As significant, though, are the various uses of local sounds on both films and soundtrack CDs, for example, a recording by Goroka-based Raun Raun Theatre for *To have and to hold*, and recordings from the Trobriand Islands for *In a Savage Land*.

Tony Mitchell discusses two films by Hong Kong-Australian director, Clara Law that were released in Australia: *Floating Life* (1997) and *The Goddess of 1967* (2001). *Floating Life* emphasises music composed by Davood Tabrizi and performed by members of the Chinese Opera Arts Orchestra together with western-style keyboard, guitar and percussion. Following the two central protagonists – a Japanese man and Irish-Australian woman – as they travel in Australia, Jen Andersen's music in *The Goddess of 1967* employs Japanese shakuhachi and ken tieu, Vietnamese dan trahn, plus violin, tin whistle, 'whirly' and Romany-style vocalisations. Both films, Mitchell argues, draw on music to carry significant emotional content of key scenes, although the effect is achieved in different ways. These musical explorations effectively assist Laws's ongoing engagement with themes of migration, cultural dis/placement and diaspora.

This section concludes with Jon Stratton's discussion of several significant films engaging with multiculturalist ideals in Australia. Stratton argues that mainstream Australian cinema has not yet come to terms with the cultural mix understood as reality for young, urban-dwelling ethnic audiences. Stratton concludes that, with few exceptions, Australian films that represent multiculturalism have largely accepted and reproduced Anglo-Australian hegemony in Australian society and this is supported in the film music. Discussing primarily the source music used in *Head On* (dir: Ana Kokkinos, 1999), *The Wog Boy* (dir: Aleksi Vellis, 1999), *Looking for Alibrandi* (dir: Kate Woods, 2001) and *Fat Pizza* (dir: Paul Fenech, 2003), Stratton connects rock music and Australian film with "core-periphery multiculturalism", distinguishing 'skips' from 'wogs'. It may be that these issues can be tracked differently in less mainstream films, the short film sector and documentaries as subjects for further studies. Meanwhile, Stratton challenges Australian feature filmmakers to a more inclusive model of 'multicultural' Australia in their selections and uses of popular source music.

Note

1.   Inhabitants of the New South Wales city of Newcastle.

Chapter One

SOUNDSCAPES OF SURF AND STEEL:
Blackrock and *Bootmen*

SHANE HOMAN

Imagine a film about a place you know well. You know what it looks like, you know what it sounds and smells like, you know other places near it and the experiences you have encountered there. (Joyce, 1996: 44)

Newcastle, situated on the New South Wales coast 150 kilometres north of Sydney, is a city that has always been troubled by its identity. Since its settlement as a port and series of coal mining towns in 1797, Newcastle residents have been preoccupied with its perception by outsiders in general, and by the neighbouring metropolis of Sydney in particular. This preoccupation has been shaped by gender, class and economics on both sides and has waxed and waned along with cycles in manufacturing booms and busts:

Newcastle has long been mythologised, both externally and internally, as a town of 'hard men', of 'working class heroes' with a tradition of intransigent unionism, of battling sturdy survivors who have overcome constant economic reverses (economic and natural) by drawing on their sense of community and spirit (Metcalfe, 1994). These representations, as masculinist and exclusionary and partial as they are, are deeply sedimented in local consciousness, part of the shared vernacular meanings and symbolic understandings of Newcastle that merge with its material landscapes to create its place of identity. (Rowe, 2001: 56)

The romanticism evoked by oral and official histories of the shipbuilding, textile, steel and coal industries 'forging' the city's character is matched by similar well-worn narratives about the integrity of its working class 'battlers'. Offering commentary on real Newcastle events, *Blackrock* (dir: Steven Vidler, 1997) and *Bootmen* (dir: Dein Perry, 2000) present radically different perspectives of the city. The release of both films occurred during a period of substantial reconfiguration of the city's traditional sense of itself, with the closure of BHP's raw steelmaking plant in 1999, leading to the loss of approximately 8200 jobs, exacerbated by the layoff of mineworkers elsewhere (ibid). At the same time, the city council began long-term projects designed to position Newcastle as a 'post-industrial' city, with culture and tourism integral to both re-investment and re-imaging strategies (Stevenson, 1998). The films, then, appeared at a crucial time for imagining Newcastle's post-rust belt identity, as well as forming part of a long-standing historical 'chip on its shoulder' about its regional and national value. The film music tracks contributed significantly to such a project.

Music has formed many of the cultural signposts of Novocastrian history. *The Newcastle Song*, performed and written by Bob Hudson, charted at Number One in March 1975 as a satire of local masculine rituals – car cruising along the 'main drag', Hunter Street, tests of bravery between male car owners, and the relentless search for 'chicks'[1]. The Star Hotel riot of 19 September 1979 – a battle between drinkers and police over the closure of a favoured live music pub, resulting in dozens of arrests – was documented in song by Cold Chisel's Don Walker (*The Star Hotel*, 1979). With fourteen police injured, 31 arrests and two police vehicles upturned, the event has entered into Oz (Australian) Rock folklore (see Homan, 2003: 102-108). The city has always been proud of the number of pubs and clubs offering live rock and pop. Indeed, Newcastle can be regarded as the archetypal city/template of Oz Rock mythology – hard rock bands, powerful sonic attacks underpinned by virtuosity in the best 'guitar hero' traditions, playing to hard-drinking and hard-to-please working class audiences (ibid: 13). The 1990s successes of local 'heroes' The Screaming Jets and silverchair assure them a place in the Oz Rock pantheon, and reinforces the bonding between male cultural sites and identities (pub, fan, performer). In the best working class mythic tradition, music remains a popular option of escape from Newcastle, as one of the forms of cultural activity the city is 'good at'.

In this chapter I argue that music plays a vital role in bringing these historical and cultural factors into play in *Blackrock* and *Bootmen*. Both films set the space of the city as a place of local affections and struggles, and emphasise the different kinds of images of the city. As argued above, representations of Newcastle as place of investment have been intimately tied to the flows and forms of industry and capital. The practices of representation emphasise a visible and dominant masculinity, reinforced by cultural success (eg silverchair) and sporting pride (the Newcastle Knights rugby league team). Here I wish to explore how music assists in each film's construction of masculinity where, in different ways, Newcastle's past continues to haunt its present.

Blackrock

It is fair to say that 1970s and 1980s Australian films were not much interested in tales of suburbia. One of the few exceptions, *The FJ Holden* (dir: Michael Thornhill, 1977), a "suburban road movie in which the protagonists … get nowhere, trapped in the maze of Sydney's western suburbs: Bankstown, Panania, Chullora" (Dermody and Jacka, 1988: 119) remains the filmic companion to *The Newcastle Song*, with its deadening portrayal of male bonding through worship of the car and a Toohey's New stubbie[2]. *Blackrock* can be included in the 1990s' 'renaissance' of suburban storytelling that encompassed both positive and very dark depictions of the Australian suburb: *Romper Stomper* (dir: Geoffrey Wright, 1992); *The Sum of Us* (dir: Geoff Burton/Kevin Dowling, 1994); *Muriel's Wedding* (dir: PJ Hogan, 1994); *Metal Skin* (dir: Geoffrey Wright, 1995); *Idiot Box* (dir: David Caesar, 1996); *The Castle* (dir: Rob Sitch, 1997); *Erskineville Kings* (dir: Alan White, 1998); *Head On* (dir: Ana Kokkinos, 1998); *Praise* (dir: John Curran, 1998); *Two Hands* (dir: Gregor Jordan, 1998); *The Boys* (dir: Rowan Woods, 1998) and *Dirty Deeds* (dir: David Caesar, 2002).

As film critics and academics such as French (2000) and Flaus (2001) have observed, many Australian films reflect wider cultural understandings of gender in their treatment of contemporary gender relations, with women secondary to male friendships and male activities. For Philip Butterss, "*Blackrock* is a film about mateship, above all else", arguing that like *Romper Stomper*, *Idiot Box* and *The Boys*, the film "suggest[s] that the young men need to make a choice between mateship and a relationship with a woman" (1998: 44, 45).

Mateship, and its role in reinforcing communal (male) bonds in youth subcultures, became a central issue in police, media and community understanding of the events related to theatrical productions of *Property of the Clan* and *Blackrock*. The death of fourteen-year-old Leigh Leigh on the beach near North Stockton Surf Club in 1989 has been the basis for sustained debate and investigation on a number of issues. Initially, her repeated rape and murder did not produce an obvious suspect. The failure of a quick identification of the perpetrator(s) provoked nation-wide, misinformed media interest that reflected poorly, to say the least, on the Stockton community. The arrest and sentencing of teenager Mathew Webster for Leigh Leigh's murder did not silence those who believed he did not act alone at the beach party. Later investigations by the Newcastle University's Legal Centre, acting on behalf of Leigh's mother, provoked an initial NSW Crimes Commission inquiry, followed by a Police Integrity Commission (PIC) investigation into the case's five investigative officers, with recommendations by the PIC in 2000 to dismiss the detective leading the murder investigation, and disciplinary action taken against the other officers (Barrett, 2000). Subsequent media portrayals of the tragedy, two plays and a feature film, have prolonged local discussion, reheating debates about the portrayal of the teenagers within broader debates about social and police attitudes towards sexual violence[3].

Indeed, the plays and the film ask how the excessive male bonding rituals of the car and the surf relegate women to explicitly domestic or sexual roles. The *Blackrock* beach culture bespeaks a traditional Australian leisure culture where women "are either physically barred or their participation is circumscribed by a melange of rules, conventions and attitudes which ensure that these activities remain the preserve of men" (Summers, 1975: 71). For the young women, physical activity is confined to unquestioning sex at the beach or in the back of a panel van (a milieu also portrayed in *Puberty Blues*, dir: Bruce Beresford, 1981). For the young men, the strength of their connections with each other remains unquestioned. The central character of Jared in *Blackrock* is pivotal in making these discourses explicit. As a character with a girlfriend from outside the beach subculture, Jared shows some willingness to explore other options to male/female relationships. After the events leading to Tracy's (the character of Leigh Leigh) death, there is recognition at the end of the film of establishing a deeper connection with his mother (played by Linda Cropper), who fears she has 'lost' him for good.

Given the obvious local sensitivities, the stage and film representations were important to correct media misinformation about the Leigh Leigh case, and to provide a forum for local reflection on events, at some distance to the earlier prosecution controversies and town portrayals. *The Property of the Clan* was written by the late Nick Enright and performed by Freewheels Theatre in Newcastle in 1992 and NIDA (the National Institute of Dramatic Art) in 1993. After revisions, the play was renamed *Blackrock* and performed by the Sydney Theatre Company in 1995 and 1996. Like the plays, the film was controversial on several accounts. Assurances from both writer and director that the film was not based on Leigh Leigh did not correspond with the choice of Stockton and Newcastle as the principal sites for the film's events. In addition, the character of Tracy in the film shared the name of Leigh's cousin, causing the family further concern (Carrington, 1998: 153).

Enright wrote the *Blackrock* screenplay for director Steven Vidler, once a student of Enright's at NIDA[4]. The early scenes of the film present the audience with a montage of suburban 'lad culture': fights over girls, car burn-outs and 'doughnuts'[5], Tooheys New, and the proud parading of Ricko's Holden Sandman, the 1970s panel van of choice for dedicated surfers[6]. Through these scenes, the intense friendship between seventeen-year-old Jared and Brett Ricketson ('Ricko'), his older 'best mate' returning from up the coast, is depicted and reinforced through Ricko's preference to hang out with his mates rather than catch up with his girlfriend.

The opening scenes in *Blackrock* set up a mixture of waterscapes and water sounds: swimmers and surfers catching waves, with industrial sites in the background; kids catching the (ten minute) ferry from school back to Stockton; waves crashing amidst ship horns and passing freight cargo, reinforcing the city's seaport origins. The surf is an important part of the soundscape, with Jared surfing; the surfboard ritual of Ricko's funeral; and as a continual backdrop to various conversations within the film. The early scenes also reveal the way the music track underwrites the dominance of the male characters, unleashing The Cruel Sea song *Teach Me* (1995) to accompany the ferry scene and Ricko's arrival. The song segues neatly into Beasts of Bourbon's *Saturated* (1997) as Jared gets a tattoo to (literally) mark Ricko's return. The breathy singing in Primary's *Like Others Do* (1997), during the fashion photo shoot that Jared skips in favour of preparing for Ricko's 'homecoming' party, is a rare female presence in the music track.

The surf club party scenes are dominated by Sidewinder, whose exegetic presence elsewhere in the film is transformed into a diegetic one, performing as the surf club band on the night. The Canberra-originating five-piece provides the aggressive, fuzz guitar rock required as emblematic of the party's display of sexual and other tensions. An act well known to national youth radio station Triple J listeners and a constant on the 'indie' festival circuit (Dogbite, Homebake, Big Day Out), Sidewinder anchor the music track (and *Titanic Days* [1997] emerged as a minor hit with the release of the film).

A few exceptions to the 'wall of source sound' are provided by composer Steve Kilbey, lead singer/writer and bassist with The Church. His first opportunity to compose for an entire film, Kilbey adopted an uncomplicated approach, employing traditional rock jamming techniques to screen developments:

> *Basically you have a cut of the film in front of you and you write as you watch it – I think that is really the only honest way of doing it ... Tim [Powles] and I were watching a scene where two protagonists [Ricko and Jared] were having a fight along a cliff... Tim was playing drums and I was playing guitar and when they were pushing we were trying to go with it. We would surge it and then come back down with it. That was the way the whole thing was written.* (Kilbey in Dicks, 2002: online)

Kilbey has enjoyed a reputation in Australia, Britain and the USA for crafting memorable pop melodies meshed with twin guitar effects reminiscent of the 1960s' Rickenbacker sound of The Byrds and The Beatles. Later Church albums were also praised for their ethereal lyrics and sound (for example, the 1988 USA hit *Under The Milky Way*). These trademark elements are evident in many of *Blackrock*'s reflective moments. In the surf, Jared seeks escape from fights with his mother and moral quandaries presented by the surf party events; he enters another world under Newcastle's breaking waves. This is signified by Kilbey's use of heavily phased guitar and synthesiser. An increasingly louder combination of digitally remixed surf noises and synth chords dominate Jared's nightmares over decisions about past and future relationships. An inner world of doubt and tension is effectively produced as an important counter to the 'certainties' of Jared's public life.

It seems the international standing of Kilbey as a craftsman of pop/rock melodies counted for little in the broader strategy of the music track:

> *Due to the success of* Romeo & Juliet *I think everyone who makes a film now wants to have a successful CD. So with* Blackrock *they indiscriminately chucked on all these songs, trying to get a hit album going. It ended up being a weird cross-section of music and I think it really interfered with the flow of what I tried to do... I personally would have preferred it to be just incidental music all the way through, but every three minutes a bloody rock tune suddenly blasts on for about ten seconds, simply so they could feature it upon the CD.* (ibid)

Anahid Kassabian notes that compiled scores offer "affiliating identifications [that] depend on histories forged outside the film scene, and they allow for a fair bit of mobility within it" (2001: 3). *Blackrock* does not offer a series of songs and performers that directly connect with the times of the Stockton event in 1989, instead offering a collection of mid-1990s performers that represent a who's-who of Australian indie rock. Only three of its songs could be said to have previous lives as mainstream hits (Mental As Anything's *Live It Up* [1985]; and Irish band The Cranberries' *No Need to Argue* and *Zombie* [both 1994]). In an era when soundtrack sales have become vital to film company profits, this choice may not make commercial sense but is astute in a subcultural sense. The majority of songs are chosen from 'indie' (independent) labels and bands: silverchair, Tumbleweed, Rebecca's Empire, Shihad, The Clouds, Ben Lee, Swirl, Died Pretty and Sidewinder. This lineup makes creative sense in breaking from older media and music industry understandings of the Oz Rock tradition based upon ageing 'rebels' like Jimmy Barnes (Cold Chisel) and Angry Anderson (Rose Tattoo). It allows youth to take ownership of the film, in keeping with the director's wish that "young kids, males seventeen to twenty-five especially" see the film (Vidler cited in Margetts, 1997: online). These bands represent an important generational and generic break with the usual Oz Rock 'working class hits' soundtrack (The Angels, AC/DC et al). Furthermore, as a relentless wall of sound, the music track is far removed from critic and filmmaker Philip Brophy's accusation that most film music is "just dripping, romantic, true kitsch" (cited in Caputo, 2003: 116).

The identifiably local music track succeeds in meshing the film's characters with the audience's music knowledge. However the use of two Cranberries songs – at two important junctures in the film – questions just how 'mobile' musical meanings can be. *Zombie*, a 1994 global hit, accompanies Jared's turmoil as he is shown pictures of the Tracy's mutilated body by the police. The audience is asked to forget the song's previous commercial histories and meanings, with its obvious references to the Irish Troubles ("it's the same old theme, since 1916"). Instead, the song is connected directly to the filmic events:

> *Another mother's breaking heart is taking over*
> *when the violence causes silence*

Zombie assumes the burden of textual speech, with "the song as voice-over" (Garwood, 2003: 116) articulating characters' thoughts and scenic mood. Yet the song jars not just against the rest of the overtly Australian material that provides some synergy with its local audience; it asks the viewer/listener to 'forget' its past commercial flows and different circulations of meanings. Questions about the extent of meaning mobility will be revisited in this chapter's final section.

Metal Heavy

> *Listen to the city as though it was music and to music as though it was the city...* (van Leeuwen, 1999: 4)

Lacking jobs, money and any form of status in the city, young people in Blackrock have "got nothing else, but heaps of time", as Ricko points out. Jared's emerging talents as a photographer are presented as a detour to a bleak future of drinking, surfing and unemployment. Escape through the arts is the central theme in *Bootmen*, in which director and choreographer Dein Perry offers a tale reflecting his own rise from steelworker to tap dancer/choreographer/director. The opening scenes present the audience with the cultural divide between industry and the arts worked throughout the film: the soft, sepia-tinted glimpses of Super-8 footage of brothers Sean and Mitchell being congratulated by their mother after winning tap contests as young boys. This family history is quickly interrupted by a heavy guitar riff and an industrial landscape: overhead shots of coal tankers waiting to enter the Hunter River; a motorbike roaring along the docks as Sean rides to his job at the steelworks[7]. From the outset, the 'soft' environs of artistic activity are juxtaposed with the 'hard' nature of steel, hard hats and industry.

Living in the shadow of the steelworks, the dancing skills of both Sean and Mitchell – and their liking for Linda, aspiring dancer and full-time hairdresser – are quickly established in the audition scene for a producer seeking talent for a Sydney stage show. His father Gary, still mourning the loss of their mother, rejects the subsequent offer to Sean of a dancing job in Sydney at "eight hundred bucks a week". With "no security at the steelworks anymore", Sean makes it clear he will not follow his father's path to "work forever and forever in the steelworks, amen". Sean's decision to go to Sydney is ultimately not much of a gamble, given the steady trickle of retrenchments at the steelworks. Brother Mitchell explores a shadier path of crime, stealing and selling cars to fund his dream of purchasing a large rig that will offer his independent path out of Newcastle's options.

In similar ways to *Blackrock*, much of the sound track is provided by the foregrounding of suburban sounds usually pushed into the background: pushbikes, motorbikes, cars, pub noises, blaring televisions, distant and close beach sounds. *Blackrock* is dominated by the sounds of Ricko's Sandman; the hard revving of Mitch's Ford provides the auto sound track in *Bootmen*. These sounds of the everyday, consistently written off as irritable 'noise' within contemporary cityscapes (see Schafer, 1977), are co-opted to reinforce the masculinity of landscapes.

Ben Goldsmith has discussed both the literal and discursive meanings of noise that can be applied to 1990s Australian films. For Goldsmith, the sound design of *Metal Skin* and *Idiot Box* invoke the musical meaning of noise as "cacophony, dissonance... nonsense" (2001: 117). Further, "noise and melody [is used] as a disorientation mechanism to force the spectator to question and avoid easy assumptions about plot, characters and their own investment in the film[s]" (ibid: 130). *Romper Stomper* is another in this collection that employs the "acousmatic scream, the wail of the repressed, patient, unloved, finally demanding to be heard" (ibid: 122). *Blackrock* also clearly fits this category, as a film that feeds a series of corrupted signals into the mainstream; in various ways, the "hoons across the water" are able to present their own sounds and ideas against the social and media distortion of events.

Sounds and memories avoided or repressed in *Blackrock* (defined by the haunting images and sounds of Jared's dreams) are confronted and co-opted in *Bootmen*. The steelworks, the source of unpleasant and dangerous work (or even worse, no work) becomes more than the backdrop to dance routines. The topography and industrial 'noise' of the site is pushed to the

27

foreground, evident in the scene in which Sean 'notices' the array of sounds around him: pipes, grinders, steel walkways. Situating the perspective of music and social distance in films, what is usually Ground (the minor, surrounding soundscape) becomes Figure (the predominant sound(s) which the audience identifies with) (van Leeuwen, 1999: 23). That is, rather than using place to enable us to think about the sound and music tracks, the place *becomes* the music in an assortment of ways.

One of the problems for live rock musicians is the acceptance of their sounds as intrinsic to their activities, and not merely regarded as 'noise', a by-product of their playing (Homan, 2003: 162). Dein Perry has asked his audiences to accept a similar notion – that the 'unmusical' noise of the steel site lies at the centre of *Bootmen*. The 'natural' rhythms of the workplace can be transformed into the more surreal set-pieces of the various dance company member auditions. Aluminium toilets, steel pipes, metal stairs, and steel meshed walkways all form the basis of individual routines.

A clever series of connected shots reveals how the film encourages the audience to think of everyday sounds as possessing their own rhythms. While Sean is rehearsing for his stage debut in Sydney, Mitch is revealed hot-wiring another car to steal and sell. These events, portrayed as happening simultaneously, provide a useful connection between the real and the staged: Sean's one-two steps are repeated with Mitch's one-two combination of electrical sparks as he tries to start the car. This call-and-response routine, a familiar part of tap routines in Hollywood musicals, produces an engaging juxtaposition of sounds, reinforcing the divergent choices made by the brothers.

Differences between the staged and the everyday are also revealed in the constant concern about the tappers' inability to be properly heard, particularly when the rock band joins the company. This is resolved through Sean's re-discovery of Mitchell's 'boot mike' invention after his brother's death that allows a narrowing of the acoustic distance between the taps (usually heard in gaps of silence between music) and the audience. The placement of small microphones on the tap boots, linked to the main PA system, is an ingenious solution in explaining the artificial enhancement of the tap routines throughout the film, in the face of other noises. Of course, such technical difficulties are forgotten in the final, 'live' performance staged at the steelworks, where extra guitars and horn sections creep into the final danced sequences, in addition to a syncopated industrial grinders sequence composed by Cezary Skubiszewski[8].

In some ways, *Bootmen* revisits a longer filmic tradition that encourages a rethinking of industry sounds and labour, dating back to the silent film era. Chaplin's *Modern Times* (1936) is a famous critique of the disconnection between human and machine, with piano accompaniment underscoring the factory workers' dislocation from industry rhythms. The Industrial Revolution, in regulating labour and leisure time, has its corollary in the development of Western music's bars and beats, in regulating musical time (Schafer, 1977; Tagg, 1984).

Time plays out in a range of ways in *Bootmen*. First, the film is part-elegy to the traditional workplace sounds and rhythms of a vanishing industrial era – as van Leeuwen (1999: 39) has pointed out, the sounds of the industrial age are succumbing to those of the electronic. More practically, the film reveals how particular workers trade labour time with an enforced increase in leisure time (mass steelwork redundancies). Second, individual and collective timing are crucial to successful tap routines ('routines' attesting to the need for precise repetition and memory). The need for conformity of beats is entrenched in the slogan of Sean's dance teacher, Waldo: "keep it simple, and no improvising!" Part of the battle with the dancers' band later in the film (detailed below) derives from the battle about musical time – who will provide a stable musical anchor, and who is allowed to syncopate/improvise[9]. The explicit solidarity of the steelworkers and dancers in the face of adversity is also presented as a problem, constraining the individual brilliance and ambitions of Sean. The final sequences of the film resolve this tension, displaying tight team choreography, while showcasing Sean's own routines.

Bootmen possesses a more conventional popular song music track, with an eye to soundtrack album sales. This becomes evident early in the film, as The Living End's *All Torn Down* accompanies footage of Sean commencing his bike ride along the F3 highway to Sydney. The refrain of the chorus reinforces Sean's abandonment of his Newcastle ties to try his luck in the 'big city' – against his father's advice. His new job in Sydney provides the only conventional tap routine in the film, which is quickly intercut with a Newcastle pub rock scene of heavy rock and moshpits. Paul Kelly's *Tease Me* (1997) and *Nothing On My Mind* (1998) were minor Australian hits, as were Grinspoon's *Better Off Dead* (1999) and Leonardo's Bride's *Even When I'm Sleeping* (1997). 'Indie' bands with mainstream success contribute short bursts from lesser-known songs: You Am I's *Junk* and *Rumble* (both 1998); and Regurgitator's *Strange Human Being* (1999). The only theatrical nod to the legacy of Hollywood dance is provided by the frustrated guitarist in Newt's band, who performs a short, cynical rendition of Irving Berlin's 1929 number, *Puttin' On The Ritz*.

Sounds of masculinity

Previous writers have observed that gender discourses are central to both films. *Blackrock* in particular can be regarded as one of a series of Australian films that are "first and foremost, critiques of protest masculinity" (Butterss, 1998: 42)[10]. The displays and settings of masculine behaviour lie at the core of Tracey's rape and death on the beach, contextualising the 'code of silence' by the boys about the event. Throughout the film, women are consistently ignored (Jared's mum; the boys' girlfriends) or sexualised (photo shoot; depictions of Tracey as a 'slut' before and after her death). We can also add the recurring subtext of alcohol as central to bloke culture. *Bootmen*'s screenplay features several invitations to "knock off and come to the pub": during dance auditions; after the footy (rugby match); while dad, Gary, reflecting on a home without his wife, "got pissed in front of the telly again". The combination of 'classic' Oz Rock/'cock rock' scenarios provide the setting for pivotal moments in both films – drunk Linda sleeping with Mitch after a pub gig; Tracey's death after a beer-soaked surf dance. These events and dialogues are brought into even sharper relief by the highlighted absences of parent figures, in Jared's case, the absence of his angry father in his life; for Sean and Mitchell in *Bootmen*, the implied loss of stability wrought by the death of their mother.

If the characters of Jared, Ricko and their mates engage in a form of hyper-masculinity that observes the stereotypes of surf culture (smoking, surfing, drinking, sex), Sean and Mitchell in *Bootmen* offer more direct gender binaries. Within the 'feminine' world of dance, the viewer is continually reassured by signs of the brothers' masculinity: Sean's motorbike and Mitchell's Ford; their shared love of playing and watching rugby league; and, in Sean's case, references and jokes about a long history of local girlfriends. An underlying fear of homosexuality is confronted several times in the film, signalled by several brandings of the brothers as "faggots" and beatings suffered by other cast members. Attempting to recruit another dancer working as a bouncer in a nightclub, Sean reassures him that "no one can call you a poofter – you stare at tits all day long". Claims are also made that tap dancing brings invaluable benefits in landing girlfriends; "girls jump on you if they know you're in the show". The masculinity of the boys in *Blackrock* derives from a well-established assemblage of teenage deviant behaviour, in a sense fulfilling expected roles within the surf subculture. For Sean and Mitch, deviancy is defined by the challenge to ignore Newcastle male traditions of education, class and work.

How are such discourses of gender presented sonically? Distinctive instruments and sounds draw audiences into understanding distinctive sexualities. Hollywood has a long and dubious history in scoring women as "the object (plot-space) of man's desire (she provokes the primal – the "natural" – in him), the bearer of affective (private sphere) values" (Kassabian, 2001: 36). For van Leeuwen, the 'soft' private sphere of women characters are portrayed by "softer instruments such as strings and woodwind… it seeks to sound 'delicate', 'gentle', 'passive', 'inward looking' and so on" (1999: 117).

Both films observe these longstanding Hollywood movie traditions of music as semiotic code for understanding gender. The number of instances in which the score overtly denotes 'woman on screen' is striking. In *Bootmen*, Linda's on-screen presence is noted by soft synth sounds in the beach scene with Sean. The stereotypical role for women as nurturers and gatekeepers of the aesthetic is further underlined by the breathy vocals of Deadstar's Caroline Kennedy (*Don't It Get You Down* [1998]) playing on the radio as Linda gives Sean a new, highly stylised haircut in her salon.

The vulnerability of the Leonardo's Bride's chorus – "I love you even when I'm sleeping, you're everywhere" – provides a syrupy context for Mitch's funeral in *Bootmen*. The chorus also reinforces Sean's comments in mourning that he continues to see his brother "everywhere". The funeral scene in *Blackrock* is similarly dominated by an explicit female voice of mourning, with The Cranberries' *No Need To Argue*, a song about the loss of a relationship transposed to summarise the loss of Tracy. Both funeral songs are rare scenes of individual and collective contemplation, coded as passive – feminine moments within a soundscape of masculinity.

These gendered patterns of sound are evident throughout both films. In *Bootmen*, *Nothing On My Mind*, with its unusually harsh, bravado lyrics from Paul Kelly, accompanies the scene where Mitch is knocked out and has his car stolen by the competing car racket gang. Another Kelly song, *Tease Me*, is an obvious choice in establishing a suitable atmosphere of sleaze in the nightclub scene (with semi-clad dancing girls in cages) as Sean recruits another dancer for his company. Reminders that it is a 'real blokes' story regularly puncture the camp aesthetic underlying many Hollywood dance films. Rehearsing in hard hats and factory boots, one dancer states what some of the doubting blokes in the cinema are probably thinking: "you look just like the guy from the Village People" – a comic reference to the Village People's 'construction worker' gay character from the 1980s. This explicit recognition of the danger of their work being essentialised as feminine is offset by the steelworks, which ensure a properly masculine setting.

The addition of a rock band to Sean's vision of the steelworks tap show is an important plot development. 'Newt's band' is invited to provide the music for the dancers, after much debate within the troupe[11]. At first, Sean is troubled that the band displays all the characteristics of 'cock rock'[12]: they are far too loud and engage in classic rock stage posturing, while their songs are dominated by long lead guitar solos. This leads Sean to ask: "is Bon Jovi's music appropriate?" Much riffing between the band and dancers ensues, with a wall of power chords and heavy drums. Gradually, the band is harnessed into the collective purpose and sound of the ensemble, with individual solos used only to emphasise tap routines. The inclusion of the band is important in 'selling' the *Bootmen* concept to the cinema public. The presence of long hair and power chords places the dancing within familiar rock contexts of duelling solos and exaggerated individual virtuosity with feet and hands. It is one of the few instances in the film where rock comes to reinforce order and structure, rather than as an icon of disorder and chaos.

Authenticities of Place

> *Bootmen is a long way from Fred Astaire in* Shall We Dance? *It is a little like Broadway Melody meets Grunge.* (Leonard, 2000: online)

Bootmen and *Blackrock* depend heavily upon sound and music to make particular connections between characters, events and spaces. Both are part of a longer tradition of harnessing particular music genres for specific effects. As a genre of rock, grunge has been too willingly lumped with broader evocations of place:

> *The new economy some say was invented in Seattle, USA. In fact, Seattle in the 1990s brought the world many things such as grunge, Microsoft, the Internet and at the end of the decade, the anti-WTO protests of 1999. These influences affected Australia too. Australia had a new musical generation with bands like Silverchair, who like Seattle's grunge musicians, were 'born global', thanks to Microsoft and the Internet.* (Harcourt, 2002: online)

Written by a government trade economist, this paragraph encapsulates the usual tensions between the local and global: the political, cultural and economic milieu of Seattle is depicted as both unique, but open to adoption and adaptation. Grunge is not just a typology of sounds (heavy drums, distorted guitar, tortured vocals) and cross-categorisation (borrowing equally from punk and heavy metal), but also a mythology about spaces, people and ways of life. Placed well away from the centre(s) of American life, Seattle's isolation fed into the alienation and aggression of its youth to produce a distinctive subculture of 'indie' musicians (Nirvana, Pearl Jam, Soundgarden, Mudhoney, Tad) that defined themselves firmly against shiny cosmopolitanism[13]. This mythic narrative ignores many other ingredients of the 'Seattle sound' (the role of the Reciprocal Recording studio and the Sub Pop recording label; assorted local venues, individual ambition and creativity), yet the success of Nirvana's *Nevermind* in 1991 produced a residue of global grunge signifiers: chequered lumberjack shirts, torn jeans, Doc Marten shoes, long hair and a hyper-ordinary nihilism summarised as 'slacker' culture.

Alternative musics and ideologies like grunge thrive partly on post-industrial landscapes. Newcastle shares with Seattle a distance from the cultural and industrial centre that produces a geographic and social distance. "As it moves through a Seattle fog", *Blackrock* has been described by one reviewer as "the voice for disenfranchised youth with the heartbeat of Seattle blues" (Margetts, 1997: online). The surf subculture of the Stockton 'hoons' display their own coded 'slacker' identity: chequered flannelette shirts and long hair, and an anger and aggression that is rarely articulated, but finds expression in moments of physical and sexual violence. The inclusion of silverchair – 'Nirvana in Pyjamas' as the Australian music press had earlier unfairly labelled them – on the music track also provides a generic signpost for those with lesser knowledge of grunge and its local exponents.

Rock cultures are defined by systems of tastes, with identities constructed by attachments to genres and corresponding lifestyles. To be authentic to its performers and fans, rock has to solve the problems of communication ("how and of what the music speaks") and community ("to and for whom the music speaks") (Grossberg, 2003: 93). *Blackrock* director Steven Vidler argued that he "could have made a film of gritty, pseudo-documentary realism ... we were at great pains to make a movie that reflected the energy of the kids" (DVD interviews, 2003). Producer David Elfick has gone further, claiming that the film "is the late 90s *Rebel Without A Cause*... it's about the music, and energy and violence" (ibid). It is curious, then, that none of the film's characters discuss favourite bands or venues. Music is only presented as a backdrop to events, not embedded in networks of friendships, or micro-ideologies of resistance as part of their everyday lives. Even a "gritty, pseudo-documentary" (Vidler, op cit) cannot do justice to the complex histories and motives of local subcultures. Yet it remains unclear how music acts as the social glue of a community that has rejected (and been rejected by) wider social networks.

Bootmen's layers of artifice – a theatre show transformed to the screen as a series of 'live' performances enhanced by studio dubs and effects – present other problems of communication and community. This 'pretending to pretend' extends to performances of masculinity that deny local (and Australian) histories of gender, art and work. The burden of communicating how music is linked to the transgressions of the 'hoon' subculture in *Blackrock* is assumed by the sound track. In *Bootmen*, there is no doubt that the main characters also transgress; yet themes about the possibilities of alternative identities and belonging are worked through various plot devices, with the main characters frequently forced to confront and deny local limitations.

It makes sense, then, to return notions of authenticity within both films back to depictions of place. Older symbolic representations of Newcastle as a hard 'steel city' endure, with some reassertion of community: despite their reservations in *Bootmen*, the locals ensure Sean's show at the BHP steelworks is sold out. Perhaps the most valuable theme to emerge from both films is that individual redemption through cultural activity remains contingent upon the constraints of history and locality (cf. *Billy Elliot*, dir: Stephen Daldry, 2000). Despite the ways that difference is presented as binding alternative communities (for example, through assertions in both films that grunge and tap is not 'proper' music or dancing), wider structural problems are unresolved. Sean's and Mitchell's father remains at the steelworks to confront looming redundancy; the small community of *Blackrock* (and Jared) are left to confront their own demons about violence, gender and community. This is exacerbated by the problem of communication, which is better described as a problem of little or no communication: all the characters conceal their emotions, with the gap filled by 'noise' of various kinds. As 'smokestack economy' films, *Blackrock* and *Bootmen* offer insight into the benefits, and limits, of the local in the face of social and economic change. Yet, as the people of Newcastle have found out, how these changes are represented is equally important.

Notes

1. The song provoked a sequel, *Rak Off Normie*, by Mureen Elkner, where the hero of *The Newcastle Song*, Normie, is told in no uncertain terms that "he hasn't got what it takes". The song charted nationally at Number Six in June 1975.

2. Beer sold in a short-necked bottle, popular with working people.

3. The Leigh Leigh case remains much studied in university criminology courses as an example of shoddy police process, borne out by the NSW Crime Commission and PIC investigations.

4. As a NIDA graduate, Vidler worked in many Australian television dramas, including *Police Rescue* (aired 1990-1996); *Janus*; *Heartland*, and *Halifax f.p.* He has acted in a variety of films: *Robbery Under Arms* (dir: Ken Hannam/Donald Crombie, 1984); *Incident At Raven's Gate* (dir: Rolf de Heer, 1988); *The Umbrella Woman* (dir: Ken Cameron, 1986); and *No Worries*(dir: David Elfick, 1992). The graduation film from his Swinburne Film School studies, *Hell, Texas and Home* was nominated for an AFI award in 1995.

5. Tyre burnings on the road caused by vehicles driven around in circles.

6. With its long body, the Sandman panel van was an obvious choice of vehicle for transporting surfboards. Its other name – and enduring mythic legacy – entailed its use as a 'shaggin wagon' – a portable bedroom for young men and their girlfriends.

7. These opening shots remain a favourite of local university students when searching for appropriate footage to discuss local and media representations of Newcastle.

8. A Polish migrant, Skubiszewski has composed for several Australian films: *Lilian's Story* (dir: Jerzy Domaradzki, 1997); *Two Hands* (dir: Gregor Jordan, 1998); *The Sound of One Hand Clapping* (dir: Richard Flanagan, 1998); *La Spagnola* (dir: Steve Jacobs, 2000) and *The Rage in Placid Lake* (dir: Tony McNamara, 2003). He has also written music for Australian television, notably the Channel Ten 2003 mini-series *After The Deluge* (dir: Brendan Maher). Skubiszewski has won two AFI awards for Best Original Music Score, with *Bootmen* and *La Spagnola* in their years of release.

9. Tensions about the extent of improvisation are also a recurrent theme in *Strictly Ballroom*, a 1992 Australian film portraying front and backstage rivalries of professional dance contests.

10. Bob Connell's term 'protest masculinity' was developed to describe "exaggerated claims to potency" and a "pressured exaggeration of masculine conventions", particularly evident in working class male youth and characterised by "violence, school resistance, minor crime, heavy drug/alcohol use, occasional manual labour, motorbikes or cars, [and] short heterosexual liaisons" (Connell, 1995: 110, 111).

11. This includes a joke about general perceptions of rock as an unskilled art form: 'Johnno' reassures Sean that Newt has 'trained at the Con' – not the 'Conservatorium of Music, Sydney', but at the local 'Conley School of Guitar'.

12. A term defined by Frith and McRobbie to summarise the "explicit, crude and often aggressive expression of male sexuality" in rock (1990: 374).

13. Of course, Seattle forms part of a grander tradition of specific historical junctures of geography, economics and communities producing distinctive sounds and scenes: Liverpool and San Francisco in the 1960s; London and Detroit in the 1970s; Manchester in the 1980s; Austin, Texas in the 1990s. The origins of sounds and subcultures has always been debated – for example, see Blunt (2001: 150-153) for a discussion of theories arguing that the sonic template for grunge was provided by a series of 1980s Australian bands (The Scientists, Feedtime, Mark of Cain, Lubricated Goat).

Chapter Two

NEW–AGE NED:
Scoring Irishness and
Masculinity in *Ned Kelly*

HELEN O'SHEA

Critical changes have taken place in understandings of both the Irish and the masculine components in Australian cultural identity and this is clearly signalled in their representations in Australian popular culture. This chapter considers the ways in which the musical scores of two film versions of the Ned Kelly story – Tony Richardson's 1970 *Ned Kelly* and Gregor Jordan's *Ned Kelly*, released in 2003 – construct the mythic anti-hero as both Australian and Irish, and in doing so reinforce a notion of an Irish component in an Australian cultural identity. While both films use source music based on late 20th Century constructions of an (historically inaccurate) Irish–Australian music culture, the contrasting ways in which the scores use musical tropes of Irishness demonstrate significant changes in Australian identifications.

Ned Kelly: Historical Figure, Legend, Myth, Icon

The exploits of Ned Kelly's outlaw gang are familiar to most Australians – the horse-stealing, holding up coaches and banks, the killing of three police and the friend who had betrayed them, Ned's plan to derail the train load of police sent to hunt them down, and the final, doomed figure of Ned Kelly in armour and helmet advancing through the morning mist to his eventual capture at Glenrowan. These events have been commemorated in songs, stories, poems, artworks and films (see Bertrand, 2003) and even before Ned Kelly's capture in 1880 his adventures and his defiance of authority were celebrated in popular ballads. He had become a legend, his story passed around and exaggerated by word of mouth, during his lifetime. After his death, the Kelly legend entered the realm of myth as aspects of his story were emphasised for the way in which they reflected contemporary concerns about the inequities of the land laws, for example, or the ineptitude and corruption within Victoria's police force, and more widely for the way in which a man who saw himself and his family (particularly his mother) as the victim of oppression and prejudice and who was resourceful and resilient in avoiding capture and eloquent in his self-justification.

Ned Kelly, born in 1855 to an ex-convict father from County Antrim (in present-day Northern Ireland) and the daughter of free settlers from County Tipperary, was raised on a small farm in northeastern Victoria, where a relatively large concentration of poor Irish selectors had taken up land. The Selection Acts of 1860 to 1869 had promised land for all but, by the time loopholes in legislation had been addressed, the best land had gone to wealthy squatters, leaving selectors battling to survive on unviable properties. Tensions between selectors and squatters expressed elements of class, ethnic and religious conflict, as the poor selectors tended to be Irish Catholics while the squatters were not. The police force, which protected the squatters' interests, included many Irish Catholics who Ned Kelly and his gang regarded as traitors to their class and heritage.

The story of Ned Kelly as an Irish–Australian working-class hero – anti-authoritarian, fighting for justice, irreverent, skilled at bushcraft, horse riding, shooting, fist-fighting, and drinking – flourished among the lower social classes, while in bourgeois society he was regarded as a murdering thug. Class identification in Australia is not clear-cut, however, and the values Ned Kelly represented were embraced as those of a rough-and-ready Australian type.

The concept of an Australian national type based on an idealisation of the Australian-born itinerant rural workforce of the mid to late 19th Century has been known, since Russel Ward's 1958 work of the same name, as 'the Australian legend'. The idea that the typical Australian is a hard-living, rebellious and fair-minded bush worker of Irish heritage has been challenged in recent decades by feminist historians and by radical changes in the Australian workforce and in social policies such as multiculturalism. However, it is still accepted by many (including many politicians) as the basis for an 'Australian way of life', and still called upon to promote products such as beer or farm vehicles. The Australian Legend and its iconic figures – the convict, the shearer, the gold-digger, the bushranger – are no longer accepted as historically accurate representations of contemporary Australian values. They are understood as myth, rather than history, and popular culture now depicts a more diverse set of characteristics as typifying Australians. Such myths retain an iconic power, but one that is undercut by parody, as demonstrated by the squad of giant Ned Kellys along with other Australian icons at the Sydney 2000 Olympic Games opening ceremony, or satire, as in the movie Ned (dir: Abe Forsythe, 2002), marketed as "a riotous comedy that ties the Kelly legend to a tree, shoots it in the groin and leaves it to die bleeding, like the dog that it is" (video sleeve).

An Irish Component in an Australian Collective Identity

It is often said that one in three Australians have Irish ancestry, although how that Irishness is defined is not always clear. Historian David Fitzpatrick argues that the proportion of Australians of Irish heritage has been greatly exaggerated (Fitzpatrick, 1984: 30). A more important question might be *why* Australians should be inclined towards a collective identity with a strong Irish component. The widely accepted notion of a significant Irish component in an Australian national identity was promoted not only by the Catholic church but is also in part the work of both radical nationalist cultural critics and of more conservative historians. The notion that Australian values had been formed by the rugged, independent-thinking, hard-drinking, rural workers of earlier generations finds its most cogent articulation in Ward (1958), whose account emphasises the influence of the Irish, whom he depicts as fair-minded, rebellious, anti-authoritarian, and fond of gambling and boozing. One of the main arguments of Robert Hughes' more recent and widely influential Australian history, *The Fatal Shore*, is that the harsh punishment of Irish convicts, and an uprising instigated by Irish political prisoners in 1804, imprinted on subsequent generations of working-class Australians a belief in "English oppression and Irish resistance" (1988: 195).

Historian of the Irish in Australia, Patrick O'Farrell, like Hughes and Ward, maintains that Irish values were imprinted on Australian society in general. O'Farrell, however, perceives a recent change in the reputation of the Irish in Australia:

> The idea of being 'Irish' has undergone a remarkable recent transformation from being identified, historically, with poverty, ignorance, low social and occupational status, sectarian Catholicism, drunkenness, disorderly behaviour. It has recently become a fashionable asset, representing charm, sociability and conviviality, mild social radicalism, fun and entertainment, possessing some of the essential ingredients of the popular Australian self-image. By 1995 it was politically correct to call the Irish 'delightful'. (2000: 330)

O'Farrell claims that Australians' embrace of a collective identity more Irish than English in character was entirely "a product of Australia's swing to multiculturalism" (ibid). There are other important factors, however, not least in the changing political relationship with Britain. A sense of betrayal was felt towards Britain following the fall of Singapore to the Japanese in World War 2, and Britain's negotiations throughout the 1960s to join the European Economic Community. In addition, (Anglo/Celtic) Australians felt the need to distinguish themselves from Englishness, first in a colonial, and later in a post-colonial context. All of the above weakened Australians' notion of England as 'home', as did the impact of the post-war immigration program and Australia's strengthened trade and military alliance with the USA, together with the diminished threat of a declining Catholic church. At the same time, Irish–Australians had become integrated into Australian middle-class society from where they had achieved political and commercial leadership. By the time a more secular and pluralist society emerged in the 1970s, the special relationship with Britain was a thing of the past. At this time, nationalists drew on a by now familiar mythology to define Australia against the encroaching political, military and economic influence of the USA. The exaggeration of an Irish element in Australia's musical heritage featuring in the repertoire of the nationalist-oriented bush bands of the 1970s was one manifestation of this revived need to define an Australian identity against that of an outside entity (see Smith, 2001).

This chapter, in dealing with musical representations of the Irish component in an Australian national type, raises the question of what kind of material a film composer draws on in order to communicate recognisably 'Australian' or 'Irish' musical ideas.

Music and Identification

The focus of this chapter is the way in which specific film music scores variously signal 'Irishness'. How we understand this process depends on how we understand the process of identification and its relationship with musical experiences and texts. If we consider certain familiar musical events – the bugle call that signals the start of a hunt, the piped carols that tell shoppers they should be buying for Christmas, the triumphant march that announces the conclusion of the marriage ceremony – it seems a common-sense conclusion that music is a kind of language, even a 'universal language'. These are learned associations, however, for music in general does not act as a language. Musical performance is non-denotative – that is, sounds in music do not invoke specific things or ideas (as language does) but depend upon the signifying processes of language in order to take on meaning (Shepherd and Wicke, 1997). This is also the case with the affective or emotional connotations of musical events: hearing a major key as happy and a minor key as sad is a learned response, for example.

The premise on which this chapter proceeds is that music is always socially constructed. That is, music does not 'reflect' or 'express' social groups and their values but, through historical and discursive narratives, these associations develop over time. Thus music comes to represent an identity such as, in the case of the Ned Kelly films, an Irish–Australian collective identity. Film scores of necessity deal in these musical representations, often simplified to the point that they function as aural iconography, musical shorthand implying conventional meanings that an audience experienced in interpreting popular cultural texts – whether consciously or otherwise – will quickly recognise.

Music offers experiences that enable us to place ourselves in particular imaginative cultural narratives (Frith, 1996: 124) such as those of the nation. While nationalist movements have sought to establish unified cultural identities based on revised histories, the notion of a homogeneous, shared culture has been widely discredited in favour of a position that recognises that such identities are the names we give to the different ways we are positioned by, and position ourselves within, the narratives of the past (Hall, 1990: 225). As I argue below, these narratives (which include collective identities, stereotypes, concepts of masculinity and femininity) are not fixed but change over time according to contemporary priorities.

An illustration of this metaphorical relationship and its historical and discursive genesis – that is, in a body of ideas that over time have become accepted as 'common sense' – is the way in which certain kinds of musical genres, timbres, modalities and instruments have come to typify Irishness. There are two types of music that have been used in recent movie scores to convey characteristics associated with stereotypes of the Irish, and both are found in the blockbuster *Titanic* (dir: James Cameron, 1997). The first is the melancholy soprano wail that throughout the movie gives voice to emotions of pain, loss, heartbreak, longing, and romantic love. The second is the lively, vigorous sound of Irish dance music that accompanies scenes of earthy celebration, pranks and high spirits: jigs, polkas, and reels played on instruments we recognise as 'Irish' (although their presence in the film is anachronistic) and the sound familiarly heard from bands in Irish theme pubs around the globe. These twin musical representations of Irishness, also employed in the music tracks to the Ned Kelly films, have a long history.

Irishness and Melancholy

At the beginning of the 19th Century, cultural nationalists enlisted music to support the notion of cultural unity in a culturally divided Ireland as a prerequisite to the formation of a nation independent of English colonial rule. Collectors, including Edward Bunting, published transcriptions of harp tunes and song airs, believing that they had survived centuries of English occupation unchanged and expressed the unique culture of the ancient Gaelic nobility, a view that endures in popular representations of Irish traditional music as expressing characteristics that are essentially and exclusively Irish (and very ancient). This aristocratic music was emblematic of a ruling class, not 'the folk' (as in other European nationalisms), and the implication was that the Anglo–Irish gentry, many of whom were the driving forces of Irish anti-colonial movements, were the obvious future leaders of an independent Irish nation.

The most popular settings of this music were those of Thomas Moore, who adapted old Irish airs for voice and piano and set them to his own sentimental lyrics (*The Last Rose of Summer* is a well-known example). This gentle, melancholy music, characterised by high-pitched singing (for soprano or tenor), modal or (when transferred into diatonic scales) minor keys, with lyrics that lamented the failures of generations of Irish people to assert their independence, was the drawing-room version of Irishness that appealed to the Anglo–Irish ruling class, who performed it on uilleann pipes (which they had developed from the cruder instruments of indigenous itinerant musicians) and the harp (again, an adaptation of the instrument used by indigenous itinerant musicians up to the end of the 18th Century). One of Bunting's objections to Moore's interpretations was that he had changed their lively style of the old airs into a "drawling dead, doleful and die-away manner" (quoted in White, 1998: 43). In Moore's songs, the imputed national character was transformed from spirited to plaintive.

Musical identities are always constructed imaginatively, and within discourse. In this case, Irish music was thought to reflect the true nature of Irish people, as spiritual, melancholy and emotional – and thus implicitly incapable of either defeating the English colonisers or of ruling Ireland. In other words, it was a representation of Irishness deriving from a colonial viewpoint. This view of the Irish people closely reflects representations of the Irish in colonial discourse as the feminine 'other' to Britain, most influentially by English poet and cultural critic Matthew Arnold in the late-19th Century (see Cairns and Richards, 1988).

While Moore's songs have remained popular in bourgeois art-music circles, this strand of Irish music has only recently been adopted as an internationally performed popular music within the music-industry category of Celtic Music, which comprises an ill-defined spectrum of musical practices that accompany a new version of Celticism. When we hear the voice of Enya (or her Norwegian substitute, Sissel, in the music track of *Titanic*), when we hear the drawn-out melismatic notes of the uilleann pipes, or the recently invented low whistle (which has a similar range), we hear the sound of a revived Celticism that represents Celtic peoples as melancholy, sentimental and feminine: the gifted losers delineated by Matthew Arnold in the 19th Century.

A Vigorous, Masculine Irish Music

In the mid-19th Century, a second type of music was adopted as a vehicle for a more politicised nationalist movement that was in complete contrast to the drawing-room airs of Thomas Moore. It is a masculine version of Irish music and is typified by the vast output of Thomas Davis, who set his incendiary political verses to popular Irish song airs. One of his most enduring songs, *A Nation Once Again*, is often performed in Irish pubs today.

Nationalism, itself a masculinist discourse, relies on the "deep, horizontal comradeship" of the nationalist fraternity (Anderson, 1991: 7). Within the political nationalist movement, Irish traditional music became a masculine field. This was once again related to colonial stereotypes, in this case the violent and drunken, irresponsible and seditious caricature of the Irishman that had festered through the centuries from the Elizabethan court to the bestial caricatures of English political cartoons and the vaudeville stage. In what postcolonial theorists call the process of inversion, this stereotype was revalued as the bold, lively, masculine national expressed in nationalist ballads ('rebel songs').

It has only been in the revival of Irish traditional music since the 1950s (which coincided with a more prosperous and economically and politically outward-looking nationalism) that this dance music repertoire has been regarded as not only exclusively Irish, but capable of expressing essentially Irish characteristics and thus symbolising 'Irishness'.

The success of ballad bands such as the Dubliners in the 1960s meant that by 1970 the international sound of Ireland was a mix of political and street ballads sung in a strong, bass voice together with fast and flashy instrumental performances of dance tunes ('Irish traditional music'). The performers were patently working-class in costume, accent and demeanour. Irish ballad bands based on this model were exclusively male, exhibiting a swaggering masculinity.

Thus the colonial stereotype of Celticism that represented Irish music as reflecting the spiritual melancholy and ineffectual emotionality of the Irish was overtaken by a more masculine stereotype. This representation of the Irish as masculine re-valued a colonial stereotype that had depicted the Irish as bestial and uncivilized to a national type that was masculine in a more positive sense and expressed in 'rebel songs' and dance music.

In 1970, when Tony Richardson's *Ned Kelly* was released, Irish dance music was experiencing an international boom, aided by contemporary touring groups the Dubliners (who performed ballads and dance music in a rough-and-ready working-class persona) and the Chieftains (who played arrangements of both the older 'classical' Irish music and dance music in settings suited to bourgeois art-music audiences). The musicians who perform ballads and dance music in both the 1970 and the 2003 version of the Ned Kelly story come from this performance background: in the 1970s, fiddler Bob McInnes played in a Sydney Irish ballad band, while the Idle Diddlies have a similar group that continues to perform in Melbourne (as do the 'steerage party' musicians in *Titanic* who perform as the American 'Irish pub' band, Gaelic Storm).

Ned in 1970

In English director Tony Richardson's 1970 *Ned Kelly*, the musical score overlays the story of an Irish–Australian anti-colonial figure with an American aesthetic, a Hollywood generic sensibility and an English leading actor who can neither voice nor embody the masculinity of the iconic Australian anti-hero. As such, it throws into relief both the anti-English and anti-American feelings that were circulating at the time of the film's release.

Marketed as an "explosive frontier crime saga" (video sleeve), Richardson's direction places the Ned Kelly story within the genre of the American frontier western. The screenplay follows a man fighting the injustices of corrupt lawmen against his family and his fellow-Irish settlers. The music track emphasises the legendary status of the Kelly gang by weaving through the narrative a series of ballads written by Shel Silverstein for the movie and sung by American country music stars Waylon Jennings and Kris Kristofferson. The American accents, instrumentation (guitar and banjo) and expressions ('turnkey', 'frontier', 'ranching') all reinforce the impression that, but for a few eucalypts and kangaroos, the movie might have been from the original Frontierland of the USA.

The ballads largely occupy bridging sequences as the film cuts from scene to scene, moving the story forward (as in *Ranchin' in the Evenin'* and *Shadow in the Gallows*[1]) or entertain us while a non-verbal scene is played out (as in *Pleasures of a Sunday Afternoon*). In both cases, the songs fill in the back-story and interpret the action. Especially in the jaunty ballad *Blame it on the Kellys*, the songs undercut the violence and bloodshed of scenes of fist-fighting, armed robbery, horse-stealing and murder, as if telling the viewer to lighten up since, after all, this is only a frontier legend, a minor Western from the colonial periphery.

For Australian audiences in 1970, the Kelly legend was a serious matter both to those for whom it represented an ideal Australian anti-authoritarian type and those who feared its power to provoke anarchic sentiments. The jaunty ballads in the musical score undercut the legend's local power by universalising and trivialising it. The effect of the distinctly un-Australian style of the ballads is to position Ned Kelly as a poor cousin to the better-known anti-heroes of the Hollywood Western. At the time of the movie's release, the growing anti-American feeling in Australia (related to Australia's unpopular participation in the Vietnam War) made the American ballads especially unwelcome to Australian audiences.

41

The heroic figure of Ned is further undermined by his portrayal by a lead actor unable to convey the swaggering masculinity of the ballads. From the moment it was known that the Rolling Stones' lead singer Mick Jagger would play Ned, Australians were aghast: a puny, pasty-faced, effeminate musician *and* Englishman playing 'our' national icon? The outcry grew to contempt when people actually saw the film and found that Jagger, a charismatic performer on the concert stage, could no more act than he could ride a horse or shoot a pistol. Audiences and critics[2] responded with derision at his discomfort on the screen, his mumbled lines and inability to govern his gangly limbs.

This popular response in 1970 brings into focus the qualities of Ned Kelly that had made him a national icon from the 1870s. Kelly possessed a tough masculinity and physical courage that were valued among rural selectors struggling on their unviable small farms. His contempt for the law also appealed to the selectors' sense of injustice against a state that had promised land for all but had delivered instead a system of slow torture to the small farmers (many of convict origin, or immigrants from rural Ireland) because the best land had already been acquired by the squatters. Added to this was a legal system skewed to the interests of large landowners and overseen by a corrupt and ineffectual police force. Ned Kelly was the last of Australia's bushrangers, not only because the growth of telegraphic communications and railroads challenged the outlaw's ability to outwit the police, but also because his years of eluding Victoria's police force became a major catalyst for its reform.

Jagger's rendering of the Irish–Australian bushranging ballad *The Wild Colonial Boy*, supposedly a taunt but in effect a pensive, tentative performance, only added fuel to the outrage at such an un-Australian, un-masculine character. This song, which tells of an earlier bushranger's career and demise, is part of a second component in the score of Richardson's *Ned Kelly*: the diegetic score (that is, music produced by characters within the film-world).

An ensemble of musicians play dance music at a welcome home party for Ned, and a woman (Australian folk-singer, Glen Tomassetti) sings an Irish song, *She Moved Through the Fair*, to the accompaniment of a tin whistle played by Irish–Australian musician Declan Affley[3]. The dramatic effect of these performances (like that of *The Wild Colonial Boy*) is to reinforce the Irish identity of the Kelly gang, to locate Ned's exploits within a tradition celebrated in folklore, and to announce a romantic link between Ned and a young woman who share meaningful looks at the line "it will not be long now 'til our wedding day". (Ironically, the song is a man's lament for his bride who dies before their wedding day.) In emphasising the Irish background of Ned and his familiars, this scene uses the two musical tropes of Irishness identified above: a lively, happy dance music and a melancholy, spiritual air. Rather than revealing both the masculine and feminine sides of the legendary figure of Ned, the musical score here serves only to further emphasise the inability of Jagger and his director to convey the style of masculinity contained in the Australian legend. His lolling absorption in the woman's love song conveys only passivity, for he is obviously not going to make his lover's dream come true.

In the dramatically pivotal scene in the Glenrowan Pub, where the Kelly gang take the town's residents hostage, and are later besieged by the police before Ned's climactic shoot-out and capture, hostages and outlaws drink and dance together. The score takes up earlier references to Irish–Australia in a fast, dance-hall version of *The Wild Colonial Boy*[4], only to revert again to the iconography of the Western. Both aurally and visually, the scene evokes a Wild West saloon, complete with honky-tonk piano and dancers performing the dosey-do (a back-to-back square dance move).

Richardson's *Ned Kelly* fails to present a hero who reflects the masculine nationalism of both Kelly's 1870s and the rising nationalism of Australia around 1970[5]. Significantly, this failure is potently evident in the film's music track. The early 1970s also saw the genesis of associated cultural forms including the bush band, a version of which appears in the party and Glenrowan scenes. These bands combined the performance style of Irish ballad bands such as the Dubliners with a mix of Australian 'bush' songs (that had come into circulation due to the efforts of an earlier generation of radical nationalists in the 1950s) and Irish dance music (Smith 2001). While bush bands such as the perennially popular Bushwackers were notable for their strongly nationalist ethos, they also endorsed the notion of an Australian national character as essentially masculine and Irish in derivation. Like other successful bush bands, their membership was (then) exclusively male and their stage costumes, swagger and unrefined delivery imitated (their idea of) the legendary Australian bushmen they sang about.

The stereotype of masculinity that represented the Irish–Australian bushrangers was consistent with stereotypes of the Irish in circulation at the time the film was made. In 1970, the Irish were under the cloud of the recently erupted Troubles, and the Irish filmically represented in Tony Richardson's London, for example, were treated with hostility and suspicion. The film's popular and critical failures were not due to the inappropriate depiction of Irish–Australians but, in large part, to Jagger's inconsistency with this widely accepted stereotype. The musical score highlighted the Kelly legend's similarities with the American outlaw anti-hero, and, given the film's emphasis on Kelly's pro-Irish, anti-British stance, Jagger's English background and irrepressible accent were, at the very least, incongruous.

A 'New-Age' Ned

In early 21st Century Australia, the stereotypes of masculinity, the poor Irish and the arrogant English found in Richardson's *Ned Kelly* seem crude and anachronistic. Such ways of thinking about masculinity, about ethnicity in Australian society and about national identity (or identities) have all been challenged since 1970. To make a film like Richardson's in 2003 would have been unthinkable. Gregor Jordan's *Ned Kelly*, based on Robert Drewe's novel *Our Sunshine* (1991), offers a pensive, introspective Ned, a man with a conscience and a deep need to be valued; a private, sensitive man – despite a screenplay that selects episodes from the outlaw's career almost identical to those in Richardson's film. Two additional strands in the screenplay are taken from Drewe's novel: a sexual affair between Ned and a squatter's wife (which Jordan depicts, somewhat incredibly, as a romance) and a scene of childhood heroism and acclaim that haunts Ned in moments of crisis. The result of both is to suggest a complex hero in whom the desire to be 'good' and socially recognised struggles with his rage against injustice and treachery. While Jordan's film adheres to the familiar myth of the bold, masculine anti-hero, his Ned (like Drewe's) has a complex interior life and exhibits a kind of post-feminist masculinity that emphasises his emotionality and sensuality and has him listening and responding to the women in his life. Ned's complexity and interiority are reinforced by Klaus Badelt's musical score, which draws on both the stereotypes available in Irish music (the melancholy feminine and the vigorous masculine) discussed above.

Since 1970, the idea that the Irish played a crucial role in forming an Australian national identity has gone relatively unchallenged, but stereotypes of the Irish themselves have changed a great deal. Irishness in Australia was once associated with rebels and rabble-rousing, working-class labouring men, Catholicism, poverty, living rough and drinking hard, gambling and swearing (most of which are characteristics of the general Australian type identified by Ward [1958] and critiqued by others). Several developments in the 1990s changed ways of thinking about the Irish: the Celtic Tiger economy, which challenged the stereotype of the Irish as ignorant and poor; a new type of Irish immigrant (highly educated and ambitious professionals); the increased traffic between Ireland and Australia; the many thousands of backpackers in Australia's coastal cities; and the advent of the Irish theme pub. While these theme pubs drew on stereotypes of Irishness that were in many ways familiar in Australia (hospitality, alcohol, premodern décor, charming workers) they also appealed to the middle-class and especially to middle-class women. They were respectable public places, in contrast to the working-class masculinity of Australian pubs where immigrant Irish workers had gathered in the 1970s (and where women were not welcome).

By the 1990s, one quarter of the Australian population were born outside Australia (Daniel, 1994: 233). Irishness had become almost a default ethnicity for those without a truly 'ethnic' heritage (O'Farrell, 2000: 330). The concept of masculinity had also undergone significant revisions in the face of challenges from feminism, a more feminised workforce, and government social policies supporting such changes. The 1990s in particular saw new versions of masculinity dramatised in popular culture and sold as style to consumers: the 'new lad', the 'meterosexual', the 'sensitive new-age guy'. Men could seek to please their women, use cosmetics, dress for sexual success, even eat quiche, without diminishing their masculinity, or necessarily losing the respect of other males. The sensitive male hero has become familiar in movies aimed at male audiences. One example is *Braveheart* (dir: Mel Gibson, 1995) which, like *Titanic*, uses the tropes of masculine and feminine Irish music (notably, in the theme to *Braveheart* the more lyrical and tuneful Irish uilleann pipes are featured in preference to the Scots bagpipes). In each case, the music is scored by James Horner, whose choice of instrumentation, orchestration and simple, melancholy melodic themes are closely followed by Klaus Badelt[6] in his score for Jordan's *Ned Kelly*. Badelt was a film music and commercials composer in Germany before moving to the USA in 1998 on an invitation by Hans Zimmerman with whom he collaborated on many Hollywood productions (including *Gladiator* [dir: Ridley Scott, 2000] and *Pearl Harbour* [dir: Jerry Bruckheimer and Michael Bay, 2001]).

Heath Ledger's Ned Kelly fits masculine stereotypes: unlike Jagger, he is tall, strong and muscular; he rides and shoots competently and shows an unsentimental admiration and empathy for women. While he fights to protect his mother and sisters, he also shows respect for his married lover and listens when she speaks. Ledger's Ned apologises to the first man he shoots, gives money to his supporters and upbraids his brother for acting like a "common thief". Like Robert Drewe's Ned, he is sensitive and self-reflective. His Irish characteristics entwine the two stereotypes: he is irascible and violent, articulate and musical, generous and charismatic, but also has a melancholy side, and the film (with perfect hindsight) suggests it is his fate to be misunderstood, persecuted and finally destroyed.

Gregor Jordan brings forth Ned's interiority and sense of doom both dramatically (through voice-over) and visually (through images of bare trees and a harsh, desolate landscape) and through contrast with the technical superiority of the police (telegraph and trains). Of at least equal power is the musical performance of Ned's brooding interior and his life-devouring exterior. In 1975, Laura Mulvey proposed the notion of the "male gaze" in which she identified a "triple" gaze – of the camera, of the hero toward the heroine, and the spectator identifying with the hero – and linked it with male voyeurism, fetishism and sadism. Changes in filmic notions of masculinity have brought about subtle changes in the nature of the male gaze: a consciousness and responsiveness to women's viewpoint that both appeal more to the female spectator and allow the male to accept a wider definition of the masculine.

The film music track is one important way in which this change has been achieved, even in films for a predominantly male audience (such as *Ned Kelly*) as well as those marketed more to women (such as *Titanic*). This is particularly true in through-composed scores. In Tony Richardson's *Ned Kelly*, the effect of ballads that comment on the action is to distance the audience emotionally from the hero. This relatively open relationship between perceiver and score results in what Anahid Kassabian terms *affiliating identifications* that 'open' the psychic field, whereas a composed score, like that of Badelt and Horner in the films mentioned above, narrows the psychic field, conditions *assimilating identifications* that "draw perceivers into socially and historically unfamiliar positions" (Kassabian, 2001: 2). In Badelt's score, Ned's interiority, his foretold doom and his Irishness coincide in the sweet melancholy of a string ensemble and woodwind (low whistle and the occasional oboe) in predominantly minor keys. Both Badelt's melodic range and his orchestration resemble Horner's score for *Titanic* and reflect more about Hollywood conventions than they do Australian or Irish-Australian elements.

45

In addition to Badelt's original music score, 'traditional' musical numbers include arrangements of Irish dance tunes (reels *The Morning Star*, *The Star of Munster*, *Laington's* and the *Kesh Jig*, performed and arranged by The Idle Diddlies and Blackberry Jam). Performed by an anachronistic 'pub band' in the lively atmosphere of the Imperial Hotel, a neutral meeting place where both police and selectors congregate, the music emphasises the Irish heritage common to both groups. As Heath Ledger's Ned later tells his hostages in the Glenrowan pub: "We're all Irish boys, selectors' sons … It's Regina versus us."

Elsewhere, however, Gregor Jordan uses Irish music to subtly reinforce the outlaws' case that they are the victims of prejudice and injustice. The song *Moreton Bay* (performed by Bernard Fanning, leader of popular Australian rock band Powderfinger) is an Australian ballad sung to an Irish air and relates an Irish convict's homesick lament and outcry against cruelty. Sung by another historically inaccurate performance ensemble to Aaron Sherritt as he contemplates his treachery, and reprised in the following scene when the outlaws confirm his betrayal, the song reinforces the interpretation of these events as a matter of tribal loyalties. In his infamous 'Jerilderie Letter', Ned Kelly summarises this song as if it were historical fact.

Even more indicative of the subtle ways in which the music track reinforces Jordan's efforts to win audience sympathy for Ned is the scene in the Glenrowan Pub. Where Richardson had played up the revelry in the dance scene mentioned above, Jordan edits this to a short sequence. The music that accompanies more of the intense vigil preceding the shoot-out with police is the slow, quiet solo voice of the concertina (the only musical instrument that historical accounts mention). The air played is *Na Connerys*, an Irish song about three brothers transported to NSW for political crimes. The significance is not the authenticity of the instrument or the song played, so much as the ways in which (especially in comparison to Richardson's soundtrack) Jordan gives us a Ned Kelly whose Irish identification is reinforced less by the vigorous dance music than by the melancholy lament of a tenor voice or the concertina and lyrics (or implied lyrics) that evoke the Irish as unjustly persecuted.

The diegetic music (played by people inside the film-world) is remarkably similar in both films, as well as in *Titanic*, in which 'Irishness' is performed by bands that are replicas, not of musical ensembles of the 1870s or (in the case of *Titanic*) the 1910s, but of the Irish ballad bands that first appeared in Dublin in the 1960s and have recently experienced a revival in the Irish theme pubs established globally during the 1990s. Also anachronistic in all cases is the presence of young women drinking and dancing in pubs. In the two more recent films, the anachronisms are entirely consistent with those in the now internationally ubiquitous Irish theme pub.

Conclusion

Ned Kelly, in 2003, was less an Irish–Australian and more a Celtic–Australian insofar as the representation is one identifiable more with an internationalised Celtic cultural sensibility than with the specifics of a nationally identifiable group. Ned's masculinity was not that of the rugged individual celebrated in the Australian Legend, but a version of masculinity that has adapted to the concerns of women and is more sensitive and reflective. In giving us a Ned Kelly unafraid to display aspects of femininity, director Gregor Jordan has opened up the male gaze identified by Mulvey and allowed a masculinity inflected by feminism to enter Ned Kelly's film world. This shift has been achieved with the benefit of a music track that emphasises 'feminine' elements of Celticism and, by these means, an additional layer of gendered complexity is offered to Australia's iconic masculine hero. As such, Jordan addresses both an Australian and an international film community using a different approach to Richardson. Jordan's universal themes of social justice, love and loyalty are explored using elements identifiable to audiences in the new millennium.

Notes

1. Cue titles given to tracks on soundtrack album released 1970.
2. International critics continue to pan the film. See for example Walter Chaw's one-star rating review accessed at
   http://filmfreakcentral.net/dvdreviews/nedkelly1970.html.
3. According to Hayward, Declan Affley with Dave de Hugard "recorded songs and instrumental pieces for the film's soundtrack but their recordings were discarded in preference to material by Waylon Jennings and Shel Silverstein" (2001: 149).
4. Performed by bush band Wild Colonial Boys, a band formed in Sydney in 1969 and a significant predecessor for subsequent Australian bush bands (see Hayward, 2001: 134).
5. A significant element of which was a revival of the Australian film industry (spearheaded by the Whitlam government and key figures such as Philip Adams) via educational establishments such as the National Institute for Dramatic Arts and the Australian Film and Television School (later including Radio), funding sources and tax breaks, and other initiatives.
6. With additional music by Ramin Djawadi and Geoff Zanelli.

Chapter Three

HAUNTINGS:
Sound Track Representations of Papua New Guinea in *To have and to hold* and *In a Savage Land*

PHILIP HAYWARD

O ver the past ninety years a series of Australian films have projected various fantasies, anxieties and, of late, shades of nostalgia for Papua New Guinea. Central to these has been the history of Australian colonial experience. The southeastern section of New Guinea (the area known as Papua) was established as a British colony in 1884, with the Dutch claiming the western section and the Germans, the northeast. Heavily staffed by Australian personnel, the British colonial imprint created a frontier of opportunity for Australia in the late 1800s and early 1900s. Following its seizure of German territories during World War One, Australia took over administration of the whole of the eastern part of the Island in its own right[1], making it one of the last of the 'old guard' imperial powers and intertwining the territories of Papua and New Guinea (PNG) and Australia in a history of exploration, exploitation and eventual withdrawal. For much of Australia's period of administration, writers, photographers and filmmakers created bodies of work that stressed the marked differences of Papua New Guinea's indigenous cultures from white western norms and/or placed intrepid white explorers, administrators (and occasional misfits) in perilous straits that they overcame with resourcefulness and racial confidence. These themes, more or less blatantly, promoted and enshrined a doctrine of white supremacy and of the 'white man's burden' of colonial responsibility.

The earliest Australian films of Papua New Guinea were made by photographer/filmmaker/adventurer Frank Hurley. Hurley's documentary *Pearls and Savages* (1922)[2] played to appreciative audiences in Australia during the 1920s and presented striking images of the northern island to Australians. Hurley followed *Pearls and Savages* with two fiction features, both made in 1926, *Hound of the Deep*, shot on Thursday Island, and *Jungle Woman*, shot in Dutch-controlled west New Guinea. Despite the latter's lurid, if predictable, plot – involving the kidnapping of a white woman and a pitched battle in which the white characters emerge victorious – both films met with critical indifference and limited box office success. It was over thirty years before another Australian feature film was set and filmed in PNG. This was a joint Australian-French co-production directed by Lee Robinson and Marcel Pagliero in 1954. Revealing a degree of uncertainty as to how to pitch the film to international audiences, the film was released in France as *L'Odyssee du Captaine Steve*, as *Walk into Paradise* in Australia and, somewhat confusingly, as *Walk into Hell* in North America. The film starred popular Australian actor Chips Rafferty as a patrol officer involved in an expedition for oil, accompanied by a female malaria researcher. Drawing on the deepest clichés of West meets 'primitive other', the film pits Rafferty against 'witch doctors', whose influence wanes as the protagonists convince locals of the efficacy of modernity and western ways.

While *Walk into Paradise* was the last Australian fiction feature shot in PNG prior to independence in 1975, a series of documentaries were also produced in the immediate post-War period[3]. The majority of these represented aspects of the Australian administration and resource exploitation of the country. Amongst other subjects explored by filmmakers was the theme of PNG's readiness (or otherwise) for self-government. The nation's attainment of independence produced a shift in documentary production. The Australian government agency and/or business sponsored productions of the colonial period were superceded by a series of less didactic/functional films produced with the assistance of bodies such as Film Australia. The first of these was Denis O'Rourke's *Yumi Yet* (1977), which offered a multi-perspectival representation of the processes and ceremonials of PNG's transition to statehood. A subsequent film, *Ileksen* (1978), funded by the PNG Electoral Commission, used similar techniques. O'Rourke's third PNG film, *Shark Callers of Kontu* (1982), had a more traditional anthropological subject. His fourth and (to date) last PNG film, *Cannibal Tours* (1989), turned the anthropological gaze on western tourists and their behaviour. Documentary team Bob Connolly and Robin Anderson also undertook a sustained engagement with aspects of Australian colonialism and its aftermath in the prize winning trio of feature documentaries centred on the Leahy family: *First Contact* (1982), *Joe Leahy's Neighbours* (1988) and *Black Harvest* (1992).

O'Rourke's work was also influential on Papuan-born Melbourne-resident independent filmmaker Mark Worth. While working on a documentary about canoe makers on Manus Island[4] in 1985, Worth approached David Bridie, the vocalist and keyboard player with Melbournian avant garde rock band Not Drowning, Waving (henceforth NDW) to discuss working on a music track for the film. The two formed a continuing relationship that encouraged the band to explore aspects of cross-cultural collaboration with Papua New Guinean musicians, and this continued from 1986 to 1996, when the band broke up[5]. One of the main outcomes of this enterprise was the band's *Tabaran* album, released in 1990. Worth remained a close associate of the group during this period, making a film clip for NDW's

PNG-themed song *Up in the Mountains* in 1986 and directing a documentary of the production of the *Tabaran* album and the band's 1989 visit to PNG, which was screened on SBS TV as part of their 'Masterpiece' series in 1992.

Worth and NDW's fascination with PNG and West Papuan issues reflected a broader interest in these topics amongst inner-city Melbournian cultural groups during the decade[6] which their activities served to amplify. Another outcome of this cultural focus was independent film and video director John Hillcoat's feature film *To have and to hold*. Like Worth, Hillcoat also had a sustained relationship with a leading Melbourne indie rock act, Nick Cave and the Bad Seeds, having shot a series of music videos for them and also directed Nick Cave in the lead role in the violent prison drama *Ghosts ... of the Civil Dead* (1989).

To have and to hold (1996)

To have and to hold has been succinctly described as "a haunting *romance noir* about love guilt, passion and obsession" (unattributed, 1996: np). The film's melodrama is as intense and humid as the climate it represents and is scattered with sudden, shocking outbursts of violence. The narrative is centred on Jack (played by Tcheky Karyo), a middle aged French resident living on the East Sepik river in PNG[7], who is struggling to come to terms with the death of his wife Rose. During a brief visit to Melbourne he encounters a novelist, named Kate (played by Rachel Griffiths), who bears a marked resemblance to Rose. The two return to the Sepik where Jack's life and personality unravel as Kate appears first to flirt with and then decline to be a substitute for Rose (unlike the female protagonist of Hitchcock's *Vertigo* [1958], a film to which *To have and to hold* bears a number of resemblances) and his idealised memories of Rose are challenged by the images he discovers on videotape. Simultaneously, Kate experiences crises as she struggles to deal with Jack and negotiates the backdrop of *raskol* culture[8] and dissolution of general law and order that Hillcoat uses to typify PNG.

The score for *To have and to hold* combines original music, written by Hillcoat's long-term musical collaborators Nick Cave, Mick Harvey and Blixa Bargeld, and pre-recorded tracks. The film's music attracted favourable critical comments upon release and won the production an Australian Film Institute 'Best Original Score' award in 1998. Harvey has commented that Hillcoat initially approached Cave and Bargeld to provide a score "in the old school style, more along the lines of [what] Bernard Herrmann would do" (quoted in Gee, 1999: online). The reference to Herrmann and "old school" traditions of scoring is significant here, since the film's brooding melodrama is more akin to styles of 1950's cinema than more contemporary genre productions. But, as Harvey correctly identifies (ibid), his final orchestral music more closely recalls the classic Hollywood neo-Romanticist scoring tradition analysed by Flinn (1992) than Herrmann's more modernist work on seminal films such as *Psycho* (dir: Alfred Hitchcock, 1960).

In terms of the division of duties in the score, Harvey has stated that the production company originally:

> asked Nick and Blixa to do the soundtrack ... Nick was obviously meant

to supply the more melodic element and Blixa to work on making music out of the machine noises and so forth, and they were meant to kind of overlap somewhere, where the noises and music all became one. (ibid)

Cave and Bargeld invited Harvey on to the project on the strength of his keyboard and arranging skills, and his contribution – together with his production of the final sound mix with co-producer Gareth Jones – helped combine Cave's melodic ideas and Bargeld's sound compositions in a unified score. In drawing these elements together, Harvey identifies that he worked with a strong sense of traditional western scoring practices, stating that:

It must relate to what must have been theatre music in the past or even writing music for ballet or opera, what that would have been like in the past. You're writing music to the choreography of editing or even quite specifically to the choreography of movements and action that's going on up there. (ibid)

The most prominent elements of the score are string and woodwind passages. The oboe is principal instrument in several cues and harp and piano also feature. The orchestral music includes several cues repeated with variations, most notably the waltz love theme that initially accompanies Jack's and Kate's dancing and romancing in Melbourne and recurs at various points in scenes of their relationship. The orchestral passages range in style from functionally brooding underscore (featuring low-pitched drones) to brief, almost parodic, lushly romantic pieces (such as the sequence accompanying Kate's introduction to Jack's bedroom – CD track 3, *Candlelit bedroom*) and the Herrmannesque flourish of 'slippery glissandi' at the end of the sequence accompanying the killing of Sal (CD track 17 – *Murder*)[9]. These orchestral sequences are interspersed with more 'experimental' sound compositions, several of which (CD tracks 4, 13, 14, 15, 16) incorporate flute (and/or blown shell sounds) that function somewhere between score and atmos, serving to unsettle and stress the otherness of PNG for the expatriates who are the centre of the narrative. The sources of these samples are not identified on the CD, film credits or video print.

Despite suggestions during pre-production that Cave intended to collaborate with PNG musicians to produce music for *To have and to hold*, the only extended (and identified) piece of PNG music included in the film is provided by the (Goroka [PNG] based) Raun Raun Theatre (RRT). Their track is referred to as *Mourning Song* on the CD, the notes for which credit it to a recording in Melbourne in November 1995. RRT member Hitch Loape has provided a different account however, identifying it as a traditional song from Morobe Province entitled *Sido*, recorded during the Warana Festival in Brisbane in September 1995. Loape has also stated that the track was included on the CD without RRT's permission[10].

In addition to these elements of original and PNG-sourced music, a pre-recorded song plays a prominent role in the narrative, Scott Walker's performance of Bob Dylan's *I threw it all away* (originally recorded on Dylan's 1969 album *Nashville Skyline*). Walker's version was recorded specially for the film and was produced and arranged by British composer Barry Adamson. The song is introduced during a wake for Jack's recently deceased wife, Rose, where it is played on a cassette recorder and heard with all the noise associated with analogue recordings and lo-fi playback. The song subsequently serves to invoke her memory at various stages in the narrative. The lyrics (modified slightly from Dylan's original recording) are a clear statement of loss and regret that are singularly apposite for the film (complete with suitable topographical references as metaphors). As the opening verses express:

> *Once I held her in my arms*
> *She said she would always stay*
> *But I was cruel*
> *I treated her like a fool*
> *I threw it all away*

> *Once I had mountains in the palm of my hand*
> *Rivers that ran through every day*
> *I must have been mad*
> *I never knew what I had*
> *Until I threw it all away*

The version of the song used in the music track is suitably 'filmic', featuring a stirring string and woodwind accompaniment, echoic drums and piano with Walker's characteristically low–pitched, vibrato-laden voice prominent in the mix (in a style not dissimilar to Cave's own – although far more controlled and pitch accurate) and dripping with resigned regret.

The song is used in various ways. It features diegetically, on a well-used tape played on several occasions, and is also performed by Rose and an unnamed local woman. Rose's performance provides a shocking affront to Jack. On a videotape that Jack watches after Rose's death, he sees her wearing a glamorous red dress that he had bought her but which she had refused to wear for him. She is shown at Sal's bar, heavily drunk, singing the song in a slurred, ironic version, taking on the persona of someone who "threw it all away" and emphasising the final verse, as a direct message to Jack:

> *So if you find someone that gives you all of her love*
> *Take it to your heart, don't let it stray*
> *One thing is for certain*
> *You will surely be a–hurtin'*
> *If you throw it all away*

Finally, after Kate has left him (and PNG), Jack hits on another prospect. The film shows us Jack at Sal's bar watching a young indigenous woman wearing Rose's original – and, by now, fetishised – red dress. Looking at Jack she is singing along to a tape recording of *I threw it all away*. Initially nervous, her confidence grows as she observes Jack's response (as he views her blurred image through his glass) and, as her facial expression lightens, her vocal is dropped out in the mix and Walker's voice fills the sound space as she lip-synchs the song and the film ends.

Together with the contributions of the film's scoring team, sound designer Dean Gawen also played a notable role in the production. The sound track approximates an aural 'humidity' at various stages through placing background ambient sounds – most notably insect noises – high in the mix, 'crowding' the characters and their speech. Further aural 'pressure' is applied in the film through the prominent presence of ceiling fan and electric generator noises at various points in the narrative (elements that mark Bargeld's contribution to the score). Atmos, diegetic sound and music[11] often blur in the film, such as the early sequence where the string-section opening to the initial 'jungle location' sequence is abruptly displaced by insect noises and an acapella choral sequence, only to emerge under it and grow in intensity to an integrated section before the insects and acapella parts are faded out altogether (CD track 2, entitled *The jungle of love*). Various sounds used in the film were sourced, without permission (or subsequent payment) from Steven Feld's CD recording of human and environmental sounds *Voices of the Rainforest* (1991), a recording made in the Bosavi community's area of the Southern Highlands region[12]. Together with the usage of RRT's *Sido* (discussed above), this suggests – at very least – a cavalier attitude to cultural rights and ownership of Papua New Guinean recordings that neatly mirrors the colonialist sensibility that permeates the film.

Throughout the film Jack is haunted by the spectre of his lost, idealised love. A broader haunting surrounds this, the memory of (neo-)colonial power and privilege that Jack and his fellow expatriates have enjoyed and that is now haunted by the return/revenge of the repressed local population who circle at the edges of lit and visible spaces in the film. The film's score – which nostalgically revisits the already nostalgicist canon and codes of classic Hollywood screen music – provides a type of interior aural melodrama to the small group of expatriates.

The reiterated version of *I threw it all away*, implicitly pulled from the youthful past of its middle aged male characters, mournfully expresses loss, with Walker's own moody melancholy (enacted in his own career as a troubled 'existential' pop star) permeating his song and Adamson's arrangement of it. The PNG 'characters' – if such a term does not flatter their sketchy renditions in the film – have no such musical realisations. As 'nature', part of the fabric of jungle PNG, the sounds of their voices are blended in with atmos and location.

In this formation, the *raskols* (paradoxically) function as 'culture' and, in the aurally decultured landscape Hillcoat provides, have no convenient local signifier. The music track thereby defaults to entirely foreign referent, British-Caribbean ragga tracks – most notably *Gangster Bone*[13] – which is presumably meant to imbue the image of the *raskols* with the toughness of Jamaican-derived 'yardie' gang culture (for those who can enact such a decoding), or else simply serve as generic 'black gang music'. In the latter, ghosts of colonialism also linger: black is other, cultural difference within that ethnocentrist category is unimportant – oppositional otherness is all the same, a haunting of whiteness.

In a Savage Land (1998)

The title of Bill Bennett's film is deliberately anachronistic, in that it derives from a common western usage and sensibility in the period in which its story is set, the late 1930s and early 1940s, a moment immediately prior to the outbreak of the Pacific War. The film was inspired by two sources. The first was the experience of pioneering anthropologist Bronislaw Malinowski in the New Guinea Trobriand Islands in the 1920s, which resulted in his seminal publication *The Sexual Life of Savages* (1929). The second was Bennett's family background. As the film's press kit states:

> *The film's genesis goes back 35 years, when an eight year-old Bill Bennett found a rusty trunk belonging to his father, who served as a war photographer in Borneo and New Guinea. In the trunk were some photographs of the people of the Trobriand Islands which, the young Bennett was told, were called "The Islands of Love" because the women were rather liberal with their affections.* (Unattributed, 1998: 6)

Quoting Bennett, the press kit continues:

> *I became intrigued with this place at university and when I started to read more about it, the whole notion of sex and freedom within a 'primitive' culture fascinated me, but my reading confirmed my suspicions that it was more complex than was perceived, with strict social and moral codes.* (ibid)

These comments serve to identify an initial, inspirational nostalgia, the opening of a "rusty trunk" from which emerged images from Australia's colonial past, which in turn lead to an encounter with Malinowski's writings and a fascination with the inspirational place of both – the Trobriand Islands. As all this suggests, the film was a highly personal project, co-researched, written and produced with Bennett's life-partner Jennifer Bennett during an extended period in the mid to late 1990s.

Drawing on the issues of gender, sexuality and social and moral codes that the Bennetts explored in their research and writing, the final film modernises its source references by making the relationship and gender/power issues between two married, white Australian anthropologists Evelyn and Phillip Spence (played by Maya Stange and Martin Donovan) the focus of the narrative, with their interactions with the Trobriand Islanders providing the frame and context for the tensions between characters. While the Trobriand Islanders emerge from Bennett's film with more complexity and dignity than the local population represented in Hillcoat's feature, they do not cross over to becoming characters and therefore do not inhabit the narrative space of the cluster of expatriates that the film focuses on. Like *To have and to hold*, *In a Savage Land* has a love tension at its core that becomes amplified in the exotic 'other' space of its setting. In Bennett's film the Spences' marriage falls apart due to differences and rivalries, most specifically, Evelyn's desire to be acknowledged as a researcher equal to her husband. Following her husband's death, and a period of intense mourning (described below), she begins a relationship with an American trader, Mick Carpenter (played by Rufus Sewell), which is almost immediately interrupted by the arrival of Japanese invasion forces.

Deciding to appoint an Australian composer to the project, an obvious choice suggested itself. As Jennifer Bennett has stated:

> *David Bridie was the perfect composer for this film ... because he came to the production with a vast knowledge and understanding of PNG*

music already, yet he was also an established and highly regarded composer of more conventional scores. Our brief to him was to find an appropriate blend between the two types of music ... (ibid: 10)

Bridie has commented that his production method was "totally different" from his (and the industry's) usual approach:

because normally I would be composing the score myself, but here, in some ways, I'm recording and compiling and then, maybe at a later date, overlaying and fusing some of these sounds together. (ibid)

The process of "recording and compiling" was also highly unusual for a film composer since Bridie chose to spend an extended period in the Trobriands, familiarising himself with the local music and recording local artists with field equipment (with the assistance of Cairns-based PNG percussionist Ben Hakalitz). Bridie has described the recording process in the following terms:

Ben Hakalitz and I slept in an open-air hut by the beach, venturing out in the cool of the evening to a local clearing. The whole village as audience followed, one by one the different performers came over to the microphone. Everyone fell quiet and each artist performed, the children watching in respectful awe as their Uncles and Aunties sang old songs. Laughter erupted during hip thrusting dances or some little play, probably at our expense.

Other days were spent recording ambience – layers of insects, conch shells, ocean waves, short wave radio, generator and Ben playing percussion on old biscuit tins, 44 gallon drums and other odd things that made up part of the film set. (1999: 2)

Bridie's approach went beyond the functional in that he recorded a considerable volume of local music (beyond that necessary for score compilation). A selection of this material was issued as a bonus disk accompanying the first run of the soundtrack CD. Entitled *Wosi: Music of the Trobriand Islands, PNG*, this was described in its CD sleeve notes as "untouched Trobriand songs, mostly not included in the film score"[14].

The music track for the film comprises a mixture of orchestral sequences, cues adapted and developed from location recordings and a 'needle-drop' track used diegetically – Joe Loss and his band, featuring Chick Henderson, performing *Begin the beguine* (1939)[15]. The orchestral pieces were written by Bridie, arranged by him with his long-term collaborator Helen Mountford and conducted by Andrea Keeble. While Bridie's liner notes to the CD soundtrack provide a description of the orchestral sequences as "all dark strings, sad chord – oboes, clarinets and horns", the orchestral score combines both brooding underscore and two distinctive love themes, one that accompanies the initial scenes of Evelyn and Phillip flirting and courting in Adelaide (which is repeated with variations) and a second theme accompanying the blossoming of the later relationship between Evelyn and Mick in the Trobriands. The sequence used to accompany the arrival of the Japanese ship provides the most marked contrast in style by using standard Hollywood musical exoticisms to convey the cultural difference and threat of the arrival. The short passage mixes pentatonic melodies with an underlying rhythm derived from that used to signify 'Red Indians' in popular US culture from the late 1800s on and later adapted by Hollywood to signify additional 'others' (such as the natives of Skull Island in *King Kong* [dir: Merian C Cooper/Ernest B Schoedsack, 1933], scored by Max Steiner).

The film opens with a reflective flashback sequence that sets the tone of the film and serves to offset the main narrative of Evelyn's and Phillip's relationship. Together with screen images showing boats arriving on a beach at dusk, the sequence communicates an insight into the mood of the film and the lead character's perceptions through a sound passage that mixes atmos, music and voiceover to produce a delicately emphatic impression. The sequence begins with insect and water noises and a low sustained tone. A female vocal sample joins the mix, high, prominent and unmistakably non-western. Evelyn's narration features extended pauses in which the vocal samples briefly reassert themselves before subsiding as her voice intones:

> I once met a man – not my husband – another man ... You look back on a life, what will you take with you? ... For me, I'll take the smell of a pearl shell, freshly opened, one late day at the beach ...

Interspersing this poetic fragment with the evocative vocal sample (and supporting sound mix), the film expresses a cultural duality, attraction and vacillation between the West/western sensibilities and the [as yet unspecified] exotic 'other' of the narrative.

The use of layered, processed passages of Trobriand music and location sound within a western-derived textural collage is the aspect that most clearly resembles Bridie's previous work with Not Drowning, Waving[16] and on some of the tracks he recorded with Tolai (East New Britain island) singer George Telek on his eponymous 1997 album and *Serious Tam* (2000)[17]. These passages occur at various places in the film's narrative, predominantly as short moodsetters. Some of the more striking of these are included at key points. The sequence showing Evelyn's and Phillip's arrival in the Trobriands, for instance (track 3 on the soundtrack CD), conveys the characters' excitement, beginning with a breathy loloni flute melody (signifying cultural difference) and bustling drum rhythm (suggesting movement) before intensifying with the addition of further percussion and a harmonium texture that fills out the sound as the couple meet the community for the first time. Evelyn's voluntary incarceration in a cage after the death of her husband is a pivotal point in the film, one where she attempts atonement by mourning her husband in a traditional local manner. Eschewing a melodramatic orchestral cue, the music for the cage sequence is provided by extracts of high, undulating vocal melodies, provided by the Luya Hed Hi Meris, mixed with shakers, bird calls and insect noises, providing an eerie, unsettling mood to convey the intensity of the drama.

The film includes many scenes of local life and culture. These provide the pretext for the film's location in the Trobriands and the diegetic subject of Evelyn's and Phillip's studies. One of the more striking aspects of these scenes (for the current analysis) is the manner in which they are not – predominantly – accompanied by diegetically realist locational atmos. Instead, they are accompanied by sound collages that include appropriate atmos along with sequences of vocal, percussive and flute music that derive from the cultural sphere of Trobriand life together with samples of music from other parts of PNG. These are, in the main, *associatively* synchronised to image sequences, rather than having a necessary, literal (and/or veracious) connection. While the images of rituals, dances, social and work interactions may suggest themselves to a western audience as quasi-documentary material, the audio tracks for these sequences work in a more commercial filmic manner, as suggestive mood pieces that thematically colour exotic locations.

Ghost Tracks

The films discussed in this chapter share a preoccupation with the past and include narratives in which the death of a partner traumatises characters and leads to new pairings. Both films also feature narrations by their female leads, reflecting on their experience and providing readings of the masculine dynamics and world-views that they have to negotiate. *In a Savage Land* opens with a voiceover and collage that identifies key memories and *To have and to hold* opens with a quote from William Faulkner: "The past is never dead. It is not even past".

But, as the above analyses suggest, there are significant differences between *In a Savage Land* and *To have and to hold*. In sound track terms, the former includes elements that directly derive from the culture it represents while the latter is less implicated to any specific Papua New Guinean place and culture. Despite such differences, both films explore western fantasies, represent various aspects of nostalgia and are riven with anxieties.

Hillcoat's film represents an essentially generic 'heart of darkness' incidentally placed in a specific part of the West Sepik region. Bennett's film is imbued with a romanticism that derives from Malinowski's work, the manner in which his enterprise has been mythologised, and the re-inscription of the Trobriands as an alluring (and 'racy') domain of otherness. These cultural contexts interweave a fabric upon which an archetypal western narrative, repeatedly inscribed in feature cinema, is embroidered – that of the trials and tribulations of heterosexual romance. The fracturing of pair bonds and sanity in both films occurs within the heat and humidity of a tropical 'somewhere else', a place where cultural difference manifests itself around the characters. In this manner, Scott Walker's version of *I threw it all away* is apposite to both productions as a vignette of regret at opportunities lost and time passing. The sonic presence of the Trobriands lurks at the margins of Bennett's film – only emerging fully into the light on the 'spin-off' *Wosi* CD. The music of the West Sepik is largely absent from Hillcoat's film, represented only by melodies sourced from a recording by the Raun Raun Theatre. The sound of PNG thereby exists in the films in a ghostly manner, as ephemeral suggestions of difference and locational specificity. This, above all, illustrates how precisely the films draw on PNG to provide narratives of the post-colonial imaginary, depicting 'haunted houses' that offer confrontation and trauma for those who enter (or linger), imagining themselves as still privileged with western power.

Thanks to David Easton, Steven Feld and Don Niles for comments and discussion of the issues raised in this chapter.

Notes

1. Administering Papua under a League of Nations mandate.
2. Hurley produced an extended version in 1923 entitled *With the Headhunters of Unknown Papua*, also released in North America under the title *The Lost Tribe*.
3. See Hayward (1996: 64-65 and 68-69) for further discussion.
4. The film, entitled *Diwai bilong Ninigos*, was eventually completed in 1989.
5. See Hayward (1997) for a sustained analysis of this topic.
6. See Hayward (1997: 72-73) for further discussion.
7. The PNG sequences of the film were shot around Angoram, Tambanum and Wewak – with additional scenes shot around Cairns.
8. The culture of PNG's young criminal gangs.
9. For a discussion of Herrmann's use of this in his film scores see Leydon (2004: 38).
10. Thanks to Don Niles for this information.
11. Here I am differentiating 'atmos' as a type of audio underscore without necessary and/or specific diegetic association with diegetic material.
12. Feld contacted the film's producers after recognising sounds in the film and receiving confirmation from Garvan that *Voices of the Rainforest* had been the source of these. Feld asked the producers to make a donation to the Bosavi People's Fund and publish an apology for unauthorised usage, although neither request was accommodated. (Feld pc November 2003)
13. The CD identifies this track as performed by General Kelty but I have been unable to verify this.
14. In this regard, the production invites comparison to Terrence Malick's film *The Thin Red Line* (1998), shot in The Solomon Islands. During the production of the film, sound recordist Claude Letessier recorded several choir performances, one sequence of which was included in the final film. A selection of these tracks – entitled 'Melanesian Songs' – were included as a 'special feature' on the DVD release and were also released on a BMG/RCA CD entitled *Melanesian Choirs: The Blessed Islands (Chants from The Thin Red Line)* (1999).
15. Which is also repeated over the end credit sequence.
16. Discussed in Hayward (1997).
17. Discussed in Crowdy and Hayward (2001: 85-106).

Chapter Four

HEI-FEN AND MUSICAL SUBTEXTS IN TWO AUSTRALIAN FILMS BY CLARA LAW

TONY MITCHELL

> *The deep relation which music has to the true nature of things also explains the fact that suitable music played to any scene, action, event, or surrounding seems to disclose to us its most secret meaning, and appears as the most accurate and distinct commentary upon it.* (Schopenhauer, in Lanza, 1995: 11)

> *In Chinese there's a word which is two words but means one thing ... hei-fen, which actually is that you go to a level where you have an understanding of the whole thing which is inside of that situation and the character. A total of that situation, and the character and what happens, everything of the moment ... I think film music should be able to work as independently as dialogue in a film. You can do a lot with dialogue to create that lyrical, poetic moment and music should be able to do the same, in a different space, on another layer, so that your film is layered with all sorts of things, and music is part of that. And music should be able to bring out a lot of things you don't say in the dialogue, which is maybe the subtext, or is just something unsaid ... and sometimes silence is music.* (Law, in Millard, 2001: online)

The Macau-born, Melbourne-based Hong Kong–Australian director Clara Law employs music in particularly distinctive ways in her films. She has used the Cantonese portmanteau noun *hei-fen* (*Qi Fen* in Mandarin) to invoke the way in which atmosphere and tone combine to generate an understanding of the totality of the situations, events and characters of a film. *Hei-fen* refers to the energy in the air in a given human social situation, such as a funeral, where the *hei-fen* is usually solemn and low, or a wedding, where it may be joyful and grand. It can also change as a result of the way in which people act and react – for example, if a guest at a funeral makes a joke that cheers people up. In film, music can enhance, or even produce, the *hei fen* of a particular scene[1].

The two feature films Law has released in Australia to date, *Floating Life* (1997) and *The Goddess of 1967* (2001), contain music by Iranian-Australian composer Davood A. Tabrizi and violinist and former member of the Black Sorrows and Weddings, Parties, Anything, Jen Anderson respectively. The predominantly Chinese music in *Floating Life*, performed by members of the Chinese Opera Arts Orchestra, together with western keyboards, guitar and percussion, is an important vehicle in expressing and emphasising the Chinese identities of the film's characters. It also underscores the interior, psychological focus of the film, and complements feelings of yearning, loss and melancholy that the characters experience. These feelings are prioritised over the social and political issues of Chinese migration to Australia that the film also touches on. The music in *The Goddess of 1967* employs a Japanese *shakuhachi* and *ken tieu*, as well as a Vietnamese *dan tranh*, along with elements of traditional Irish music such as violin, tin whistle, 'whirly' and Romany-style vocalisations to allude to the identity, cultural displacement and past 'ghosts' of both its Japanese protagonist, who comes to Australia to buy a rare 1967 Citroën DS car, and the blind Irish-Australian young woman he encounters.

The music in both films extends the syncretisation of western and Chinese musical elements of three of Law's previous films made in Hong Kong and mainland China, *Farewell China* (1990), *Autumn Moon* (1992) and *Temptations of a Monk* (1993). The first of these, a harrowing melodrama about a Chinese couple's separate migration to the USA won four Golden Horse awards in Taiwan in 1990. Its music track comprised syncretic 'Chinese-inspired electronic blues' (see Mitchell, 2001) that combined a Taiwanese dialect folk ballad about homesickness for China with blues music played by a US disc jockey based in Taiwan. The two latter films were scored using ensembles of Chinese instruments, guitars and keyboards in an ambient music track by the 'godfather' of the Hong Kong musical avant garde, Tats Lau, who won a Golden Horse award at the Taiwan Film festival for his music for *Temptations of a Monk* (see Mitchell, 2003b).

This chapter explores the ways in which Tabrizi's and Anderson's musics make important contributions in radically different ways, with differing success, to the *hei-fen* of *Floating Life* and *The Goddess of 1967* in expressing the 'subtexts' of situations, the 'inner worlds' and 'yearnings' of the characters, and in embodying the prevalently melancholic but ultimately hopeful mood which both films convey.

Autumn Moon and Law's Approach to Film Music

Both the themes and the sonic architecture which amplifies them in *Floating Life* and *The Goddess of 1967* have strong affinities with *Autumn Moon*, Law's film about an encounter between a young Japanese tourist and a teenage Hong Kong girl who is about to emigrate to Canada, which won a Golden

Leopard award in Locarno in 1992. These affinities are at least partially anchored by the presence of sound designer Gareth Vanderhope who has worked on all of Law's films since *Temptation of a Monk* (Millard, 2001: online), ensuring a degree of sonic continuity as well as reaffirming Law's status as an *auteur* who has explored ongoing themes of migration and the Chinese diaspora in most of her films (see Mitchell, 1999, 2001, 2003a, 2003b).

The ambient-styled music in *Autumn Moon*, provides a salient example of the unobtrusive but idiosyncratic underscoring aspects of film music, comprising predominantly slow, repetitive patterns of instrumental music for electric and acoustic guitar, piano and fretless bass, augmented with Chinese stringed instruments the *erhu* (2 string violin), *sanxian* (3 string lute) and *ruan* (lute). Its reliance on extended amplified notes (which are frequently 'bent' through distortion and feedback) with little rhythmic pulse (no drums) gives it a 'floating' quality that sonically complements the drifting, transient and displaced state of the film's principal characters. The use of Chinese instruments also iconically expresses aspects of Chinese culture and identity integral to the journey undergone by the film's central protagonists, without ever being self-conscious, essentialist or obvious about their aural connections to Chinese characteristics. The sonic drift of Lau's music also expresses a sense of deracination and alienation in its lack of narrative melodies (echoing the film's minimal narrative), as well as being capable of expressing moods ranging from sadness to muted celebration. It is used non-diegetically and non-narratively throughout most of the film, frequently accompanying slow Ozu-like 'pillow shots' which track over the facades of city buildings, road movie-style, combining with the film's architectural facades to establish an often lugubrious mood of desertion and emptiness. Lau's music in *Autumn Moon*, performed in collaboration with Tommy Wai was released on CD in Hong Kong in 1994, two years after the film release. The CD adds a number of songs and tracks not featured in the film but is nonetheless subtly and effectively evocative and expressive of the Hong Kong wasteland and transit zone that is the film's setting, and the drifting, floating lives of its central characters, as well as its slow and sometimes directionless narrative.

Tabrizi's music in *Floating Life* fulfills a similar, though often more dramatic, function in both underscoring and commenting on the emotional and psychological dilemmas of its Hong Kong-Chinese migrant characters in Sydney and Munich. While this music was never released on CD, it won Tabrizi a Golden Horse award at the 1997 Taiwan Film festival, and an Asian Pacific Film Festival Award. A selection of Anderson's music for *The Goddess of 1967* was released on CD in 2001 but does not include any of the most important diegetic musical cues which occur in the film, especially those from existing musical repertoires. One example is the key scene in which the Blind Girl (or BG, played by Rose Byrne) visits the bar where her grandmother used to dance, and dances frenetically to a jukebox playing the Ventures' version of *Walk Don't Run* (1960). An image from this scene is used on both the Australian publicity posters for the film and the CD cover of Anderson's music from the film.

Davood A. Tabrizi and *Floating Life*

Tabrizi, a multi-instrumentalist of Iranian cultural background, specialises in playing the *kamanchec*, or Persian spike fiddle. He has composed a number of varied cross-cultural scores for Australian films, most notably his medieval-styled music, "inspired by Celtic folk music, Gregorian chant or plainsong, mining songs from the 19th Century, naïve peasant music and Scottish military music, which were fused with the eastern sounds brought back to the West by the Crusaders" (Tabrizi [1989] soundtrack CD sleeve notes) for New Zealand director Vincent Ward's 1988 film *The Navigator: A Medieval Odyssey*. A selection of Tabrizi's music for Mojgan Khadem's 2001 *Serenades* was released on CD in 2001. Khadem's film is set in the South Australian desert in the 19th Century, and recounts a cross-cultural romance between Johann (Aden Young), the son of a German missionary, and Jila (Alice Haines) the daughter of an Aboriginal woman and an Afghani cameleer (Sinisa Copic). Tabrizi's music is particularly evocative in this distinctive but rarely-screened film. The music dramatically exploits narrative and thematic interplay by contrasting traditional Afghani music and recorded European music, such as Nellie Melba singing an aria from Verdi's *La Traviata*, Bach's *Minuette in Bminor* and Christian Christmas song *Silent Night*, thereby embodying the clashes between Islamic and Christian doctrines of belief which the film explores[2]. In 1988 Tabrizi released the 'Asian roots fusion' album *Tazzad*, a series of compositions performed by himself and the Sri Lankan musicians Devendran Gopalasamy and Ram Chandra Suman, the first of which, *Bush to the City*, is particularly evocative of Australian landscape in a quasi-cinematic way. More recently, he has played violin and *daayareh* (Persian frame drum) in a multicultural ensemble featured on Tatar singer Zulya Kamalova's 2002 album *Elusive*, and composed music with saxophonist Sandy Evans and Hussain Samawi for *In Our Name*, Nigel Jamieson's play about the plight of a family of Iraqi refugees in Australia, which was performed at the Belvoir Street theatre in Sydney in April 2004.

Tabrizi's brief for *Floating Life* was also cross-cultural, requiring composition of music for the Chinese Opera Arts Orchestra comprising *erhu*, *pipa*, *guan* (a cylindrical wind instrument with reed mouthpiece), *dizi* (Chinese bamboo flute), *suona* (a reed instrument like a clarinet), *yang quin* (dulcimer), *sheng* (a reed pipe instrument) and *zhong ruan* (4 string lute) as well as percussion, keyboards and guitar. The voices of Bahar (who also sings in *Serenades*) and cast members Cecilia Lee Fong Sing (a former Beijing Opera singer, who plays Mum in the film) and Annie Yip (who plays Bing) also feature in the film's music. Apart from two diegetic moments (when a cassette tape of dance music is played on Chinese New Year, and a Spanish guitar accompanies two female dancers in a restaurant), all the music is instrumental and non-diegetic, evoking mood and atmosphere, and underscoring dialogue and action. The structural discipline with which the film is divided into chapter-like episodes focusing on different members of the Chan family is a notable feature, along with the use of monologues or voice over narrations by a family member in each episode. These obvious structural elements combined with the sparing use of Tabrizi's music assists the music track to function as dramatic counterpoint to dialogue or to express unstated moods or feelings in the characters.

Music and 'Silence'

Law also employs 'silence' – in the sense of an absence of speech or music – in a dramatic way, emphasising the sense of emptiness experienced by the family in outer suburban western Sydney, with often only faint birdsong, insects, dogs barking and distant traffic noise defining the setting. A number of key dramatic scenes also occur in silence, and most of the Chinese-box-style intertitles (perhaps evoking silent cinema) announcing the separate 'chapters' of the family members' stories making up the film, also occur in silence. This dramatic use of silence pointedly illustrates not only the sense of disorientation and alienation of the Chan family in Australia but also Law's belief (quoted above) that silence is an integral part of the music and sound design of her cinema. This resonates with Simon Frith's comments about the way silence has become valued, coveted and feared in contemporary everyday life, and associated with 'emotional intensity' in the cinema:

> *Silence has become the indicator of an unusual intensity of feeling – emotional intensity in the Hollywood film ... silence, as something valuable, to be bought, means not complete silence, but the absence of human or electronic or artificial sounds ... Because we seem to value silence, to covet it, it is perhaps not surprising that silence is now something to be feared – on radio, in seminars, on the telephone. Here silence becomes something to be filled, and music becomes that which isn't noise (i.e. silence).* (2003: 93-94)

Floating Life embodies the 'silences' of suburban Australia, particularly in relation to fear. The long sequence which presents first daughter Bing's fraught attempts to survive on her own in a hostile semi-rural Australian suburban environment is particularly fraught with silences, especially as they are contrasted with the all-pervasive background noise in the Hong Kong scenes in the film, for which the opening sequence of the film sets a benchmark. Silence functions as an indicator of Bing's pathological loneliness and self-isolation. During this sequence, silence is offset only by the sounds of the dance music played by the owner of a Chinese noodle shop on New Year's Eve in an attempt to cheer her up, and the guitar music which ironically underscores the moment when he kisses her after she rejects his attempts to cook her a romantic dinner in her home. The music in *Floating Life*, used sparingly and economically throughout, offers an important dramatic subtext to the characters and situations and is further intensified by its contrast with often long periods of silence.

Even the scenes in which we see second daughter Yen (Annette Shun Wah) in Munich are relatively 'silent', and the itch she develops as a result of what she believes is the bad *feng shui* of her apartment and that impels her to visit her family in Australia, seems the result of the noiseless disorientation she experiences in this alien European environment. The one scene in the film which offers any direct, public social comment on the Chan family's Asian migrant status occurs in Munich, when Yen sees a neo-Nazi skinhead aggressively staring at her in a shopping mall car park, and decides to confront him. An industrial hum fills the background and, as Yen walks towards the skinhead, the sounds of a *pipa* come in, followed by an *erhu*, as the skinhead leaves the precinct. Apart from providing dramatic underscoring to this confrontation, the music here seems to function as an indicator of Yen's pride in her Chinese identity (which has been compounded by her German husband telling her daughter Mui Mui that Cantonese is "not real Chinese") and her refusal to be cowed by German racism. Nonetheless critics and reviewers have commented on the lack of a social and political dimension in *Floating Life*'s portrayal of Asian migration (see Stratton, 1998, and Fung, 1998). Law has answered such observations by emphasising that:

> the approach is not a naturalistic approach. What we want to deal with is the inner worlds of the immigrants, what it's like ... to be cut off from your roots, and try to build and to plant new roots in a new soil. That actually is more important, that area is what we should focus on, instead of showing how they relate to others. (in Law and Fong i/v, 2000)[3]

The music in the film thus takes on added weight in contributing to the overall *hei-fen*, given that the predominant focus on the characters throughout is interior, psychological and spiritual. Indeed, as Dominic Pettman has noted:

> the film's depiction of actual Australians (whatever such a fraught term may mean) is fleeting and peripheral, as if they themselves are ghostly apparitions haunting the fringes of the landscape ... whereas the newly arrived immigrants are vivid and fully materialized. (2000: 76)

Music and Chinese Migrant Perspectives

This 'reverse perspective' in relation to mainstream notions of Australian identity arguably constitutes one of the film's chief values as both an important object of study as the first dramatisation of Asian migration in Australia and a landmark transnational 'Australian' film about migration (a problematic status given its transnational dimensions – see Mitchell, 2003a). The almost exclusively Chinese music used throughout the film, in which it is difficult to detect the western instruments, except for the very muted use of piano and violin to underscore Yen's monologue about her alienation in Germany, contributes strongly to this perspective.

Apart from the sparing use of an *erhu* and *pipa* in the opening credits, the first significant use of music in *Floating Life* occurs at the end of the lengthy sequence in which the Chan family settle into their new house in outer Western Sydney, and Bing has a series of disciplinarian confrontations with both her younger brothers and her parents in an attempt to enforce an ascetic regime of safety, morality and inconspicuousness based on her own rather wilfully negative experiences of migration. Bass chords emphasise the family conflict and tension this produces, and then the scene shifts to a suburban bus stop near their house where Mum and Pa are waiting to go to an English lesson in Chinatown and plan to buy some incense and paper money there, since the next day is the Day of the Ancestors. Their dialogue at first forms an interplay with the fragmentary lines from the *erhu* and *pipa*, which punctuate it, until they fail to successfully signal the bus, since Mum does not have her glasses, Pa thinks it is the wrong bus, and it passes them without stopping. As they resign themselves to waiting for the next bus, Pa announces it is no use buying incense, since Bing has forbidden them to burn it in the house (supposedly because it presents a fire hazard), and also suggests they should "follow the customs of the new village", adding that they are too far away from their ancestors to be able to reach them anyway. Mum's response is to cry silently, and the particularly plangent, minor figure the music traces at this point embellishes her sense of loss, yearning, frustration and isolation. We then cut to Munich, continuing the mood of mourning and loss with Yen saying, "Don't cry Mum" as she speaks to her mother on the phone from Sydney. The bus stop sequence plays a significant role in the film, and its emotional atmosphere is more effective for the lengthy 'silence' that has preceded it. Mum and Pa's quiet exterior isolation at the bus stop anticipates the film's later emphasis on them as the principal agents in ensuring the family find new roots in Australia by fusing their adherence to their traditional Chinese customs and beliefs with an adaptation to the 'ghost town' aspects of suburban Sydney, establishing the first step in their journey towards a realisation of what needs to be done to achieve this.

The bus stop scene also establishes the film's major theme of loss of contact with the family ancestors – something Mum re-establishes at the end of the film in the particularly moving speech she makes to the family ancestors after Bing has withdrawn from the world and become catatonic. The music functions in this concluding scene to plangently express Mum's unspoken feelings of spiritual and emotional disconnection and alienation from her family, her religion and her culture, which she and Pa manage to succeed in re-affirming by the end of the film after they buy their own house and re-establish contact with traditional Chinese customs. Here, as elsewhere in the film, the music is tightly woven into the thematic structure as well as hinting at the subtle themes of the scene.

Filial piety as a key to neo-Confucian family harmony is a pivotal theme of the film, and this is illustrated in a scene in which Pa disappears from Bing's house in order to meet up with an old friend who has recently returned from mainland China. As Yen mobilises the family to search for him, we see him with his friend, who shows Pa a picture of his ancestral home in China, which he realises he will never see again. The intertitle of the scene announces 'a House in China'. As the two old men lament a general lack of 'filial devotion' and then say farewell, probably for the last time, since Pa's friend has migrated to the USA, the *pipa* and *erhu* play a melancholic, falling figure similar to that of the bus stop scene. Mum's prayer to her ancestors in Bing's house at the end of the film, which signals a resolution of the family's problems of filial piety, has a similar interplay with music. As Mum kneels on the floor in reverence to her ancestors, and confesses, "I haven't paid you enough filial respect", we hear the subdued sounds of a gong, a *pipa*, bass flute and drone. As she goes on to talk about family harmony, the *pipa* and *erhu* combine in a rare melodic line, rather

65

than simply an atmospheric figure, to convey a sense of resolution. This use of musical resolution to convey both narrative and family resolution is echoed in the final credit sequence of the film, when for the first time we hear the full Chinese orchestra, an emblem of all the disparate family themes of the story having come together.

Floating Life is a major 'Australian' film for a number of reasons – the first 'foreign' film to be made in Australia (in a combination of English, German and Cantonese), and the first Australian film to be nominated for an Academy Award for Best Foreign Film. It won a Silver Leopard Award at the Locarno Film Festival, and was nominated for three Australian Film Institute Awards (director for Law, screenplay for Law and her screenwriter husband Eddie Fong, and supporting actress for former SBS veejay and TV announcer Annette Shun Wah, who plays Yen). But *Floating Life* was seen by very few audiences in Australia, Asian or otherwise – it ran to largely empty cinemas for little more than two weeks in the main cities, although it was acclaimed at the 1996 Sydney and Melbourne film festivals, and has been subsequently screened five times on the Australian multicultural TV network SBS[4]. It is also widely studied on Australian university curricula, no doubt partly because it problematises the notion of an Australian 'national cinema', given its almost exclusively Chinese focus and relative lack of concern with Australian issues of migration in an ultimately positive portrayal of the family's integration in Australia.

The growing body of critical writings about *Floating Life* also signals its importance, positioning it in contrasting ways: in relation to notions of an 'Australian Self' and other Australian films which deal with non–Anglo-Australian migrants as victims of a repressive, intolerant nation-state (Roxburgh, 1997); as an exploration of hybrid Australian notions of home, in contrast to the Anglo–Australian norms of home contested in Rob Sitch's 1997 film *The Castle* (Siemienovich, 1999); as highlighting Asian migrant displacement and "the diasporic condition of homesickness and the longing for belonging" (Yue, 2000: 195); from a US perspective, as a representation of an experience of immigration with Freudian overtones of mourning, loss and melancholia, which assumes that 'full assimilation' is a desirable goal (Eng, 1999); as a ritual conflict between Asian migrants and an initially hostile Australian environment which they succeed in taming (Mitchell, 1999); as a postmodern film "symptomatic of [an] uncanny and ubiquitous cross–cultural liminality" which is both Australian and Hong Kong in its identity (Pettman, 2000: 75); and, most interestingly, as an illustration of Edward Said's concepts of the 'median state' of the exile caught between homeland and new country, becoming both an 'adept mimic' and 'secret outcast', and ultimately showing that "cultural convergence can be achieved through transformation and compromise" (Ma, 2001: 157-168). Ma, an English teacher from mainland China based in Australia since 1995, is closest to the migrant experience portrayed in the film, and her reading is arguably given anchorage both by the dynamics of Tabrizi's music in *Floating Life* and by Law's implication that 'living floatingly' can be a positive experience as well as a negative one (Law, 1996: online). Law's second Australian film, *The Goddess of 1967*, has not attracted so much praise.

Music in *The Goddess of 1967*

Critical responses to *The Goddess of 1967* were decidedly mixed, ranging from Adrian Martin's eulogy of it in the Melbourne *Age* as "a fascinating, superbly crafted work ... undoubtedly one of the most exciting and ground-breaking Australian movies of the year" (cited in www.palace.net.au/goddess/reviews/) to Richard Phillips' damning critique of it on the *World Socialist Web Site* as "confused, pretentious and essentially coldhearted ... heavy handed and tiresome ... the film contains no fresh insights and is a cold and misanthropic work" (2001: online). The film won Best Film and Best Director awards at the 2000 Chicago Film Festival but many reviewers found it self-conscious, confusing, rambling and uneven in its characterisations and dramatic structure. The use of bleach bypass and other non-naturalistic visual effects, such as pixilation for the Tokyo sequences, by cinematographer Dion Beebe (whose use of contrasting film stocks, filters and levels of exposure to delineate the three settings of *Floating Life* was particularly effective) also attracted criticism. Even Fiona A. Villella's sustained, relatively sympathetic critique of the film in *Senses of Cinema* finds that:

> *ideas of story and character remain conventional and clichéd ... a series of themes ... explored in an essentially heavy-handed, overblown and clichéd style ... The 'heart of darkness' scene, in which the full grotesqueness of Grandpa is revealed in almost comic book style, is overly dramatic and indulgent ... a facile, pretentious exercise ... The Goddess of 1967 is ultimately undermined by a denial of the full clinching of style and content. Its dazzling postmodern landscape ultimately collapses under the weight of reductive and simplistic ideas of character and story.* (2001: online)

In contrast to the taut, intensely economical, episodic structure of *Floating Life*, *The Goddess of 1967* appears to meander through a series of scenes involving spectacular outback surfaces. It is a loosely defined road movie featuring flashes back and forth in time, mostly within the past life of its female protagonist, in an attempt to link her traumatic past experiences of abuse by her grandfather and fanatical Catholic repression by her mother with those of her Japanese traveling companion and integrate them into some kind of narrative and thematic synthesis. Like most film reviews, those for *The Goddess of 1967* make no mention of the film's music.

Law has stated that the film marked Anderson's first time as a composer for a feature film – although she had previously composed music for both Pabst's silent classic *Pandora's Box* (1929) and *The Sentimental Bloke* (1932) as well as contributing music to Australian features *The Big Steal* (dir: Nadia Tass, 1990) and *Death in Brunswick* (dir: John Ruane, 1991) and numerous TV documentaries and drama series, including *Simone De Beauvoir's Babies* (1997) so she can hardly be regarded as a novice. Law adds "she was like a piece of white paper... and I could try to talk her into things" (in Millard, 2001: online). The results of their collaboration are particularly evident in the film's non-diegetic music, which is a mixture of Celtic and quasi-Japanese elements, with a Vietnamese *dan tranh* (16 string zither similar to the Chinese *zheng*) standing in for a koto, along with some wordless Romany-style vocalisations from a singer called Marianella. The results are often harsh, strident and emotive, as befits the perspective of a blind girl who relies on sounds to relate to her environment and whose experiences have often been traumatic. Law has indicated that:

> I wanted the music – and particularly the voice of Marianella, to be almost like a silent observer: looking at the characters, both the victims and the predators, and watching them with love and compassion, a healing voice ... as it is, I think the music really reaches into the soul, in the same way that someone like Tarkovsky did. (Law, 2001:4)

This suggests the music is mobilised to play a particularly strong role in the *hei-fen* of the film, contributing a quasi-mystical, non-naturalistic weight and external emphasis, almost disrupting the film's suture. This is in keeping with the subjective responses of Rose Byrne's blind character who responds intensely and primarily to sounds throughout, and the use of deliberately askew back projection in some of the road sequences. The music takes on a role of external commentary that contrasts sharply with the much more subtly integrated, underscoring function of Tabrizi's music in *Floating Life*. Anderson's syncretic use of musical elements from different cultures, combined with foley sounds, is not as extensive as the homogenised 'soup' of 'world music' and contemporary western orchestral and rock elements in Peter Gabriel's (and others, as outlined in a chapter elsewhere in this volume) music track for Philip Noyce's *Rabbit-Proof Fence* (2002). It is noteworthy that there are no Aboriginal signifiers, either sonic or visual, in Law's film, thereby framing its reading of the Australian outback in exclusively European, Anglo-Celtic and Japanese terms. The Citroën and Grandpa's idiosyncratic wine making (he even attempts to make a Chateau Neuf du Pape at Lightning Ridge) are particularly strong signifiers, giving *The Goddess of 1967* a European arthouse orientation. Law's admiration of Tarkovsky is well known, and her invocation of his films in relation to the role of the music in *Goddess* seems to cement this orientation.

'Feminised' Asian Men

As with *Floating Life*, *Autumn Moon* can again be seen as a narrative paradigm for *The Goddess of 1967*. However the latter is, importantly, Law's first film in which no Chinese or Hong Kong-based characters appear, and it is in the central situation of a young Japanese man visiting a foreign country for the first time rather than in largely dual character-based narrative structure where the affinities with the earlier film lie. JM ('Japanese Man'), a Tokyo-based IT worker and vintage car enthusiast, comes to Australia in pursuit of a 1967 Citroën DS (Déesse -the Goddess of the title), and embarks on a journey into the outback with a blind Australian girl BG ('Blind Girl' – a role for which Rose Byrne won a best actress award at the 2000 Venice Film festival). Fashion model and former boxer Rikiya Kurokowa, speaking hesitant English and occasionally looking stiff and awkward in his first film role, lacks the authority of the far more assured and internationally experienced Masatoshe Nagase in *Autumn Moon*, and his characterisation is often sketchy and underdeveloped, as the use of a generic acronym for his character's name indicates. The sex scene between JM and

BG, while introducing the latter to a degree of tenderness she has not encountered in her previous rough and violent treatment by men (including her grandfather), involves a rather problematic feminisation of JM. In a study of 'the sacrificial Asian' in Australian films, Olivia Khoo (2004) compares *The Goddess of 1967* with Sue Brooks' 2003 film *Japanese Story*, where the Australian character Sandy rather ludicrously puts on her Japanese guest Hiro's trousers in order to assume the male role in their lovemaking. Law's film, she argues, involves a similar 'feminisation of the Asian man' that has been a recurrent tendency in Australian films since Peter Weir's *The Year of Living Dangerously* (1982):

> *Again, the sex scene between the two characters is rendered as a site of 'connection', with Byrne 'on top'. Cross-cultural exchange and understanding is made to be heterosexually resolvable, but only through a reconfiguration of gender relations applied to a hierarchy of race.* (Khoo, 2004: 15)

Nonetheless JM's character, unlike Hiro in *Japanese Story*, is not 'sacrificed', and contains far more psychological substance and depth than the clichéd, stereotyped and self-conscious cross-cultural Japanese-Australian outback encounter of the over-praised, multi-award-winning 2003 film *Japanese Story*, also shot very effectively by Dion Beebe. *The Goddess of 1967*, although similar in its basic narrative structure around a journey across the outback, reaches far beyond the narrow narrative and character confines of *Japanese Story*, which, as Mike Walsh has indicated, is "unfortunately limited to checking off national and racial stereotypes (Japanese men are gruff, Japanese women are inscrutable, and there is so much space in Australia)" (2003: 20). JM's character functions as a catalyst in extending BG's awareness of her world, teaching her to trust people and stop protecting herself with a gun, and also offering her a relationship based on mutual understanding. In exchange, she offers him lessons in outback survival, teaching him to trust his senses as opposed to being dependent on technology. This also involves listening to sounds, explored in a scene where BG encourages JM to listen to the insects dying on the windscreen of the car, which we later see him cleaning.

But arguably Law's fascination with the surfaces of the film's outback setting and textures of the landscape is often showcased at the expense of narrative consistency and function or character development. That said, largely driven as it is by Beebe's somewhat flamboyant cinematography, the film is much more formally experimental and adventurous than *Floating Life*, displaying a desire to take risks and break with narrative conventions in a way which makes demands on the spectator, and the use of music often embodies this break with narrative convention. But the film's ultimate narrative resolution is conventional to the point of cliché, with the two characters driving off into the sunset. There is also a superficiality about a number of sequences, such as the pixilated shots of Tokyo, which JM describes as being "like Mars", while Law has suggested rather disingenuously that:

Just showing Tokyo in a film, for example, can make a very succinct point about post-modernism. The wealth and materialism, the sense of isolation, the coolness and beauty of surfaces. It communicates all that very clearly. (Law, 2001: online)

But, lest her remarks on postmodernism be read in a positive light, it is important to note that Law has also indicated that:

for me the postmodern existence is cold and inhuman and incomplete, because we are probably very fulfilled in our material need but we are very cut off from the spiritual side and the emotional side in us. (in Thompson, 2001: online)

This restricts postmodern readings of the film's narrative and formal structure. The need for spiritual and emotional grounding and connection is a recurring theme in all Law's films, although *The Goddess of 1967* tends to approach these themes through blunt and simplistic characterisation, narrative and dialogue. Nevertheless the often fragmentary and sometimes clashing use of disparate genres and moods of music in the film could be characterised as postmodern.

Music and *The Goddess* Narrative

The pre-title sequence for *The Goddess of 1967*, comprising jump cuts in music and image, mobilises a range of musics as an index to character, situation and mood, as it chronicles JM's email communications with Australia in quest of a Citroën DS. He first appears on a bullet train in a tunnel, then we see him at various moments in his apartment preparing to feed his collection of snakes with white mice, and a heavy rock riff is succeeded by excerpts of a classical piano sonata, some flamenco guitar, a jazz orchestra, Beethoven's *Fifth Symphony*, some 1960s pop music, frenetic accordion music, a violin sonata and finally, after he has agreed to pay $35,000 cash for the car and announces he is going on holiday, some hip hop, as he dances around his apartment in snorkel and flippers. As elsewhere in the film, cuts rather than fades between the changes in music gives the music track a jagged, abrasive quality. We later learn from JM that if his snakes are unhappy, listening to Wagner's *Flying Dutchman* will help them but this use of snippets from contrasting musical genres also establishes the passing of time and mood, as well as the somewhat frenetic nature of JM's commodity fetishism and dependence on technology, and the centrality of music and dancing in the film. As Villella has indicated, this opening sequence illustrates Law's skill in manipulating *mise en scène*: "not a word is spoken as one set-piece after another, with music as a key identifying factor, reveals important plot details and peculiarities relating to JM's character" (2001: 1). But the music samples used here do not tell us a great deal about JM, who remains a relatively undeveloped character throughout the film.

After the scene shifts to Australia, animal sounds give way to more loud rock music, as the couple selling the car dance in jubilation with their young daughter after having sealed the deal. An expressionistic sequence showing the pink Déesse in motion, accompanied by statistics of its history and manufacture, is then presented to the strains of an ethereal solo violin, as

JM arrives in Australia to discover, in a horrific silent sequence, the would-be vendors are both dead as a result of a murder-suicide, and brains and blood are spattered around the house – an event which is never satisfactorily explained – and BG is now his main link to the car. We then return to the Déesse, caressed and fetishised by the camera and the recurring electric violin music, and accompanied by a quotation from Barthes's celebrated 1957 essay on the Citroën DS19 in *Mythologies*, "It is obvious that the new Citroën has fallen from the sky" (1973: 88), which serves to establish the car as a major character in the film. Reinforcing this status is an image of the pink Déesse in the Australian outback used for publicity for the film in France. A tearful JM, overawed by the car's beauty, test drives the car, which he says feels like 'flying', and tries out its famous hydraulic suspension. JM reveals that his fascination for the car dates from having seen it in Jean-Pierre Melville's film *Le Samurai* (with Alain Delon) which, as Stratton (2001) notes, was also made in 1967. Although the Melville film is not mentioned by name, it reinforces the European arthouse referencing in *The Goddess of 1967*. A later documentary sequence in *Goddess* recounts how the Déesse gained cult status in France after its hydraulic suspension, which pumps the car up, was credited for rescuing President De Gaulle in 1967 from a barrage of bullets in an assassination attempt. To BG, on the other hand, the car has more emotional connotations: it is her (rather unlikely) 'family car' and thus full of grisly ghosts from her past which she is attempting to exorcise. So the pink Citroën becomes, in Villella's words,

> a personalised vessel travelling in an alternate time-space continuum. In the film's swift and clever association of meanings, JM's desire for the ultimate material possession eventually translates into a spiritual and deep connection with BG, whose identity becomes synonymous with the Citroën. (2001: 2)

But the Citroën's central metaphorical role in the film is a ponderous one. The five day car journey the two protagonists undertake through the outback, complete with lengthy flashback sequences, accumulates a considerable amount of emotional and spiritual baggage, mostly BG's, along the way, without succeeding in synthesising or resolving it satisfactorily with the present-time narrative. Law has stated that she prefers the term 'journey film' to 'road movie', implying that the narrative 'journey' involved is primarily an interior psychological one (Millard, 2001). Anderson's solo electric violin offers a kind of sonic signpost, as in the drawn-out, tentative sex scene between JM and BG, and in a haunting sequence when BG lies outside next to a tree in the dark, watched over by a group of dingos, linking these sequences associatively to the car and the journey.

A variety of diegetic music from opera to jazz is also used in the driving sequences, sometimes with JM singing along rather tunelessly, and snatches of opera recur elsewhere in the film, contrasting with the use of *shakuhachi* in the Tokyo sequences, and there is an effective flashback sequence accompanied by violin and strings in which Grandpa tells BG's mother about the stars in the sky (a scene that is reprised when BG's mother tells the same story to a young BG). But the diversity and disparity of the music, which at times seems excessively forceful in its function as commentary, serves to further fragment an already fragmented film, which lacks the structural cohesion and control of Law's previous work. The final encounter between BG and her abusive grandfather in an opal mine in Lightning Ridge, where she intends to shoot him but eventually doesn't, lacks any real sense of convincing resolution. Ultimately the characters fail to engage sympathy in a sustained way, despite strong performances from Byrne and Nicholas Hope (Grandpa), and too often the film's narrative lacks sufficient substance, being too dependent on the visual appeal of its landscape, inconsequential exchanges between JM and BG, and overly dramatic set pieces like the one in which BG's mother burns down the family home, tries to persuade BG to die in the fire "for her sins" and kills herself.

Conclusion

Whereas Law succeeded in defamiliarising the ghost town of Australian suburbia and showing it effectively through her characters' eyes in *Floating Life*, the characters in *The Goddess of 1967* are dwarfed and overwhelmed by the outback environment and do not manage to make a comparable impact to that of the Chan family in Sydney. The *hei-fen* of *The Goddess of 1967* is arguably much less fully realised, partly because it is reaching across to widely different cultural bases from Law's familiar grounding in the Chinese cultural formations that inform *Floating Life*. At the time of writing, Law and Fong are completing *Letters to Ali*, a low-budget self-funded documentary shot on digicam about the relationship between a woman doctor and a young Afghan asylum seeker in a Port Hedland detention centre, with music by jazz musician and composer Paul Grabowsky. The impetus for this film came from an article in Melbourne newspaper, *The Age*, and Law and Fong's engagement with current Australian issues relating to immigrants and the inhumane treatment of asylum seekers seems a natural development from their concern with Chinese migration in *Floating Life*.

Law's statement that "film music should be able to work as independently as dialogue" and "bring out a lot of things you don't say in the dialogue" (quoted above) is fully realised in *Floating Life*, where Tabrizi's music functions subtly, quietly and unobtrusively to express a *hei-fen* that projects the characters' unstated feelings to the spectator. It also succeeds in charting the moods and atmospheres of the Chan family's progression from regarding Australia as a place of fear, anxiety and paranoia towards a more harmonious integration into their new environment. In *The Goddess of 1967* the psychological and narrative role the music plays is far less simple and more diffuse, particularly in its function as an extension of BG's often anxious and troubled sensory perceptions of her environment, and in its use as a 'silent observer' and an external commentary on the characters and situation. Here the *hei-fen* is a more strident one, expressing the deep-seated anxieties and traumas of both protagonists in their contrasting sensory responses to the outback environment.

The Goddess of 1967 can be regarded as a transitional film in which Law and Fong are groping towards the realisation of a narrative involving Anglo-Celtic Australian characters and situations markedly different from the grounding of Law's previous films in transnational narratives of Chinese diasporic experiences. The fully realised *hei-fen* of *Floating Life*, in which Tabrizi's music plays a major, though understated, role, is only sporadically evident in the more emphatic, varied and disparate *Goddess* narrative and the role that Anderson's music plays in it. Despite this, *The Goddess of 1967* remains a fascinating and unusual Australian film. Overall the musics and musical treatments in Law's 'Australian' films offer significant and challenging additions to Australian cinema sound tracks.

Notes

1. Thanks to Eric Chu for this definition.
2. None of these copyright-restricted musical elements are included on the CD release.
3. Interview with Clara Law and Eddie Fong by Haiyan Wang and Tony Mitchell, Melbourne, 30/6/2000.
4. SBS included a clip from the film in the montage of its output assembled to advertise the channel's 2000 Global Outstanding Achievement Award, an indication of SBS's association with the film as a co-producer, and the film's own global orientation, as well as signaling the film as an ideal example of the local production values and content of the channel.

Chapter Five

LOST IN MUSIC:
Popular Music,
Multiculturalism and
Australian Film

JON STRATTON

D*ogs in Space* (dir: Richard Lowenstein) was released in 1986, at the
height of the Hawke Labor government's concern with implementing the
population management policy of multiculturalism. The institutional structures that gave shape to the policy were founded on the recommendations
of 'The Review of Post Arrival Programmes and Services to Migrants',
usually known as the 'Galbally Report' after the chair of the committee
which provided it, Frank Galbally. The 'Galbally Report' was tabled in
Federal Parliament in 1978, the same year in which *Dogs in Space* is set.
However, the idea of multiculturalism in Australia was not new. Al Grassby,
then Gough Whitlam's Minister for Immigration, had delivered his speech
titled 'A Multi-Cultural Society for the Future' in 1973[1]. In 1974 the Ethnic
Community Councils of South Australia and Victoria were formed, followed
by that of New South Wales in 1975.

Dogs in Space is an unrelentingly white, Anglo, film – apart from one
tantalising element. Focused on one inner-city household, and centred on
the Melbourne punk scene, the film, as Tim Groves describes it, "has an
episodic narrative, covering a flow of parties, gigs, bed hopping and the
obligatory road trip spread over several months" (2003: online). In this
shared house are Sam (played by Michael Hutchence), lead singer of Dogs
in Space, Anna (Saskia Post), his lover, Tim (Nique Needles), Grant (Adam
Briscomb), Tony (Peter Walsh) and Jenny (Caroline Lee). Also, and most
importantly for my argument here, there is Luchio (Tony Helou).

Luchio is a second generation Italo-Australian[2]. While all those in the
house live in a chaos fuelled by sex, drugs and punk music, Luchio, with his
neatly cut hair and wearing shirt and slacks, is studying for his structural
engineering exams at university. Why is Luchio in this house? We never find

out. We never meet his family. We don't know why he isn't living with his parents like most 'good' Italian-background young men of his age.

The film erases all positive signs of Luchio's Italian cultural origins. In films of the 1980s and later that have non-Anglo-Celtic characters, music is used to signify their cultural difference. One example is *Moving Out* (dir: Michael Pattinson, 1983) discussed in Tan (2000). This coming-of-age film about a teenage Italo-Australian boy uses songs by Umberto Tozzi (see Mitchell, 1998). While, of course, Luchio is not narratively central to *Dogs in Space*, he gets no Italian music. The film's music is purely punk, as if an aural expression of both assimilation and Anglo crisis; an attempt to erase Luchio's cultural difference.

Where the film is sometimes derided for being formless, the music, both its Australian and non-Australian contributions, is celebrated. Reviewing Michael Hutchence's work outside of INXS (the band of which he was the singer) on the web, Rarebird typifies this distinction, writing:

> *Unfortunately the film makes little sense, it is noisy, plotless and esoteric, and is far less effective than many similar films about alienated youth. The soundtrack album, though, is something to hear … The* Dogs in Space *soundtrack sounds like a great party record – if you're throwing a real wild party.* (2004: online)

From a purely musical perspective, *Dogs in Space* appears concerned with placing Australian, and in particular Melbourne, punk in an international context. While the majority of the music is late-1970s Melbourne punk[3] by Marie Hoy, The Primitive Calculators, Boys Next Door and others, this is set beside American and English punk classics. The film has two Iggy Pop tracks, one of which, *Dog Food* (1980), opens the film and therefore provides a context for the Melbourne music and a Gang Of Four track *Anthrax* (1979). A piece by Brian Eno, *Sky Saw*, from his *Another Green World* album released in 1975, also features.

With the advent of multicultural policy there has been a limited discursive shift in the organisation of popular music in Australia, and in the use of popular music in Australian films. This is evidenced as far back as *The Heartbreak Kid* (dir: Michael Jenkins, 1993) but in this chapter I will mostly concentrate on *Head On* (dir: Ana Kokkinos, 1999[4]), *The Wog Boy* (dir: Aleksi Vellis, 1999), *Looking for Alibrandi* (dir: Kate Woods, 2001), and *Fat Pizza* (dir: Paul Fenech, 2003). *Head On* and *The Wog Boy* are both centred on Greek-Australian characters, as is *The Heartbreak Kid*, while *Looking for Alibrandi* is a coming-of-age film with an Italo-Australian lead. All these films, whether comedy or drama, exhibit similar features that are effects of Australian multicultural policy. And all these films use popular music in similar ways.

In this chapter I will be concerned primarily with the diegetic use of popular music, and not with underscored music used for atmosphere and to link scenes. I want to examine how the organisation of popular music, in an Australia dominated by official multicultural policy, is reproduced through the way music is used in films that we might loosely call multicultural – films that have non-Anglo-Celts as their main characters. Before examining more recent films, though, there are further observations to make about the model offered by *Dogs in Space* in the mid-1980s.

1980s Film Music Culture

Portrayed in the mid 1980s, the household functions in the Anglo-Celtic cultural imaginary as an expression of the Anglo crisis of confidence in the preservation of its own power, and its own cultural practices, in the face of the transformation of first generation migrants into second generation European-Australians. In terms of numbers these were predominantly Italo-Australians and Greek-Australians. Blond Anna's death from a heroin overdose could be read, perhaps, as the loss of the old, Anglo Australia, given that we are shown Anna in her parents' comfortably suburban, middle-class home. Her overdose is counterpointed with Luchio successfully passing his exams in spite of all the distraction around him.

Punk is a white musical form. Writing about the American proto-punk garage bands of the 1960s, Jon Savage describes their music as a "purely white, blue collar style, in which any black rhythmic influence was bleached out in favour of pure noise and texture: fuzz guitar, feedback, drones and whiny vocals" (1992: 81-2). In Australia the acceptance and development of punk was in part due to the loss of Australia as having a totalised Anglo, understood as 'white,' culture[5]. From the 1970s on, Anglo-Celtic domination would have to be hegemonic, negotiated. In Australia, punk can be understood as, among other things, an articulation of a crisis in an Anglo-Celtic generation which found itself dealing with an Italian- and Greek–Australian generation born in Australia and, on that basis, with as much right to claim Australian identity as the so-called Anglo-Celts (for a discussion of this term see Stratton, 1998: 38-39).

From this perspective the Richmond household in *Dogs in Space* can be read as a metaphor for 1970s/80s Australia. Richmond was an inner-city working-class migrant suburb. While the Anglos reassert their whiteness – as opposed to a southern European non-whiteness – in an existential crisis exemplified by their punk life-style, Luchio, disregarding the mayhem around him, attempts to assimilate into dominant culture and, one presumes, be upwardly socially mobile. This is compared to his mostly middle-class housemates who have dropped out of the educational system and become déclassé. Luchio's Australianness is evidenced in his Anglo–Australian pronunciation style. The film offers a comparison between Luchio's *faux*-Anglo 'respectability' and the household's first generation Italian neighbour who stands in the street and, in a strongly Italian-accented English, shouts angrily at the house's occupants about their noisiness.

Luchio's acceptance by the household comes in the form of being ignored. He tolerates their lifestyle and they let him be except for occasional visits from the women in the house. These unmotivated drop-ins suggest some degree of fascination with the exotic. The only time the men of the house take notice of Luchio is when they return from a road-trip with a lamb for him. Why a lamb? Perhaps this can be read as the punks' understanding of Luchio as a version of the Paschal sacrificial lamb; Luchio as the naive (Italian, Catholic, non-white) lamb to the slaughter in the

(Anglo, secular, white) punk household. The marker of Luchio's place in Anglo-Australian society will not come from his educational achievements, as he would like. Rather it is signalled by Leanne, the young woman from the lower-working class with whom Luchio has had some sort of brief liaison. Brought to the house by her family, Leanne sees Luchio as her ticket out of her background. She tells Luchio that, even though he is not the cause of her pregnancy, she's sure he will make a good father. Aspiring middle-class he may be, it is Luchio's Italian migrant background that allows Leanne to think that he is available to her.

Australian Multiculturalism as Context

In order to understand the Australian popular music landscape on which more recent films draw we need to revisit the development of Australian multicultural policy. Produced during the Coalition government of Malcolm Fraser, many of the 'Galbally Report's' 1978 recommendations were carried through under Bob Hawke's Labor government that came to power in 1983[6]. In *Mistaken Identity: Multiculturalism and the Demise of Nationalism in Australia*, Stephen Castles and his fellow authors describe the 'Galbally Report' as, "[t]he most complete articulation of ... conservative multicultu-ralism" (1988: 67). By this they mean that the Report emphasised the *cultural* disadvantages that caused problems for migrants, such as prejudice and language competence, rather than looking at the *structural* disadvan-tages migrants faced, that is to say aspects of the social and economic organisation of Australian society which militated against the acceptance of non-British and Irish migrants. Labor's concerns were primarily in terms of social welfare, access and equity, equality of opportunity issues, whereas the Coalition, and the Galbally Report, tended to lean towards seeing problems in more individualised terms, and in terms of the capacities of migrants to live successfully in Australia. As Adam Jamrozik, Cathy Roland and Robert Urquhart write:

> True multiculturalism, some argued, would have to be concerned not only with life-styles but also with life chances, with 'equality, justice and fairness' and not just with tolerance and understanding. (1995: 105)

A part of the problem had to do with the assumptions that underlay the 'Galbally Report', that is, that it was concerned with *migrants*, and how migrants might be best accommodated, not with a policy that would manage an ongoing culturally diverse population. The 'Galbally Report' actually presumed that, over a generation or so, the need for institutional structures to support groups from Non-English Speaking Backgrounds (NESBs) would decrease as the members of these groups assimilated into the general population. From this point of view, Australian multicultural policy might be transitory or, as Jamrozik, Boland and Urquhart put it, "multicul-turalism as assimilation in slow motion" (ibid: 111).

A key feature common to both Labor's and the Coalition's image of multiculturalist policy in practice has been the emphasis on 'ethnic' groups. As Castles et al write, "Both modes of multiculturalism were part of a process of construction of ethnic groups as a focal point of social cohesion and mobilisation in Australia" (1988: 71). In this process the discourse of ethnicity became the marker of difference between those who were accepted as members of the core, mainstream culture and those migrants and their descendants identified as not completely Australian, as members of a particular 'ethnic group'.

The construction of migrants from NESBs, and *de facto* their children, as a problem that needed to be resolved, combined with a long-established understanding of assimilation in Australia as a one-way process in which migrants gave up their culture for the Anglo-Celtic Australian culture, has led to a core-periphery structure in the Australian population. One very important element of this has been the retention of power by the Anglo-Celtic population. As Jamrozik et al wrote in 1995:

> The monoculture of [the core] institutions is overwhelming. After close to half a century of mass immigration of people from non-English-speaking countries, the vast majority of school teachers, university lecturers, public servants and professionals is monolingual, notwithstanding some presence of non-Anglo persons, usually second-generation immigrants, in these occupations. (108)

Furthermore, they continue:

> Multiculturalism is evident in the arts, in music, even in some literature. However, there it seems to stop; the closer to economic, social and political power, the less cultural diversity, the more the traditional Anglo-Australian character comes to the fore. (ibid)

In this core-periphery structure, where members of ethnic groups are isolated from key sites of economic, social and cultural power, Sneja Gunew wrote in 1994 that, "multiculturalism in Australia is acceptable as a celebration of costumes, customs and cooking" (22). As we shall see, one of the acceptable customs is music – provided that it predates the era of migration and that the music is, roughly, pre-1960 and can then be identified as a part of a person's heritage, brought from the country of migration. An exception is the use of Tozzi's songs in *Moving Out*, including his popular track from 1977, *Ti Amo* (which retains this title in its Anglicised version). However, as a film made in Italian and English, without subtitles, and early in the new multicultural environment, *Moving Out* does not fit within the mainstream multicultural filmic discourse. The best comparison is, of course, *Looking for Alibrandi*, a film on a similar theme made almost twenty years later.

The Skip/Wog Divide in Film Narratives

Experientially, the core-periphery structure of multiculturalism is replicated for the second generation in what we could call the skip-wog divide. Skip, or Aussie, and wog are the vernacular translations of the more formal Anglo-Celtic/migrant distinction. In both, the terms designating the more powerful, hegemonic group, skip and Anglo-Celtic, came into use later and signal a certain denaturalisation of that dominance. 'Wog' was the term applied to the second generation during their school days, roughly the 1960s and 1970s[7]. Nick Giannopoulos, who subsequently began the *Wogs Out Of*

Work stageshow in 1986, and later starred in *The Wog Boy*, "was called a wog, and teased about the rich food in his lunchbox, the cut and crease of his home-stitched jeans, the smell of his lustrous hair" (in Castles, 2003: online). Giannopoulos was born in 1963, three years after his parents migrated to Australia. Later, George Megalogenis recalls:

> *I learned the word "wog" when I changed primary schools in 1972. That was the year that stung. The year I felt isolation before my time.* (2003: 8-9)

He goes on:

> *The boy braggart in me was finally quelled after two-and-a-bit years of being told I was a wog. As silly as it seems today, when I was young I thought I wasn't a real person. That is what being a wog in a very white school felt like.* (ibid: 9)

Not feeling real was the existential equivalent of not being regarded as a 'proper' Australian[8]. In *The Wog Boy*, Giannopoulos (Steve) has a flashback to being a schoolboy and told he is a wog by the 'real' Australians. His reaction was different to that of Megalogenis:

> *By his teens, Nick's torment has morphed into something more functional – rage. And in this, he enjoyed safety in numbers. Richmond High was full of Greek-Australians. "We were angry at everyone," he says. "Angry at being called wogs. Angry at our mothers being made fun of. Angry we couldn't get Australian girlfriends – they were all after surfie guys. Angry that the Big M milk ads only had blond-haired, blue eyed guys on them – that the media in general was not acknowledging the true state of what Australia was".* (in Castles, op cit)

This anger, born of powerlessness and exclusion, is one aspect of Ari's anger in *Head On*, and in the novel on which the film is based, Christos Tsiolkas' *Loaded* (1995). Talking to his brother's Anglo, liberal, university student girlfriend in the kitchen of their share-house, Ari says:

> *I'm all for racism, I tell Janet, moving slowly towards her, rolling my eyes and putting on a mean motherfucker sneer, dropping my voice very low. I think every whitey deserves to get it in the throat, I whisper in her ear. How about you? she counters, moving away. You're white. I just look at her. I'm not white, I'm a wog. You're white she insists. I say nothing because the conversation is boring.* (in Tsiolkas, 1995: 5)

Loaded, and *Head On*, are pervaded by Ari's anger at being constructed and categorised in ways about which he feels ambivalent. As the narratives of the texts proceed, so he is positioned increasingly as gay rather than straight. And he is a wog but told he is white and yet does not feel 'fully Australian'. Whatever that is, it is what skips/Anglo-Celts feel, not wogs.

The two ambivalences are united in Ari's desire for his brother's new house-mate, the fair haired, blue eyed George in the book, Sean (Julian Garner) in the film – the name change no doubt to reaffirm the character's impeccable Anglo-Celticness[9]. Ari (Alex Dimitriades) finally discovers that George/Sean finds him attractive. However after they have had sex Ari becomes overwhelmingly angry and hits George/Sean. A fight ensues and Ari is kicked out. The book is clearer about what is going on here than is the film. Ari feels trapped in a skip/wog power dynamic. George doesn't understand the complexities of Ari's background: Greek but Australian. When Ari's anger explodes and he hits George, George feels rejected. Here, in a metaphor, is the Anglo-Celtic/migrant divide and also, in Ari's feelings of subservience, the feminisation of the wog.

What I am showing is how the fracture, the power dynamic, which is central to the organisation of Australian multiculturalism, is reproduced through the film texts I am discussing. In *Head On* the anger produced by the dynamic is one of the film's motivations. In *The Wog Boy* the anger is transformed into humour. In *Looking for Alibrandi* the anger is repressed by way of a concentration on Josie's sweet character and the quality of her relationship with her mother. Nevertheless the anger is present and we should briefly examine this subtext before proceeding to a discussion of the music.

Josie (played by Pia Miranda) was born out of wedlock. When her mother, Christina (Greta Sacchi) was seventeen she had a brief affair with Michael Andretti (Anthony LaPaglia), the second generation son of the Italian next-door neighbours. The Andrettis moved from Sydney to South Australia before Christina found out she was pregnant. There is a family secret, a curse as Katia (Elena Cotta), Christina's mother and Josie's grand-mother, puts it – though she will never be clear about what this curse is. Katia had migrated to Queensland with her husband Francesco. It turns out that Christina is not Katia's husband's child but rather the daughter born of Katia's love affair with an Anglo-Australian, Marcus Sandford, and raised by the always-resentful Francesco. Here, as in *Head On*, sexual relations can be read as a metaphor for the migrant situation in Australia. Katia is unloved by her Italian husband, but loved by the Anglo-Australian, Marcus Sand-ford. However, she cannot leave her husband, her culture, as Marcus asks, meaning that she cannot assimilate by giving up her cultural background and taking on Anglo-Australian culture. Christina is brought up apparently Italian in Australia but actually half Anglo-Australian, that is, she is forced to see herself as 'Italian,' as a wog, because of the Anglo-Celtic/migrant divide, when, in fact, much of her cultural make-up is Anglo-Australian.

Read in this analogical way, Josie is the product of Christina's illegiti-mate relationship because, from the point of view of the dominant Anglo-Celtic culture, migrants are supposed to assimilate through the second generation. The most effective sign of second-generation assimilation would be their marriage to Anglo-Celts. Having a relationship with another second-generation Italo-Australian is inappropriate (read illegitimate) while, because of the way the skip-wog divide works, it is practically inevitable. The book from which the film was developed was set in the present of its publication date, 1992. Josie, herself now seventeen, would have been born in 1975, three years before the time of *Dogs in Space*, the Galbally Report, and during the formal development of multicultural pol-icy[10].

Josie has a teenage romance with the Anglo working-class Jacob Coote[11] (Kick Gurry) but refuses to have sex with him. It is worth thinking about Josie's female desire for Jacob in relation to Ari's feminised desire for

George/Sean. Like Ari and George/Sean, Josie and Jacob break up, not least because he just cannot understand the complexities of Josie's Italo-Australian life. (However, at the end of the film, with the commercial need to provide audiences with a happy ending, there is some suggestion that they might reconcile.) The barrenness of Josie and Jacob's relationship expresses an attitude to the skip/wog fracture that runs through both the book and the film of *Looking for Alibrandi*. In the film Josie breaks the blond, Anglo Carly's nose with a history book (one volume of Edward Gibbon's *A History of The Decline and Fall of the Roman Empire* [1776-1788]) when Carly calls her first a wog and then – the clincher – a bastard. Josie rings her father to come to the school to help when Carly's father threatens to sue her. However, Josie cannot bring herself to tell Michael that she has been called a bastard so she just tells him that she was called a wog. Michael's response is that she needs to get used to being called names. Michael is the migrant success story, second generation and a barrister. Yet even he is not quite assimilated. Telling Josie she needs to get used to being called names suggests that he has achieved as much as he has by not reacting to the insults thrown at him, not that he hasn't been called a wog. While the dominant narrative of *Looking for Alibrandi* is Josie's acceptance of her Italian heritage, one secondary narrative concerns Michael Andretti's acceptance of his own Italian heritage, and its Italo-Australian reproduction in his daughter.

The clearest expression of the skip/wog fracture and its effects is to be found in Lee Taylor, one of Josie's best friends. She is Anglo but from a 'deviant' background; her father is an alcoholic. It is Lee who corrects Josie when she claims "We're masters of our own destiny" by retorting:

> That's rubbish. If your father's a dustman, you're going to be a dustman and if your father's filthy rich, you're going to be filthy rich because he'll introduce you to his rich friend's son. People breed with their own kind, ... the rich marry the rich, Josie, the poor marry the poor. The dags marry the dags and the wogs marry the wogs. (in Marchetta, 1992: 144)

This is where core-periphery multiculturalism, combined with the policy of ethnicising people into more or less institutionalised groups, has led us.

Rock Music and Australian Film

We now need to turn to the landscape of popular music in this multicultural order. The popular music charts in Australia are dominated today by what is a predominantly American hegemony, expressed in male vocal groups, female singers influenced by African-American R&B, and rap artists. At the same time there is a strong Australian rock tradition. In his chapter on Australian popular music in *Popular Music and Local Identity*, Tony Mitchell, following Graeme Turner, suggests that there is an "absence of any recognisable indicators of national identity in Australian music, especially the music marketed abroad" (1996: 208). Elsewhere I have criticised this position, suggesting that there are at least two traits that have characterised Australian rock music (Stratton 2003; 2004a). One is its whiteness, the historical lack of an African-American aesthetic input – a lack that can, in part, be related indirectly to the White Australia Policy[12]. The other is the importance of the ballad tradition to the form that Australian rock music has taken most obviously in the 1970s and 1980s pub rock era; if you like, the important connection between Slim Dusty and Cold Chisel.

What is important for my argument here is the recognition that Australia does have a particular popular musical history and that this is white, Anglo and Irish derived. Furthermore, its formation and historical dominance in Australia has been a function of Anglo–Celtic hegemonic power[13]. In the semiotic system of Australian popular music this white rock is identified as Anglo-Celtic but also as characteristically Australian. It is the continued naturalisation of this music as Australian popular music that has enabled it to be not only unmarked in an international context but also unremarkable, that is, its cultural specificity could not be written about, in a local, national context. This is the white, Anglo-Celtic, Australian rock that, within the spectrum of Australian popular music, Australian punk bands from the Saints to the Boys Next Door (Nick Cave's first band), to the other bands in *Dogs in Space* took to its bleached-out limit. This is the music which, in the films made under the impact of Australian multicultural policy, signifies both white, Anglo-Celtic culture and, because of its hegemonic dominance, Australian culture.

There appears to have been a modest shift in Australian feature films over the last ten years from a tendency to use American, or English, music as an apparently unmarked musical signifier, that is as seemingly having a universal significance, to using Australian rock and thereby signalling the Australianness of the film. Even in *The Dish* (dir: Rob Sitch, 2001), with its nostalgic celebration of the American space landing, there are two Russell Morris songs, including *The Real Thing* (1969), and the Loved Ones classic, *The Loved One* (1966). The use of Australian rock in films helps reproduce its position as an aspect of the hegemonic culture of Anglo-Celtic Australia. Exemplifying the shift to the use of Australian rock we can compare *The Heartbreak Kid* with *Looking for Alibrandi*. *The Heartbreak Kid* (dir: Michael Jenkins, 1993) uses the Neville Brothers' *True Love* (1992), The Persuasions' reworking of The Troggs' *Love Is All Around* (1967), U2's *One* (1992) and a reworking by the Australian musician Stephen Cummings of Elton John's *Teacher I Need You* (1978). In contrast, eight years later, *Looking for Alibrandi* uses tracks by Killing Heidi, Lo-Tel, Spiderbait and Endorphin, among others, with comparatively little non-Australian music. All these are artists that musically knowledgeable young Australians will identify as 'locals'.

This Australianisation of the mainstream popular music used in Australian films has led to a heightened sense of the play around the core-periphery, skip-wog fracture. Thus, for example, Josie's Australianness is signalled by the constant use of Australian rock as background to scenes she is in: Spiderbait's *Dinnertime* (1999) when she and her friends drive to Bondi, Magic Dirt's version of (American) Liz Phair's *Supernova* (1994) when Josie is riding on the back of Jacob's motorbike, silverchair's *Miss You Love* (1999) when Jacob and Josie almost have sex. In contrast, Josie's mother, grandmother, and friends, when they are positioned as Josie's Italian heritage, are given Italian-style continuity music or, and I shall discuss this below, actual Italian music. Thus, the problem that Josie has to resolve, her wogness in relation to her Australianness – itself a consequence of the distinction between those who are 'proper' Australians and those identified as migrants – is reproduced and played out in the quarantined way the music in the film is organised.

In this regard it is rewarding to think about Michael Andretti. When Andretti picks up Josie and Jacob in his car the radio is playing the Australian band Even's *No Surprises* (1998), another piece of white rock[14]. The lyrics include the line "I come out clean but I wear my disguises" which suggest Andretti's assimilatory shift from his Italian heritage. When Josie and her father are together in his apartment the music-over is The Church's *The Unguarded Moment* (1981). This is another piece of white Australian rock that implies the Australianness, and assimilatory shift, of both characters as well as suggesting the new depth of their relationship.

Most interesting here though, is Andretti's CD collection. In the book we are told that he "hates all modern music, except Billy Joel" (Marchetta, 1992: 163). As a New York Jew, Joel has a specific American profile not necessarily considered mainstream. In the film Andretti has a large Santana collection. What does Santana signify, apart from mainstream, adult American, Latino-blues–rock[15]? In the United States Santana has become a major, long standing and mainstream recording artist with his mix of African-American, Latin and rock influences. Contrarily, in Australia white rock has taken on board few if any non-Anglo-Celtic influences, reflecting an assimilation demand that non-Anglo cultures should be considered unsatisfactory (uncivilised?) and should be given up in favour of Anglo-Celtic Australian culture. Unlike Santana's cultural syncretism, Andretti's choice, and for that matter Josie's, is more complex: a choice between asserting their wogness and limiting their assimilation and chances for upward social mobility, or attempting to assimilate, knowing that their wogness will always hold them back.

In *Head On* the use of music similarly reproduces the Australian core-periphery, skip-wog, multicultural organisation. However, the place we need to start is with *Loaded* which, if possible, makes even greater use of music than the film. Ari's music likes are semiotically complex, spanning both his gay/straight and Greek wog/skip ambivalences. He tells us that the Jackson Five's 1970 hit, *I Want You Back*, is "a supreme moment in music history" (in Tsiolkas, 1995: 19). This track, with its insidious bass riff and shouted chorus by a young Michael Jackson before his voice dropped, has long been a disco favourite. From its inception in the 1970s disco has been an integral part of gay night-life[16].

In relation to *Head On*, we need to distinguish disco from the late 1980s and later dance music of house, and especially trance and its related genres. Ari likes disco a lot and another of his favourite tracks is Sister Sledge's *Lost In Music* (1979). Also a track by an African-American act, it celebrates dancing as a solution to the problems of mundane living:

Responsibility
To me is a tragedy
I'll get a job some other time, uh-huh...

The band plays so very tight
Each and every night, uh–huh
It's not vanity
To me, it's my sanity I could never survive

With these lyrics it is understandable why Ari should like the track so much; it offers him dance as an escape from his intractable identity problems.

On Ari's perfect tape, the one he has made for his Walkman, six of the tracks are African-American disco and Tamla Motown. For Ari, disco connotes a simpler, probably happier because less complex, time. Ari comments on the AIDS sufferer who is dancing for money:

He is spinning on the roof of the van looking for heaven, finding
jubilation in the gospel of disco music from a time when you could put
your dick into anything and not worry what you might find. (ibid: 78)

Ari has a gay man's nostalgia for disco as evocative of a time before HIV/AIDS.

One of the strongest early scenes in *The Wog Boy* involves Steve (Nick Giannopoulos) and his best mate, Italo–Australian Frank (Vince Colosimo) dancing at a disco to The Bee Gees *You Should Be Dancing* (1976) in the style of John Travolta in *Saturday Night Fever* (dir: John Badham, 1977). The scene is part of a retrospective look at Steve's life. Having accepted the Aussie schoolkids' classification of himself as a wog, Steve is determined to become the best wog he can. Travolta as Tony Manero is, understandably, his idol. Steve and Frank get off with Norwegian and Czechoslovak netballers. These wogs are so good that they can make it with the blond European women. This is a defining moment of wogdom. Through disco nostalgia from the mid-20th century, and after, the Anglo-Celtic Australians' fear that the wogs are here to get the Anglo-Celtic girls is defused by, first, having the girls they get as not Australian and, second, using the nostalgia of disco as a way of deflecting the feelings of anxiety for the Aussie males that this scene might otherwise conjure. Moreover, a part of the ideology of disco was the community of the dance-floor[17] – everybody could share in the same ecstatic dance experience. In this way, then, the use of disco in *The Wog Boy* helps to make Steve and Frank less threatening and allows viewers to continue to think of the film as a comedy.

Ari's tape contains one New Zealand track by Split Enz and little Australian. The exclusion of Australian rock suggests its Anglo–Celtic hegemonic force. The music in the film functions more obviously than the book and along similar lines to *Dogs in Space* and *Looking for Alibrandi*. From the electronic rock of English duo Lunatic Calm's *Leave You Far Behind* (1998) to the Saints's classic Australian punk of *Know Your Product* (1978), Ari's taste in music is whiter, harder and only a little more Australian than in the book. However, where in *Loaded* the music suggests Ari's uncertainties, in the film the music more clearly reproduces the discursive organisation of the multicultural order – core–periphery and skip–wog – that provides the basis for his ambivalence about his Australianness.

In *Head On*, from the point of view of the Australian multicultural experience, it is significant that Ari likes African-American music. In the Greek club, Ariadne asks Ari what he would like the band to play. His response, typical of his ambivalence about his ethnic identity, is Jimmy Ruffin's *What Becomes Of The Broken Hearted?* (1966). Peter announces to the table, "my brother wishes he was black" (ibid: 73). Ari is upset with his brother and gets angry. Yet Peter is right: being African-American is a fantasy solution for Ari. Rather than dealing in the hybrid compromises forced on someone constructed as an Australian wog, he would, seemingly, be both a clear-cut member of a racial minority and have a distinct culture. The irony is to be found in the high number of tracks on Ari's perfect tape which are, in one sense or another, creolised and ambivalent: the rock influence in Prince's *Little Red Corvette* (1982), the white, melodic pop influence in the Four Tops' *Walk Away Renée* (1968), the African-American blues influence in the Rolling Stones' *Gimme Shelter* (1970), and so on.

In *Head On* Ari meets Sean at a gay dance club playing trance. Mitchell argues:

> the more than 90 per cent rate of imported dance music played at most parties turned the Australian house and dance party scene into a weightless featureless terra nullius of simulated and displaced origins. (1996: 202)

While the Greek club he visits earlier in the night privileged his ethnic, wog identity issues, Ari's sexual identity issues are also signalled. Ari dances the *tsiftelteli* with Ariadne to respected rebetiko bozouki player and composer, Markos Vamerakaris' *Your Two Hands* (1932). The *tsifteteli* is a belly dance performed predominantly by women. That Ari dances it subtly suggests, perhaps, his ambivalence about his sexual interests. When Ari's crossdressing Greek-Australian friend, Toula, turns up at the club, shocking the conservative patrons and embarrassing Ari, s/he dances the *tsifteteli* on her own, thus making a spectacular statement about her sexual identity that reinforces the effect made by her transvestism. It is, though, the gay club that allows the privileging of Ari's sexual identity issues. The Greek club had a band playing Greek music (music originating from Greece) the gay club fades ethnic identity back in the mix, playing electronic dance music without vocals. This is a featureless music to be lost in, music to lose one's personal identity and, as the scene shows, couple up for anonymous sex. All are apparently equal; here in multicultural terms, sexuality and sexual taste predominate. Sean makes the mistake of taking Ari out of this environment, taking him home where the issues of his wogness, and Sean's Anglo-Celtic whiteness, reassert themselves.

From the point of view of Ari's wog-Australian identity issues one of the most evocative scenes takes place early on in the night, before he has left his parents' house. In *Loaded* Ari tells us that his mother is second generation born in Australia. His father is a first generation migrant. Ari's mother puts on a vinyl record, Kevin Borich's *Gonna See My Baby Tonight*, which was a hit for the La De Das in 1971. It reminds her of her youth. She dances what Maria Papas describes as "a kind of lazy version of the *tsifteteli*" (pc 2003)[18]. Ari's mother is merging her Greek heritage with her Australian origin in a way that Ari finds difficult to do: after all, the Australian multicultural policy that evolved when Ari's mother was an adult seeks to partition ethnic cultures from Anglo-Celtic culture on the grounds of keeping the 'purity' of each. Ari's father comes into the kitchen and is upset with what he sees. He takes off the La De Das and says that if you're going to dance a *tsifteteli* you should play *tsifteteli* music, by which he means that Greek dances should be performed to Greek music. Ari's father is here not so much observing the organisation of Australian multiculturalism as affirming his cultural heritage. He puts on Yiorgos Dalaras's *Mi Mou Thimonis Matia Mou* ('Don't Be Angry With Me, Darling') (1991) and starts to perform a different dance, the *hasapiko* (butcher's dance), with his daughter. He then coaxes Ari to join him. Ari dances the *zembekiko*, a male dance. Indeed, Ari shows that he doesn't just know how to do this dance but can effectively inhabit it. He obviously knows and loves his Greek heritage but at the same time despises himself as an Australian wog and doesn't like to show his cultural knowledge.

Ethnicising Music

In order to understand how non-Anglo music functions in the films I am examining, we need to appreciate how non-Anglo music is positioned in the popular music landscape of Australian multiculturalism. Mitchell observes:

> *many local 'ethnic' music groups* [remain] *trapped in local community 'ghettos' partly caused by the rather solemn and tokenistic image inherent in the concept of Australian multiculturalism.* (1996: 191)

As we have seen earlier, music and dancing designated as ethnic are acceptable as an exemplification of heritage. They are, then, acceptable as something to be displayed but are not considered to be an element in the composition of Australian culture itself. This, as we have seen, is thought of hegemonically as synonymous with Anglo-Celtic Australian culture. Since the advent of the discourse of 'world music' in the 1980s, ethnic music is now put into this category, as a cursory look at the racks in almost any general CD store will show[19].

The consequence of the way Greek-originated and Italian-originated (and indeed all non-Anglo-American commercialised) musics are con-structed in the multicultural order is that they are considered legitimate only as minority music, as heritage music, and it is only in this way that they can function in Australian society. This makes all the more remarkable Joe Dolce's 1981 hit *Shuddup You Face*. Dolce is a second generation Italian-American who migrated to Australia in the 1970s. *Shuddup You Face* has a jaunty, Anglo-pop styling. Voiced by Dolce, its Italianness comes from the pronunciation style and 'broken' English, marking the female protagonist as a first generation Italian migrant. Still the biggest selling Australian single, it is also still the only popular Australian song to acknowledge Non-English-Speaking migration to Australia. Dolce tells an intriguing story. In October 1981 he received a Radio 3XY silver chart award:

> *I attended the awards ceremony dressed as the 'serious' artist, Joe Dolce, with* [partner] *Lin Van Hecke, accompanying me as my bespectacled secretary. As I took the podium I declined to accept the award as a protest*

against the way ethnic people have been treated in Australia, did a short speech, and very haughtily, we both walked off. There is a stunned silence. Backstage, I quickly changed into my Italian hat, grabbed my mandolin, and a grovelling 'Giuseppe' quickly ran back on to grab the award apologising for his 'serious' alter–ego.[20]

It is the requirement that, in Australia, Giuseppe should grovel that has made Ari and many other wogs so angry.

Ethnic music in Australia serves as a signifier of migrant origin. Thus, later musical developments are not discursively acceptable. There is no Greek techno, or Greek rock for that matter, in *Head On*, certainly none in *The Wog Boy*, and no recent Italian popular music in *Looking for Alibrandi*. There is no Greek-Australian or Italo-Australian music in these films. Australian compositions that utilise a language other than English, or musical forms drawn from other cultures are considered a peculiarity in Australia and lacking in worth, being neither properly Australian nor Greek/Italian and having no other possible status. As we shall see in a moment, the only exception to this rule is the use of 'ethnic' music from within the dominant, Anglo-Celtic Australian, order and music identified as 'world' music[21], this classification also being made by that dominant order.

Ari has two Greek songs on his perfect tape, Sotiria Bellou's version of *Sinnefiasmeni Kiriaki* ('Cloudy Sunday') (1947) and Manos Loizos' *O Thromos* ('The Road') (1999). Both songs are heard in *Head On*. *Sinnefiasmeni Kiriaki* is sung by the woman in the Greek club toilet and *O Thromos* is played by the Turkish taxi driver who picks up Toula and Ari. This song, as the taxi driver explains, is overly political, about youth and the struggle for freedom from dictatorship. In *Head On*, Ari's nihilistic self-loathing is privileged and he is dismissive of the lyrics' politics. Both are significant items of popular music from the post-Second World War era. *Sinnefiasmeni Kiriaki* was written by Vassilis Tsitsanis during the German-occupation and recorded by Bellou, a renowned singer of the post-war period shortly after the end of the war. Like Vamirakaris, Tsitsanis and Bellou worked in the Greek musical style known as *rebetiko*. This music, making use of Turkish and other eastern melodies, was associated with the Greek working class, and with anarchism and communism. It was the music played by the *Rebetes*, people who considered themselves outsiders to the social order. Both the *zembekiko* and the *tsifteteli* are closely associated with *rebetiko*. There is, then, a density of signification in the use of this music in *Loaded* and *Head On*.

In the Greek club all the music played by the real-life band, the haBiBis, is, according to their website:

very classic and traditional. None of these songs have been modernised or westernised. They are all very authentic sounding village songs – the type of songs our parents [first generation] *might have listened to.* (2003: online)[22]

That Ari, Ariadne and the other Greek wogs in *Loaded* and *Head On* identify with *rebetiko* helps to understand how these characters use their own cultural heritage to produce an assertive personal identity in an

Australian multicultural society where they are constructed as wogs and excluded from the dominant culture.

At the same time, from the point of view of the dominant, Anglo-Celtic Australians, this music would be regarded as world music. Mitchell describes a 1989 album by Sirocco called *Port of Call* that appropriates instruments and musical forms from many cultures and also includes a section that "simulates musically the journey of the tall ships from London to Australia" (1996: 191-2). Mitchell argues that:

> *It is difficult to interpret this musical representation of the British invasion of Australia as anything other than a celebration of colonialism, and one which places all the other exotic and multicultural musics Sirocco appropriates in a similarly colonialist context.* (ibid: 193)

Constructing Ari's musical heritage as world music has a similar colonialist effect.

Within this general context we can think about the music that frames *Looking for Alibrandi* and is played on Tomato Day or, as Josie calls it, National Wog Day, at the beginning and end of the film. Josie's mother, grandmother and friends are all working in the yard making tomato puree while listening to *Tintarella di Luna* ('Moon Tan'). Rejecting her heritage, Josie attempts to take off the record and put on some heavy rock. She is howled down and made to put the record on again. *Tintarella di Luna* was a hit in Italy in 1959/60 for the well-known singer, Mina[23]. It is an Italian pop song influenced by American popular music of the time. In other words, it is, itself, a creolised cultural object which, in *Looking for Alibrandi*, works within the discourse of Australian multiculturalism, and thus is used as the legitimating signifier for the origin and heritage of the film's Italo-Australians. In other words, this piece of Italian popular music is ethnicised. At this point we can make a distinction between hybrid and spontaneous musics, that is, the kind of deliberate hybridisation that treats all non-Anglo musical themes and instruments as elements from which a new piece of music can evolve – although usually framed by a characteristically Anglo musical form such as that which Mitchell describes in *Port of Call* – and music that has evolved relatively spontaneously out of the mixing of cultural forms. While it could be argued that *Tintarella di Luna* shows the effects of American cultural colonialism, it cannot, itself, be considered a colonialist enterprise.

Over the film end credits another version of *Tintarella di Luna* is heard. This one is by the Australian rock band, Happyland. Happyland is a side project for Janet English of Spiderbait and Quan Yeomans of Regurgitator. Available on the soundtrack album for the film, we have another intriguing exception to the rule partitioning Anglo-Celtic Australian culture from Non-English-Speaking cultural influence. In Happyland's updated, punked-up version we have a very small beginning for the ethnic creolisation of Australian culture. Happyland's involvement in this project may have been influenced by Yeomans himself being the second-generation son of a (north) Vietnamese-born mother and an Anglo-Australian father.

Before leaving this discussion we should note that the lyrics of *Tintarella di Luna* make it an interesting choice for the film. The song tells of a girl who moon-bakes, getting a tan the colour of milk. When there is a full moon she becomes completely white. And her white skin makes her the most beautiful woman of all[24]. In the Australian context the song can be read as a comment on the wog's impossible desire for whiteness, for acceptance within the Anglo-Celtic Australian hegemony.

Looking for Alibrandi ends on Tomato Day a year after its narrative commencement. Dean Martin's *Volare*, a hit for him in the United States in 1958, is on the record player. Here, we have another example of successful American creolised assimilation. Martin, a second generation Italo-American born Dino Crocetti, sings a Neapolitan song in English.[25] Josie takes the record off and puts on *Tintarella di Luna*, thus suggesting that, through her year of travail she has come to an acceptance of her Italian heritage. But the scene becomes more semiotically complicated as she takes her grandmother and begins to do the twist, an African-American dance popularised by Chubby Checker (whose track, *The Twist*, was released in 1960). Immediately the others stop work and start twisting. Thus, in the scene where authentic Italianness is signified by the music regardless of its complex provenance, these Italians demonstrate the incorporation of American culture into Italian everyday life by performing an American dance – one which is also well-known in Australia as a consequence of the post-war spread of American youth culture.

Rap, or the Lack of It

Music constructed as ethnic is accepted within the multicultural order as an aspect of the identification of wogs as opposed to skips or Aussies. In the multicultural musical landscape the music which is understood to be threatening – if not to the order itself then within that order – to white, Anglo-Celt Australia is rap. Here we have a history in which rap has taken over this role from reggae. John Castles explains that Bob Marley's 1979 concert in Adelaide, "became the inspiration for No Fixed Address and a generation of CASM [Centre for Aboriginal Studies in Music] bands" (1998: 16). In Australia, reggae was adopted by indigenous people who felt that the music gave them a connection with other oppressed black people. As Castles remarks:

> By embracing reggae as an expression of solidarity with black people everywhere, NFA [No Fixed Address] presented its Aboriginal audience with the possibility of a way out from under this oppression. (ibid)

To position this development we should remember that 1979 was a year after the presentation of the 'Galbally Report'.

Until the advent of multicultural policy, the societal divide in Australia was understood to be between the indigenous people and a unified, apparently homogeneous, Australian population. In multiculturalism, as we have seen, the divisions based on claims of race and ethnicity have become more complex. With the waning of reggae in Australia as an oppositional musical force, its place has been taken by rap. Rap started to gain importance as an Australian musical form in the early 1990s. In 1992, Sounds Unlimited released *A Postcard from the Edge of the Underside* and the following year Def Wish Cast released *Knights of the Underground Table*. Rap is not identified solely with Aboriginal oppression. Both Sounds Unlimited and Def Wish Cast came from the western suburbs of Sydney. As Mitchell writes:

> The Western suburbs have continued to provide the main historic centre of hip hop in Sydney, partly owing to the strong concentration of non-Anglo migrant communities such as Greeks, Italians, Lebanese and Vietnamese, whose youth have been attracted by the oppositional features of African-American hip hop and adopted its signs and forms as markers of their own otherness. (1996: 194)[26]

In Australia rap remains the music of oppression, its makers and consumers characterised as refusing to comply with the organisation of Australian multiculturalism. Of the groups most usually associated with Australian rap, the Lebanese – felt by many to be the most oppressed of the wog migrants as the group least able to make inroads into the Anglo-Celtic institutional core of multiculturalism – are the ones most tightly identified with the music.

In the discourse of the multicultural order, rap has become the music of the angry wog, relegated, according to Mitchell, to "an 'underground' subculture" of the mainstream music industry (ibid: 193). However it is still hardly present in Australian film. There is no rap in the angriest of the films I have been looking at, *Head On*, and only a brief, joke rap by Giannopoulos in *The Wog Boy*. The recent film where one would be most likely to find rap is *Fat Pizza*, the film made to capitalise on the success of the comedy series of the same name that screened on SBS through 2002/3[27]. *Fat Pizza* is not 'politically correct'. Its characters don't want to be 'good ethnics' or to assimilate. The guiding light of *Fat Pizza* is Paul Fenech, a second-generation Maltese-Australian. In the series, as in the film, Fenech, going by the name Paul Falzoni, works as a pizza delivery boy for Bobo (Johnny Boxer), a forty year old Italo-Australian virgin who lives with his mother and runs a pizza shop, Fat Pizza. Working with Falzoni is Sleek The Elite (played by Paul Nakad).

Fat Pizza adheres to the conventions about the use of music that I have been identifying, albeit with a seemingly knowing awareness – that is, in this film the common filmic technique of using music to help identify particular groupings of people is taken to a self-conscious, almost parodic, extreme[28]. The bikies are given hard rock music, Bobo always has Neapolitan crooning as his underscore in the shop, the dance sequences have house, trance and thrash punk dependant on the club's clientele.

Sleek The Elite is also the name Nakad uses as a professional rapper[29]. Nakad is of Lebanese descent. In Australia, Lebanese-Australians are members of one of the most stigmatised and alienated groups in Australian society. Anglo-Celt Australians tend to think of stories about 'Lebanese gangs' in Western Sydney's Bankstown, and the 2000 series of gang rapes by young men of Lebanese extraction which are now used to give credence to these stories. Chris Johnson describes Sleek's work this way: "Sleek the Elite, particularly, raps proudly of inner-city life, multiculturalism and racism in a thick, Lebanese-Australian accent." (2004: online) In the television series, Sleek regularly raps in his pizza delivery car, adding to the sense of subversion in a show that pillories sacred cows indiscriminately and mercilessly. Sleek's use of rap suggests his defiance in face of dominant attitudes to people of his background. However, in the film, Sleek's rapping is reduced to an early cameo when we first meet him. Elsewhere in the film the rap used is so low volume as to merge with the disco/house music forming the general backdrop. In other words, it would seem that rap has moved back underground (into underscore rather than music-over or 'overscore'). This makes the film more palatable, less confrontational and threatening, for an audience that might be larger than for the SBS series, specifically, an audience with more Anglo-Celts.

Since the advent of multicultural policy, there has developed a clear organisation of popular music in Australia. Rock is identified as white, as Anglo-Celtic, and also as the hegemonic 'typically Australian' musical form. Music from outside the British-American-Australian rock nexus, the music from the non-English-speaking world, is constructed as world music and, more specifically, as the heritage music of Australian NESB migrants. The core-periphery structure of Australian multiculturalism keeps a strict partition between 'Anglo-Celtic' and 'migrant' cultures. The consequence is that Australian popular music does not incorporate elements from the musics of Australia's NESB population. This strict division is reproduced and naturalised in films that portray Anglo-Celtic and migrant, skip-wog, relations. Australian rap, which has become the angry music of refusal of this ordering of multicultural Australia, is as yet hardly to be found in Australian films, something that may be a consequence of the attempt to find Australian films a mainstream, Anglo-Celtic audience.

The lack of rap music in Australian films that represent multiculturalism suggests the extent to which these films, even those made by non–Anglo-Celtic directors, have accepted and reproduced the dominant understandings of multiculturalism – the understandings which reinforce Anglo-Celtic hegemony. It is clear that, to a significant extent, this has been driven by commercial constraints informed by a conservative view of Australian film audiences as dominated by the Anglo-Celtic majority. With certain honourable exceptions, such as the Greek music used in *Head On*, the songs used in most Australian films are ones that a young, and early middle-aged, Anglo-Celtic audience can easily leave the cinema humming. However, even a cursory examination of the websites inviting feedback on *Fat Pizza* suggests a large, youthful and ethnic audience looking for films that reflect their frustration, and indeed anger, at the ways non–Anglo-Celts continue to be minoritised in Australian multicultural culture. How Australian filmmakers respond to such feedback will be worth examination over the next decade of Australian cinema.

Notes

1. Also, the institutional signs of the breakdown of the Australian incorporatist ideology of assimilation can be found much earlier, in the establishment of the Italian welfare organisation Co.As.It (A Community Organisation for Italians and Australians of Italian Descent based in Carlton, Melbourne) in 1967 and the Greek welfare society in 1969 (Castles et al, 1988: 60). Whitlam's government set up the Australia Assistance Plan which, as Jean Martin describes it in The Migrant Presence (quoted in Castles et al: 61), provided the vehicle by which the scattered groups of migrant

and migrant-oriented welfare organisations could move towards the centres of political power and also acted as a catalyst to the development of more integrated and articulate migrant organisations.

2. The term 'Italo-Australian', like other terms such as 'Greek-Australian', can be used to mean a number of quite different things, for example, that the person so described has come from Italy and is now resident in Australia, or that they have Italian parentage and were born in Australia, or that one of their parents is Italian, or of Italian heritage, and the other is Anglo-Celtic Australian. In this chapter, for the sake of space, I will use the term accepting these slippages, the consequent vagueness and the ideological work that the slippages perform.

3. See Riley (1992).

4. Ollie Olsen was musical consultant for *Dogs in Space* and played in the 1970s Melbourne punk band Whirlywirld, and was also musical consultant for *Head On*.

5. Compared to the United States there is still little published work on the construction of whiteness in Australia but see, for example, Hage (1998) and Stratton (1999). An overview of discussions of whiteness in Australia can be found in Ganley (2003).

6. Castles, et al wrote that, at the beginning of the 1980s, "two out of every ten Australians are first generation immigrants" (ibid: 25). Of these "37 percent of the foreign born population were from Britain and Ireland, while a further 37 per cent were from Europe" (ibid). In 1976, a couple of years before the timeframe depicted in Dogs in Space, the total number of second generation Australians was 2,276,330 or 16.8 per cent of the Australian population (Siew-Ean Khoo et al, 2002: 9). By 1996 this figure had risen to 3,389,962 or 19.1 per cent of the total population. Of these, 1,444,444 came from British backgrounds, 334,048 were of Italian heritage and 153,876 had Greek forebears. Second generation Lebanese, who we will want to discuss in relation to Fat Pizza, came eighth, numbering 82,582, but we need to remember that this figure does not distinguish between Christian and Muslim Lebanese (ibid: 11).

7. There is an instructive website for Australian wogs, called Woglife, started in July, 2000, at http://www.wog.com.au/default.asp.

8. For Megalogenis, "There are three phases of wogdom: cowed, cocky, and connected" (2003: 7). Megalogenis suggests that feelings about wogness are individual, rather than the culture that has constructed the person as a 'wog.' He writes:

   The third phase of wogdom occurs when you are happily Australian. However, not everyone wants to get there. The Wog Boy, a box-office hit in 2000, was not a bad film. But it wasn't a good one either... The movie missed the point because it celebrated the second phase of wogdom. It was a dated indicator that we had already surpassed. (ibid: 11)

9. Sean is an Irish name. This is not the place to discuss the history of the incorporation of the Irish into Australian whiteness. However, the use of an Irish name suggests a subtle unsettling as the Irish, while now generally accepted as white, were once not acceptable (for a history of the whitening of the Irish, see Stratton 2004b).

10. Melina Marchetta's book, *Looking for Alibrandi* (1992), the basis for the film, uses much older musical reference points such as Janis Ian's *At Seventeen* (1975). Marchetta has Josie inform the reader, "My name, by the way, is Josephine Alibrandi and I turned seventeen a few months ago. (The seventeen that Janis Ian sang about where one learns the truth)" (4-5). Also, Marchetta's musical references are not Australian: Elton John's *Crocodile Rock* (1972) and "a slow Elvis song" are played at the School Dance (54); Josie listens to the Irish U2, "to the words written by, perhaps, a modern-day poet" (260).

11. There is an intriguing resonance with James Cook in the name and Jacob goes to school at Cook High.

12. The term used to stand for a set of laws restricting immigration by people of non-European descent (who were forced to undergo a dictation test in a European

language). The White Australia Policy was federally actioned from the cornerstone Immigration Restriction Act passed in 1901 and was still in operation 50 years later.

13. From this point of view the finalists in the 2003 Australian Idol competition assume great importance. On the one hand there was Shannon Noll, the Anglo boy from the New South Wales bush whose vocal phrasings were clearly pub-rock originated – he even covered Jimmy Barnes' *Working Class Man* (1985). On the other hand there was Guy Sebastian, inheritor of a mix of Portugese, Sri Lankan (this probably means Sinhalese) and Indian ancestry and born in Malaysia, whose musical influence was mainly African-American gospel and R'n'B. The division between core and periphery Australia, the old and the new, could not have been more clearly delineated. In the end Guy, clearly the better singer, won the popular vote.

14. Thank you, Kristen Philips, for recognising this song.

15. Carlos Santana was born in 1947 in Autlan, Mexico. His father was a mariachi violinist. In 1955 the family moved to Tijuana, near the American border. In 1961 Carlos moved to San Francisco, with his family following the next year. Santana learnt to play the blues on guitar but he plays with Latin influences.

16. See, for example, the history of disco in Brewster and Broughton (2000: chapters 6 and 7) and Haslam (2001: chapter 3). Andriote (2001: 23) tells us that disco was often called 'the gay sound' in its early days and that: "Even at disco's peak, Billboard estimated that at least 50 percent of the [United States] nation's dance clubs were gay" (84).

17. Andrioti reiterates this idea when he writes that, "From the beginning, disco music and discotheques themselves united like-minded people in a shared experience of physical exuberance" (2001: 79).

18. I would like to thank Maria Papas for her invaluable help with my understanding of the Greek music and dancing in *Head On*.

19. On the development of the discourse of world music see, among others, Feld (1994: 257-289) and, more generally, Taylor (1997).

20. This story comes from Joe Dolce's web site at
http://www.starnet.com.au/dwomen/SYFStory.html.

21. This discursive situation is what caused such problems for the classification, and consumption, of Not Drowning, Waving's *Tabaran* album on which the band worked with musicians from Rabaul, Papua New Guinea. See, most importantly, Hayward (1998).

22. See the haBiBis's home page at http://www.sprint.net.au/~jomal/habibis/. Indicating how they are positioned in Australian music, the band tells us that they "are regularly heard at the major folk and world music festivals around Australia."

23. For some reason, perhaps because of copyright, the version used in *Looking for Alibrandi* is a replication of the original by the Italo-Australian artist Gina Zoia.

24. My thanks to Amanda Third for translating the lyrics for me.

25. Volare is the English version of a song written by Domenico Modugno called *Nel Blu, Dipinto Di Blu* which won the San Remo song contest in 1958. Modugno is credited with modernising Neapolitan song.

26. See also Maxwell (2001). For a rather different take on Australian hip hop, see Iveson (1997).

27. The abbreviation SBS refers to the television channel of the multi-lingual Special Broadcasting Service. This was set up as an outcome of one of the recommendations of the Galbally Report and started broadcasting in 1980.

28. Fenech is quoted as saying, "With stereotypes there's an element of truth in them... as long as you have fun with them and aren't nasty then it's okay." http://www.smh.com.au/articles/2003/03/31/1048962698529.html?from=storyrhs.

29. Sleek The Elite's official website can be accessed at http://www.sleek-theelite.com.au/bio.htm.

Section II:
MUSICAL SOUNDS

The chapters in this section examine sonic engagements that incorporate music and those sounds that can be interpreted as music. While film production industry structures tend to separate music from sound effects and atmospheres and dialogue, this is becoming increasingly problematic in the context of Australian practices that use musical sounds as music and effects. The section opens with an overview chapter discussing sounds associated with sexuality in Australian film, then explores vocal performance in dialogue, the creation of aural spaces through sound effects and atmospheres, a 'world music' approach to recorded sound, and production collaborations between sound and music personnel.

Bruce Johnson's and Gaye Poole's chapter is a wide-ranging investigation into Australian cinema's approach to sexuality and the way in which film music engages with such narratives, events and obsessions. Through an overview of films prior to the period of concern in this volume (that is, post-1990), the authors argue that sexuality was presented in a limited fashion prior to the late 1960s, then was shown as "a harmless romp" and has only relatively recently matured in its representational approach. Furthermore, music and sound, they argue, are "powerful means of conferring significance and affect on what is seen" and operate in various styles in Australian cinema. Following an overview of approaches and films, the authors focus on more detailed discussion of *feeling sexy* (dir: Davida Allen, 1999), *Walking on Water* (dir: Tony Ayres, 2002), *The Boys* (dir: Rowan Woods, 1997), and *Japanese Story* (dir: Sue Brooks, 2003).

Melissa Iocco's and Anna Hickey-Moody's analysis of the sound and music tracks for Rolf de Heer's *Bad Boy Bubby* (1993) places emphasis on the musical and sonic contribution to this powerfully affective film. The film's impact arises largely from industrial noise, aggressive dialogue and claustrophobic soundscape added to a range of musics. The authors argue that the film is sonically memorable particularly through its affective use of silence, sound and quotable dialogue, especially drawing on repetitive phrases and vocal inflections, as well as the use of binaural microphones to enhance these effects. By these means, sound and music, the authors demonstrate, play crucial roles in the "construction and re-construction" of the central protagonist's subjectivity.

Mark Evans's chapter focuses on Andrew Dominik's gangster/crime film *Chopper* (2000) arguing that, drawing on the considerable talents of sound-aware personnel in the film team, the film is exceptional to generically similar films that tend to draw on pre-recorded source songs. Rather the music is strategically placed within a soundscape of sound effects, ambient noise, background conversations, on-the-air sounds and dialogue. These effectively both place the viewer within the confined spaces represented on-screen and assist in identification with the central protagonist, however reluctantly, and his violent actions and approach.

In her discussion of the music track for *Rabbit-Proof Fence* (dir: Phillip Noyce, 2002) created largely by Peter Gabriel, Marjorie Kibby reveals a complex mix of musical timbres and textures that are significantly enhanced by sounds recorded by Andrew Skeoch and Sarah Koschak of the environmental recording team Listening Earth. Kibby argues that Noyce and Gabriel used the score "to construct the environment – specifically the landscape – as a character that plays a key role in the narrative events". Gabriel's score (and soundtrack album tracks) interweaves musicians and instruments from various locations with Aboriginal music and environmental sounds to produce musical washes that offer an empathetic context for the narrative, and evoke a generalised 'sound of Australia'.

Concluding this section, my chapter on Ray Lawrence's critically acclaimed *Lantana* (2001) offers a production study conducted retrospectively with key personnel who worked on this award-winning film. The chapter centres on quotes from interviews conducted with director Ray Lawrence, music supervisor Christine Woodruff, original music track composers and mixers, Paul Kelly and Shane O'Mara plus Bruce Haymes, Steve Hadley, and Peter Luscombe, and supervising sound designer Andrew Plain. Two main issues arise from the research: namely, the collaborative approach to the film-making process, and the creative input by sound and music personnel involved in construction of specific cues and overall sound and music tracks.

Chapter Six

SCORING:
Sexuality and Australian
Film Music, 1990-2003

BRUCE JOHNSON AND GAYE POOLE

Cinematic sexual practices ... retain their longevity because of the viewer's fascination with sexual intimacy. (Wilson, 1994: 34)

Throughout its history as a mass medium, film has refracted and constructed the changing sexual imaginary. With its larger-than-life sensuous intensity and its ubiquitous public accessibility, the portrayal of sexuality in film has become perhaps the most sensitive and instantaneous register of the morés of society. It has also diversified with the enlargement of the general discourse of sexuality, becoming implicated with issues of gender, desire, class, race, age, heterosexuality, male and female homosexuality, cross-dressing, socio-historical contexts, and the relationship between spectator and representation (Hayward, 2000: 326). The Australian film *Dance Me To My Song* (dir: Rolf de Heer, 1998) boldly ventured into the hitherto taboo area of sexuality and physical disability. Debates about what may be represented publicly in the way of sexuality, and the complementary or competing claims of aesthetics and morality, are now primarily activated by film. In Australia, we have recent experience of this in controversies over the film *Romance* (dir: Catherine Breillat, 1999). The relationship with violence has been equally controversial, as in the suppression of *Baise-Moi* (dir: Coralie Trinh Thi and Virginie Despentes, 2001).

The connection between Australian film and sexuality was signalled as early as 1918, when Raymond Longford's exploration of sexual hypocrisy, *The Woman Suffers* (dir: Raymond Longford, 1918), was banned. From the early 1920s the limits of public discussion of sexuality were probed in such locally made movies as *Know Thy Child* (dir: Franklyn Barrett, 1921), *Circumstance* (dir: Lawson Harris, 1922), *Should A Doctor Tell?* (dir: P.J Ramster, 1923). In 1926 a poster for the local film *Should A Girl Propose?* (dir: P.J Ramster, 1926) provided a cameo of the consciousness of the young modern female to whom such films addressed themselves, and in which sexual initiative is complicit:

> *The modern girl jazzes, smokes, indulges in athletes* [sic]*, enters law and politics, and, in short, does most things a man does, and in most things does better. Why should she not propose?* (Pike and Cooper, 1981: 170)

This 'Indian Summer' of enlarged sexual discourse in Australian film was brought to an end by both industrial and socio-political developments. The nostalgic retreat to traditional values following the Great Depression, the atrophying of the Australian film industry during the 1930s and the advent of the Second World War were significant forces in this change. In the period immediately following that war, Australian audiences were swamped with US films attempting to reclaim a social order in which the woman's place was in the home. Women who were to be found outside authorised domestic spaces came to no good (*Mildred Pierce*, dir: Michael Curtiz, 1945) or were presented as literally alien and grotesque, as in B-Grade sci-fi films of the post-war decade such as *Cat Women of the Moon* (dir: Arthur Hilton, 1953). Courtship was largely a process of domesticating the woman, concluding musically and visually with the promise of 'happily ever after'. Procreative sexuality was so much a given of happy marriage that it could be presented on screen by the most indirect means, constrained by protocols of public and cinematic discourses. The power of such mediations made sexuality itself both invisible and inaudible. Sexual activity began with an embrace, a kiss, then became a fade-out and a musical motif ascending to climactic resolution.

Among the relatively few Australian feature films made during this period, *Sons of Matthew* (dir: Charles Chauvel, 1949) presents a model of the representation of sexuality against which we can measure subsequent changes. In a climactic scene, its function in consummating marriage becomes complicit in the building of a culturally homogeneous nation. Shane and his brother Barney have been vying for the affections of Cathy. Amidst a violent storm Shane rescues Cathy from a flooded river that threatens both the central characters and the settlers' land itself. Shane's passion erupts in an extravagant declaration:

> *You think I'm going to let Barney marry you, and spend a lifetime of nights thinking of you in his arms? You're going to be my wife and bear my sons because that's the way it was meant to be and neither you, nor I, nor Barney, can do anything about it ... You and the earth Cathy, that's all I want.*

This is accompanied by a musical sequence in the western orchestral tradition that underlines and foreshadows the triumph of will and destiny (the first section above: defiant brass), then romantic tenderness (strings) converging towards a procreative marital union. The homology between heterosexuality, its visual and musical representation, the society that validates it through marriage, and the fertility of an Anglo–Saxon nation of which that marriage is the microcosm, is complete.

That homology, once normative, has since been ruptured. Socio-cultural homogeneity, marriage and heterosexuality have become centrifugal, strangers to each other. And, we shall argue, so have the musical/acoustic conventions of their representation, particularly in relation to sexuality. Even in *Sons of Matthew*, these conventions of sexual representation achieved two outcomes that were in some tension. They both occluded sexuality and filled it with approved significance. Sexuality was so thickly mediated, that it became a set of meanings rather than a physical reality. Sex was a look between two people, a verbal sparring, a visual symbol like the waves washing over Burt Lancaster and Deborah Kerr in *From Here to Eternity* (dir: Fred Zinnemann, 1953) or exploding fireworks in *To Catch a Thief* (dir: Alfred Hitchcock, 1953). This indirect representation was reinforced musically. Just as the visual action was masked behind a symbolic language, so were the physical sounds of sexuality transformed into music. The realities of sex were made to disappear behind a set of symbolic conventions that define its meaningfulness – the waves, the fireworks or a complete fadeout, with the music of harmonised connection and completion. We don't see Lancaster and Kerr having sex, but we know what it means to them when they do.

The seachange in sexual attitudes that is generally dated from the late 1960s began to manifest itself in Australian film with the revival of the local industry in the 1970s. *Alvin Purple* (dir: Tim Burstall, 1973) was one of the most commercially successful Australian films of the 1970s, perhaps because it made no inquiry into the ambiguities and tensions of sexual politics, as indicated in Sandra Hall's 1973 review: "It is cheerfully sexist, unashamedly mindless and in the *Carry On* manner, leaves no innuendo unexploited ... it is bountiful in full frontals and happy vulgarity" (reprinted Hall, 1985: 13). The success of *Alvin Purple* generated a spate of opportunistic and superficial exercises in the new explicitness, as in John Lamond's films, including *ABC of Love and Sex - Australian Style* (1978) and *Felicity* (1979). In such films, sex was a harmless romp conducted outside the responsibilities of the marriage contract that traditionally authorised it. In 1985 Hall declared: "Middle-class sex, marriage and divorce have never been of overwhelming interest to Australian film-makers" (Hall, 1985: 101).

Hall's assessment tends to be confirmed by the fact that while the *Oxford Companion to Australian Film* (McFarlane, Mayer, Bertrand: 1999) has separate entries on religion and food, there is none for sex. Yet in *Australian Cinema* (1994) Debi Enker recognises a range of filmic forays into sex and romantic love and in particular a motif of mismatched lovers in films such as *Monkey Grip* (dir: Ken Cameron, 1982), and *Far East* (dir: John Duigan, 1982), to which we could add numerous instances including *Proof* (dir: Jocelyn Moorhouse, 1991). Compared with French and American cinema, Enker identifies a negative pattern:

> *Examining romantic relationships between men and women in Australian films is illuminating, if only as a guide to the filmmakers' collective discomfort with heterosexual love stories and scepticism about the possibility for enduring passion.* (Enker, 1994: 218)

In a 1980 essay entitled 'Personal relationships and sexuality', Meaghan Morris declared: "At the centre of the representation of sexual relationships in Australian cinema is the mark of an impossibility of some kind" (Morris,

1980: 142). This "impossibility" is implicit in our argument that Australian films of the 1990s manifest a movement towards literal explicitness and away from symbolic clarity in the representation of sexuality. Its significance is as impenetrable as lantana, the eponymous plant in a recent film in which sexuality is entangled with the genre of guilt and concealment: the thriller. And this process is accompanied, and even defined, by the collapse of a straightforward homology between sexuality and music, which becomes tentative and multivocal, or simply falls silent – again the opening scene of *Lantana* (dir: Ray Lawrence, 2001) exemplifies the point – in a kind of dismayed confusion as to how sexuality functions in human relationships.

One of the earliest shadows to fall across sexuality in a major post-war Australian film was in *Jedda* (dir: Charles Chauvel, 1955). Jedda is an indigenous Australian woman brought up in a white household. She becomes fascinated by a full-blooded Aborigine, Marbuk, who arrives at the cattle station looking for work. He abducts her but is ostracised by his own people. Caught between the two cultures, the two are driven to desperation and are killed in a cliff fall. While the scenario placed the sexual tensions at what was then a comfortable distance from mainstream society, it was nonetheless prescient. Its troubled portrayal of sexually focussed cultural conflict has been rearticulated in ways more familiar to the later sense of cultural diversity that produced films like *Aya* (dir: Solrun Hoaas, 1991), *Dead Heart* (dir: Nick Parsons, 1996), *In a Savage Land* (dir: Bill Bennett, 1999), and *Japanese Story* (dir: Sue Brooks, 2003).

In the meantime, sexual dysfunctionality has become less easily quarantined to the cultural 'other'. In *Don's Party* (dir: Bruce Beresford, 1976) we see the beginnings of Morris's "impossibility", with middle class marriages fretted away by distrust and cruelty. Following a honeymoon with the possibilities of explicit sexuality, and with the increasing consciousness of gender politics, there were increasingly sophisticated critiques for the probing of this newly exposed and minutely inspected site of social interaction. In *The FJ Holden* (dir: Michael Thornhill, 1977) suburban heterosexual relationships are sexist and soulless; in *Long Weekend* (dir: Colin Eggleston, 1979) the husband's bleak consolation to his wife is that "weak as you think I am, I'm all you've got". With *Thank God He Met Lizzie* (dir: Cherie Nowlan, 1997) the sexual narrative begins where romantic comedies had once ended: the decision to marry. But the only portrayal of sexuality is through flashbacks in which the future husband, Guy, has sex with the woman he once lived with; marriage to Lizzie is a pragmatic compromise for husband and wife. In *Passion: The Story of Percy Grainger* (dir: Peter Duncan, 1999) the real love of Grainger's life is not a wife but his mother. In *Muriel's Wedding* (dir: PJ Hogan, 1994), the bleakness of suburban marriage is summarised in the images of Muriel's mother staring at the coffee cup rotating in a microwave and, later, a backyard lawn incinerated just before she suicides. It is dismaying to explore Australian films since the 1980s and to discover how few celebrate a successful sexual relationship within a marital framework[1]. *The Year of Living Dangerously* (dir: Peter Weir, 1982) includes a 'courtship' side-plot that has echoes of the *Sons of Matthew* model in that the heterosexual couple survive life-threatening perils, moving towards a reunion ("I don't want to lose you"), that intimates the permanence of marriage. It is notable in this context that the love scenes incorporate a traditional romantic musical motif[2]. In *Return Home* (dir: Ray Argall, 1990) we are presented with a happy couple in a well-established marriage and business partnership in Adelaide, in studied contrast with the life of the brother who returns from the Melbourne rat race.

More generally, however, Australian films dealing with sexuality since the 1980s are almost unremittingly negative. It would include the sexual panic of *Lonely Hearts* (dir: Paul Cox, 1982) and the breakdown of marriage in his *My First Wife* (dir: Paul Cox, 1984); sexuality as a site of boredom, opportunism and hysteria in *Peter Kenna's The Umbrella Woman* (dir: Ken Cameron, 1987) and *Love Serenade* (dir: Shirley Barrett, 1996); sex as disruptive to middle-class life in *The Last Days of Chez Nous* (dir: Gillian Armstrong, 1992); the aggressive skinhead sex of *Romper Stomper* (dir: Geoffrey Wright, 1992); sexual harassment in *Brilliant Lies* (dir: Richard Franklin, 1996); rape and murder in *Blackrock* (dir: Steven Vidler, 1997). Even such apparently disparate films as the smut comedy *Pacific Banana* (dir: John Lamond, 1981), *Monkey Grip* (dir: Ken Cameron, 1982) and *Floating Life* (dir: Clara Law, 1995) share the premise that sexual liberation has become detachment at best, alienation at worst, an instrument of sexual politics. Disaffection with heterosexuality generated discussions of alternatives to the authorised but now joyless model. Jane Campion explored sexual fetishism in *The Piano* (1993) and bisexuality is all but explicit in *Sirens* (dir: John Duigan, 1993). The most debated alternative to conventional sexuality has been, not surprisingly, homosexuality, but the genial example of *The Sum of Us* (dir: Geoff Burton and Kevin Dowling, 1994) is less representative of the treatment than the self-loathing which pervades *Head On* (dir: Ana Kokkinos, 1998).

Only *Better Than Sex* (dir: Jonathan Teplitzky, 2000) seemed to find a 'wholesome' model of sexuality. An encounter between Cynthia and the metrosexual Joshua leads to several days of unembarrassed sexual bonding. Its libertarianism recalls *Alvin Purple* but with a political equipoise missing from the masculinism of the 1970s. Apart from the 'he said/she said' format, the point is dramatised when Joshua is modelling a wedding dress for his sexual partner Cynthia, a dressmaker. Interrupted by the arrival of one of her friends, he displays not the slightest embarrassment: he is, we might say, entirely comfortable with his feminine side. Yet even this narrative about frank and equally balanced sexuality leaves questions. Part of this is to do with the unique profile of the male actor: could anyone but the extraordinarily varied persona of David Wenham get away with this cross-dressing without compromising his screen masculinity? Apart from this, the carefree music score, strongly featuring lounge music, underlines the fact that the action takes place within a hiatus in everyday life. Joshua is waiting to depart Australia in a socio-economic vacuum free of financial worries and domestic routines. The film portrays a life-style, not a life. Perhaps this is why it ends on a slightly uncertain note, as Joshua and Cynthia prepare a little nervously for some kind of commitment. The bond has been sexual. Is that enough, or does the ending point to something necessary in a relationship, but as yet undefined, something 'better than sex'?

Sexuality and Music in Australian Cinema

By the end of the 20th Century, Australian film seemed adrift between sexual explicitness and meaningfulness. Since the sound track is one of the most powerful means of conferring significance and affect on what is seen, this dilemma is particularly audible in music and sound. The point can be briefly exemplified through films listed above. At the beginning of *Jedda* the lonely life of station owner's wife is described as lying between the voices of the station Aborigines and those coming through the pedal radio. Jedda is initially drawn to Marbuk by his 'singing' her to his camp and, following the onset of her attraction to him, her cultural conflict is dramatised when, while practising the piano, in her head tribal chants and didjeridu gradually intervene and finally overwhelm the piano, leaving the young woman shaking her head and covering her ears as if to drive the sounds out of her consciousness. Such musical dichotomies have become something of a formula in love narratives entangled with cross-cultural encounters, as in *The Year of Living Dangerously* (dir: Peter Weir, 1982) and *Dead Heart* (dir: Nick Parsons, 1996). In *Muriel's Wedding* the banality of the beanbag seduction scene is emphasised by the diegetic sounds and music coming from the television set and other domestic sources. In *Love Serenade* the melodramatic Barry White love songs fit the characters' exhausted romantic clichés; *Head On*, *Monkey Grip*, *Romper Stomper* and *Blackrock* all at various times use music that reflects the alienating milieu. Narratologically more complex is *Making Venus* (dir: Gary Doust, 2002), a documentary film about making a porn film, but the music is for the most part confined to the diegesis of the innermost narrative, and exemplifies the porn genre unproblematically.

Much of this is diegetic sound and music, adding little to the narrative other than a straightforward confirmation of the milieu, as in the relatively unimaginative *Dust Off The Wings* (dir: Lee Rogers, 1996) which discloses little change in the bleak situation of sexuality within Sydney's surfing culture since *Puberty Blues* (dir: Bruce Beresford, 1981). Sexual dissonance is explicit in an account of a sexual episode by one of the surfers to his mates (39'00)[3]. There is negligible exploitation of the distancing potential of extra-diegetic music, which simply echoes the style listened to by the characters, so much so that at one point the two are indistinguishable. As one of the surfers drives down the coast we hear apparently extra-diegetic 1970s-derivative rock accompanied by set-piece surfing, and 'on-the-road' footage. The fit between this music and the surf action is emphasised when we realise that some of the former is actually from the car radio. Where sex is accompanied by music it is borrowed from some other zone of the subculture, as at 7'33" where brief glimpses of a sexual encounter on a beach at night use fragments of 'drug' music, concluding a male vomiting. The message simplistically establishes sexual relationships as a secondary component in the male surfing culture: at 2'40", a sexual encounter elicits a post-coital "Mm, great huh?" from the woman, which is interpreted by the man as a reference to the surf conditions, to which he immediately heads off. The message is that simple and the music does nothing more than crudely underline the point.

While generationally (and aesthetically) at the other end of the spectrum, *Innocence* (dir: Paul Cox, 2000) deploys music in a similarly direct way, establishing a fit between visual and musical. In this film of an autumnal revival of an affair, both men – the husband and the lover – are musicians in ways that complement the triangular relationship. The husband John leaves the domestic sphere to attend choir practice, a music of public sociability. Andreas, the lover, is an organist who plays in private, linking him with Claire in a way that John's choir activities do not. The extra-diegetic music functions similarly. At 13'00" a recollected sexual encounter between the youthful lovers is both visually and acoustically layered, with elegiac 'classical' guitar over train noise. With the visuals this suggests something recalled in sad tranquillity. As elderly lovers they are later seen in an affectionately self-conscious sexual encounter, intercut with remembrances (19'30"). The two timeframes are brought together musically, with simple piano music, to classical guitar, then layered with strings. The tenderness is unequivocal, the fit with the music is undisrupted. This montage of recollections is reprised at 56'00", now mingled with images of death. Andreas dreams in hospital. The sound of the train is heard again, with its intimations of the journey, but the 'music' is now the tolling of the bell; the 'journey' is to death, though not as it turns out, his. Visually, the intercutting of past and present erotic contacts between the lovers emphasises the difference between flaming youth and old age. But the theme also involves the idea of continuity of identity and subjectivity, manifested in the reawakened sexuality, accentuated by the capacity of music to confer significance on otherwise disconnected events. As a whole, the movie suggests a harmony between sexuality and love, but only outside the mainstream of life. Claire declares that she hasn't had sex with her husband, whom she finally leaves, for decades. The erotic reunion of the lovers, underlined musically, becomes a fleeting recovery of something long gone, and cut short by death, a love that comes too early or too late to be part of the main business of life – a kind of *liebestod*.

All these films present a relatively straightforward relationship between sexual image and sound: good sex – sweet music; bad sex – ugly music. More interesting is music and sound deployed in tension with the visuals, thus problematising rather than underlining the meaning of what we see. Even the carefree world of Alvin Purple came to recognise the hidden threat in sexual liberation. That world was invoked in the sequel *Melvin: Son of Alvin* (dir: John Eastway, 1984), a connection emphasised by the use of Brian Cadd's *Alvin* song in flashback clips. Musical intertextuality was also crucial in signalling the concealed dangers of sexuality in a scene in which Melvin is in a swimming pool, prelude to yet another sex romp. His pursuit by a naked woman, visually represented by an aroused nipple projecting above the water, is underscored with the 'shark' theme from *Jaws* (dir: Steven Spielberg, 1975), comically layering this erotic image with menace. This more complex relationship between visual diegesis and auditory extra-diegesis can be achieved in a number of ways to complicate sexuality. Apart from incongruous extra-diegetic music layered over a scene as in the example just noted, a serial juxtaposition is exemplified in *Brilliant Lies*. A case of sexual harassment brought by Susie against her boss, Vince, is traversed by a history of childhood molestation of the victim and her sister by their father. The opening credits and music, *Harassment Tango* (Nerida Tyson-Chew), evoke period 'screwball' comedy in the style of *I Love Lucy*. With a self-consciously 'zany' musical exclamation mark concluding the sequence, we feel we are in the uncomplicated fantasy world of the mid-20th Century. This adds to the shock of the bitter and very contemporary monologue about harassment immediately following, accentuated by the realisation, emphasised by later flashbacks, that the antagonists grew up in an era of such apparently greater innocence. We shall explore the semiotic possibilities of the 'frame' further below in the discussion of *feeling sexy* (dir: Davida Allen, 1999).

Apart from incongruity between music and action, even more complexities are produced by blurring the distinction between music and other sounds, both diegetic and extra-diegetic, in a way that produces dissonance. The ambiguities of sexuality are often parallelled by a sound track in which ambient noise and music become difficult to distinguish, as in the train sound and the tolling bell in *Innocence*. More frequently, however, it parallels a dissonance in sexuality itself. In general, the underscore of *Brilliant Lies* is a straightforward descant to the theme of sexual abuse. The dissonance of the opening scene of sexual harassment is enhanced by an underscore that combines conventional music with sound effects, a device paralleling the developing tension throughout the film. At 40'00" a poignant recollection by the sisters of their childhood molestation is underscored with slow, elegiac music enhancing the mood of fragile and wounded innocence. At 65'00": the molestation is again recalled, even more painfully because it is in the presence of all siblings and the father. The music is now overlaid with jarring industrial sound effects. The connection between Susie's childhood sexual trauma and the vigour of her litigious pursuit of Vince is suggested by the reintroduction of this acoustic device in the final version of the harassment episode, with music, harsh noises, dissonant chords, slowed voices (76'00"). There is nothing disjunctive between sound and image here – the jarring, distorted brutality of the sexual episode is matched by the sound.

Because musical accompaniment is so much a part of traditional film grammar, withholding it at key points becomes in itself a statement, a meaningful absence. Bill Bennett exploited this in *Kiss or Kill* (dir: Bill Bennett, 1997):

> *I started to think about not having music at all and just going with sound ... When I had a look at the first cut I thought that there was nothing music could do that we couldn't do just as effectively with sound.* (Bennett, 1999: 261)

The absence of music declares that the grammar of film, and of the lives it represents, is disturbed. When the key point is sexuality, then one of the linchpins of human relationships is called into question. One pattern over the period under investigation is the dissolving of the musical screen between the audience and the representation of sexuality, like the symbolic visual mediations. Acoustically we are thus deprived of affective clues that might clarify the significance of the experience. The toilet blowjob in *Dust off the Wings* (42'00") and the foreplay in *The Boys* (dir: Rowan Woods, 1997) (11'40") exemplify the absence of the usual musical cues, leaving random noises of everyday life and occasional coital sounds.

Lantana (discussed in detail elsewhere in this volume) exploits the potential of such techniques to throw an arc of meaning across the whole film. In contrast to the working class couple Nik and Paula, the sexual lives of the middle class characters are profoundly troubled. The inability of the central couple, Leon (a police detective) and his wife Sonja, to communicate physically lies at the heart of the plot. The film opens with Leon in an act of sexual infidelity with Jane. Their uninhibitedness is accentuated by the daylight and their position on top of the bed covers. Acoustically this is parallelled by the absence of any musical masking of their noises, producing an unillusioned auditory focus on sexuality. This acoustically unmediated physical contact recurs in another sex scene between the two, and in an episode where Leon injures himself when, while jogging, he bumps into a stranger (who reappears later in the film). The vivid intensity of all these physical encounters is accentuated by the absence of an underscore, emphasised by its resumption when the episodes conclude. By the film's end Leon and Sonja have moved towards a new level of mutual understanding, and in the final scene they dance together, a staple metaphor of ecstatic reconciliation and resolution. The logic of their dynamic, however, would make such a conclusion implausibly facile. As one viewer observed, "If she'd kissed him at the end [I] would have walked out" (Cordaiy, 2001: 60). Rather than a dance of triumphant reunion, the two are guarded, and ambivalence is sharpened by what the film has already established musically and acoustically. Dancing signifies, as earlier articulated by the Latin dancing instructor who had scorned Leon's terpsichorean woodenness: "This is about sex – about a man and woman groin to groin. Get it?" It is about physical contact as an elegant metaphor of sexuality. The couple's diffidence as they attempt to conduct this concluding dance stands in cautionary contrast to the unmediated coital noises of the adulterous opening. The "impossibility" seems obdurate.

The ultimate withdrawal of acoustic cues is silence. At this point sexuality becomes inscrutably mute spectacle. Following Bill Bennett's music-free sound track in *Kiss or Kill*, in his next film, exploring liminal sexuality, he enlarges the range of acoustic devices along a spectrum ranging from traditional deployment of music, through something between music and noise, to silence. *In a Savage Land* (discussed in detail elsewhere in this volume) won AFI awards for sound and for David Bridie's original music that, like other cross-cultural films discussed here, syncretised western and non-western styles (Roche, 2000: 125). Evelyn, a young anthropologist, marries her former lecturer, Phillip, with whom she then conducts fieldwork in the Trobriand Islands in the late 1930s. The complex politics of the anthropological gaze emerge particularly in representations of sexuality, underpinned and nuanced by the sound track, including silence, all of which chart the failure of the conventional model of Western marital sexuality. At 5'00" Phillip proposes to Evelyn. The motives behind the proposal, however, suggest the ambiguous dynamics underpinning marriage. He is in the position of power and the marriage will also enhance his professional opportunities. These problems are barely suggested potentialities, however, so that the scene appears to be a set-piece overture to a happy-ever-after relationship. Phillip's on-his-knees proposal and the swelling pastoral strings constitute a traditional convergence of episode and music affect.

Their relationship then becomes a counterpoint to the relationships between the indigenous islanders. Beginning at 12'58" a sexual episode between Evelyn and Phillip follows immediately upon a daylight scene of a noisy massed courtship ritual among the islanders, which the anthropologists have witnessed with the appearance of dutifully scientific detachment. In an abrupt shift we see them that night at foreplay fully clothed on their bed. There is no music, and even sexual noise is so restrained as to be barely audible, an acoustic metaphor for the awkward modesty framing the relationship. An ellipsis jumps from this fumbling intimacy to the next morning, acoustically proclaimed by apparently local music. The transition emphasises the invisibility and inaudibility of the sexual life at the heart of this exemplary model of western marriage. It is a conspicuous contrast with a later scene (28'34') involving an indigenous couple in a small cave pool. Again, there is no music, but their loud, unembarrassed sexual vocalisation has an almost musical antiphonality that emphasises reciprocity and symmetry. The parallel between these two scenes is also underlined by the fact that each is spied upon by a representative of the 'other'. The sex scene between Evelyn and Phillip is intercut with shots of two native children looking at them through the window. Later Evelyn intrudes on the couple in the pool by taking a photograph, which ultimately has fatal consequences.

One of the film's themes is the effect of the anthropological 'gaze' on both subject and object. The moment of this gaze is also the moment that should be of ultimate privacy: sexual intimacy. What Evelyn sees and photographs results in the fatal disruption of the life of the local people, and irreparably disrupts her own 'civilised' conceptions of sexuality. At 34'00", a second sexual episode with her husband is now less restrained, and this is suggested acoustically. No swelling strings, as in the marriage proposal, but physical noises, and a sexual position that Evelyn saw in the two native lovers. The straight-laced Phillip cannot keep up with his wife's intellectual and sexual growth. Her next sexual encounter is with the American trader, Mick (1.25'00"). The foreplay is open and unembarrassed, and appropriates the romantic orchestral musical style of the original marriage proposal. Evelyn's shifting cultural loyalties are played out sexually, and the state of play is articulated by a complex interplay between music, sound and silence.

The foregoing has sketched a broad range of relationships between the representation of sexuality and the sound track in Australian films since the 1990s[4]. Each of the following individual case studies exemplifies one or more of those models of sexuality and their acoustic articulation, presenting interview material with directors, sound editors and composers, conducted by Gaye Poole specifically for this chapter[5]. All quotes, unless otherwise cited (or where two interviews have been conducted with the same interviewee), are from these interviews. *feeling sexy* explores marital sexuality; *Walking on Water* (dir: Tony Ayres, 2002) takes us outside heterosexual marriage; *The Boys* is in the tradition of 'protest masculinity'; and *Japanese Story* is the most recent contribution to the theme of cross-cultural sexuality.

feeling sexy

In a bleak landscape of marital sexuality, *feeling sexy* finds its way to a positive outcome yet it is far from simplistic, and arguably regards its own resolutions with something of an ironic, if affectionate, smile. And this distance is established musically. The story follows a middle class couple, Vicki and Greg, from marriage in the 1970s through the trials of child-raising, the descent into staleness and stale-mate, and the wife Vicki's attempts to revive romantic sexuality. It is her success that distinguishes the story from other marital alienation films. In the words of producer Glenys Rowe, it is "an ode to marriage". Lisa French wrote that it "connects sex with growth, imagination and partnership" (French, 2000: 15). The trick lies in fantasy.

Even before the wedding, the couple exhibit warning signs, as he expresses irritation when she playfully interrupts his medical studies. The marriage that follows is a narrative of sexual tension: a crying infant and a husband who cuts his toenails in bed while boring his wife with work talk. Brief moments of rapturous expectation, as during foreplay (14'00"), are interrupted by a crying baby and other episodes of banality, aggression and desperation, and by 15'40" Vicki's bedtime overtures are being rejected. At the same time, within three minutes of the film's opening, the importance of fantasy to Vicki had already been established as she imagines her coming marriage. The soft-focus erotic scene she conjures up suggests perfume commercials with equally formulaic music[6]. Already there is a clear hint of the ironic nuance that music can bring to the narrative, as its saccharine romanticism underlines the uncritical glibness of the fantasy, which itself is completely at odds with the increasingly mundane and tense actuality from which it springs.

The filmmakers regarded the music as playing an equal role with the visuals in unfolding the film's subtexts:

> *We had the music specifically designed for the film. Basically it was a collaborative relationship between the film composer* [Claire Jordan] *and the film director.*

Extra-diegetic music is used sparingly and therefore to more striking effect, particularly during scenes that take Vicki out of marital sexuality in actuality or in her imagination. Bored, she seeks stimulation as an art teacher, becoming involved with a student. Sexual contact in the back of his panel van (19'20" and 20'05") is accompanied by a moody bass line. An erotic encounter with him in her home (22'00") is underscored with ominous music, interrupted by the husband's return. Yet the film's genial willingness to complicate its own tone and teeter on the edge of farce emerges in a second encounter with the student (23'17"), with the same music, but interrupted when a child kicks off the handbrake of the car outside. The absence of extra-diegetic music from marital sex is striking. When at 21'25" the husband makes a successful sexual overture, the only sound is that of children interrupting the moment. Later, after Vicki confesses her sexual transgression to her husband, they have sex (25'00") in sullen and tearful silence. It is brutal and rape-like. Feeling sexy seems not to be an option.

The edginess of the music accompanying the adulterous episodes, its absence from marital sex, and its romantic lushness during Vicki's fantasies, are important markers of her negotiations with her own sexuality. Its nuances and ambiguities matter, according to Allen: "Yes, the music was intended to be the white line on the road so to speak, to keep the audience where I wanted them to be". At the marriage's nadir the music is more of a qualifying statement than a simplistic complement to 'feeling sexy'. From 29'00" jaunty and perky 'new leaf' music underscores an apparent reconciliation following her revelation of infidelity. Fantasy scenes recur, interspersed ironically with sex scenes with the husband. The visual and musical glibness of these fantasies is now emphasised by the intercuttings, and by what has passed between them. The music rings hollow, then, dropping darkly to the lower register, first signals the tenuousness of a 'new' life. This drop alerts us to small visual signals of dissonance that might otherwise have gone unnoticed, such as a toy accidentally going into the washer with all the dirty laundry, amid her desperate domestic bustle. She's trying to make it work but the two individuals remain out of alignment. In the shower (37'00") with her husband he remains unresponsive. In bed (38'00"), he puts a pillow between them. The domestic energy gives way to a sad stillness as she stares at a blank page, no longer able to paint anything on it.

Painting has become her way of articulating her fantasies. Following a series of real and fantasy encounters in such places as the public swimming pool and the back of a car, she projects her imaginative life onto one of the rooms of their own house and, through a change in the music, we realise the redemptive possibilities this brings with it. Already suspicious because of Vicki's confessed infidelity, her husband becomes angry at a new episode of solitary secretiveness. Who's she seeing this time? She answers by taking him into the unused room in their house where she has covered the walls with vivid paintings and erotic messages to her husband. This spatial reconciliation of fantasy and domesticity is the turning point in the relationship and in the film, and a new kind of music marks the shift. Neither fatuous romantic cliché nor ominously dark, the music is now of a kind that has not been heard hitherto: almost 'ambient', with a non-cadential tranquillity rather than narrative compulsion. Fantasy has been brought into her marriage.

Yet the film's willingness to play on the borders of romance and irony save it from an implausibly facile resolution. At 43'00" she starts actively fantasising again. The music's mood is ambiguous, and the fantasy becomes playfully caricatural as she lustfully re-imagines a service station attendant in revealing overalls as he phallically pumps petrol. "Not again," groans her husband but, later that evening, he appears mustachio-ed in a playfully similar manner, then takes on the stereotype of a continental *roué* from a B-grade romantic film. This shared playfulness seems to produce a harmonisation but, if fantasy energises the marriage, it also leaves the film with a slightly quizzical smile that saves it from simplistic complacency. Fantasy is, after all, finally fantasy. In the words of Davida Allen:

> *I made the film with a message that the imagination is the most powerful tool Vicki has and she can use it to keep her marriage alive ... It is not meant to be dogma ... I am not a preacher ... It is a fairy tale, not a church sermon.*

The closing credits roll to the music of *Que Sera Sera*, which itself constitutes an unwittingly ambiguous comment on the action not simply for what it says, but for the glibness of its lyric in a film which has shown a healthy suspicion of the glib[7]. Questions about the intended significance of this song led into a thicket of possibilities. Its choice generated artistic differences among those involved, a "political nightmare" according to Allen. The orchestral music was by the Australian Youth Orchestra Camerata project, the leader[8] of which was disdainful of the choice, as Rowe has commented:

> Que Sera Sera *didn't fit the orchestra leader's idea of quality music. The orchestra leader was interested in pure music, whereas we were interested in soundtrack music. We wanted a singalong song. The leader had contempt for our desire to use* Que Sera Sera.

Rowe wanted "great walk-out music":

> *It was very successful in that way. When we did radio interviews for the film it would be picked up immediately and played during the interview. It makes a difference to the success of the film. We looked at millions of different songs. It was all about audience reception. Everyone knew the song already, and for those who didn't it had a 'good time' feel.*

She denied that it was chosen "as a commentary on what had gone on in the film". Yet every well-known song carries connotative luggage, and Rowe also argued that one reason for the choice was for "all those historical associations". The most cinematically specific of those associations is *The Man Who Knew Too Much* (dir: Alfred Hitchcock, 1956) in which the Academy Award winning song, by Jay Livingston and Ray Evans, played a significant role. Contemporary audiences, however, don't need to know that source to pick up the retro flavour of the closing credits and the music, which have an almost cheesy innocence. The song is a touch faster than the Doris Day original (as Rowe says, "we would have been conscious of not wanting it to drag"), and the sax lead is slightly saccharine in its vibrato and declamation. It is almost entirely instrumental apart from the last ten seconds or so, when what sounds like the actors (Porter and Tamblyn Lord) sing along, in the manner of an undesigned afterthought, as if casually singing over something they are hearing on a radio. Together with the big wind up, it suggests the kind of comfortable 'golden oldie' schlager music that finishes a night of old-style dancing. And the colour and layout of the final credits, like the opening credits of *Brilliant Lies*, suggest cartoons of the 1950s. All these evoke a shared memory of a more innocent era.

Whether intended or not, it is difficult not to read into the closing credits and its song some suggestion of an era past, a message that younger audiences might find unfamiliar. Rowe was conscious of a generational divide among those participating in the project:

> The arrangements with the Camerata Orchestra ... most of the filmmakers in the scheme (to match filmmakers with the orchestra and give them experience of working together on film music) were young ... and experimental ... whereas Davida was an established artist. We were much older than the other filmmakers.

In relation to the film as an ode to marriage, Rowe added:

> Not all young people are familiar with the idea that marriage and family are not just a series of Kodak moments ... So we felt we had to be careful with how we presented those ideas.

The couple persist and the music at the end lifts the mood to one of a possible future: a *possible* future, rooted in an idea of marriage that has diminished credibility in the contemporary world. For all its erotic energy and optimism, *feeling sexy* is a complex and ambivalent statement in a genre all too quick to take simplistic positions – whether positive or negative. Music is an essential tool in inscribing this highly nuanced message and, whatever forces intersected the path of *Que Sera Sera* into the film's closing credits, it leaves us with questions about the status and chances of marital sexuality. Desire and design can take us just so far. What will be, will be.

Walking on Water

Although *Walking on Water* won the 2002 Gay and Lesbian Award at the Berlin Film Festival, homosexuality is only one of several extramarital sexual relationships in the film. Indeed, rather than emphasising the distinctness of these relationships, one of the major points made by the film is the way a range of such models can share meaning and function. If we take sexual expression as the polarity to death, then it may be understood as an attempt to counteract grief's burdensome effects. When it was screened at the Taipei Film Festival in 2002 the Chinese title of *Walking on Water* translated as *If you love me kill me*; it focuses on how people deal with loss and grief. Early in the film a young man, Gavin, dies from AIDS–related illness. His housemates Anna and Charlie try to assist in a dignified and less painful death but the massive morphine overdose does not work to plan. After the funeral the two lives spin out of control as they deal with their grief; simultaneously we see reactive behaviours: illicit sex and illicit morphine use.

Director Tony Ayres' attraction to the script was "a hierarchy of grief – who is allowed to grieve, who is not allowed to grieve – especially in the position of a friend where there's no lover who has the natural role of chief widow" (Cordaiy, 2002: 65). Much of the film's tension arises from the jostling for position in this grief hierarchy. The film treats grief not as a shared process of comfort-giving but as the extremely solitary experience that it is. Sex is life-affirming; the opposite of death. It connects people with their aliveness in the midst of being immersed in death. *Walking on Water's* 'grief sex' occurs around the "disorganisation and despair" phase defined by Bowlby as one of the stages in recovery theory (Bowlby, 1980; see also Kubler-Ross, 1984; Parkes, 1986; Raphael, 1984).

Sex remains a taboo topic in relation to bereavement, possibly the last sphere in which this is so (Danbury, 1996: 145). The film captures this sex/bereavement taboo in Charlie's plausibly intense disapproval and sarcasm on finding Simon in bed with Anna: "Yeah, we're as happy as Larry here ... your wife is on the phone". Anna's need for 'grief sex' coheres with Raphael's idea that sexual 'acting out' may occur as "a consequence of bereavement... this may occur as an attempt for body comfort and care, as a discharge of tension, as the acting out of particular conflicts" (Raphael, 1984: 168; see also McKissock and McKissock, 1995: 48–49).

We have discussed the role of music in conferring meaning upon otherwise disconnected events. This affective power is linked to sexuality in the extra-diegetic music for *Walking on Water*. The circumstances of the death leave everyone grappling for responses to it, and what follows is an exploration of the diverse ways in which bereavement is mediated in a group of people who have relatively little in the way of shared ritual. The group, comprising Gavin's flatmates, Anna and Charlie, and Charlie's lover Frank, is augmented with the arrival of Gavin's mother Margaret and brother Simon and his wife and child. Diverse sexual morés signify the heterogeneity of the group. Apart from being a mix of hetero- and homosexual identities, there is also tension between metropolitan and provincial attitudes to morality. Sex, that is, means many different things.

Yet while it divides them, it also temporarily becomes one of many otherwise unrelated ways of expressing and sometimes sharing the experience of grief, as in the unlikely pairing of Anna and Simon. And the burden of making that point is wholly borne by the extra-diegetic music, particularly in a sequence that includes a scene of 'grief sex' (49'40 to 52'00), accompanied by melancholy string quartet music, blending with coital noise, and intercut with the scenes of Charlie taking morphine. This sequence is visually diverse and discrete, with only the linking underscore imposing thematic unity. That is, these disparate forms of conduct are all responses to the same thing: grief. It is the music, therefore, which establishes the meaning of the sex. It is a grief response, having the same significance as Charlie vomiting after morphine, and reading Gavin's will, along with all the other vignettes framed by this music. None of these has any visible connection with the others, but music signals the common significance of mourning. Significantly, then, when the intense grief has been sexually exorcised, so has the meaningfulness of sexuality, and so has the music. At 60'00" there is again a sexual encounter between Anna and Simon. But this time there is no music to confer meaning. It has become soulless and mechanical, and a moment later she abuses him and Charlie. Sexuality is a provisional and fleeting consolation. Music not only discloses a pathological, albeit therapeutic, meaning in sexuality, but then empties it of meaning by falling silent.

Composer Antony Partos (AP) confirmed the centrality and the role of music in the grief sex scenes:

> AP: *The music in the grief sex and morphine montage represents a real turning point in the film. It occurs at the film's central point in its structure and involves the two main characters each dealing with their grief in their own self-destructive manner. The music is used to link these scenes and tries to provide some sort of release not only to the characters but the audience as well. Up until this point the composed music has been restrained in length and very introspective/internal. Having said that, the music for this montage is not fully blown or climactic in any sense. Rather I tried to make it have a certain sense of resignation, almost fatalism about it.*
>
> ...
>
> *The music acts as some sort of counterpoint to the passionate lovemaking and deliberately does not score the 'action' but rather the emotion behind the action. The instrumentation is kept rather simple with piano, very small string ensemble, plucked double bass with some added synthesised textures. These textures are added to emphasise the blurring of the morphine and to internalise some of those feelings. The instrumentation and stylistic approach I would say is of a postmodern take on the slow movement to a Mozart piano concerto. Mozart could sum up incredible emotion with a deceptively simple theme and I guess that I instinctively tried to approach this scene from the same perspective.*
>
> Gaye Poole (GP): There is a second sex scene between Anna and Simon but there is no music this time – we thought it was a more soulless sex scene. Music seemed to endorse/construct the meaning like this: the therapeutic value of the first sexual encounter as opposed to an attempt to make the second encounter more alienating in terms of the sound production.
>
> AP: *I totally agree with your reading of this scene. The reason why music works for the first sex scene and not the second is because the first time was about the release of grief. The second sex scene was simply a fuck and lacked the emotional response. So music would have been totally inappropriate for this scene.*

In another sex scene, Charlie, Frank and others watch a gay porn video. Partos argues that the choice of source music from a library music CD, rather than a scored music cue, was designed to emphasise the "crassness" of the scene and "its self-destructive nature" linked to "the latent anger between Charlie and his partner".

The Boys

When actor John Hargreaves was presented with the Byron Kennedy Award by colleague Chris Haywood in 1994, he observed that, whereas Hollywood had its screen couples like Doris Day and Rock Hudson, Cary Grant and Irene

112

Dunne, Australian cinema had Hargreaves and Haywood; he wondered what this said about Australian culture (Mortimer, 1999: 287). The tension between homosocial bonds and heterosexuality raises the issue of "protest masculinity", a pattern of conduct "arising from the childhood experience of powerlessness, and resulting in an exaggerated claim to the potency that European culture attaches to masculinity" (Connell, 1995: 111). Its causes range from the absent or monstrous father (Butterss, 1998), through heterosexual inadequacy, to marginalisation by class or economics (Connell, 1995; Butterss, 1998). Its manifestation has been described as "a divided consciousness – egalitarianism and misogyny" (Connell, 1995: 118). Connell suggests that protest masculinity is an exaggeration of hegemonic masculinity by those who have no other access to power, or as the title of Butterss' article puts it "When being a man is all you've got" (Butterss, 1998). There is a long tradition in Australian films of homosocial relationships, including authorised all-male communities like the armed forces or sporting teams. More recently attention has turned to more monstrous manifestations of the phenomenon such as rape and other forms of sexual violence, including *Shame* (dir: Steve Jodrell, 1988) and *The Accused* (dir: Jonathan Kaplan, 1988).

Two of these, *Blackrock* (discussed in detail elsewhere in this volume) and *The Boys*, have been more or less based on fact, and the main characters display aspects of protest masculinity. Screenwriter Nick Enright commented on the primacy of the bond between the boys (the co-rapists) in *Blackrock*:

> You have to ask why so many rapes like that are communal ... They would be more honest just fucking each other, because that's what they want to do. They're not gay but their emotional interest is in each other. They're virtually sharing body fluids. (in Butterss, 1998: 44)

One of the rapists, Ricko, explains to his mate Jared why he killed the girl: "Then she bites me. Bites me like a dog. No bitch does that mate". It is this combination of the homosocial and the misogynist, fuelled by social and sexual impotence, which also drives *The Boys*. Brett Sprague has recently emerged from a year in prison, where his sexual desire has been annihilated. He comes home to unemployment, a new sexual politics that destabilises his dominance, and the attentions of the local police. Reviewer Ed Scheer summarised the connections between social and sexual impotence, protest masculinity, and the film's through-line:

> the character of Brett Sprague just released from prison is the catalyst for an unseen crime against an unknown girl. This is the only event he can effectively orchestrate after a day of failures and diminutions in his personal power base. The turning point occurs at the moment he realises he is impotent. (Scheer, 1998: 29)

Brett's vengeful anger echoes Ricko's: "There's no way out. You fuckin' do what they're trying to do. You fuckin' do it to them". A significant difference between the two films, however, is that while *Blackrock* begins with the crime then tries to untangle it, *The Boys* ends as it is about to be committed. Brett speaks the final words as the boys, watching from their car, see a woman waiting for a bus late at night: "Let's get her". Partly because of this narrative structure, the unfolding of the logic linking socio-economic desperation to sexual violence gives the later film a permanent and unsettling sense of dread that is far more disturbing than the spectacle of the rape and murder in *Blackrock*. The film is about monstrous possibility becoming inevitability. The sense of imminence is parallelled by the composition of the frames, the lighting, the sets, the establishment shots, all of which have the same decentred, unresolved character. The suggestion is of something threatening hovering just out of sight, an event or object about to be disclosed, spaces waiting to be filled with dreadful explanation.

Editor and sound editor Nick Meyers reported that this edgy suspensefulness was carefully built into the editing of sound as well as image:

> Gaye Poole (GP): *Our overwhelming sense of the sound production in* The Boys *is that it creates a permanent sense of imminence – that is a sense of being in suspension – something about to happen. There is not the usual drive or build in the sound track ...*

> Nick Meyers (NM): *There is a lot of that in the edit as well – shots held a bit longer than normal – the usual rule is to cut before the beat, but in* The Boys *we were often cutting on the beat or on some percussive moment ... [so this produces a] sense of waiting built in, the whole thing about structure of film is that you're waiting ...*

The working brief defined for the band The Necks encouraged the diffuse atmospheric approach, suggesting that they are playing an endless introduction to something, which has been one of the band's signatures since its debut album, *Sex* (1989). Meyers has emphasised:

> *I was the music editor as well ... the way the music worked,* The Necks *came and saw the film while we were cutting it and they just wrote ... they came on set they saw rushes and various cuts ... that's when they wrote so when it came time to do sound we had their tracks. The Necks' music is based on repeating patterns, quite appropriate for a film about men perpetrating violence against women – particularly appropriate for a film about Brett who comes home from jail only to pick up where he left off – menacing his brothers. There is nowhere for the tracks to go ... the soundtrack ... is one kind of mood that just builds in intensity.*

There is relatively little straightforward extra-diegetic music, so that the narrative is deprived of one of the usual developmental markers that say: here is something happening, and the music tells you what it means. According to Meyers:

> *Without having music you're not guiding the audience and that is not very reassuring for the audience – it doesn't have a layer of romance ... It wasn't right for this film to start feeding music in.*

When music is present, it is confusingly allusive, disconnected, detached, often enhancing the disturbing indeterminacy of the film's mood by confusing the distinction between noise and music. A briefly sustained chord at 111'00" is, like much of the 'music', difficult to distinguish from other ambient industrial sounds like electric doors and road noise. Like the visual composition, the effect is of something meaningful but evasive, just out of ken. Meyers recalls:

> *The Necks also did atmospheric effects ... We were chasing the tonal quality of the sound effects ... you're not quite sure where the effects stop and the music starts because a lot of the effects have a musical quality and some of the music is used like sound effects.*

It is a testament to the skill of the filmmakers that in a film about violence, there is almost none on screen and yet the sense of it is far more chilling than in films that revel in the spectacle. The sound track is decisive in achieving this. Likewise, sexuality is central to what drives Brett, yet there is not one explicit sex scene. And again, the soundscore (music plus sounds) is essential in evoking the sense of profound sexual anxiety. At 44'00" there is the beginning of brutal foreplay between Brett and his girlfriend Michelle. The boys are partying, and their record of the heavy metal band Arm can still be heard in the other room. Meyers observes:

> *The cut gets quite chaotic and strange there ... It's supposed to be about things going out of control though Brett has created that state. He wants to re-establish control so ... they are flirting in a brutal way and the music dips down, disappears when the close-ups of his eyes and lips* [appear], *and then it disappears when we go outside ... It doesn't resolve, it fades away.*

The foreplay leads towards a sexual encounter that occurs outside, against a wall. The music of the party record is now inaudible, and all that is heard is the low sound of wind in this flat suburban wasteland of built shapes, incongruously framed against trees and sky. The corner of a roof opposes rather than balances the branch of a gum tree, separated by a patch of blinding blue sky. The leaves are still; it is a windless day, so that the sound of the wind, plus a high-pitched hum, suggest a sourceless, ceaseless threatening energy. Meyers identifies that:

> [The] *scene is pretty much held together with the sound. Once we're in the shed it becomes quite natural with the sound and the cutting ... It does get you wound up. Alan Lamb, that's his* [recordings of the] *sound of wind in high tension wires. Alan Lamb is into the sound of high tension wires. He has built his own high tension wires (his 'wire farm') so he can record them. We might have dropped them back to next to nothing. We were trying to get a still moment, and then when we get back into the shed we're back into raw naturalistic sound, coming back to something very raw. And especially for the violent scene – no music – heightened a bit by the washing machine scraping on the floor. Sam* [Petty, Sound] *recorded the washing machine scraping.*

The couple go into the shed for sex but Brett can't get an erection. This is the pivotal moment, "the turning point", as Scheer called it. The outlet for this energy now moves towards increasing levels of sexual violence and ultimately murder. There is no music, just the sound of physicality out of shot, and the suggestion of an aircraft passing heedlessly overhead, so high as to be invisible, just a sound, telling of other unrelated worlds, other

115

Figure 1: Brett (David Wenham) receives an offer in The Boys *(1997).*

potentialities from which Brett will remain irredeemably excluded and distant.

Japanese Story

In terms of the nexus between music and sexuality, *Japanese Story* offers a distinctive conjunction between duration, sexual expressivity, music and intercultural explorations. Among the accolades for *Japanese Story* were 2003 Australian Film Institute awards for Best Original Music Score and Best Sound, and Film Critics Circle Award for Best Original Music[9]. Elizabeth Drake has interwoven and layered "elements of Japanese culture (Japanese instruments, modes, folksong and ritual) with western orchestral instruments, tonality and harmonic composition" (CD notes *Japanese Story*, 2003). An extended sense of 'real life' duration is typical of all the key scenes: the getting sand-logged scene; the waterhole scene; the viewing the body and airport farewell sequences and as well the sex scenes. With the film's score Drake consciously tried "to create a space so that the sense of duration could be achieved" (i/v 2003a).

Sandy is a geologist assigned to accompany a young visiting Japanese businessman, Hiromitsu, on a tour of inspection of mines in Western Australia's Pilbara. After a screwball comedy/mismatched couple opening, the two are forced to cooperate after their car sinks into desert sand and can't go further. Intense frustration, miscommunication and irritability give way to wild jubilation as they free themselves from the sand. The mood of sexual possibility intensifies as they travel the long drive to the next overnight stop. Drake's timing for the singing accompanying the first sex scene (in the hotel) was determined by a wish:

> *to create the connection between sexuality and the unconscious – the*
> *'desire for the Other', although those are terms I get anxious about, but*

this is part of my signature work – to create something outside our comprehension.

Prior to this moment Sandy has been prickly, resistant, and intolerant of Hiromitsu. For his part he has arrogantly treated her as his driver, rather than the geologist she is. Misperceptions on either side mean that they have a long way to travel to achieve intimacy and understanding. So, to move the character from "being stuck", not a very nice person and "in her own world", Drake introduced the singing voice (jazz singer Shelley Scown) in the hotel room to signify the point at which Sandy "was moving somewhere else". Drake believes that it was only through her sexuality and moving towards his foreignness that Sandy could effect the shift of "moving outside her own known boundaries".

Musical construction of the sex scenes involved extended discussion between director (Sue Brooks) and the composer centred on the roles of the instruments and the part they played in the overall texture of the music, particularly in the first sex scene. Drake expressed very specific intentions for her instrumental affect at particular moments: for instance, in the sex scenes, the strings were left as clean and unadorned as possible, to try to give "a little bit of a blank canvas for the sex scenes". There was anxiety that an excess of vibrato would preempt the disclosure of intimacy between the characters so the musical emotionalism was kept to a minimum. Later, following Hiromitsu's accidental drowning in a waterhole, the strings are used prominently and in a major key – "to counter the grief".

In the hotel room the balance between the bass drum and the strings was changed, giving the drum prominence, because Drake thought the "string and vibrato carry a lot of emotion whereas the drum is more percussive and insistent" (i/v, 2003b). As they played with volume and vibrato, the drum and the shamisen became more important, Drake comments:

It was all about texture and how one chooses a texture. I know that Sue Brooks used the expression 'dropping down' – it refers to the assistance of the bass drum.

As Sandy takes her clothes off Drake "tried to make the music more dissonant" (i/v 2003a). This subtle musical dissonance coincides with the moment of her sexual initiative and his sexual passivity. Here she literally wears the pants – she puts his black suit trousers on leaving the fly undone, moves toward the bed and straddles him. He is passively waiting. Drake did show the scene to a female Japanese friend who said, "Oh, not another passive Japanese man". Such a comment betrays discomfort with possible western perceptions of stereotypical Japanese male passivity in relation to sexually assertive western women.

Drake's re-orchestration of the Okinawan folk-song *Chinsagu No Hana*, with the voice, shamisen, koto and percussion, together with a western string orchestra, is used both in the scene in the hotel bedroom scene and for the entire final quarter hour of the film[10]. This forges a connection between the couple's first sexual encounter and the final theme of transformation through difference. While this first scene is more rhythmic and

Figure 2: Hiromitsu (Gotaro Tsunashima) and Sandy (Toni Collette) at the waterhole, in Japanese Story *(2003).*

repetitive, the second sex scene is much more melodic. In full midday sun, on a blanket on the ground, he kisses her – he is above her. We do not see them engage in sex but the next scene is late afternoon, they lie naked, his clothes neatly folded and hers strewn.

Discussing this moment of intimacy the composer reported that she "slowed the folk song right down". To signify that she was going into his world the singing voice (of Scown) was introduced; to promote the idea that "Sandy was hearing the folk song in her head". At this moment Drake uses a reference to the koto:

> *I wanted something more Japanese – it came from some passionate place in me – though now this is not totally logical – it goes across the scene when we see them naked. It might be that I felt that it should go as far as possible into the Japanese world.*

In a follow-up interview Drake clarified: "I do think there is something about using a foreign language – I think there is desire there – that's more my idea" (i/v 2003b). Here the koto acts as a musical anaphone for linguistic difference[11].

The boundaries between the central protagonists, and between them and the landscape, are most dissolved at this stage; this merging was reinforced by cinematography (deliberately out of focus), sound design (sounds of nature) and score: here Drake wanted "something hazy and heat-filled", the "sense of feeling the heat, the molecules moving very fast ..." (i/v 2003a).

Placed between the two sex scenes, the diner scene in which the pronunciation of desert/dessert is negotiated accelerates their intimacy. It is a scene that is in its own way musical – stressing the rhythm, cadence and colouring of language. By the later 'In the Mirror' scene (when Sandy gazes into her raw, new self in the mirror) we understand that Sandy has internalised the cultural, linguistic and sexual transformations. She is utterly naked at this moment but saturated with the gravity of discharging her responsibility to Hiromitsu. There is a reprise of the melody from the waterhole just before they have sex, Drake notes:

> The cello refers to the folk song melody; when she looks in the mirror we also used cello. When she is washing she is looking at herself with all that inside her.

Music is being used consciously here "to build the layers of what is going on inside a person". In a film whose characters are largely 'out of their depth' – culturally, expressively and finally, literally – layering and duration and accumulation are central to the film's sonic and visual meaning.

Characteristic of the collaboration between Sue Brooks, Sue Maslin (producer), Alison Tilson (writer) and the composer were the debates about whose role it was to resolve things. Drake emphasises film music's bossy capability for resolution:

> Alison got cross with me – "you've resolved the scene (musically) before the writing has resolved it" ... I said I put in two notes – when (Sandy's) mother realises [that Sandy has suffered her own loss][12] ... This is a constant discussion ... whether you're doing too much resolution (with the score) – those are the issues – whether something is resolved or whether it goes on and on.

It is, however, in the Okinawan tradition to repeat sanshin motifs over and over. So dominant was this sequence that the film was "actually cut to that folk song" (Chinsagu No Hana)[13]. In the long final sequence the audience knows more than the characters, Drake argues:

> the layers allowed each [element] – the wife, the letter, all these things are coming to the surface. It is like a sequence – it has all been set up and now it's coming out beyond what each character expected.

By the end both Sandy and Hiromitsu have moved to open-heartedness, an intimacy beyond sex and death. They have shared a rare human connection in their desert landscape journey 'off the map'.

Conclusion

The sexual relationship in *Japanese Story* is redemptive. Yet he dies, and leaving an already established family in Japan. As with almost every other Australian film we have referred to made since 1990, the traditional links between sex, marriage and cultural compatibility have been questioned, if not actually severed. While the visual and acoustic representation of sexuality has become ever more explicit, it has also reflected a nervous confusion about the role, meaning and status of sexuality in the mediation of relationships[14]. In any event the musical component of these cinematic representations has served to emphasise the disjunctions. The straightforward fit between romantic consummation, sexuality and lush strings has been disrupted. As sex itself is complicated by a range of emerging dynamics that traverse the old models, so music in one way or another has registered the dissonance, what Morris described as the "impossibility" underlying Australian screen representations of sexuality.

119

Note: In preparing this chapter the authors assembled and consulted a bibliography of more than fifty items relating to individual films and the more general issues under discussion. While too extensive for inclusion here, the full bibliography has been retained and can be emailed to interested researchers. Enquire at b.johnson@unsw.unsw.edu.au or gpoole@waikato.ac.nz.

Notes

1. Our discussion will be confined to feature films enjoying general public distribution. While movies like the French film *Romance* obviously close the distance visually between feature films and pornography, in Australian productions such extreme explicitness is still confined to films of the kind available in sex shops or in 'adult' sections of video stores. Pornographic film is a major industry. Apart from having its own aesthetic (including, significantly, in terms of sound and music), it was recently reported that in Los Angeles more than 10,000 are made each year, compared with the Hollywood feature film average of 400 (Marriott, 2003: 4). These are an important area of study in the representation of sexuality but take us beyond the parameters of this chapter.

2. The statement that a piece of music evokes a particular repertoire of meanings, as for example 'romantic' in the sense clearly implied by the context here, obviously goes to the heart of the vexed issue of music affect. It presupposes an 'interpretive community' within which there is general consensus regarding the meanings of particular musical signifiers. For the purposes of this essay we have of necessity taken for granted a certain level of such consensus among the readership; not to do so would make it impossible to conduct the discussion. We could, for example, refer to 'lush strings', but any such adjective invites the question of what 'lushness' means when applied to strings, since it is affective rather than analytically musicological. Yet it is reasonably safe to assume that the readership of this book will know what it means. To expect that a cultural discourse can be developed that would have a universal interpretive community is a vain (in both senses) discursive imperialism that we would imagine is now bankrupt. It would also be to write as though the subject of music affect itself had never been addressed by music scholars, while in fact it has an extensive literature. Most recently Tagg and Clarida (2003) have published the results of decades of research in this area, compiling what amounts to an extraordinarily detailed 'dictionary' of music affect. In relation to our phrase 'Traditional romantic musical motif', for example, their work provides what is in effect a descriptive taxonomy of what such music may be expected to sound like (see eg the discussion of 'string padding' pp170-172, or refer to the index for various kinds of 'romantic love' motif).

3. Where it seems useful for reference we have given approximate timings, taking the opening credit as zero.

4. See note at end of this chapter re extended bibliography.

5. The following interviews were conducted by Gaye Poole from Sydney to locations as indicated:

    Allen, Davida (2003) Brisbane, 17/10 (pc)
    Drake, Elizabeth (2003a) Melbourne, 18/11, telephone i/v
    Drake, Elizabeth (2003b) Melbourne, 26/11, telephone i/v
    Meyers, Nick (2003) Sydney, 19/11, telephone i/v
    Parker, Laurie (2003) Sydney, 9/11
    Partos, Antony (2003) Sydney, 4/11 (pc)
    Rowe, Glenys (2003) Sydney, 21/10, telephone i/v

    The following interviews were conducted by Gaye Poole from Hamilton, New Zealand:
    Drake, Elizabeth (2004a) Melbourne, 14/6, telephone i/v
    Drake, Elizabeth (2004b) Melbourne, 16/6 (pc)

6. For discussions and documentation of such 'formulaic' music see Tagg and Clarida (2003: index entry 'Advertising', pp856-857).

7. Coincidentally, the same song bookends the recent Jane Campion film *In the Cut*, previewed at a Q & A session in Sydney on 9th November 2003. In a discussion with the American co-producer and sound supervisor Laurie Parker, Gaye Poole discovered that she was unaware of its use in Davida Allen's film, but that the reasons for its selection included both nostalgia and irony, which we are suggesting are at least implicit in its function in *feeling sexy*. It is relevant to the comments regarding younger audiences and the song's "historical associations" that one of the questioners, presenting herself as an aspiring film composer and enquiring about the song, was unaware of the song's provenance.

8. Who asked to remain nameless.

9. In 2004, Best Feature Film Score in the APRA-AGSC Screen Music Awards and also nominated for the ARIA award for Best Original Soundtrack/Cast/Show Recording.

10. Thanks to Philip Hayward (pc) for the ethnomusicological detail that Elizabeth Drake's description of her adaptation of *Chinsagu No Hana* constitutes a departure from traditional Okinawan practice. Nonetheless, we are documenting here the intention of the composer and the proposed music affect on the target audience. In Drake's words, "It was never my intention to produce an 'authentic' traditional version of this folk song. My intention was rather the opposite, to emphasise the shifts that take place through cultural displacement... My interest... was more from a Western minimalist point of view."

11. The term 'anaphone' is derived from Philip Tagg's sign typology of music, and may be described as the musical equivalent of an analogy; see most recently Tagg and Clarida (2003: 99-101).

12. Sandy had previously been dismissive of her mother's ritual of pasting funeral notices into a scrapbook. When Sandy presents her mother with Hiromitsu's death notice (in a silently eloquent moment), her mother registers that Sandy now understands grief and the necessity of ritualising loss.

13. As an outcome of a discussion between *Japanese Story* producer Sue Maslin and Gaye Poole at the12th Biennial Conference of the Film and History Association of Australia and New Zealand, Canberra, 2-5/12/2004, the following illuminating insights arose. Despite selling to 22 countries *Japanese Story* has not achieved distribution in Japan. The sales agent Fortissimo Films has made extensive attempts to sell into Japanese markets. One of the reasons for the refusal is explicitly to do with the music. Maslin argues, "In particular the music is unacceptable to the Japanese because it was based on an Okinawan folk song". She also commented on the significance of the introduction of *Chinsagu No Hana* in both the first sex scene and the last long grieving/funeral sequence as "all about both scenes being very elemental", dealing with the forces of "eros and thanatos". Further, Maslin informed Poole that the editor of the film, Jill Bilcock, utilised "the Sakamoto version of *Chinsagu No Hana* as a guide track. Music is crucial to Jill before the score is composed"; she actually "cut the whole film (in rough cut form) to the Sakamoto version". This constituted a considerable risk on the part of the film's key production/creative team because, at this relatively late stage of the process, Elizabeth Drake had not yet received Sakamoto's permission to rescore his work for the film. Ryuchi Sakamoto's version of the song is consistent with his synthesiser-oriented, rock/Japanese world beat style and represents a repopularised form of the folk song. Drake's rescoring is a further step beyond these versions.

14. How far this corresponds to the distinctive expectations and realities of Australian life is a question for another study, though the most recent survey of sex in Australia certainly suggests parallels (see Smith et al, 2003).

Chapter Seven

"CHRIST KID, YOU'RE A WEIRDO": The Aural Construction of Subjectivity in *Bad Boy Bubby*

MELISSA IOCCO AND ANNA HICKEY–MOODY

We make our lives in identifications with the texts around us every day. Many of these texts are music, yet we continue to think of them as background, perhaps absent from consciousness, perhaps entertaining, perhaps annoying, but in all cases ultimately innocuous. (Kassabian, 2001: 14)

The industrial noise, aggressive dialogue, claustrophobic binaural soundscape and the range of music featured in *Bad Boy Bubby* (dir: Rolf De Heer, 1993) is anything but innocuous. Signaling a marked move away from insipid approaches to film music tracks, already critiqued by Anahid Kassabian above, this chapter explores critical intersections between film sound theories and the aural construction of subjectivity in *Bad Boy Bubby*[1]. First, the chapter investigates the affective employment of binaural microphones in *Bad Boy Bubby* and examines the role of such tools in crafting the spectator's journey. It is argued that the employment of binaural technologies choreographs an intense, claustrophobic atmosphere in *Bad Boy Bubby*. Second, the emphases placed upon sound, speech, and particularly silence within the first half of the film, are examined in relation to the construction of a pre-Oedipal soundscape and the perverse relations between Bubby, his mother Flo and his Pop[2]. Finally, the chapter explores some uses of music in creating emotional intensity in key moments in the film where sonic connections are made between Bubby and the 'outside'. It is argued that these moments open new possibilities of spectatorial identification, interpretation and affective response and a movement towards film *auratorship*[3], rather than spectatorship, is posited.

The film clearly divides the sound track into two distinctive sections, namely: inside the flat where the soundscape predominantly comprises silence, limited dialogue and the occasional background drone and screech of invisible machinery; and outside the flat where the sound track is saturated and rich with both diegetic and non-diegetic sound and music. *Bad Boy Bubby* also offers a unique listening experience centering on the protagonists' social activity that is structured around the reproduction of idiosyncratic linguistic statements and styles. Examples can be heard through Bubby's sonic and kinesthetic (re)constructions of his lived experiences performed on stage with his rock band, and through his linguistic mimicry during his encounters with others. There are several occasions in the film where music and sound are privileged in the text. As such, they play particularly crucial roles in the construction and re-construction of Bubby's subjectivity. Indeed, the manner in which music and sound carry the narrative of the film text as a whole is remarkable, as examined in this chapter.

Filmed in and around the streets of Port Adelaide, South Australia, *Bad Boy Bubby* was a critical success both nationally and internationally[4]. While the film is certainly visually memorable (for example the notorious mother and son sex scenes, clingwrap *motif* and Bubby's performance on stage with a blow-up doll) the film is also sonically memorable, particularly through its affective use of silence, sound and quotable dialogue. The film is an exploration of a man-child's – the 'Bubby' of the film's title – journey of self-discovery after his escape from a life of confinement and abuse. Through its fragmented yet thematically familiar narrative[5], *Bad Boy Bubby's* employment of sound and silence works to create a powerful and often unsettling aural experience.

Bubby (played by Nicholas Hope) is a thirty-five year old man who lives with his mother, Flo (Claire Benito), in a dirty, dark, sparsely furnished warehouse flat. Bubby's mother bathes him, feeds him, beats him and has sex with him. At the point of the film's commencement, Bubby has never left the flat nor had contact with anyone besides his mother, their tormented cat and the cockroaches that dart about their home.

After a series of strange events – which irrevocably augment Bubby's vocabulary and repertoire of pronunciation styles and phrases – Bubby ventures 'outside' for the first time. Here, the range of sounds, including music, that Bubby experiences, become focal points for both the listener and Bubby. He is consistently drawn to music, to people who love music, and even begins 'singing'/rapping for a struggling rock band. Furthermore the film's evocative use of Handel's *Largo* at key moments supports the film's emotional intensity largely through sonic elements. Through such devices, Bubby's subjectivity is sonically and aurally constructed.

Binaural Mics, Claustrophobia and Crafting the Reader's Disgust

Through key scenes such as: Bubby's incestuous sex with his dependent and abusive mother; Bubby pissing his pants under the gaze of Jesus; cling wrapping[6] his cat, Mum and Dad to death (and having a go at cling wrapping himself) the first half of this film actively works to disrupt spectator pleasure. Indeed, in *Bad Boy Bubby* the viewer's disgust is crafted, an effect primarily achieved through the use of binaural microphones.

Binaural mics produce a detailed kind of stereo sound, employing one microphone for each ear. Each microphone performs an analogous function, recording music and sounds with two tiny omni-directional microphones at the entrance to either of the protagonist's ear canals. These microphones are usually built on an artificial human head that includes the thickset ridges of the outer ears in order to adapt the frequency balance of sounds depending on the direction from which they derive. De Heer states:

> *A pair of miniaturized radio microphones and transmitters were built into a wig ... worn by Nicholas Hope, the actor playing Bubby. This way each scene was recorded ... from the perspective of the main character.* (Production notes, 1993: unpaginated)

Binaural microphones construct an aural position in a soundscape, as their recordings are detailed and therefore exactly located in relation to sonic frequencies and directionality. Binaural mics track the distance of sounds from their aural position and identify the sound's location (in front, behind, left or right of their position). Both channels of binaural recording are kept isolated from each other in the recording process and through to the sound track playback in the cinema[7]. This facilitates a crisper and more specific sound than stereo, in which the two channels are often mixed or manipulated away from their location in production. The specificity of binaural sound is, by its very nature, a definitive aspect of the listener's journey and the construction of a protagonist's position within a film text. The employment of binaural microphone technologies in film is relatively new. For fifty years, following trials in a French opera, the novelty and intensity of binaural sound remained relatively untapped in cinema. *Bad Boy Bubby* is one of the first feature films released to employ binaural microphones as a key feature of the sound track[8]. As De Heer recalls, on set the use of binaural mics:

> *forced a completely different approach to sound. Instead of attempting to eradicate the usual exterior-to-the-scene sound, we encouraged them, even supplemented them, by doing things such as opening windows and doors, turning machines on, having crew members off set making sounds and so on. This was so that the perspective of the introduced sounds, matched the sound that was organic to the scene.* (ibid)

It can be argued that the technology of binaural microphones works to increase audience identification rather than encouraging critical distance from the film text (Miller, 1997: 30). Just as the use of music, for example punk music in Geoffrey Wright's 1992 release *Romper Stomper*, engenders an audience response to the film as being "objectionable ... appalling and ... repellent" (Stratton, in Miller, 1997: 29), the intimate re-creation of humblingly human sounds, such as gurgling, eating and urinating in *Bad Boy Bubby* ensures repeated disruptions of the viewer's experience.

Binaural mics make conscious the pedestrian sounds of the everyday, challenging Claudia Gorbman's assertion that "the volume, mood and rhythm of the sound track must be subordinate to the dramatic and emotional dictates of the film narrative" (1987: 76). Binaural microphones record changing spectral characteristics or frequency responses in minute detail and, as such, they are able to emulate the directions and imperceptible qualities of particular sounds. Thus, tiny shifts in frequency responses, phase and sound levels are made available to the human ear. The spectator or, more appropriately, 'aurator', then employs this data to localise sounds.

In order to craft a cohesive synchronicity between Bubby's journey in the film text and the spectator's journey, de Heer and sound designer James Currie (who had worked with de Heer on several previous films) designed and used an original set of binaural microphones, creating an intense, claustrophobic soundscape within which the listener is (literally) aurally positioned between Bubby's ears. The spectator's journey and the protagonist's journey are aurally and, at times, visually in sync.

In the context of De Heer's *Bad Boy Bubby*, the affect of this sonic containment and at times excessive over-amplification seems nauseating. For example, as Bubby fastens cling wrap around his skull, the viewer's aural hemisphere in drawn into a muffled, uncomfortable tension. If fear is a sound, then the billowing, crackling, rustling, 'underwater' noises of being enfolded in cling wrap exemplifies it. (Or munching the foul milk and bread drowned in sugar that your deranged mother slops in front of you.) Fear is also conveyed by the noise of the world outside the door – the world where one must wear a mask. When Bubby takes his first tentative steps outside the flat, wearing a First World War style gas mask, the disconcerting screeching sounds, previously heard only from inside the flat, grow louder and intensify. Combined with Bubby's slow breathing through the mask, this moment of sonic claustrophobia amplifies the terror of the everyday in Bubby's world.

Given that binaural microphones are designed to produce surround sound of exceptional specificity and intensity, Bubby's movements within the film take the listener into a sonic gravitron as they are immersed in intensities usually overlooked in a film text. Sounds that would usually be marginalised in a sound track are loud, too close for comfort and unnervingly persistent in *Bad Boy Bubby*. The listener endures a second sugar-crunching moment while hearing Bubby's parents debating his name. Bubby's father, Pop (Ralph Cotterill) protests to Flo that she has chosen "a stupid name for a stupid kid". The listener hears Bubby crunching his sugar and bread *over* his parents' frustrated dialogue.

The overlay of pedestrian noises on top of dialogue challenges Michel Chion's assertion in *The Voice in Cinema* that voice and dialogue in the cinema sound track are the most privileged sites of aural significance. Chion argues that cinema is characteristically 'vococentric' and that "in every audio mix the presence of a human voice instantly sets up a hierarchy of perception" (1999: 5). In *Bad Boy Bubby*, the listener experiences exactly the extent to which the under-stimulated Bubby has privileged aurality (quite broadly) in his subjectivity. Additionally, as listeners to the binaural sound, Bubby's aurators are afforded the opportunity to undertake his sonic adventures.

When Bubby discovers the small group of Salvation Army singers standing in a line, Bubby approaches each singer in turn, staring with

125

fascination at their faces, attempting to look into their open sonorous mouths. After moving from the deepest-pitched male voice to the highest-pitched female voice, Bubby joins the end of the line of singers and begins singing along in his own atonal high voice, improvising the tune of the hymn. This scene not only attests Bubby's lack of socialisation and thus his nonexistent sense of individuation. It also illustrates Bubby's libidinal relationship to sound through his willingness to 'lose himself' physically and sonorously in the moment by 'plugging' his disorganised singing and self into the end of singers' harmonised line[9]. In this scene, and throughout *Bad Boy Bubby*, the hierarchy of human, dialogic sounds constructed by Chion is dismantled, as the masticating sounds produced by Bubby's mouth engage the spectator over dialogue and Bubby's actions become completely determined by his textural, tonal love of and immersion in sounds.

For Bubby, the amplified soundscape of daily life is the defining feature of his subjectivity. Deprived of visual and social stimulus, save for the aforementioned ritual abuse administered by his mother, Bubby's aurality is afforded considerable power. The constant tick of a clock, far away industrial screeching sounds, a constant eerie hum and the repeated scratch of Bubby's spoon and sugar in his bowl provide a disturbing substitute for the characters' sparcity of dialogue.

"The fuckin' kid's tryin' to be me again": Dialogue and Voices in *Bad Boy Bubby*

You filthy little cunt. You dirty little shit! I'll send you to hell, just you see, you'll go to hell, and your eyes will fall out and your prick will fall off you dirty little slime! (Flo in *Bad Boy Bubby*)

Bad Boy Bubby contains some of the most offensive, memorable and humorous dialogue heard in an Australian film. While dialogue is a prominent feature of most contemporary feature films, and certainly features extensively in academic film analysis (see Kozloff, 2000), de Heer's *Bad Boy Bubby* accords dialogue – and the performance and *sound* of dialogue – a special significance. There is minimal dialogue in the first part of the film, and much of the dialogue is about Bubby and spoken indirectly in Bubby's presence. Starved for human contact, Bubby retains every word spoken about him and, indeed, most indirect speech he comes across. The intonation of his mother's and father's voices combine with the textures of the soundscapes Bubby moves through to be privileged in the construction of Bubby's character. Words, voices, sounds and noises are all radically decontextualised by Bubby. He reinvests sound, be it the spoken word or the hiss of a cat, with his own, generally very literal, interpretation. As such, Bubby's subjectivity is constructed aurally and later comes to be re-staged through sound as Bubby takes to the stage as a peculiarly neo-punk blues band frontman.

From a psychoanalytic film theory perspective, the use of silence, sound and minimal dialogue in the first part of the film constructs a fantasy of pre-Oedipal containment, as Bubby's perverse life of confinement and abuse with his mother is established. There is little dialogue or narrative action and the pace is suffocatingly slow, the scenes difficult to watch, and the minimal and eerie sound track challenging to listen to.

This use of less obvious sound is an effective (and affective) way to illustrate Bubby's life of confinement and ignorance (both blissful and terrifying) with his mother. Kaja Silverman (1988) has explored the relationship between psychoanalysis, sound and the female voice in cinema[10]. Silverman argues that the female voice is often represented as an ambivalent "sonorous envelope," attesting "to the divided nature of subjectivity" (1988: 72). The sonorous envelope stems from a fantasy of infantile containment, before the infant can engage in language and understand identity. Here, the mother's voice is imagined as either a comforting blanket of sound or a suffocating, entrapping web: in both cases the child is imagined as "trapped within the vocal continuum of the Maternal voice" (ibid: 74).

Although the difficulties of applying psychoanalytic theories to film – as a historically, culturally and personally contingent medium – have been well documented[11]; Silverman's ideas still hold some relevance to the representation of the mother-child relationship in *Bad Boy Bubby*. Although he is 35 years old, Bubby is constructed, or fantasised, as being in a stage of infantile containment. Bubby's mother meets all his physical needs and keeps him confined in a small space, almost as if he were in a perverse nursery or a dark womb. The industrial hum and distant screeching are the sounds that create the suffocating blanket surrounding Bubby. This is the soundscape that the aurator identifies with the perverse mother-child relationship between Bubby and Flo, associating Flo's lawless maternity with erratic, eerie sounds and suffocating silence[12].

That said, Flo's dialogue seems to challenge Silverman's ideas surrounding the sonorous maternal envelope and the role of the mother's voice in fantasies of pre-Oedipal containment. Neither strictly associated with maternal sound nor paternal meaning, Flo's voice oscillates between. Although Flo is given the ultimate verbal authority, her dialogue signifies the static, unchanging relationship she maintains with Bubby, certainly up to the reappearance of Pop. Bubby is locked into stasis, imprisoned in a desirable, seductive and yet confining maternal bond. Bubby's relationship with Flo can be read as the place *from which* the narrative progresses.

Once Bubby meets Angel (Carmel Johnson) the similarities and differences between his mother and his lover's voices are worth noting. Although Bubby is first drawn to Angel because she physically resembles Flo (being overweight and large breasted) her voice creates the more conventionally feminine, caring and 'maternal' voice missing from Bubby's perverse soundtrack of life. The softness and 'femininity' (higher pitch) of Angel's voice both contrast to Flo's aggressive and abusive tones and statements, while also overwriting Flo's perverse feminine voice (the voice we hear during the incest scenes) with a more acceptable and less gender ambiguous sound. In the scene where Bubby (now in his 'Pop' persona) states, "Pop wanna see Angel's tits", Angel responds, "I'll show Bubby". When Bubby continues on in Pop's gruff tones, Angel protests – "I don't hear Bubby!" While Bubby speaks with many voices, Angel 'finds' Bubby and in some ways singularises his voice through coaxing his 'true' voice from him. Bubby's 'true' or 'original' voice is the higher pitched and softer, hesitantly toned voice one associates with a vulnerable or scared child.

The bizarre Oedipal triangle introduced upon Pop's arrival into the flat engenders shifts in the tone and timbre of voice and dialogue by the characters. The change in what the characters say and how they say it, particularly in the case of the character Flo, is testimony to the gendered relationship between speaking, power and authority in a sonic medium such as film.

Within the exclusive and dyadic mother and son relationship, Flo's voice oscillates between comforting and abusive and, in both cases, the desired effect is to keep Bubby dependent on his mother. The only soothing, comforting words or 'maternally sonorous' sounds heard in the first part of the film are during the scenes of incestuous sex between mother and son. "Such a good little boy", "that's a good boy" and "good boy Bubby" are some of the 'comforting' statements heard throughout the sex scenes between Flo and Bubby. Juxtaposed with the visual of Flo astride Bubby as he fondles her saggy, doughy breasts, the soft reassuring sound of Flo's voice, in this context, is downright menacing. Furthermore, Flo's bossy and abusive statements such as "don't move!", "be still!", "don't you bloody forget it!" and "by Christ, I'll beat you brainless!" ensures that the spectator is not only drawn into this perverse relationship, but that there is little escape: even if you close your eyes, you'll still hear the sounds.

Following Silverman's psychoanalytic argument, Flo loses verbal authority and verbal control when Bubby's Pop returns after a thirty-five year absence. The tone of Flo's voice changes when she addresses Pop. Here, as opposed to her manner of address to Bubby, she is polite, flirtatious and apologetic. Flo utters phrases like "I'm sorry, we don't get very many visitors, would a sherry do?" and "you always were a charmer!" When Pop caresses Flo's breast, she expresses a new-found modesty and insecurity signaled by her question, "you don't think it's too big?" Silverman states the male voice is given status and authority by identifying "the mother with sound and the father with meaning" (1988: 75) and by "stripping the female voice of all claim to verbal authority" (1988: 77). While Flo's dialogue is not confined to the realm of 'sound' over Pop's 'meaning', Pop's voice and utterances do take control of the filmic plot upon his arrival. That said, Flo's voice and character can be heard as deconstructing what Kassabian (2001: 68) critiques as the two gendered positions of desire defined by the female's Oedipal situation in film. Using Kassabian's claims for assimilating and affiliating identifications in film using sound, we can see that Flo's voice and character allows for multiple points of gendered construction and identification. Kassabian argues:

> unlike assimilating identifications, affiliating identifications can accommodate axes of identity and the conditions of subjectivity they create. They can permit resistances and allow multiple and mobile identifications. (2001: 139)

Flo's voice flows between aggressive and dictatorial associated with a 'masculinised' voice of authority, and submissive and coy and hence more stereotypically 'feminine'.

The arrival of Pop also alters the vocal and linguistic catalogue available to Bubby, leading to irrevocable changes. Pop speaks to Bubby, and about Bubby, in tones and with a vocal texture that Bubby has never even imagined. Once left alone in the flat, Bubby's vocal experimentations include a recreation of Pop's aggressive, dictatorial tones. Bubby (re)constructs his father's Irish brogue and adopts his criticisms as a mantra: "Christ, kid, you're a weirdo... Christ, kid, you're a weirdo".

Following this strangely fractured Oedipal trajectory[13], Pop takes control of the filmic plot and becomes Bubby's main point of identification, imitation and impersonation. Jealous of Flo's affections towards Pop, Bubby tries unsuccessfully to win back the attentions of his mother by dressing in Pop's clothes, speaking in his gruff manner, adopting his pronunciation style and even pasting on a false beard with pieces of his own cut hair. When Pop notices Bubby's attempts he grumbles, "The fuckin' kid's tryin' to be me again". Bubby's adoption of Pop's drunken slur, raspy laugh, catalogue of profanities and bawdy humour demonstrates the extent to which Bubby's subjectivity through his identification with Pop is sonically constructed: Bubby *hears* his identification with the Father figure.

The affective power of Pop's verbal abuse and name calling, including "so long as he ain't a poof", "you got a mental condition or somethin'?", "ya mad bastaad!", "shoulda been left to dieeeeh!", is significant in terms of constructing Bubby's fractured, vulnerable and victimised subjectivity. The continued abuse Bubby endures, both inside and outside the flat, ensures that the spectator/listener experiences an uneasy sympathy towards this melancholy character. This sympathy is directly related to the construction of Bubby as a victim of familial and social abuse that is, to a great extent, verbally administered. A sense of satisfaction is experienced by the aurator when Bubby quickly learns to retaliate his aggressors through *talking back*, particularly through the imitation of vocal texture and delivery of other characters' words.

In *Bad Boy Bubby* the perverse enacting of Oedipal conflict through the mother-father-child triad is further exaggerated with a reconstruction of the classic Freudian primal scene[14]. While psychoanalytic theory and much film theory overemphasises the role of voyeurism and scopophilia in fantasies surrounding the primal scene, *Bad Boy Bubby* reminds us that the sounds of sex are just as powerful and suggestive as the sight of sex. Elizabeth Weis has theorised the possibility of eavesdropping as an "aural analogue of voyeurism" (1999: 79).

The psychoanalytic concept of voyeurism has been central to feminist psychoanalytic discussions of male subjectivity and film ever since Laura Mulvey's 'Visual Pleasure and Narrative Cinema' (1975). Weis asks, however, "if voyeurism is such a fertile subject for film, to what extent is there an aural equivalent?" (1999: 79). *Bad Boy Bubby* explores this aural equivalent when, after being scolded by Pop for spying on his parents having sex, Bubby listens in, or 'eavesdrops' on the encounter. It is Pop who verbally frames Bubby's eavesdropping by angrily calling him a "sexual pervert" when he discovers Bubby watching and listening.

129

In this case, Bubby's eavesdropping also works to construct his subjectivity in terms of child-like curiosity. Weis argues

> One narrational function of eavesdropping is to literalize a metaphorical or psychological gap between the listeners and speakers. In most cases children's eavesdropping involves exclusion from the adult world... Their exclusion from adult life is by definition one of innocence because they lack certain kinds of knowledge. (1999: 85).

Bubby's 'innocence' is characterised by a lack of knowledge and socialisation. In terms of the Oedipal fantasy, after Flo's rejection of Bubby when Pop arrives, Bubby is symbolically and literally thrust into the 'outside' world. In this case "the eavesdropping trope thematizes the child's incomplete comprehension of the world including the mystery of sexuality and the threat, real or imagined, of parental rejection" (ibid). Furthermore, the sounds of sex and Bubby's act of listening reminds the aurator of the uneasy juxtaposition between Bubby-as-child and Bubby-as-man, blurring the lines between innocence, perversion and listening pleasure.

Sound, silence and speech in the first half of *Bad Boy Bubby* explore how Oedipal dynamics are imagined or fantasised as being constitutive of a perverse masculine subjectivity. In this case, the fantasy or discourse of the Oedipal triangle affects Bubby's subjectivity in ways that promote masculinity and subjectivity as consciously constructed and performed through sound.

"Bubby is the Apprentice Roadie": Feeling Through Music, Sensing Through Sound

> music is the vehicle for encompassing a number of aspects of human desire. (Magowan, 1997: 110)

The use of music in *Bad Boy Bubby* is intense, distinctive and powerful. Sound and music both play particularly crucial roles in the construction and re-construction of Bubby's subjectivity. Bubby's participation in music plays a crucial role in his understandings and reconstructions of self as well as being a key component of the narrative. In a manner comparable to Scott Hick's *Shine* (1996) the power of music to Bubby's expression of mental and emotional anguish is a key feature of *Bad Boy Bubby*'s narrative and one of the film's defining features. Loud pulsating music is also a feature of the film. From the blaring organ-playing of the Scientist just before Bubby is told to do away with God and "take responsibility for who he is" to the dreary pulsating bagpipes in the harrowing rape scene in the jail, loud pulsating music is used for moments of existential angst as well as violent assault[15]. Indeed, music is invoked to express concepts and emotions in a way that film dialogue does not. Here we focus on the use of two musical elements variously constructed by composer Graham Tardiff: Handel's *Largo* and the *Bad Boy Bubby Blues*.

The film's signature piece, Handel's *Largo*[16] is one of the most obvious examples of the emotive and affective use of music in *Bad Boy Bubby*. Written by George Frideric Handel in 1738, what is now termed the 'Largo' is one of the composer's most cited works, although it was originally written for a now-little known opera *Serse* (or *Xerxes*) and comprises the melody of the opening aria *Ombra mai fù*. The work is slow and melancholy[17], centering on string and organ. Extracts of *Largo* can be heard at three points in the film: the first time only briefly through headphones placed over Bubby's ears. This is another moment where the listener is drawn into Bubby's aural hemisphere, suggested here more explicitly through the prop of headphones[18]. The members of the band have just discovered that Bubby is the 'Clingwrap killer' they have read about in the newspapers. By placing headphones over Bubby's ears they pacify and exclude Bubby as they argue over what to do with this child-like murderer. The audience experiences this peaceful sonic moment with Bubby, as the organ sounds that Bubby hears are privileged over the anxious male voices of the band members. In this case *Largo* works to soothe the disoriented, confused Bubby, much like a lullaby. The listener is rudely awakened with Bubby when the headphones are torn from his head and the band members drag Bubby to his next destination.

The second time *Largo* is heard for a longer time occurs about midway through the film when Bubby returns to the flat and must reassess how he will cope in the outside world. The music begins quietly prior to this scene as Bubby lays on the ground, kicked by a group of women, who take him for a sexual pervert. The music continues as Bubby returns to the flat in a state of desperation and despair. This is when the piece has its most powerfully melancholic effect and affect. Bubby lies next to the chalk outline of the mother he murdered and sobs. The combination of sight and sound convey the film's broader concepts of alienation, loneliness and despair in contemporary society.

In its final usage at the film's conclusion, *Largo* is played over a montage of shots, including Bubby and Angel making love, Angel giving birth, and an aerial shot of Angel and Bubby's home in the industrial suburbs of Port Adelaide. The repetition of the signature piece here creates a sense of hope in the face of adversity. Bubby and Angel have a little patch of 'paradise' (whatever that might be) in an industrial wasteland. There is a sense that this is not a 'happy ending' and, despite the music's repetition at this seeming narrative resolution, the mood remains somber and uncertain and there is little sense of closure or finality.

Another example of the film's use of music in order to signal a key moment in Bubby's subjectivity is through the *Bad Boy Bubby Blues* song that the band sings to Bubby as they travel in the back of a van towards their next gig.

Tell you a story sad but true
Tell you a story about you know who
A boy called Bubby sitting right over there
Bad boy Bubby with the wild, crazy hair
Bad boy Bubby
Bad boy Bubby Blues
Got them Bad Boy Bubby blues
From my head right to my shoes

This spontaneous song is not only a celebration of Bubby's peculiar and particular circumstances and appearance. Up to the point at which this song features in the film, Bubby had only experienced rejection, hostility and violence in the 'outside' world, predominantly in the form of verbal abuse[19]. Everything he had heard up to that point informed him that this was a world where he didn't belong, a world where he was a foreigner, unable to speak or understand the language. The glee on Bubby's face when he hears himself referred to in the *Bad Boy Bubby Blues* song is notable as he joins in with the singing, awkwardly at first, and then lets out a howl of sheer joy expressing his inclusion and acceptance into this social group.

Bubby's performances as the band's 'frontman' include phrases, actions, profanities, sounds and melodies he encountered during and since his life with Flo. In many ways Bubby is restaging his lived experiences and restaging the Oedipal nightmare of his 'childhood'. In doing so, the listener experiences a kind of *déjà écouté*[20]. At first Bubby's vocal delivery is erratic, unpredictable and impromptu. The stage lights during one particular performance change quickly from green, to red, to orange, casting dark coloured shadows across his face. As Bubby's performances with the band continue, his mimicry becomes more repetitive, familiar, 'performed' and rehearsed. The band performs in bigger venues and the crowd members dress and speak like their hero Bubby, and even know the words to the now familiar songs. The sense of approval and acceptance Bubby experiences though the crowd's enthusiastic and vocal response is important to Bubby's sense of belonging. Furthermore, the change from erratic chaotic words and sounds, to rehearsed familiar and performed words, suggests Bubby's acquisition of language and verbal communication since his departure from Flo and the 'inside'. This 'acquisition' is important to the film's fantasy, and creates a dialogue with the ideas of Jacques Lacan (1977), in terms of the acquisition of subjectivity through language.

French psychoanalytic linguist Julia Kristeva has argued that 'discourse' is limited by language, its denials, structures and rules. She says, "discourse is a complex psychological event that cannot be reduced to what I call the *symbolic* dimension of grammatical categories and their organisation" (1995: 109). Bubby's own 'discursive' capacities extend beyond conventional discursive structures demonstrated in several scenes through his ability to understand the normally unintelligible groans, screeches and contorted expressions of a group of people with cerebral palsy. Bubby becomes accepted by, and popular with, this group and becomes an object of desire for Rachel, who also has cerebral palsy. Bubby's ability to understand and interpret the desires and opinions of this group illuminates Bubby's transcendence of these "denials, structures and rules" limiting that which can be expressed by the spoken word. This is a fantasy of transcendence enabled through another fantastic figure – that of the 'wild child' or 'innocent' through the improbable character of Bubby.

Conclusion

From Bubby's beginnings in the dank and dirty flat with his mother Flo, to his experiences with the 'outside' world, Bubby's most significant moments and encounters in the film are characterised by diegetic and non-diegetic music, sound and speech. While it can be argued that *Bad Boy Bubby* is structured according to fantasies of suffocating pre-Oedipal containment and traumatic post-Oedipal socialisation, the use of sound, rhythm and music are also a source of creative connections and possibilities, not only for the character Bubby, but also for the aurator experiencing the film.

Within the film text, music, sound and speech not only work to enhance representations of Bubby's perverse subjectivity and masculinity, they also create a dialogue with theoretical ideas such as Kristeva's regarding the 'semiotic', alongside contemporary explorations in film sound theory (see Kassabian, 2001; Coyle, 2001; Flinn, 2000). Furthermore, the various deployments of music, sound and speech in *Bad Boy Bubby* also work to actively constitute the construction of Bubby's subjectivity and create meanings, connections and possibilities which effect and *affect* film-hearing experiences.

De Heer's intense and evocative soundscape in *Bad Boy Bubby* echoes the earlier avant garde film scores of Philip Brophy that have been described as "the organization of more complex spatio–temporal relationships ... [that] broadly experiment ... with methods which have the potential to extend and enrich the vocabulary of film sound production and perception" (Samartzis, 1998: 50-1). Indeed, the authors would go so far as to contend that, while Caryl Flinn has cogently argued "scholars have been slow to acknowledge the contributions sound makes to film narrative, desire and overall signifi-cation" (2000: 9), *Bad Boy Bubby* as a text pushes film theory toward investing intellectual force into theories of listening and hearing. The same kind of intellectual force that Kassabian has noted being previously directed toward "'reading' in literary studies and 'spectatorship' in film studies" (2001: 65).

Through positing the notion of 'auratorship' to theoretically engage with the significant and affective ways in which music, sound and speech are employed in *Bad Boy Bubby*, this chapter moves towards a comprehensive aural analysis of film soundscape[21]. *Bad Boy Bubby* invites spectators to cover their eyes and listen. The grim realities of Bubby's life and his drab visual surroundings are overshadowed by the unnervingly detailed and intense binaural soundscape as well as diegetic and non-diegetic music. Accompanied by complex negotiations of identity, power and gender con-ducted through dialogue, *Bad Boy Bubby* offers a rich and productive site for sonic inquiry.

Notes

1. The authors approach this analysis of critical intersections from a feminist, post-structural perspective. As such, the theorisation of music and identity conducted in this chapter draws upon psychoanalytic theories of masculine subjectivity and feminist scholarship of the early 1990s that explored masculinities in crisis and the disruption of spectator pleasure. This chapter explicitly moves beyond the frame-works established by this theoretical base, while also drawing upon aspects of this perspective.

2. This examination is undertaken through exploring the film's take on the Freudian Oedipal mother-father-child triad of psychoanalytic theory. For examples of psycho-analytic readings of popular, particularly horror, films see Williams, L (1996);

Clover, C (1992); Creed, B (1993); Schnieder, S. J (ed) (2001). For a more general approach to psychoanalysis and film see Allen, R (1999); Mulvey, L (1975).

3. The terms *aurator* and *auratorship*, as far as the authors of this chapter know, have not previously been used in the analysis of film sound or in film sound theory.

4. Recognised in awards including the Grand Special Jury Prize and the International film critics' award at the 1993 Venice Film Festival and three AFI (Australian Film Industry) awards in 1994, including best actor (Nicholas Hope), best director (Rolf de Heer) and best screenplay.

5. Thematic consistencies are evident between *Bad Boy Bubby* and Werner Herzog's *The Enigma of Kaspar Hauser* (1974) in terms of the 'wild child' motif. See also Malone, P (1996).

6. Plastic film used for food cover and storage.

7. The production of truly binaural sound playback requires a number of somewhat complex and expensive processes that allow loudspeaker amplification of binaural sound while retaining the aforementioned 360-degree realism. (A less expensive, and not as effective [hence rarely employed] approach to binaural sound is ambiophonics, produced through the use of a baffle between a pair of closely-spaced loudspeakers.) The cost of the technology required in order to build binaural microphones and to undertake the production of binaural sound has limited the employment of this technology. Binaural microphones were first trialed in 1881 on the stage of the Paris Opera using double telephone lines to transmit the Opera to its subscribers. Since this somewhat low-tech but innovative beginning, binaural ear trumpets were used in the First World War by the British Air Force to locate enemy planes and in the 1920s experimental binaural radio broadcasts incorporated a pair of frequencies, with listeners tuning in on a pair of crystal radiophone sets. At the 1939 World Technologies Fair, the binaural dummy head "Oscar" was featured as a major attraction, with showgoers lining up to don Oscar's binaural headphones and experience sounds in the room where Oscar was placed. A number of manufacturers are currently working on improved binaural playback via crosstalk-cancelled loud-speakers, a technology that will see the use of binaural sound expedentially increase.

8. The binaural microphone headset used in *Bad Boy Bubby* was constructed and supplied by Fred and Margaret Stahl.

9. Bubby's joining the end of the singing line, and his doing so, can be conceptualised through Gilles Deleuze and Felix Guattari understanding of desire in terms of intensities, flows and mechanic assemblage (Deleuze and Guattari, 1983). Bubby 'plugs' himself into the end of the choir 'machine', creating a new 'assemblage' of voices, one that is no longer perfectly harmonised but rather reflects Bubby's awkward attempt at, and desire for, belonging.

10. See also Flinn (2000) for a discussion of the female voice in *film noir* and Kassabian (2001: 61-89) for a discussion of constructions of femininity and spectator identifi-cation in and through film music.

11. See, for example, Shaviro, S (1993); Crane, J.L (1994) and Freeland, C.A (2000).

12. This soundscape is revisited later in the film when the band Bubby joins creates a tense, dark and moody atmosphere as, on stage, Bubby reconstructs his experiences inside the home and his abusive relationship with Flo and Pop.

13. Susan Hayward writes,

> In referring to the Oedipal myth, Freud seeks a means whereby he can explain a child's acquisition of 'normal' adult sexuality ... The male child who is first bonded to his mother (through the breast) imagines that he is a united whole with her ... He become aware of the illusory nature of his unity with his mother and yet still desires unification. The desire for the mother is now sexualized. He is, however, aware of the father whom he currently hates because of his 'lawful' access to the mother, and he, the child, does not ... he now moves to identify with the father and sets about to complete his social-sexual trajectory successfully by finding a female (m)other – that

is someone who is just like his mother. The Oedipal trajectory thus involves identification with the father and objectification of the mother. (1997: 254-255)

Bad Boy Bubby draws on, twists and subverts a number of tropes from psychoanalysis. While Bubby's movement from a powerless position within an incestuous relationship with his mother, to imitating his father to get his mother back, to falling in love with the overweight Angel with her tits 'like mum's', echoes the Freudian stages of 'normal' male development, Bubby's trajectory moves anywhere but towards 'normal' adult male sexuality and subjectivity and in fact encourages us to question whether it is possible for such a status to exist.

14. According to Freud there is a 'primal scene' from which the male child's Oedipus complex develops. This scene is one in which the child either witnesses or imagines its parents having sexual intercourse. Barbara Creed has explored the predominance of primal scene 'phantasies' in horror films. Creed uses the term 'phantasy' over 'fantasy' in order to emphasise the Freudian subject as a protagonist engaged in the activity of wish fulfillment and to avoid the connotations of whimsy associated with 'fantasy' (1993: 6). Creed states that these "phantasies are about origins: the primal scene represents to the child its own origins in its parents' lovemaking; the seduction phantasy is about the origin of sexual desire" (1993: 17). Creed's analysis, however, is limited to a structural psychoanalytic framework. This framework has been problematised by film theorists such as Shaviro,S (1993); Crane, J.L (1994) and Freeland, C.A (2000). This chapter notes the importance of moving beyond a structural psychoanalytic approach to film, sound and subjectivity.

15. At one point, Bubby is arrested, taken to jail and placed in a cell. In a surreal scene, he hears the loud, droning sound of bagpipes. In a mixture of wild agony, curiosity and ecstasy, he begins shouting, jumping and pounding on the prison wall. Bubby is dragged out of his cell, where he sees a group of kilted bagpipe players assemble and face him at the end of the corridor. Bubby is placed in another cell, where a naked and dirty male prisoner (named "the animal" in the film credits) promptly rapes him. The scene is made all the more violent and disturbing by the loud drone of the bagpipes that persist. Bubby grimaces in pain and shock, and then surrenders to the sexual attack, 'playing dead' as the violent and repetitive thrusts of the rapist match the pulsation of the bagpipes.

16. Performed by the Adelaide Symphony Orchestra. The aria is sung by Emperor Xerxes in praise of a plane-tree for providing shade, and causes amusement for hidden onlookers.

17. Although in its original form, this piece was indicated for Larghetto tempo and was presented in Handel's only humorous opera. Curiously, the aria has been more recently used in sanctimonious contexts, and this may well have informed Tardiff's usage.

18. The sound of music, in this case, is conventionally described as diegetic – that is "music that is produced within the implied world of the film" (Kassabian 2001: 42). The distinction between diegetic and nondiegetic sound, a distinction that Kassabian argues grossly reduces film music to either 'in' or 'out' of the narrative (ibid), has been blurred in this scene. The music is both *in* the narrative (Bubby listens to it through his headphones) and *out* (the music drowns out the dialogue and draws us into Bubby's moment of pure sonic bliss), challenging the diegetic and non-diegetic dichotomy and thereby serving as extra-diegetic. Another example of this complex use of sound can be heard when Bubby enters a printing shop and is drawn to the sound of the printing machine. The film allows the spectator to experience Bubby's blissful moment as he closes his eyes in a mixture of ecstasy and relief at the rhythmic and pulsating sound. In this scene we become Bubby as the screen blacks out to leave only these sounds. Again the sound is both *in and out* of the narrative, in that its draws us into Bubby's moment and yet away from the other actors and dialogue.

19. Bubby hears a variety of profanities directed at him once he goes outside such as

"fucking greedy bastard" and "fucking poofta bastard" by the football yobs that drive by in the car, "fucking idiot" by the tree lopper, "fucking smart cunt" by the policeman and "mad bastard" by the service station attendant.

20. The authors have used this term as a sonic alternative to the more commonly used *déjà vu*, substituting the French *écouté* (heard) for *vu* (seen). In English speaking contexts the term *déjà écouté* has more commonly been used in popular music reviews to describe the unoriginality or familiarity of music (*déjà écouté* – "I've already heard it"). The authors apply the term in the film sound analysis here as a way to describe the conscious repetition of sound in order to produce a particular effect/affect for the listener.

21. There is a range of sonic directions opened up for investigation in *Bad Boy Bubby* that we have not been able to explore within the boundaries of this chapter. Possible future research directions include: creative resonances between academic philosophies of Existentialism; capitalism and the factory soundscape as constructed in *Bad Boy Bubby*; and the important relationship between tonality, vocal texture, accent, meaning and message in the organ-playing Scientist's speech in the film.

Chapter Eight

THE SOUND OF REDEMPTION IN *CHOPPER*: Rediscovering Ambience As Affect

MARK EVANS

Many recent Australian films have been characterised by soundtracks that have involved near continual use of popular pre-recorded music. Mary Ann Doanne has argued that "sound is never absent (silence is at least room tone)" (1980: 166). However the use of (largely rock-based) music in Australian urban crime films such as *Two Hands* (dir: Gregor Jordan, 1998) and *Garage Days* (dir: Alex Proyas, 2002) has created a style of aural barrage sound track that, in many ways, has advanced the assaultive narrative of the movies. Yet in director Andrew Dominik's gangster/crime film *Chopper* (2000) – clearly a candidate for such a sound track – the opposite sonic construction has been employed.

This chapter argues that the predominant sound design of *Chopper* is based on the use of ambience[1], atmospheres and effects; or, in terms of recent Australian film sound, on the sound of redemption. That is, redemption in the sense of deliverance and liberation; a liberation from Australian sound tracks that bombard the audience with an aural intensity that supposedly matches the drama/violence on screen. In *Chopper* the sound track is freed to operate with subtle and carefully premeditated nuances. The use of such subtlety not only enhances the often very disturbing action of the film but also contributes substantially to the character development of the main protagonists within the movie. The soundscape of *Chopper* may appear initially minimal yet, as will be demonstrated, the sonic landscape is a complex web of sound effects, ambient noise, background conversations, dialogue, atmospheres and on-the-air sounds. Analysis of sound design in *Chopper* and similar films[2] may assist in breaking contemporary Australian film out of its sensory overload approach to sound track creation, and help it see past the ever-present temptation offered by pre-recorded music.

The following analysis will pay particular attention to key scenes within the film as markers of general sound design philosophies. Place-based soundscapes are used throughout the film to help make sense of action and motivation, context and source, as well as to heighten the reality and ferocity of the drama. What makes the movement away from pre-recorded music within *Chopper* all the more absorbing is the backdrop to the project itself and, in particular, the personnel involved in creating it.

Research for this chapter includes quotes by sound designer Frank Lipson. All such comments, unless otherwise indicated, are taken from an interview with Lipson conducted by Dan Freeman (via email, 9/9/2003).

Chopper's Milieu

The film *Chopper* is based on the life of Mark Brandon Read, a notorious criminal colloquially known as 'Chopper'[3]. Read was born in Melbourne, Victoria, in 1954 and was first arrested at the age of 17. Read went on to spend 23 years of his adult life in prison, convicted variously of attempted kidnap (of a County Court judge), wounding with malicious intent, shootings, assault and arson. He was also acquitted of a murder charge on the grounds of self-defence. Read himself suffered numerous beatings, was stabbed, and had his ears sliced off in prison. His flamboyant character and public exploits made him a favourite subject for the Australian media. On release from Pentridge Prison in 1991, Read published his first book *From The Inside: The Confessions of Mark Brandon Read*. This colourful account of his life story became a best seller and, nine books[4] later, Read has sold more than 300,000 copies and become one of Australia's most successful authors[5]. Although interviewed by writer/director Andrew Dominik and lead actor Eric Bana in the lead up to filming, Read had no direct involvement with the making of *Chopper*. Nor is the film a direct account of his book or life, and he received no payment for the sale of film rights.

Writer/director Dominik was born in New Zealand and moved to Australia at the age of two. A graduate of Swinburne Film School, Dominik went on to establish himself as an innovative director of music videos for clients such as Crowded House, Jenny Morris, Diesel, James Reyne, The Cruel Sea and The Church. His videos garnered MTV awards and ARIA nominations. *Chopper* was Dominik's first feature film. The connections between *Chopper* and the music industry are notable. Along with Dominik, producer Michele Bennett has had a long involvement with the music industry, producing videos for INXS and U2. Co-producer Michael Gudinski – founder of Mushroom Records – is widely known within Australian popular music. Executive Producer Al Clark had experience in Virgin music and film divisions in the UK before moving to Sydney to produce films (notably, Stephan Elliott's *The Adventures of Priscilla, Queen of the Desert* [1994]). Given the strong connections key personnel have with the music industry, it was conceivable that the music track to *Chopper* would represent another extended advertisement for Australian bands (as is the case in *Two Hands*). However, the divergence from such a model is noticeable, and no doubt due in part to the involvement of composer Mick Harvey.

Harvey is best known as the multi-instrumentalist collaborator with avant garde rock identity Nick Cave. Having played a pivotal role in the

Cave-fronted Boys Next Door (1977-1980), Birthday Party (1980-1983) and Bad Seeds (1984 onwards), Harvey developed his passion for experimental sounds and textures, both in subtle and not-so-subtle forms. Indeed some critics, like Nathan Bush, credit Harvey with providing the "intricate and atmospheric arrangements that have brought to life Cave's lyrical narratives" (2003: online). Harvey went on to release two solo albums, *Intoxicated Man* (1995) and *Pink Elephants* (1997), both of which paid homage to French composer Serge Gainsbourg through radical translations and versions of his work. Gainsbourg (1928-1991) was a singer/songwriter for television, advertising and film music tracks. His work often contained bitingly cynical, humorous and/or lurid lyrics, leading to it being frequently censored – or simply not released[6]. Alongside his commitments to Cave's projects, Harvey also began to dabble in composition for film and television. In the late 1980s he composed scores for German television productions, including *Identity Kid* (dir: Ed Cantu, 1988). Harvey subsequently composed scores for numerous feature films and documentaries, and the score for *Chopper* represents his tenth major film score. Other films Harvey has worked on include *To have and to hold* (dir: John Hillcoat, 1996) and *Australian Rules* (dir: Paul Goldman, 2002).

Harvey's music does not stand alone in *Chopper*. Rather it blends with, incorporates, and influences the other elements of sound design. Thus, of pivotal importance to the final construction of the *Chopper* sound track was Frank Lipson, who has worked as a sound editor and designer since 1976. Despite Lipson's long list of film credits, including *He Died with a Felafel in his Hand* (dir: Richard Lowenstein, 2001), *Romeo and Juliet* (dir: Baz Luhrmann, 1996), *Snow Falling on Cedars* (dir: Scott Hicks, 1999), *Metal Skin* (dir: Geoffrey Wright, 1994) and *Romper Stomper* (dir: Geoffrey Wright, 1992) – the last two yielding AFI awards for him – Lipson acknowledges the collaborative working practices that produced *Chopper*, particularly through Dominik's involvement:

> *The Director Andrew Dominik was an amazing person to work for. He is the most 'sound aware' director that I have had the pleasure of working for ... truly inspiring. He was every part a member of the sound team, in fact he was in the cutting room every single hour of every day with us.*

This contextualisation of the production team involved in the sound of *Chopper* is significant for several reasons and highlights the intimate attachments several members have to the Australian music industry. These connections, many over several decades, may easily lead to the use of existing Australian popular music as the dominant feature of the sound track. Such a construction would also fit with recent sonic excursions in this genre of Australian film (such as *Two Hands*). At the same time, the combined involvement of Harvey and sound aware director Dominik with Lipson ensured *Chopper* could move beyond tough crime stereotypes, and use sound to reinforce the murky, unsettling world of the film. What follows is a discussion of the way key moments in *Chopper* are established and enhanced via a brave new approach to crime/gangster film sound tracks.

Pulsating Pentridge

After the opening scene with Chopper in prison, our musical introduction to the film comes rather wryly with the Cole Porter hit, *Don't Fence Me In* (1944) accompanying the credit sequence. Neither Australian nor 'criminal', the sound of Porter's song provides an immediate departure from any previous expectations the audience may have about the sound of *Chopper*[7]. However, rather than being totally unrelated to the mood of the film, *Don't Fence Me In* provides an insight into the as-yet unmet Chopper character – albeit a clichéd introduction. The song sets him up as somewhat of a dreamer, an (out)sider, a free spirit unable to conform to society's norms. Moreover, combined with shots of Pentridge Prison in Melbourne, it serves as "comic allusion" (Smith, 2001: 408); the ironic juxtaposition of the prison images with the music establishes the black humour that pervades the film. Much of this dark humour comes via the main character in the film, yet it is this slightly offbeat introduction that paves the way for the audience's reception of his particular persona. The song also initiates a subtext running through the film, that of Chopper's desire for land, "lots of land", in order to remove himself from the caged environment and relocate to Tasmania (where Mark Read himself now resides).

Chopper's caged environment is initially evoked through the clever manipulation of dialogue emitted in three ways: via a television, spoken outdoors, and spoken within a prison cell. The scene cuts between Chopper recording the television interview outside in the prison yard, and watching the broadcast interview on a small television in his cell with two guards. As they watch the program Chopper interjects comments and questions to the guards. The sound of Chopper's voice is manipulated to suit the visuals, with a tinny representation of his voice coming out of the television, a voice thick with reverb (resonating within the concrete walls) in his cell, and a voice mixed with outdoor sounds in the prison yard. At this early stage of the film, Chopper's voice is mediated, bounded, constructed and, perhaps most importantly, different. The different effect of filtered sound is thrust on the audience, raising questions about which represents the more 'real' sound. Which will be the voice that the audience can trust? The mediated sound of television news and current affairs, packaged, edited and presented by respected community voices, often invokes authority, yet Chopper's real-time commentary on his own television appearance immediately calls into question the place of his mediated communication throughout the movie. What is evident at this early stage is that all of Chopper's dialogue is caged. Whether he is outside in the prison yard or inside his cell, his voice does not possess the freedom his dialogue would have us believe he enjoys. He is bound by the prison walls, by cell walls and gates. His voice emanating from the television is edited by others, and transmitted via trebly speakers that denude the strength of his voice. The constraints of his sound, and that of those around him, are the dominant sonic premise on which the sound track is built.

The sonic environment of Pentridge Prison involves the near-constant drone of television and/or radio in the background of the mix, usually broadcasting greyhound racing or other sports coverage. This combines with the constant murmur of voices, shuffling of feet, rattling of keys and locks etc, to create an unsettling audio atmosphere for the film. The anonymous acousmatic[8] prison banter distracts the audience and occasionally the protagonists, as threats and alliances develop. Background sounds are filtered, contained and ambiguous. There is also a considerable blending, even bleeding together, of these sounds of prisoners, guards, radios, televisions – the aural concoction becoming indecipherable and, by implication, potentially explosive. The overall impact of this sound offers a slightly mysterious and very intimidating context for the action. Prisoners appear simultaneously oblivious to the noises surrounding them yet overtly conscious of who is where, doing what, to whom. This subtly suggests differences in sensory phenomena: the eyes may be shut or distracted but the ears never close. Such a construction of sound layers was carefully designed, according to Lipson:

> We went to great lengths in creating the atmospheres in the gaol. We spent three days at Pentridge prison with a small group of ex-prisoners, where we recorded many different tracks for background use. Our reason for recording there rather than in a studio was to get the right atmosphere for the prisoners who were performing. We also recorded activity tracks, race calls and general yelling out etc.

Due to the constancy of sound within the prison, and the rises and falls in its intensity, the gaol appears to 'throb', to have its own life[9]. As will be noted later, this 'throb' connects prisoners together and follows them into the free world. Characters become demarcated by their ability to move away from this sonic environment, or, in the case of Chopper himself, become contextualised by it.

Ambient Stabbings

Two scenes that reveal the judicious use of ambient sound for affect are the prison stabbings of Keithy and Chopper. Moreover, through their sound design, the scenes depict the separation of prison life from that 'outside'. A violent stabbing scene would generally create commotion in the outside world, signalled through screams, cries of pain and fear, and perhaps rescuers and police. Yet, in the prison world of *Chopper*, these events occur with little dramatic sound accompaniment and signposts. Once again the film demarcates a sonic environment within Pentridge that is vastly different to that outside, mainly due to the heightened use of ambient sound.

During Chopper's stabbing of Keithy there are various tinkles, voices and echoes present, although the voices of Chopper and Keithy dominate the soundscape. The group of other prisoners present, like the audience, are merely spectators to the 'theatre' unfolding before them. Tension and violence are portrayed via heightened foley effects[10], which also contribute to the oppressiveness of the environment, every sound expanded and suffocating the aural environment. For example, the accentuation of cigarettes being lit and inhaled 'draws' the audience into the impending violence. The constant sound of keys jangling in the background also raises the tension of the scene by positing questions about the guards' whereabouts. As Keithy is stabbed, the television commentator[11] – to this point merely a contributor to the ambient murmur – is mixed much louder in the sound mix to reflect the climax of the onscreen action, coinciding neatly with the stabbing as the highlight of the cinematic action. The heightened squelching and slopping of Keithy's blood, prominent in the mix, highlights the violence and visceral nature of the act. Meanwhile the dripping tap that has been present in the background of the mix throughout the scene increases slightly in tempo, both propelling the drama of the scene and indicating the impending termination of Keithy's life.

Notably, the ambient sounds so prevalent throughout the prison only retreat when the scene changes to show detectives interviewing Chopper in the prison warden's office. The outside world, where actors must face consequences, is devoid of the paranoia and ambience and constancy of the prison world. Such absence of familiar ambience discomforts Chopper, whose character thrives on a mesh of sound denoting the presence and activities of other people, on the inseparable blend of truth and fiction, and on security found in densely layered soundscapes. To escape this, his narrative on how the incident unfolded involves a visual and sonic flashback to the scene, where he is able to use those visual and sonic layers that best suit his version of the story. Without the murkiness of the prison world, and its sonic undercarriage, Chopper's ability to reconstruct events, and himself, would be greatly diminished.

This sonic undercarriage is also used to show Chopper's dominance and level of control within various scenes. The density of the ambient sound track creates opportunities for clarity and fuzziness as required. Such is the thickness of this soundscape that definition between sound elements can also become blurred, as Lipson noted:

> The scene where Chopper gets stabbed by Jimmy in the [indoor] exercise yard is entirely sound effects based, although one could easily assume that what you are hearing is music … There were several instances in Chopper where this [blurring between music and effects] was the case.

Such a blurring is only possible due to the thickness of the ambient sound layered throughout this scene, and much of the film. This layering of ambience and effects largely occurs at an almost subconscious level, influencing the mood of the film and the audience's relation to the characters (particularly Chopper). As Lipson noted, "There are several scenes where we edited small metallic pings on Chopper's eye blinks … [They are] almost subconscious sound effects but effective nonetheless" (ibid). These pings add intensity to Chopper's character, highlighting the heightened subtleties we are led to believe he perceives. Somewhat alternatively they also provide a release for the viewer, the high treble sound adding a comedic, almost cartoonish, lightness to his persona.

Subtle manipulations of the music track provide dominance and control for characters, without the need for obvious bursts of pre-recorded music to guide the audience. The lack of pre-recorded music keeps the viewer immersed in the diegesis longer, effectively maintaining the discomfort of viewers through their suspension of disbelief, with no irrelevant music to jar them away from the context being constructed. Furthering their discomfort is the subjective positioning this creates, with no sonic breaks available to objectify the diegesis or present it from another angle. The audience thereby becomes bound to Chopper's interpretation of events and even his experience of them.

During Jimmy's knifing of Chopper, it is Chopper who remains in control – despite being on the verge of death. This is enacted sonically via the presence of low frequencies surrounding Chopper and his bodily movements. By comparison, Jimmy's stabs occupy a small aural spatiality, and sound rather insignificant. There is a brief moment where Chopper appears vulnerable from the repeated attack – expressed through a high-pitched string sound – before suddenly retaliating with a fierce sonic thump as he grabs Jimmy in a strangle hold and forces him to drop the knife. At this point, low frequencies – heard as deep drones and bass tremors – return to fill the sound track. These 'sub bass tremors' were largely Lipson's contribution: "Andrew is not fond of them [due to their overuse in some genres, especially science fiction, and the risk of cliché] and it was my pushing in that direction in a few scenes, and him giving in, that saw them end up in the mix".

An addition to the stabbing of Chopper is the use, especially post-stabbing, of non-diegetic music to highlight the drama. The effectiveness of this orchestral music is that it represents Chopper's bodily injuries. While still in control of the situation – in that he prevents Jimmy from killing him – Chopper cannot control the loss of blood and threat to his life that the stabbing poses. Thus the dominance of ambient sound, so useful to Chopper throughout the film, is displaced by orchestral sounds that overtake the soundscape. After the stabbing, the string chords held in sustained dissonance are notable for their tempo as much as their dissonance. The slow tempo of the music here suits the routineness and boredom of prison life, while simultaneously representing the gradual draining of Chopper's life. High-pitched, atonal strings contribute to the tension and suspense of various scenes elsewhere in the film, without providing any overtly distinct character empathies. The lack of resolution in the orchestral sound in the post-stabbing sequence complements Chopper's surreal visions, as well as conveying a sense of tension and foreboding that arises as a result of the stabbing.

In My Father's House

The diegetic world constructed around Chopper's father's house provides background information regarding Chopper's upbringing and, in a sense, connects him to the prison world from which he has come. His father's house interior (first encountered on Chopper's initial release from prison) contains a similar ambience to that which was constructed in Pentridge prison. Although not as pronounced, the connection of the two sonic worlds is notable. For example, the television in the background of the soundscape replicates the constant murmur of the television/radio heard in prison. The television is mainly low in the mix although when his father starts to laugh at Chopper – normally as a result of his own jokes – the canned laughter of the audience is mixed up, enforcing the ridicule and isolation experienced by Chopper. Such "on-the-air" (Chion, 1994: 76) sound can change radically without notice, and does so here without overly jarring the listening experience. There is a connection here to Oliver Stone's *Natural Born Killers* (1994) that uses a similar technique in providing sitcom-based sound effects and laughter over graphically violent and misogynistic imagery[12]. In *Chopper*, the effect is used less for dramatic emphasis and more to estrange Chopper from his father, thereby creating a certain empathy from the audience for his situation. What the scene shows, largely through the heightened atmospheres and effects of the sound track, is that Chopper's father clearly has personal and social issues too, which facilitate both tension and grudging acknowledgement between them. It also posits Chopper's domestic life, and presumably his upbringing, as being closely associated. Thus a contextualisation of Chopper's violent life is ascertained to some extent via the parallel of two soundscape environments.

A similar bond is created after Chopper's release from prison when he visits Jimmy's small suburban apartment to clarify whether Jimmy is planning to kill him or not. Jimmy's apartment, aside from the many visual and social representations presented, contains a sonic environment analogous to that of prison. Once again television is present in the scene although greyhound races on screen are not initially matched with audible sound. As with the prison setting, there are numerous voices in background that, despite their placement in the sonic mix, are nonetheless quite intrusive. Phrases such as, "I'm sick of the sight of you!" pierce through the domestic soundscape of the apartment. Displaced from their point of origin these verbalisations become sonic markers of the emotion and intensity present at this point in the narrative, despite the relative visual calmness. Other more non-descript terse interchanges and verbal tones[13] fill out the background of the soundscape.

The key moment within the scene has a direct link to those acts of violence that were depicted in prison. As Chopper reaches the climax of his nervous anxiety and aggression towards Jimmy, ultimately pulling out a gun and threatening to shoot him, a kettle in the kitchen reaches boiling point. The piercing whistle of the kettle synchs with Chopper reaching his boiling point, demonstrating sonically his inability – or at least intense internal struggle – to control himself and not resort to extreme violence. Coinciding with this, arguments and accusations from other apartments build in volume and intensity as Chopper holds the gun to Jimmy's head. The tension and drama of this scene are pre-empted by baby cries and deep sub-sonic throbs. Overall the scene reflects once again the dominance of atmospheres and effect sounds in creating suitable accompaniment to violent and distressing diegesis.

Conclusion

Chopper is striking for its lack of prerecorded music and instances of its use are restricted to the 'social' interactions of Chopper in the outside world. The vast majority of prerecorded musical excerpts occur at Bojangles nightclub where classic Australian rock songs are heard and assumed to be emanating from a jukebox somewhere in the club. It is these songs that are included on the film's soundtrack release. Only two other instances of prerecorded music exist in *Chopper*. The first is when, on release from prison in 1986, Chopper and his girlfriend Tanya are in her bedroom. Here gentle rhythm and blues styled music plays in the background. The other occurs as Chopper talks with the 'dirty' detectives in an unnamed pub. In this example the music is so backgrounded (mixed low volume) as to be virtually indiscernible. Thus prerecorded music in *Chopper* is marked by its lack of prominence in the mix, even the Bojangles examples, and the fact that all occurrences of it have some (at least suggested) diegetic source.

In many ways the *Chopper* CD soundtrack release (2001) is evidence of the visionary approach to non-musical elements in the film. The CD product released in conjunction with the film not only features music from classic Australian rock bands Cold Chisel, Rose Tattoo, The Birthday Party and The Saints, but also includes sound excerpts from the film, and themes composed by Harvey. A review of the soundtrack release noted that compiler Mark Opitz:

> has used the movie itself and the songs from the movie, to create an emotional ride as confronting and challenging as the film's subject matter. He's used Chopper's words and action to set up the songs and he's used the songs to add to the weight of the words. It's a relentless, powerful journey. (Unattributed, 2003: online)

Such an observation highlights how the strength and confronting style of the film was created largely through the sonic elements. The world of the film is needed to "set up the songs", given that *Chopper* represents a film where pre-recorded music is a minor player in the overall milieu of the sound track. Popular music tracks or songs, especially those normally marketed on CD soundtracks, are largely absent from the film. More importantly music is largely absent from the violence of the film. Yet the film is not marked by silence. Rather it communicates a complex matrix of layered foley, atmospheres and sound effects, culminating in a disturbing, yet richly rewarding, sonic experience. In this way, rather than stipulating an intended audience reading, the absence of music allows the violence and deception of *Chopper* to critique itself.

The final scene of the film represents the most salient, and indeed silent, sonic commentary on the film and Chopper's character in particular. Following the shooting of Sammy the Turk, and the associated trial, Chopper is imprisoned and watches himself represented on a current affairs television program that profiles his misdemeanours and character. It is this scene that is cut into the opening scene discussed above, except here the viewer has had the entire movie to assess Chopper's bravado, and to ascertain whether the voice emanating from the television or the one speaking to guards within the cell, is the most appropriate sonic representation of his character. After watching himself on television in the company of two friendly guards, the guards are forced to reluctantly shut him in at lock down. As the door to Chopper's cell is closed, the particularly thick atmosphere track disappears and the ambience subsides. Chopper is left alone, the ambience has diminished, the effect is gone. Chopper has come full circle in his journey. Able to comment on his own life, to confess (albeit elaborately) his sins, we hear more than we see that redemption has come to Chopper, and silence can finally reign.

> Thanks to Jerome Madulid, Gareth McCarthy, Zane Pearson and Dan Freeman for their various engagements with the sonic world of *Chopper*.

Notes

1. Ambience is used here not as a synonym for 'atmospheres', as is often the case in film sound, but as a deliberately created sonic milieu. This environment, constructed at low volume levels and often placed in the background of the mix, has a direct lineage to the work of Brian Eno (and others) who pioneered the Ambient music genre in the 1970s and 1980s (Hayward, 1998: 32ff).

2. It may be argued that such a movement has already begun. Crime thriller *The Hard Word* (dir: Scott Roberts, 2002) draws on composer David Thrussell's extensive experience in electronic and industrial music to create textures appropriate to the film.

3. Different theories abound over the origin of this nickname, one of the most favoured being that it comes from Read's trademark of cutting off people's toes. Read himself traces it to when his ears were cut off (at his own request) in Pentridge prison.

4. Not including the children's book authored by Read, entitled *Hooky The Cripple* (Pluto Press, 2002).

5. Read continues to enjoy "celebrity gangster" status, featuring on the cover of *The Bulletin*'s expose into Australia's underworld war which, at the time of writing, had involved 22 deaths (Shand, 2004).

6. See http://www.francevision.com/nsltr/vf14/gains.htm and Bart Plantenga (1996) 'Serge Gainsbourg: The Obscurity of Fame', http://www.wfmu.org/~bart/sg.html.

7. The song is, in one sense, an easy option for directors/producers seeking instant recognition. It was used in several prominent Australian commercials for products such as cars during the 1990s, and continues to be used in Australian film – featuring as the opening track in the 2004 film *Go Big* (dir: Tony Tilse), while visuals follow the main protagonist running late for work and eventually settling into her cubicle environment.

8. Michel Chion (1994: 71-73) uses this term to discuss sound that is heard but not visualised on screen.

9. For further reflection on the construction and use of such an organic sound design, see Evans (2004).

10. Gerard Long, highly respected in the Australian film industry, was foley artist for *Chopper*, with Steve Burgess foley recordist and mixer.

11. Interestingly the commentary itself is rather non-descript. It would appear to be sporting commentary of Australian Rules Football yet, despite being mixed extremely loudly at the moment of the stabbing, the sound is melded with Chopper's yell, deep bass sounds, and the overriding effects sound of the stabbing itself making it largely indecipherable.

12. Thanks to Zane Pearson for this observation.

13. Sarah Kozloff (2000: 51-56) usefully notes that the way dialogue is spoken is often more insightful than the words used.

Chapter Nine

SOUNDS OF AUSTRALIA IN *RABBIT-PROOF FENCE*

MARJORIE D KIBBY

Based on Doris Pilkington-Garimara's autobiographical novel, *Rabbit-Proof Fence* (dir: Phillip Noyce, 2002) tells the story of three Aboriginal girls who, taken from their family under a policy of raising children of mixed blood in a non-Aboriginal environment, return home by following the rabbit fence[1] for nine weeks through outback Australia. It is a powerfully simple story, and it is economically told. Dialogue is sparse, and the visuals emphasise the vast loneliness of the empty spaces. The score provides a density, driving the narrative, commenting on the action, and positioning the audience in relation to the conflicting aspirations unfolding on the screen. Chris Doyle's cinematography frames the landscape as a focal point of the narrative, and the music track gives that landscape a voice.

A 'True Story'

It is impossible to separate Noyce's film from the social and political context that inspired it and in which is was produced and released. Released at a time of widespread sensitivity to Australia's colonial past and an awareness of how history influences the way Australia defines itself as a nation, the film necessarily added to the ongoing debate in Australia over the Stolen Generation and the role played by the Government in the separation of Aboriginal families and erasure of the Aboriginal heritage of children taken from their parents.

The fact that the movie posters bore the subtitle 'A True Story' and the film opens by declaring that it is "a true story" heightened debate over the 'correct' reading of Australia's black history. Key personnel in the public debate were Keith Windschuttle, author of *The Fabrication of Aboriginal History, Volume 1* (2002) and Robert Manne, author of *In Denial: The Stolen Generations and the Right* (2001). Writing in the *Sydney Morning Herald* Manne says that:

> Rabbit-Proof Fence *is not only a remarkably accurate account of a dark episode in our history. As it suggests, a simple story of the seizure and the escape of three young "half-caste" girls can take us, if we are willing*

to open our eyes, to an understanding of the racial fantasies and phobias and to the genocidal thoughts that masqueraded as policies for the welfare of Aborigines in Australia's interwar years. (Manne, 2002: online)

A year later, in the *Washington Post*, Manne argues:

The pain of child removal lives on in the memories of almost all Aboriginal families ... Rabbit-Proof Fence is far from being propaganda. Rather, this simple story ... is a sober, historically accurate account. (Manne, 2003: online).

Windschuttle compares *Rabbit-Proof Fence* to Noyce's 2002 adaptation of Graham Greene's novel *The Quiet American*, opining that the anti-Australianism of the former film outdoes the anti-Americanism of the latter (Windschuttle, 2003: 12). Windschuttle says that rather than being a true story, it is a "combination of a fictionalised memoir" and the "contentious" 1977 report into the Stolen Generation by the Human Rights and Equal Opportunity Commission (ibid). In criticising "the consensus reached by the university-based historians of Aboriginal Australia" and the support of this view "in the media, the arts, the universities, and the public service", Windschuttle offers the explanation that:

They have inherited a self-critical, morally sensitive culture that readily becomes incensed at breaches of its own ethical rules. This is why they are so willing to believe authors who discover injustices such as those alleged to have been perpetrated against the Aborigines. (ibid: 18).

Political figures also publicly debated the issues raised by the film. A former leader of the Australian Liberal Party, John Hewson, expressed the view that:

[Australian Prime Minister] *John Howard and his ministry should, as a matter of compulsion, take the first opportunity to see and discuss the movie* Rabbit-Proof Fence ... *they should then immediately say 'Sorry!' along with, and on behalf of, the rest of us.* (Hewson, 2002: online)

Peter Howson, the Minister for Aboriginal Affairs in Australia in the 1970s, criticised *Rabbit-Proof Fence* as an "attempt to give credibility to the now discredited stolen generation thesis" (Howson and Moore, 2002: online).

A major problem in making a film of Pilkington-Garimara's story was the divided audience, ranging from a polarised but relatively informed Australian audience, to a relatively un-informed and less politically aligned international audience. A solution to this problem was to "speak in a universalising language of emotions" (Hughes D'aeth, 2002: online) and to do so via a marketing campaign described as "dubious and meretricious" (Simmons, 2003: 42). "Before I'd seen a single frame of *Rabbit-Proof Fence* I was drowning in a sea of marketing spin-offs and moral blackmail," claims one reviewer (Mills, 2003: online). There was the (inevitable) soundtrack album, the book, a film tie-in addition, Mambo tee-shirts, two trailers, a website, a 'making of' documentary titled *Follow the Rabbit-Proof Fence* (dir: Darlene Johnson, 2001), the screenplay, postcards, posters, a study guide for schools, and a massive launch campaign that involved transporting hundreds of media and other personnel to Sydney for a Fox Studios screening and multiple 'premieres' in Aboriginal communities. Noyce admitted that he'd "learned the lessons in marketing and casting that Hollywood teaches" and said that he used those skills "to sell an indigenous story into the mainstream" (in Mills, ibid). As a result, the film operates as both a factual account of a specific lived experience, and as a story whose narrative devices ensure the audience is emotionally caught up in that experience.

The true/story divide was emphasised by the decision to cast girls from remote Aboriginal communities, and with no acting experience, for the leading roles:

> We realised that the best kids for this particular movie were coming from the north-west of Western Australia, towards the coast, where the real story took place. Because in that area so many of the Aboriginal people are still in contact with traditional lifestyle and law, so there's a whole different body language and feeling and spirit about the people, which we needed. (Noyce in Gurr, 2002: online)

In another interview Noyce observes:

> Our only chance was to have the audience invest in this incredible journey that they took; so there are two journeys – the characters' and the audiences'. And we hoped people would invest in them even more because these were not professionals. So that was always planned, but we had an uphill battle. (in Edwards, nd: online)

Everlyn Sampi, Tianna Sansbury and Laura Monaghan left their homes for the first time and travelled to Perth for the filming. Everlyn in particular is shown in *Follow the Rabbit-Proof Fence* to have found her new life difficult. During rehearsals she ran away twice, and with her mother's agreement was placed in a boarding school near Perth, which she reportedly hated. As part of the massive publicity campaign, the *Today Show* on Australia's television Channel Nine ran a daily report on the making of the film in the week beginning 7th December 2001. James Thomas interviewed Noyce as part of the report, and confronted him with the parallels between the story of the filmmaking and the story of the film. "Picture this," Thomas says, "A white man enters a remote Aboriginal community with the best intentions, takes three girls out of their community and promises them fame and fortune. Does it sound familiar?"

Noyce wants it to sound familiar. Though few in the audience will have had similar experiences, the film asks that they make the imaginative leap to empathise with the characters. The controversial US poster did this explicitly, asking, "What if the government kidnapped your daughter?" Noyce responded to Thomas that we live in a different world, but the intense colour-charged cinematography and, significantly for this chapter, the affective power of the sound track draw us into the world of the rabbit-proof fence.

A Sonic Character

In discussing *Mad Max* (dir: George Miller, 1979) Ross Harley talks of how the sound track adds a "sonic dimension to character and narration" to the extent of effectively generating a "sonic character" (Harley, 1998: 17). In *Rabbit-Proof Fence* director Noyce and composer Peter Gabriel use the score to construct the environment – specifically the landscape – as a character that plays a key role in the narrative events. In doing so they produced a music track that suggests a tapestry woven from the sounds of the world. Linked to the Australian locations it supports, this music track becomes an integral part of the film, representing a 'sound of Australia'. The soundtrack album closely follows the film score. Additionally, reviewers remark on this: "Unlike *Birdy*... the songs bear more of a resemblance to traditional film scores" (Customer review Amazon.com).

Gabriel was one of the founding members and the lead singer of the rock group Genesis. He left the group for a solo career in 1975 and has since made a name for himself through his efforts to bring different styles of international music to the attention of the West and his support for human rights, particularly through Amnesty International. Real World, the record company he founded in association with WOMAD (The World of Music and Dance), promotes and distributes musicians from various non-western locations, and his own music constructs complex instrumental soundscapes drawing upon diverse musical traditions. Gabriel composed the scores for *The Last Temptation of Christ* (dir: Martin Scorsese, 1988) and *Birdy* (dir: Alan Parker, 1984). When Noyce began to discuss a score for *Rabbit-Proof Fence*, Gabriel insisted that it be a collaborative work with David Rhodes and Richard Evans. Rhodes has been associated with Gabriel's band for over twenty years as a guitarist and co-writer. Multi-instrumentalist Evans has produced and engineered many projects at Real World records. Gabriel, however, is listed on the film credits as the primary composer and the soundtrack CD, titled *Long Walk Home – Music from the* Rabbit-Proof Fence, is credited to him, with Evans and Rhodes credited on two tracks[2].

Gabriel proposed building the music track largely from natural sounds that Noyce would record for the effects and atmosphere tracks of the film (Gabriel, nd: online). Gabriel saw possibilities for integrating the sound effects track and Aboriginal musical elements into the score. As Noyce describes it, Gabriel said, "I want to do a score that comes out of the earth. I want to do a score that expresses the Aboriginal oneness with the land" (in St George, nd: online). Interviews with both Noyce and Gabriel after the film's release repeat the sentiment that the birds, insects, wind, rain, animals and running water were authentic sounds that Noyce "recorded, or could have recorded" while shooting the film. (Gabriel, nd: online). However, Andrew Skeoch and Sarah Koschak, who form the environmental recording team Listening Earth, state on their website that in mid-2001 they were contacted by Real World who requested copies of their recordings "for use in a 'small' soundtrack project that Peter was working on" (Skeoch, 2003: online). As Skeoch points out, while Gabriel had anticipated using environmental recordings gathered during the making of the film, "gathering good nature recordings is not as easy as sending the recordist out to get something while the rest of the crew take a coffee break". Listening Earth's recordings became the raw material from which Gabriel's team constructed the 'sound of Australia' that accompanied the girls on their journey home.

The Landscape

The emphasis on the landscape in *Rabbit-Proof Fence* is not a novel idea. The "foregrounding of the unique Australian landscape [has been] a key feature of Australian films over the past twenty-five years" (Rayner, 2000: 27). Looking back over films from *Picnic at Hanging Rock* (dir: Peter Weir, 1975) to *The Tracker* (dir: Rolf de Heer, 2002), the codification of particular features of the landscape as defining elements of national culture is an established tradition in Australian cinema. Gibson maintained that the landscape was not just a regular 'character' in Australian film narratives, but it was often the central or dominant one (Gibson, 1983: 50). He argued that Australian films both highlight the uniqueness of the landscape, and draw a connection between the natural environment and national identity. The aspects of the landscape most often connected to Australian identity are those of the outback – vast, desolate, remote, harsh. "The idea of the intractability of Australian nature has been an essential part of the national ethos" and the concept of the land as an unknowable but respected adversary became "the structural centre of the nation's myths of belonging" (Gibson, 1994: 49). More recently the profound connection between Aboriginal people and land has been recognised.

The projection of the newcomer's mythology onto the landscape gave rise to the trope of the "great Australian silence" which was evocative of the experience of strangeness and displacement felt by the colonisers. This silence, "audible and epistemological, was an effect of colonisation" (Belfrage, 1994: online). The perception of silence was an extension of the idea of 'terra nullius' where the country was declared uninhabited because it was inhabited by unfamiliar people. The stillness signified not so much an absence of sound but the presence of a silence coloured by unfamiliar sounds. It was expressing the absence of expected familiar sounds, and negating indigenous sounds. The idea of the great Australian silence denies that "the landscape's acoustic heritage has been maintained by the Aboriginal people's singing of their land for over 60,000 years" (Bandt, 2001: online). In discussing her soundwork, *Mungo*, sound artist Ros Bandt comments:

> *The land's geography defines the acoustic shell. An ever changing soundscape emerges from the interplay of the flora, fauna, the weather patterns and the passage of human beings. The land is a container for the sound, its past, its songs, its flora, its fauna, and its original inhabitants.* (ibid)

In *Rabbit-Proof Fence* the land regains its voice.

The Role of the Sound Track

The sound track historically has been conceptualised as playing a subservient role in film narrative. Burch regretted that "sound plays the role of a 'poor relation' of the image" musing that perhaps he was writing ten years too soon, and that one day he would see the ability to "organise successfully and totally a soundtrack both internally and relative to the image, to create a total sound texture" (Burch, 1985: 209). Gorbman (1987) referred to narrative film music as "unheard melodies", music that inconspicuously contributed to the mood and atmosphere of the film without intruding on the viewers' conscious experience. However the mutually dependent marketing of films and music began with the producers of sheet music and the exhibitors of silent films, and has advanced along with cultural and technological changes to a point where the score is a marketing tool of tremendous economic importance (Smith, 1998). Henry Mancini, John Barry and Ennio Morricone, amongst others, brought the film score to the foreground in marketing terms. The growth of modern entertainment conglomerates and the increasing importance of music subsidiaries to their profit levels, has motivated film producers to use the music track to create a market for both the film and the soundtrack album. The net effect has been that in many contemporary films the music is far from 'unheard', conversely, it is an important part of the film experience. This is evident in *Rabbit-Proof Fence* in terms of its music track as well as its cross-media marketing.

Rabbit-Proof Fence begins with sound. The screen is black as an 'indigenous' soundscape fills the air. Aboriginal singing underscored by the muted drone of ancient instruments accompanies titles that tell how, in Western Australia in 1931, the Aborigines Act gave the Chief Protector of Aborigines, Mr A. O. Neville, legal guardianship of every Aboriginal person in the state and the power to remove 'half-caste' children from their parents and the influence of Aboriginal culture. Molly takes up the story, speaking in her native language and translated in subtitles. As the camera flies across the red-gold landscape that will play such a significant role in the film, Molly explains that the film is a true story of herself, her sister Daisy and their cousin Gracie from the Jigalong mob, who were desert people living off their land when white men set up a supply depot there to support the building of fences to stop the spread of rabbits onto grazing land.

The introduction of the landscape as the only visual accompaniment to this narrative information creates a causal link between the landscape and the score. This connection is magnified through the film where we see only the bush or the desert and take from the sound track clues to the motivations and emotions of the characters, or the progression of the narrative. This connection is one element suggesting that it is the land itself that is speaking, but other techniques enhance this suggestion such as the use of stereo imaging and directional effects so that the sound seems to emanate from the landscape, the use of natural sounds of birds, wind and water as a leitmotif commenting on the action, and the integration of computer manipulated environmental sounds into the score so that the land is always aurally present just as it is visually present.

Audio Effects and Environmental Sounds

The score uses surround sound imaging to noticeable effect. Different ambient effects occupy various speakers. For example, in the cinema release mix, distinctive, natural wildlife sounds come from the rear speakers throughout the film and people and vehicles move across the soundstage, both creating a concrete experience of the space in which the narrative unfolds. This physical experience is emphasised during key moments in the narrative. For example, on their first morning in the dormitory at the Moore River facility, the girls are woken by a thumping stick on the wooden walls, and the sound moves distinctly from speaker to speaker, enhancing the feeling of disorientation and enclosure and echoing the predicament of the children on-screen. In another scene as the children are saying grace the sound moves with the camera from the girls in the right front, to the nuns in the left rear, to all of the children in surround sound as the camera pulls back and up to show the whole room. The directional effects also build up a sense of off-screen space particularly through the use of 'natural' atmospheric sounds combined with computer-manipulated tones that allude to vaguely familiar, organic sounds. When the girls are transported by train to the Moore River Aboriginal Settlement, the huffing train sounds are set against a dense background of electronic sounds that provide a sense of foreboding that is emphasised by the movement of the sound, so that the train ominously rushes on in a way experienced, not just observed.

Sounds of nature are used throughout the film. Leaves rustling, soft animal noises, sounds of cooling stones, earth settling after the heat of the day, and the whisper of water are used not just to create atmosphere, but also to comment on the narrative and underscore viewers' emotional responses. The early scenes of the Aboriginal women teaching the girls to track a goanna are accompanied by bird and animal noises of the bush, and accompanied by soft percussive sounds. When the girls run from the Moore River camp through the rain, the sound track carries the intrinsic noises of the landscape. Similarly, when they sleep in the bush on the first night after their pursuers have turned back, the sound track swells with the soft insect and frog noises of peaceful night. The environmental sounds suggest peace, security, and oneness with the bush. The whistling kite is specifically used as a leitmotif. The whistling kite is a bird well known in Australia for its distinctive call, though few amateur bird-watchers could distinguish it from similar species on its appearance. Its shrill call consists of a long descending note followed by a series of short, shrill staccato notes. Molly's mother Maude points out the bird in the first scenes of the film, telling the girls that it is their tribe's spirit bird. It is heard again when Moodoo begins to track the girls in earnest. Daisy has just said to the others that the tracker will catch them when there is a cut to Moodoo examining a twig picked up from the ground, and the bird's call fills the sound track. Watching the film it is difficult not to read this association as a sign that, despite having to do his job as a Government tracker, Moodoo has the girls' interests at heart. Again, when the girls have collapsed in the desert from heat, hunger and exhaustion, the bird's call is a symbol that they will find the strength to continue. It is heard again when they reach home, and Molly mimics its call to let her mother know they have arrived.

Moodoo has an ambiguous role in the film. While we see and hear stories of his successful pursuit of other runaways, he seems sympathetic to the girls' quest to return home. The relationship between screen music and the screen has been frequently discussed in terms of whether the music is 'supporting' or 'contradicting' the on-screen narrative information (Gorbman, 1987: 15). But in the case of *Rabbit-Proof Fence* the music often gives narrative information and the visuals play a supporting role. Molly is asked to empty the refuse bucket before joining the others in church, and she takes the opportunity to run away, knowing that it will be some time before they are missed and the approaching storm will cover their tracks. A wide shot of the congregation cuts to a medium close-up of Moodoo, and the sound track for the hymn *All things bright and beautiful* is modified to become an electronic pulsing reminiscent of the didjeridu. Moodoo seems to acknowledge the information contained in the music, in that the medium close-up emphasises his change in expression as the western hymn is replaced by the didjeridu as a symbol of Aboriginal spirituality, and the audience knows that the girls have left the settlement to return home.

Listening Earth note that:

> *Some of our recordings are used quite naturally, as background atmospheres (escaping from the mission through the forest), or in the case of the 'Spirit bird' (Whistling Kite). In other cases sounds have been computer manipulated by slowing them down, adding vibrato etc, until they become almost unrecognisable (Dingoes during the journey home).* (Skeoch, 2003: online).

Just as the organic bush sounds are associated with peace or tranquility, overtly computer manipulated sounds accompany scenes of greatest tension. When Molly and her mother watch the whistling kite, its call is 'natural' but when Molly, in the mission dormitory, recalls the scene in a dream the call is electronically manipulated. In the scene where the girls are taken from Jigalong, the camel's distinctive, other-worldly cry warns of approaching danger and marks a transition from natural to computer enhanced sound. In this scene every part of the sound track is working overtime – the amplified screeches of the camel, the intensified noise of the car crashing through discarded fence material, the drawn-out whistling of the wind, the increased bass and tempo of the score and the echoing pleas from the children and their mother. There is an undercurrent of vibrato running through the scene. This throbbing effect, created by rapidly varying the pitch, is used together with an enhanced bassline throughout the film but is generally reserved for creating tension at key moments.

The Sound of Australia

The effect of using naturally recorded environmental sounds and then manipulating them electronically was a deliberate strategy to enhance the atmosphere by creating a soundscape that was at once strange yet familiar. The score reinforces the experience of the Australian outback for the majority of the film's (Australian) viewers – it is familiar from media representations and popular mythology but at the same time intensely strange. Gabriel explains:

> *we took some Australian bird sounds. It is mainly a magpie that you hear. I decided we could slow that down, and get a moodier thing that was of that sound but not exactly that sound. And then Richard Evans took it into the computer and started manipulating it a bit, further slowing it down and putting a little vibrato into it. We then sink it into*

the soundtrack. One of the places that we used it was in The Return where the kids are coming back home. There's a big string section around it, but for me it is still very evocative. (Gabriel, nd: online)

At this point in the film the girls have come through the worst of the desert, and the landscape has changed to a semi-arid plain dotted with stunted shrubs, but the visible indicators of their nearing the end of the quest are few. Constable Riggs stands on the verandah of the Jigalong supply station, looking out across the horizon from which the girls approach but, in visual terms, representing little in the way of threat. Molly's mother and Grandmother are involved in "women's business" and, while the campfire scene suggests that they are preparing for the girls' return, it offers no clues to the force of their determination to resist the girl's recapture. The juxta-position of the three scenes warns of the approaching climax but it is the sound track that creates the associated tension and carries the nuances of mood across the three groups of people – Rigg's apprehension, Maud's determination, and Molly's relief and regret.

Dialogue is sparse in the film. Molly, Daisy and Gracie speak little, and even respond to direct questions with silence. Other Aboriginal characters speak economically in indigenous languages or shorthand English. The officials, from Mr Neville to the Matron at the home, speak to the point, in clipped tones and businesslike phrases. Some key scenes are entirely without dialogue. When the farmer comes to the room of the Aboriginal domestic who has given the girls shelter, and prepares to join Mavis in bed, not a word is exchanged between him and the girls hiding there. Gracie attempts to catch a train to where her Mother has moved and is recaptured but we view the scene with Molly and Daisy, crouched too far away to hear voices. The silence of the characters, combined with the dense loquacity of the score heightens the sensation that it is the land that is speaking. This perception is developed through the film by the use of environmental sounds incorpo-rated into the score, and the use of directional effects that disassociate particular sounds from specific sources. Through the film score it seems that the land is speaking. Like the 'terra nullius' myth, the great Australian silence has been exposed as a falsehood. Noyce has said that when Gabriel expressed an interest in trying to write a score that grew out of the land and the sounds of the bush, his response was:

That's perfect, exactly what we want. Something where the land seems to be speaking. Where the indigenous people in the film seem to be speaking through the music. Where the music is not something separate to the story, to the images, to the themes of the film, but seems to literally come out of the film. There's a synthesis. (in Elder, 2002: online)

However the musicians and instruments were not necessarily Australian but rather drawn from around the world. In various segments we hear a traditional North Indian drum played by Johnny Kalsi and the Dhol Foun-dation; vocals by the late Nusrat Fateh Ali Khan and the Blind Boys of Alabama; the renowned sitar player Ravi Shankar; Assane Thaim with the African talking drum; Cathy Thomson playing the sarangi, a classical Indian stringed instrument; James McNally on bodhran; Hossam Ramzy playing finger cymbals; Babacar Faye with an African drum, the djembe; plus over fifty other artists from a range of musical traditions. As a BBC reviewer of the soundtrack album *Long Walk Home* (2002) said: "The more observant among you will have noticed that the musicians mentioned don't necessarily bring Australia to mind" (Unattributed, 2002: online). However Gabriel has used mostly instruments and vocal styles that may not be instantly recognisable as belonging to particular contemporary locations or areas but instead might be understood to evoke a timeless space for a Western listener. The reviewer continues, "Gabriel's skill as producer and knowledge of the textures and timbres associated with exotic instrumentation allows this all to blend magnificently. Add to this the expert didgeridoo of Ganga Giri on most tracks and the results never allow you to be in any doubt that you are in antipodean climes" (ibid). The didjeridu by itself has become a powerful signifier of not only Aboriginality but also a particular type of spirituality connected with nature and the landscape, and of a generic Australian location (Kibby and Neuenfeldt, 1998: 67). It has also served to represent the land itself in a number of films including *Walkabout* (dir: Nicholas Roeg, 1971) and *Where the Green Ants Dream* (dir: Werner Herzog, 1984).

Listeners tend to hear the blend of world musics as Aboriginal. "*Long Walk Home* ... features 15 atmospheric, peaceful pieces that blend historical aboriginal instruments with a modern eye for emotion and drama" (Naldrett, 2002: online). "There are complex tapestries of percussion, guitars, keyboards, and instruments native to the Aboriginal cultures at the focus of the film" (Overstreet, 2002: online). Though the didjeridu is significantly featured, and clap sticks are one of the percussive instruments, 'authentic' Australian Aboriginal instruments do not dominate the score. For non-Australians perhaps, Aboriginal music is just one type of 'world music', but even for Australian audiences the score on the whole suggests 'Australia':

> I don't know how exactly to describe it, but listening to the music I hear great expanses of lonely land under the wide burning blue skies. I hear the heat of the outback, I hear the desolation felt by the children traveling across a wilderness on their own, I hear the fear that they may never make it, I hear the determination that they will. (Customer review Amazon.com: online).

One piece, titled *Ngankarrparni* on the soundtrack album, is particularly representative of the score in the way that it interweaves musicians and instruments from around the world with Aboriginal music and environmental sounds to produce music that evokes Australia. Gabriel says of the music:

> One of my favourite moments in the film is the end piece. There are two actresses who play the grandmother and mother in the film and they are... mother and daughter in real life, and they provided some singing and... did some beautiful phrases that we then laced into the track and ... in fact Stephen Hague has also worked on a re-mix of the track. It's very soulful because when you hear it in isolation it doesn't sound immediately familiar, but put on a backdrop, and there seem to be quite

a lot of ... blues type references that come through, and at a certain moment Ningala's voice has gone from a single position to totally surrounding the audience in the theatre, and then in the distance the cavalry coming over the hill are the Blind Boys of Alabama with this beautiful chant, and it's a magic moment for me. (in St George, nd: online)

The piece features the two women singing in their indigenous language, the didjeridu music of Ganga Giri, plus the sound of bluegrassy fiddles, bluesy vocals from the Blind Boys of Alabama and the voice of Gabriel himself. *Ngankarrparni* sounds like Australia – not Australia the nation state, but Australia the land. If we accept that "musical forms express a form of life that functions outside the territorially fixed mode of national attachment characteristic of nation-states imaginaries," (Shapiro, 2001: 600) then we can accommodate the idea of music that expresses an Australia that is something closer to the Aboriginal perception of it, the land as a living thing with a spirit and a voice, and accept the possibility of that Australia being represented in this score.

Gabriel's score for *Rabbit-Proof Fence* might be explained in terms of Gilles Deleuze's and Felix Guattari's concepts of de-territorialisation and re-territorialisation. For Deleuze and Guattari (1994), to deterritorialise the proprietary forces through which space is coded (as sacred space, nation-state space or otherwise) is to replace, re-contextualise or make ambiguous the language through which ownership is legitimated. The score de-territo-rialises musical instruments and styles and ambiguates them by blending them with environmental sounds, manipulating them electronically, and combining them in new alliances. Ownership of them thereby disappears and they are re-territorialised – not in terms of modern nation-states but as belonging to an ancient, spiritual place that is the land of Australia.

Notes

1. Resulting from a plague of rabbits introduced to Australia in the 19th Century, in 1901 contractors were employed to construct a fence running for almost 1200 kilometres. The aim of this rabbit fence was to divide pastoral land with human-constructed waterholes from dry uninhabited bush lands in the eastern part of the state of Western Australia. The fence was designed to prevent the spread of rabbits onto grazing land and becoming a threat to cattle, sheep and wheat farmed by pastoralists.

2. Stephen Foster (III) and Fred Gilbert are also credited on the film music track, for songs, specifically Gilbert's *The Man Who Broke the Bank at Monte Carlo* used in several films including *Lawrence of Arabia* (dir: David Lean, 1962), and Foster's *Old Folks At Home (Swanee River)*, a song first used in the 1929 film *Coquette* and frequently used, alongside other Foster songs, in television and film music tracks subsequently.

Chapter Ten

UNTANGLING *LANTANA*: A Study of Film Sound Production

REBECCA COYLE

Lantana is a weed[1] that produces both brightly coloured pink, orange and yellow blooms and prickles on its densely interwoven stems. Director Ray Lawrence's 2001 film, *Lantana*, opens with a slow tracking shot that delves into a lantana thicket to reveal details of the body of one of the central characters in the film, Dr Valerie Somers. A high-pitched overlay and buzzing drone of insect noises builds to an oppressive level, then is accompanied by drawn out chords on keyboard and guitar as the camera zooms in to reveal sections of the body. Although the opening scene and suspenseful music suggest a thriller, the narrative is as much a subtly worked drama about contemporary Australian relationships, based in Sydney and city outskirts. In the course of solving the mystery established at the outset, the film focuses on four main relationships and explores additional elements of courtship, sexuality, masculinity and Australian identity. Characters' lives interweave as the narrative uncovers the events leading up to Valerie's (accidental) death.

Lantana investigates the disintegrating relationship between Valerie (played by Barbara Hershey), a psychoanalyst, and her academic husband, John (Geoffrey Rush), who have never recovered from the murder of their eleven-year-old daughter two years previously. Valerie's disappearance is tracked by detective Leon (Anthony LaPaglia) who is undergoing a midlife crisis that upsets his wife, Sonja (Kerry Armstrong) and their teenage sons. Leon commences a short-lived affair with a woman he meets at salsa dancing classes, Jane (Rachael Blake), who is separated from her husband, Pete (Glenn Robbins), and dreams of a more exciting life. Jane lives next door to Paula (Daniela Farinnacci) whose husband Nik (Vince Colosimo) is involved in Valerie's disappearance. Of all the relationships, Nik's and Paula's is represented as the strongest and most overtly loving, despite hardship resulting from Nik's unemployment, Paula working night shifts as a nurse and the complexities of raising three children. Beyond these central partnerships, subsidiary relationships and courtship rituals are explored, for example, through Leon's detective partner, Claudia (Leah Purcell), trying to initiate a relationship with a man she has seen regularly dining at a local Chinese café (The Mystery Man, Russell Dykstra) and also the affair between a gay man, Patrick (Peter Phelps) and his married bisexual lover (Lani John Tupu). Patrick is counseled by Valerie who he challenges about heterosexual marriage until she begins to suspect that the married lover is her own husband, John. In a distressed state, she drives to her home outside the city but, on a back road, crashes her car. She calls for help from a telephone box, is picked up by Nik on his way home from socialising with mates, but panics when he takes a shortcut, leaps out of the car, and falls off a cliff to her death. Valerie's death is presented as a possible murder that the film untangles alongside the complexities of adult relationships.

Lantana's screenplay was based on Andrew Bovell's stage play *Speaking in Tongues*. Lawrence and acclaimed film producer Jan Chapman attended the opening night of the 1996 season of the play at the Stables Theatre in Sydney. Lawrence could see the potential for a film in the play and he collaborated with Bovell (who had developed screenplays for *Head On* [dir: Ana Kokkinos, 1999] and *Strictly Ballroom* [dir: Baz Luhrmann, 1992]) to produce a treatment to present to Chapman, who then accepted the challenge of producing the film. *Lantana* won several Australian Film Institute awards in 2001, most notably Best Film, Best Direction, and Best Adapted Screenplay as well as Best Leading Actor (LaPaglia), Actress (Armstrong), and Supporting Actor (Colosimo) and Actress (Blake). Paul Kelly was nominated for the Original Music Score award and Andrew Plain and Robert Sullivan for Best Sound. The sound and music operate mostly as subtle accompaniment to or background for the action and emotions conveyed by the characters, apart from key scenes (outlined below) and in dance scenes where source music is particularly prominent. The operational manner by which Lawrence (and Chapman) contracted and oversaw the film music and sound is reflected in the aesthetics of the final work, although the individuals involved and the nature of their collaborations are also evident.

In this chapter, I will draw largely on interviews with key personnel associated with the sound (and music) track as a way of discussing a cultural sociology of the film production. Interviews via email were conducted with Ray Lawrence (24/3/04 and 7/5/04) and Christine Woodruff (21/6/04). Telephone interviews were conducted with Andrew Plain (26/3/04) and Shane O'Mara (21/7/04). The analysis begins with a focus on Ray Lawrence as director, then includes information about Christine Woodruff's music supervision, leading into discussion of the original music track created by Paul Kelly, Shane O'Mara and a small ensemble of musicians, and concluding with detailed comments on the sound design and supervision by Andrew Plain. Given that my methodology relied largely upon personal interviews with filmmakers reflecting on the process a few years after actual production, excerpts of these interviews provide significant input to this chapter[2]. This approach assists my concern with the nature of the collaborative film production process and the critically important engagements of music and sound personnel in realising the director's vision for the film.

159

All quotes by film personnel, unless otherwise cited, are from my interviews conducted with them, as outlined above.

Overview of Lantana's Music and Sound

I will commence this analysis with a summary of some of the key scenes in relation to sound, then discuss the dance scenes in relation to their use of music.

Several aurally-engaging scenes feature images of lantana and this is established in the opening scene. As we enter the lantana thicket, birdcalls give way to insect rasping, buzzing and cheeping and frog croaks, ultimately loudly reverberating in a kind of 'thrumming' (reverberant low-pitched throbbing-like drone) as the sound increases in volume and thickness. As detailed parts of the body are revealed, low notes on guitar and keyboard chords take over from the insect sounds. High continuous notes play as the full body is seen lying face down, clothing in disarray, one hand with wedding ring lying palm up against the back. The dim lighting renders the scene in monochrome, in sharp contrast to the brightly coloured lantana blooms that open this scene. The details dwelt on in the image track are aided by a wash of sound in the insect noise and music sound track. The excruciating detail of the damaged body is like a Cindy Sherman 'Film Stills' image. Identifiable sounds of flies and cicadas fade in and out of this thick wash of insect noise and a buzz is heard as a bee appears in the upper frame. The sound of droning flies suggests rotting organic matter. This sound and music gives way to heavy breathing and puffing as Leon and Jane engage in sexual intercourse, and the scene cuts to a new narrative thread.

Throughout the film, insect sounds and an oppressive use of such noises are associated with various appearances of lantana thickets. Lantana connects Valerie's body with the incriminating shoe that Nik throws into a lantana thicket in a vacant block across the road from his house. Jane sees this and, the next morning, while Nik takes his child for a walk, she clambers into the thicket to retrieve the shoe. Later, she informs the police of her suspicions that Nik has been involved with Valerie's disappearance. In this scene, as Jane hides from Nik, insect sounds are again predominant, contrasted to the slapping of Nik's thong-shod footsteps, and aided by high-pitched musical suspense notes.

Insect noises also feature in a sequence of scenes where Valerie has crashed her car and she seeks help by calling John from a public telephone box outside a deserted roadside café (named Pie in the Sky). The buzz and rasp of insects, and frog croaks and calls, continue with reverberating keyboard and guitar chords. Valerie calls John three times and leaves increasingly confessional messages on the voicemail. As the headlights of Nik's car appear in the distance and Valerie hurriedly concludes her final message, short melodic motifs are heard that recur in further scenes at this location and as the search for her body develops.

The original music cues are mostly sparsely orchestrated, often featuring one or two instruments from an ensemble of acoustic and electric guitars, bass, keyboard and drums. A central theme that occurs as Leon tries to make changes in his life while pursuing the investigation, features plucked notes on guitar that step down, then rise up, and recur several times before being joined by keyboard. The theme stays within a narrow range of notes, and is variously accompanied by other instruments to flexibly adapt to different scenes. While several cues are jazz-inflected, the final credit sequence is accompanied by a swirling, triumphant electric rock cue that melodically and harmonically suggests narrative resolution.

The music cues for the dance scenes at the salsa classes and club are not signaled as particularly significant in their own right. Appropriately, in this regard, Lawrence argues that he had no real knowledge of Cuban dance music prior to working on *Lantana*. Nevertheless, the use of salsa music in the film reflects two significant aspects about music and dance in Australia. First, there has been interest in Latin-American music reaching back to 1913 when Australia experienced "a craze for the tango as a stage and social dance" (Bendrups, 2003: 393). However Dan Bendrups argues that, "there was little understanding of the cultural origins or significance of the tango … or later popular Latin-American music or dances" (ibid). Second, the representation of salsa dance classes – to which Sonya brings Leon in an effort to renew his interest in their relationship – reflects a more recent interest in salsa, a fast-paced dance style that Bendrups notes is "characterised by a syncopated bass line" (ibid). Salsa is a 'Latin' style that developed in New York City among Cuban and Puerto Rican immigrants and American jazz musicians. The word salsa literally translates as 'sauce' although John Storm Roberts argues that it is also "used by Cuban musicians in the sense of 'spice' or pep" (1999: 187).

Although salsa became popular in North America in the 1970s, it was introduced largely through a new wave of Latin American immigrants (especially from El Salvador) to Australia in the 1980s. In the 1990s, Bendrups observes, salsa "dominated the output of Australian 'Latin' bands" and attracted audiences through its cross between Cuban and jazz musics, giving it "intercultural appeal" and coinciding with "the return of couple dancing as a leisure activity" (2003: 394). In the 1990s, too, the French-Spanish folk group Gipsy Kings achieved international popularity and their hit number *Bamboleo* (1990) was included as a standard for 'Latin' bands in Australia (and its use in the *Lantana* club scene acknowledges this status).

The dance tracks are listed in the table overleaf, in relation to the scenes they accompany. Lawrence's usage of these 'Latin' tracks as well as his approach to creating *Lantana*'s original music track have informed the film's overall outcome.

Director's Vision

Since 1975, Ray Lawrence has won awards as a director of television commercials in Australia and internationally. His first feature film, *Bliss* (1985), based on Peter Carey's novel and screenplay, explored magic realism and met with mixed reviews although it won AFI awards for Best Film, Best Director and Best Screenplay in 1986 and was screened at international film festivals. Lawrence has continued to work as a commercials director in the USA while also writing screenplays.

Table 1: Scenes Using Source Music[3]

Scene	Narrative content	Track title, composer, performer
Scene 1	Leon driving from motel, finds Jane's earring.	*Permisso Que Llego Van Van* (1999) Juan Formell Los Van Van
Scene 2	Salsa class (music continues into) Leon jogging, holds chest.	*Descarga Total* (2000) Isorlando Valle Maraca
Scene 3	Jane dances at home. Chats with Paula re affair with Leon.	*Respeta mi Tambo* (1998) Pablo Justiz Los Naranjos
Scene 4	Salsa class – Leon arrives late. Sonja and Jane dance. Teacher reprimands Leon for sluggish dance. Second dance track as class practises.	*Que Sabes Tu De Amor* (1998) Hiran Calvo Juancyto Martinez *Snowdrop* (2000) Adrian Van De Velde Ego featuring Elizabeth Wei
Scene 5	Salsa club with live band. Sonja flirts with dance teacher.	*Opening* (1995) Lazaro Valdez Bamboleo
Scene 6	Narrative resolution – lantana bush; Jane dances by herself; Pete drives off; mystery man greets Claudia; Patrick watches lover's happy family interaction; Nik and Paula tickle kids; John looks out to sea; Sonja hugs Leon and they dance.	*Te Busco* (1993) Victor Victor Celia Cruz

Lawrence is circumspect about his serendipitous choices of music, especially source music, in *Lantana*. In the following interview, he refers to his own musical background as "limited – I used to play drums in a marching band at primary school". Indeed Lawrence argues that, "Most of what I know about music has come from putting commercials together" and he draws upon the same approach in film production, that is, "I mainly talk in terms of emotions (major/minor)". Overall, Lawrence used different approaches to the two main categories of music required for *Lantana*:

> *The Latin music was part of the story. I just had to find it. Paul Kelly's score was something else. I wanted it to feel like a hot, wet and sticky Sydney summer.*

In further questions to Lawrence, I asked:

> *RC: How did you select Paul Kelly as the composer? (Based on his songwriting oeuvre? Or competitively? Audition tape?)*

> *RL: After I made* Bliss *in 1984 I had heard some of Paul's songs. We met and I asked him if he'd like to score my next film. Which happened to be* Lantana *in 2000. At about this time I heard a track from one of Paul's more recent albums called* Melting. *This was the basis for our initial discussions. He then went away and came up with a motif, which we kept to, throughout the score. It was played in different ways, but was*

Figure 1: Sonja (Kerry Armstrong) dances to Bamboleo *at the salsa club.*

mostly there in some form or another. The whole score was improvised in a couple of jamming sessions with his band. Then it was a matter of cut and paste! Nothing was ever written down. There was no sheet music. It was a very organic process that required a lot of trust. And it worked out well enough for us to be going to do it again on my next film.

RC: How did you select the Cuban dance numbers – is this a particular interest of yours?

RL: *I had no knowledge of Latin music. I got hold of a lot of albums (from EMI then I went to a record store) and started to listen. On the seventh album there was this track that just sort of said something emotionally for me. This was Te Busco; we hadn't shot a foot of film. I didn't know where it was going to go. Or what they were singing about. I just loved the sound of it. They could have been singing about their crops for all I knew. I didn't even know the singer [Celia Cruz] was famous in Latin countries. It was pure instinct.*

RC: What role did you mean the Cuban dance cues to play?

RL: *The Latin music was part of Leon and Sonja's journey to try and put some life back into their relationship. A lot of couples go to these salsa classes.*

RC: Latin dance has been associated with sex and sexuality – was that in your mind when you selected the dance numbers?

RL: *Yes.*

RC: How did you choose the specific tracks for particular sequences eg in particular the final slow dance? Was it based on musicians and what you knew about the track, or more tied to rhythm, tempo, etc?

RL: *It was all done in a very organic, intuitive way, by feel.*

RC: How did you shoot the dance sequences – eg using a temp track?

RL: *No I managed to pick all the tracks I wanted and it was all shot to play back.*

RC: How difficult were copyright clearances on the dance tracks?

RL: *Yes!!! The reason that* Te Busco *isn't on the album is because we just couldn't find the author Victor Victor and his publishing company was in the process of changing hands etc. It was impossible without deadlines.*

Lawrence was assisted in the task of copyright clearance by music supervision on the project.

Music Supervision

Lantana's music track, including source and original music, and soundtrack album, were overseen by music supervisor Christine Woodruff. Following several years working with copyright agency the Australian Performing Rights Association, Woodruff worked on many features, short films, documentaries and television dramas and is now a well-established music supervisor in Australia. Woodruff recalls that the requirements of her work on *Lantana* were specific to the film:

CW: *In Australia, because of the size of the industry, the role of the music supervisor tends to be more 'multi-functional' than it is in the US where the supervisor may do no music licensing at all. I do a LOT of licensing; it would be hard to survive just doing the fun creative bits in Australia. I don't write or perform music but I can do anything else required to ensure the music for a film comes together. Amongst other things, I liaise with director, producer, composer, sound department et al, arrange recording sessions, budget, research and suggest songs for particular scenes. I have a lot of publishers' samples that are useful for finding copies of songs or new songs (for example, the Snowdrop track in* Lantana*). I may also work on the soundtrack CD, putting the deal and the package together with the record company. The job requires a lot of plugging away. Oftentimes you have to uncover mysteries. For example, if a writer has fallen out of their publishing deal, they've changed manager or lawyers, they have moved to a different country... Some of the music in* Lantana *was not represented by Australian publishers, and tracking down a couple of them entailed multiple emails, faxes and phone calls.*

RC: So how did you approach the clearance for the *Lantana* tracks?

CW: *A number of the Latin tracks were owned by a Cuban company called Ahinama Publishing and Recording Company, a Cuban company now based in Los Angeles. They were very keen to have us use the music in the film and most helpful. In another case the record company was a little less responsive until eventually I made a personal visit when I happened to be in New York. The guy I met with was also a concert promoter as well as record company and publisher, so I had to jump in with my requests between his phone calls to venues and sound system providers etc. Then when we were in the final throes of licence paperwork the company was sold to another major company so it all got rather complicated. But with the help of a very friendly lawyer in Miami we did get it sorted in the end.*

RC: How were the tracks found?

CW: *There was a Latin music advisor Frank Madrid who found some of the tracks in his collection and then there may have been suggestions from a dance teacher as well as from Ray himself. Once the tracks were found, then we had to work out an appropriate approach. Not being an expert in the area of Latin music I was not aware, for example, that Los Van Van had been labeled 'the Cuban Rolling Stones' so this 'superstar status' had to be taken into account. It's certainly easier when the artists are represented in Australia, rather than dealing with record companies overseas.*

RC: Can you tell me more about the *Snowdrop* track by local artist Adrian van de Velde?

CW: *I found this on a publisher's sample from Origin Music (who are a local publisher representing local writers as well as overseas catalogues). I wanted a local electronic or jazz track and they had a number of these in their catalogue. It was a very minor part of the music for the film.*

RC: How were the tracks used during production?

CW: *I had worked with Jan Chapman before and she was very organised with the music. I saw the script before pre-production so I could get clearances in time for production. We had to clear a couple of back-up tracks in case the ones we wanted did not come through. The back-ups had to work for the dance though. In the end, all the tracks were cleared for the dance performances on set, and that was because I had what I needed well before production.*

RC: What sorts of decisions were made about the soundtrack CD?

CW: *In Australia we decided to release a soundtrack CD [with EMI] with just Paul Kelly's music; it made for a more coherent album as the Latin tracks (apart from Te Busco) were really incidental/source use in the film. However the UK release of the soundtrack CD included the Latin tracks as well.*

RC: In Australia, we are often hampered by music budgets, and copyright clearance costs can eat into overall music budgets. How do you deal with these kinds of negotiations?

CW: *It's the job of the record companies and music publishers to maximise the income from the copyrights they represent on behalf of* *artists and writers so I will tend to say "this is how much I can afford to pay" – so that they can decide if they want to be part of the project at that rate, rather than have them come back with a quote I can't afford. I have seen an increase in music budgets and it's not unusual to pay say $10,000 for a well-known track for a low budget feature but there are no set rates and prices can get stratospheric for really big songs. It really depends on the value of the song in the market, who owns it, and how it is intended to be used.*

RC: What role did you play in negotiations between Ray Lawrence and Paul Kelly?

CW: *I was involved in early meetings. Ray had it in mind to work with Paul and I have known him and his manager for many years. Paul was given a copy of the source tracks, and he came to spotting sessions in Sydney with Ray, Jan, Karl (the editor) and myself. The first spotting sessions were not very specific – more general notes – but I took pages of notes from them. Then Paul came back with a song that became the main musical motif for the film, and it went from there.*

Woodruff's recollections of the process involved in the original music production are elaborated on by Paul Kelly and Shane O'Mara.

Original Music

During pre-production, Lawrence and Chapman approached Kelly to write the original music for *Lantana*. In production notes released by Palace with the film, Lawrence argues that:

When Paul composes his music it is always completely emotionally in sync with the story he's telling so I had always thought it would be interesting to have him do a film score.

Kelly is a well-recognised Australian singer/songwriter who has worked in rock and pop, bluegrass, country and other musical genres, although *Lantana*'s original music represents somewhat of a departure in style. Kelly was attracted to the idea of writing a film score that did not require writing lyrics:

Words are always the hardest part of song writing. I always have many more music ideas that often never become songs. So, it is a relief to be able to just make up music without words. (ibid)

Kelly worked with regular collaborators Shane O'Mara (guitar and mixing), Bruce Haymes (keyboards), Steve Hadley (bass) and Peter Luscombe (drums) with whom he has played from the mid-1990s, notably in an experimental music band, Professor Ratbaggy. Kelly recalls:

When Ray Lawrence asked me to do the music for the film I came up with several simple motifs which I played on the guitar for him. We were looking for a riff that held both tension and tenderness. (Kelly [2001] *Lantana* soundtrack CD sleeve notes)

After viewing a rough cut of the film in a rehearsal studio the music team improvised some early ideas and developed a musical motif or theme that would recur through the film. Kelly argues that:

We were just groping towards something without having a hard and fast idea about it. I watched the film a few times and just worked on a couple of short little motifs and played them to Ray and there was one he liked in particular. (ibid)

On his return to Melbourne, Kelly started working with long-term collaborator Shane O'Mara on these ideas. O'Mara is a graduate of the Victorian College of the Arts, where he studied classical guitar and composition, and has extensive recording and touring experience with many diverse musicians. Kelly notes:

We thought we would just try and keep things really simple so I got five people together including the drummer, bass player, keyboard player, Shane on guitar and myself. We just had this one little motif that we started with and we improvised for quite a while until we had a kind of rough shape of music. (in Palace Films [2001] *Lantana* production notes)

Motifs based on the D chord seemed most attractive to Lawrence and Kelly asked the musicians to improvise around that chord. In the final music track, the only departure from this chordal focus was the final electric rock cue. Kelly recollects:

[In the recording studio] we just played all day and we did some really long pieces, not even watching the pictures, just playing around these motifs. Trying to play these few little themes in many different ways. We came away from that with a couple of hours of music and since then, with Ray and Jan, we've just really been cutting and pasting out of that. We would move stuff around to fit the pictures, sometimes we would also record some new stuff over the top. But really, the music we played on that one day has really been like our quarry and we have just gone into there and dug out the ore and then made little pieces out of it. (ibid)

The production of the specific filmcues[4] by Kelly and O'Mara was then one of extraction and streamlining:

Our process was mainly one of subtraction – cut and paste with emphasis on the cut. Why use five instruments when one or two of them are doing the job? (Kelly [2001] *Lantana* soundtrack CD sleeve notes)

The style of the cues reflects the collaborative nature of the musical process that was used to generate and modify the film music. O'Mara notes that the production process of the music was followed by a negotiated post-production procedure:

The way we did the music was a simple idea. It was Paul's idea to play some pieces that could be used wherever they were needed. So we came up with two 20-minute jams. But this didn't work out because it was too much information for Ray. What he liked was the essential D chord and a couple of motifs. So we took it back to my studio, and Ray, Paul, Jan and I picked bits we liked and placed them in pertinent spots. We had them on Pro-Tools on separate tracks so I was able to isolate the drums, for example, and use that whenever Ray wanted it to be featured.

Then what happened was that if a cue needed a longer motif or

167

something else, I produced that on the spot. So I played electric guitar overdubs, put some tremolo on, played some swelling guitar chords, and other stuff, but trying to keep the improvised feel. I have worked with Ray on music for commercials and he is very keen on the authenticity of the original performance. So we didn't work with a formal spotting session but rather on the spot.

RC: How did you work the music with other sounds?

SO'M: *For the opening scene, we constructed a little prelude in the studio. Ray wanted to keep the cicada noise there and so the music comes in later. To move from the cicadas to the music, we wanted the sound of wine glass ringing. We didn't have any brandy balloons to hand, so I found a sample of a synthesised form of this kind of ringing sound and put that in to create the tension.*

RC: What was your role in post-production?

SO'M: *When the film was being mixed, Ray perceived the music to be integral to the film, and he didn't want it to be buried in the other sound. So I went up to Sydney with the music in both separate tracks and a rough 2-track version. This was the first time I had been involved this way because usually you just hand over the music. But it helped because I could change the music if, for example, something with a lot of drums in it didn't work against a scene that had a rhythm already there, or the frequencies didn't work together.*

RC: How did you think the collaboration on the music worked?

SO'M: *When the film came out, we realised we hadn't properly talked about film credits because they didn't list all five of us, and in reviews Paul tended to get all the credit. Originally we were going to come up with a band name for the credits but then we wanted all of our names listed because we all had input to the music in different ways. So the music was a departure for Paul because we weren't playing as the Paul Kelly Band – it was a true collaboration. If it had been a Paul Kelly tune, it would have sounded like that. We have since remedied the issue so it's not a problem for us.*

The flexibility offered by the generation of music in this improvisatory manner also assisted the sound design of *Lantana*.

Sound Design

In the following section, sound supervisor and designer Andrew Plain discusses his role on *Lantana* and his brief. Given the dearth of information about this role, Plain's comments are contextualised within current practices for film sound production in Australia. The detailed and lengthy nature of his observations blend technical considerations with aesthetic concerns and challenges, and reflect on the personal dynamics between those working on the film. Plain starts by talking about his original commission.

AP: *The film was in middle pre-production before I came into production – another editor had been contracted to do the mix but had pulled out.*

Although it is not unusual for sound personnel to come onto a film at this stage, producer Jan Chapman and Ray Lawrence were worried about the change of personnel because they wanted more involvement than we usually expected. They wanted me to read the script and pass comment on a couple of scenes about whether there would be trouble with sound. Not so much stylistic things but logistical problems. They were concerned about what they should be miking. In some ways it didn't really matter because Ray is fairly dogmatic about the way he shoots – he's very definite about what he wants to do.

RC: In the production notes for the film [released by Palace Films, 2001], Ray says that he prefers filming on real locations rather than basing everything in studios. How did that affect your role?

AP: *He was certainly like that on sound. The sound recordist [Syd Butterworth] is one he used on* Bliss *and has used on commercials (and has since died of cancer). He was in some ways the last of a very old breed of sound recordists, for example,* Lantana *was the first film where he did not use reel-to-reel tape and he used a digital recorder. His miking style was very old-fashioned and not the way people would tend to mike today. Syd had not done much feature film work – his last one was* Spider and Rose *[dir: Bill Bennett, 1994], and that was the beginnings of Dolby sound – spreading sound around the theatre. Syd's technique tends to be wider in miking and a more naturalistic approach. Our miking keeps atmospheres away from the dialogue. When everything is coming from one speaker, it doesn't matter if the voice comes with a bit of mush when dealing with just stereo. But when we're dealing with 6-track digital sound, we generally aim for pristine, clean dialogue with nothing else behind it. We want the intensity and level of sound that you get from performance on set but nothing else. Then we can add all those things in and put dialogue up loud. Syd came from the old school and tended to mike wide, he was less reliant on radio mics [worn on the body] and it was very real miking. At first we freaked out when we did the first run through to determine ADR [re-recorded sound using actors performing in the sound studio], and we said 70% would have to be ADR recorded. Ray said, "you're kidding". He believed that what you get on the day is sacrosanct.*

So being on Lantana *was a fantastic lesson in how, if you embrace that noisy sound, then you can actually come up with something really wonderful.* Lantana *got overlooked in awards for all but location sound and that was a tribute to Syd but also to editors who enhanced that messiness rather than fought it. Ray's favourite saying was "it is what it is" and at first that would drive you insane – what does that mean? He didn't want anything in the film to be artificially imposed later on. That's kind of funny in a way because so much of* Lantana *is very stylised but that stylisation comes out of really natural sound. He's not into wizzbangery for its own sake. In the end we finished up doing about 10% ADR which is very low for a film like that.*

RC: It's becoming more common in Australia to use ADR, isn't it?

AP: *Australian sound people have embraced ADR to the point of insanity because they think it's what the Americans do. I spent some time in Canada working on a couple of American productions but the movement is away from too much ADR – what you get on set is the best spontaneous performance and only do ADR if you have to. To some extent that's to do with the fact that when stars get to a certain level, getting them back into the studio is a monumental task. But also sound people have recognised that it's difficult to get that sort of energy of the performance and the precise location sound back again. In Australia, I hope there will be a swing back here too.*

RC: You're credited at the end of *Lantana* as 'sound designer' but you call yourself a sound supervisor – what did you understand your role to be?

AP: *It's hard to tell what a sound designer is. Generally in Australia there's not enough budget to differentiate sound designer from supervisor. I have only worked on one film where the sound designer has been a separate entity, where the designer is solely responsible for working out particular sounds and moods that the film should express. On* Lantana *I did both. I tend to call myself supervising sound designer because I feel a backlash against 'sound designer'. In a way, dialogue editors right through to mixers etc are sound designers on a film. But 'sound designer' is the term directors and producers prefer because it suggests more of an artistic input. In terms of the supervisor role, I actually think there's enormous value in getting six people to work together to create a final work so the supervisory role is a thing to be commended. So my role is really supervising sound designer. I don't let any elements of sound go to mix that I haven't heard and checked in relation to what everyone else is doing. I'm the one in the end who is guardian of Ray's vision. I see my job as taking what he says to me and then going "OK, now what does that mean in terms of sound". Now that's a hard thing with Ray because he doesn't say very much.*

Our first spotting session with Ray is now legendary in the film industry – we all had to work out how to deal with each other. For a start, Jan was very nervous about changing her usual sound team. Anyway, we choofed off to the editing room and I had asked all of the sound editing team to come to the session because I believe it is important that they are all involved at this level. We did introductions and then Jan said, "So, Ray, I think you should start by saying what you want from the film," and he said, "Well, I want it to be hot and summery and lots of insects." Then there was a long pause and then he said, "So that's about it really." Then Jan got really flustered and said, "Don't you think we should go through the film?" Ray said, "Well, if we have to – I mean, I'm really sick of the film now." That's very symptomatic of Ray. He'll give you really simple instructions and say, "it is what it is", and "I don't want it to be any more or any less than that, you've just got to give that to me in sound". So you have to work out what that means. We gave him some things to listen to and he'd say, "No no no – less of that and more of that". When you got it, he was a staunch defender of it. Being in the same area he was, he would defend it or knock it on the head really fast – he'd say definitely, "No that's not right". That's different to other directors who might talk a lot about sound but in the end expect 57 different versions of the mix to choose between. When he heard something, Ray was totally precise about whether it fitted in with his vision or not. I'm not defending one approach or another but, with Ray's approach, once you found out what he wanted, you could just focus on that.

RC: So what sort of sound style did you aim for?

AP: We knew from the beginning that we wanted the opening to be deafening. By the time you got to the lantana bush, the sound of insects needed to be oppressive and overwhelming. The musicians wrote an opening piece of music but the start was dropped for the sound, and then music came in later. That carried through the whole film: we wanted natural sound capturing people and paralysing them – stuff would weigh down on them until they couldn't move and they would burst out in really unexpected ways. While Ray wanted it to be realistic sound, we could have little shifts in it. For example, the other section I really love – and again it's insect based – is where Barbara Hershey [Valerie] is in the phone-box calling for help. There's very little going on besides a whole mass of insects but if you listen to it you'll hear that there are gradual shifts and single animals 'beating' in the bush and minor variations a lot like music. We played it like music where one insect would come into prominence and then drift away and another would take over. Ray did not want anyone to say 'wow listen to that sound atmosphere' so it couldn't be too obvious. As long as we stayed within those borders, we could do all sorts of rhythmic things and orchestrate natural sounds.

RC: How did you achieve the final sound mixes? For example, the opening sounds suggest original recordings that are highly treated?

AP: There was a little bit of recording from the set but most was sounds we had recorded over the years. Also a picture editor friend of mine had recorded heaps of stuff at his girlfriend's place in Eumundi [near Noosa in southern Queensland]. We were having trouble coming up with the right kind of insect and he offered some sounds that were recorded on a mini-disk with lots of bumps and clicks but it was just the right kind of insect effect – they'd got to that incredible shrillness. When the camera dives into the lantana bush, certainly other things are happening. For example, Ray wanted creaking wood to give a sense of being trapped. But Ray hated the wood sound we played so we stretched the sounds so that they were so long that they didn't sound like wood anymore but had a pressing down effect, so that's mixed into the insect sounds. Plus there're more tracks for the opening thirty seconds than anywhere else in the film. But in the midst of this wall of sound, you can hear the sound of a bee flying in and out and this is used as a single sound in the midst of the sheer wall of sound. I thought at first that the wall of *sound was too much but then, in Queensland one time, I experienced this kind of pulsing, overwhelming cicada noise. You never believe that it could be real in the way the sound resonates and beats down on you, so that's the effect we wanted.*

RC: How did you work with the musicians and determine priorities between music and sound?

AP: *I had heaps of contact with Shane O'Mara representing the musical team – he was my best experience of working with a film musician. I had lots of liaison time with him. They did not provide roughs of cues. They told me about the musical instruments they would use and the feel of the music but nothing really definite. There were no printed mixing sheets or cue sheets – only the Pro-Tools [software] sessions. Shane had not done much film work before and so we had lots of conversations about how the music should come to the mix and, in the course of that, we discussed where the music and sound would go. We knew from these conversations the vague parameters of where music would go and what it would do there. Shane came to the mix with separate tracks of music like guitar on one, rhythm on another, drums on another, and so on, which meant he could do some secondary editing in the final sound mix. This meant that there were lots of situations in which music could move around the speakers. We could use it left and right speakers and keep it away from dialogue that was quite low and natural and realistic. We could also make the music much more part of the atmosphere of the whole film rather than imposed over the top and that worked well for* Lantana. *It was different to more traditional film music where a sting would be heard on a gun image or whatever. The music blended with the whole sound.*

So it was different to other films in the way we worked with music due to the musicians improvising and cutting afterwards, and the sparseness to it. There never seemed to be a time where there was a dispute about music and sound priorities, or it felt like we were treading on each other's toes.

RC: What sort of work did you have to do on the dance music items?

AP: *Those all came from recordings – they were problematic as far as we're concerned because we can't play with them in the Dolby encoding process where we needed 4-track and 6-track mixes (for different theatre formats). A CD plays out of left and right speakers in a home stereo but, in the encoding process, this comes out of the centre speaker exactly where dialogue is coming out of, so it's difficult to make it 'fill a room'. In the scene in the salsa club, the salsa music had to feel like it was from the live band and, when the actors move closer to the band, the music gets louder. The band was just miming to a recording so you couldn't play with live sound in the space, and the mixers* [Roger Savage, Martin Oswin, Robert Sullivan, with Syd Butterworth] *had to work a lot with the recording to make it sound live.*

While sound design is often marginalised or overlooked in film analyses,

Figure 2: Leon (Anthony LaPaglia) and Sonja (Kerry Armstrong) initiate reconciliation, as Celia Cruz sings Te Busco.

Plain's comments – combining explanation and recollection – reflect the significant role as mediator played by sound designer/supervisor.

Conclusion

The recollections and observations by key production personnel presented above suggest a lack of auteurial closure in terms of *Lantana*'s sound track. Indeed, the comments indicate a fracturing of any single authorial voice informing the sound and music texts. However, far from impeding the music and sound tracks, it is this disparity of often-understated inputs that has created impact in the audiovisual text. Rather than undermining the effectiveness of the work, the diversity of sonic aesthetic contributions attests to the power of *Lantana*'s sound.

In the end, the film leaves us with the sound of an emotionally affective song. *Lantana*'s concluding sequence follows a final scene featuring the eponymous plant, as Valerie's body is winched up the cliff. The insect sounds usually linked to lantana are drowned out by helicopter motor and propeller noises, together with dramatic music chords. Leon returns home and confesses to Sonja, "I don't want to lose you. I couldn't bear it." He lies fully clothed on the bed while *Te Busco* quietly commences. Celia Cruz[5] sings in a reflective style that amply highlights her alto voice and expressive lyrical rendition. The controlled power of her voice is suggested as she stresses key phrases and melodic movements. Her Spanish pronunciation is clearly articulated and, at various points, accompanied by low harmonising voices. In the instrumental break, a muted trumpet improvises on the melodic line. In *Te Busco*, the lyrics Cruz sings translate[6] as:

I look for you, lost between dreams
Noise from the crowd envelops you in a veil

I look for you flying in the sky
The wind has taken you like a ragged cloth
And I do nothing else but continue searching
Those familiar landscapes in such foreign places
That I cannot find[7]

While the meanings of the Spanish language words of the original recording are inaccessible to the majority of Anglophone audiences, their content is coincidentally appropriate to the song's use. Ultimately, Cruz's vocals work affectively as tone and communicate quasi–linguistically.

The song continues extra-diegetically over a sequence of narratively-concluding scenes. Jane dances, drink in hand, in her loungeroom while, outside in his car, Pete resigns himself to watching her from a distance. The Mystery Man in the Chinese café approaches Claudia to share her table. Outside another café, Patrick sadly watches his married lover kiss his wife and child. Nik and Paula are shown with their children posed tableau-style on the front garden lawn. From his stylish hillside house, John stares out to sea. Sonja lies on the bed with Leon and this scene dissolves into Leon and Sonja dancing in a tentative embrace that carefully avoids a kiss as a clichéd resolution. *Lantana*'s central mystery narrative has been solved but, just as the *Te Busco* song content is accessible primarily by sound, further developments in these lives are left for another set of stories.

Thanks to: Ray Lawrence, Shane O'Mara, Andrew Plain, Christine Woodruff, Jan Chapman and Karen Colston, Alan Hughes for assistance with technical matters, Tait Brady and Rachel Pemberton at Palace, and Philip Hayward for insights about the text.

Notes

1. While 'lantana camara' is considered a weed in New South Wales locations where it thrives in the subtropical climate, in the post-Second World War period, lantana was specifically cultivated in Melbourne gardens due to its attractive blooms.

2. Those people interviewed were assisted by additional sound personnel (eg Nada Mikas, dialogue editor; Linda Murdoch, atmosphere editor; Mark Ward, FX editor; Bronwyn Murphy and Lidia Tamplenizza, assistant sound editors) although, within the constraints of this short chapter, I have focused on sound and music personnel most critical to the overall sound and music.

3. A few extra source music excerpts are used (such as an ABC TV news fanfare in the scene where a news report reveals that Valerie is missing), although these are relatively marginal in the music track.

4. The *Lantana* soundtrack CD includes some music from the original jam session that was not included in the final film music track.

5. Born in Havana in 1924, Cruz left Cuba for the USA after the Castro Communist takeover in 1959 and has become well-known as a leading female vocalist in salsa.

6. Translation by Andrew Bartlett and Frank Madrid of *Te Busco* (I Look For You). Andrew Bovell describes the film as "a search for meaning, a yearning for meaning" (in feature documentary 'The Nature of Lantana' on *Lantana* DVD).

7. Written by Victor Victor copyright Flamboyan Publishing/Sony ATV Music Publishing LLC.

Section III:
MUSICSCAPES

T he term employed for this section heading refers to the musical styles and approaches used by musicians and composers for film music tracks. Original music composers commonly draw on a particular concept of the music and its instrumentation, arrangement and overall role for the film. However, the final product may – to more or less extent – operate as an assemblage of musical elements in the form of music cues. The chapters in this section argue that the scores offer distinct musical works for the audio-visual case studies. These chapters discuss musical films consistent with various generic approaches, from the musical balladry of *One Night The Moon*, to the vocal orchestra heard at significant moments in *Paradise Road*. Two further chapters analyse films where composers have played a major part in their music tracks and where original music is highlighted. Finally, the third section and this volume conclude with an overview of musical approaches and practices in the most recent period of Australian feature film production.

Kate Winchester examines the musical film *One Night The Moon* (dir: Rachel Perkins, 2001), a short feature film (duration 57 minutes) offering a refreshing and challenging alternative to big-budget Hollywood-produced films that have been lauded as heralding the return of the musical, such as Baz Luhrmann's *Moulin Rouge* (2002) and Rob Marshall's *Chicago* (2002). Winchester argues that, in the original concept that arose from composer Mairead Hannan's collaboration with writer John Romeril, *One Night The Moon* centred on music. The choice of singer/songwriter Paul Kelly as a lead character and also on-screen performer, together with his musical duet with indigenous artist Kev Carmody, significantly dictated the musical style and approach for the film.

Also examining a film that emphasises song and the singing voice, Jude Magee analyses the choral music in Bruce Beresford's *Paradise Road* (1997). Memorable acapella vocal orchestra cues appear later in the film, although they are an integral part of the film narrative and used for emotional impact in crucial scenes in the film, one of which is case studied in Magee's chapter. In addition, Magee discusses diegetic music incorporated into the music track including a Japanese folk song, as well as the role of composer Ross Edwards's 'underscore' music for cues in the style of Elgar and his own identifiable oeuvre.

Michael Hannan is particularly concerned with the intertextual features of Alan John's score for *The Bank* (dir: Robert Connolly, 2001). Hannan notes the film's heavy reliance on score rather than pre-recorded tracks or rearrangements, and shows the incorporation of screen composition techniques derived from Bernard Hermann and other composers. In addition, Hannan observes John's use of sacred choral textures and settings of Latin texts from the Requiem Mass to comment on action and obscure motivations of central protagonists.

Also studying an orchestral score, Catherine Summerhayes and Roger Hillman discuss Carl Vine's music for Tracey Moffatt's experimental film, *beDevil* (1993). Vine brought his background in dance and theatre music to bear in composing for this film structured around three 'ghost stories' that deal with haunting and different kinds of bedevilment. Summerhayes and Hillman highlight the degree of flexibility accorded to Vine in his compositional approach for this film. Ultimately, the authors argue, this results in a film that eschews a conventional representation of "black Australian memory".

Michael Atherton's concluding chapter draws together themes and issues affecting and informing Australian composers' film music approaches, particularly over the last decade. Atherton argues that major changes have occurred in the industry due to developments in technological tools for music composing, recording and production, and changes in operational modes by producers and directors. In this overview, based on interviews with currently practising film composers, widely differing approaches are shown to operate in the Australian film industry, and these have impacted on film music aesthetics. Atherton sees an "evolving aesthetic" in Australian film music practices arising from the last decade that may well impact on Australian cinema in the future.

Chapter Eleven

MOON MUSIC: Musical Meanings In *One Night The Moon*

KATE WINCHESTER

O*ne Night The Moon* (dir: Rachel Perkins) is a singularly unusual Australian film. Released in 2001, its originality lies in the way music is placed at the forefront of its text. Above image or dialogue, music is the primary vehicle for the narrative structure of the film. Set in the Australian outback in the 1930s, *One Night The Moon* tells the story of a farmer and his wife whose young daughter goes missing after becoming entranced by the full moon. An Aboriginal tracker (played by Kelton Pell) is called to lead the police search for the missing girl, only to be turned away by the farmer who insists that there's to be "no blacks on my land". Acting on the request of the farmer's wife, who defies her husband's prohibition, the tracker eventually discovers the location of the missing daughter. But it is too late as the daughter has perished. The story thereby follows two paths: the emotional angst of the farmer and his wife who have lost a child (and the separate ways they deal with this) and the frustration of the Aboriginal tracker whose knowledge of the land is denied. The narrative revolves around issues of race relations and the price of prejudice.

The relationship between music and drama in *One Night The Moon* blends elements from the Hollywood musical with operatic traditions. As a form of musical art, opera emerged in the tradition of literary theatre and became common across Europe. It developed as a practice that featured sung action on stage. From the 18th Century, there was a strong interrelation between literature and the performance of opera in terms of historical texts and dramatic contexts (Sadie, 2001: 427). Thus opera's main function has been the act of storytelling through music. The operatic elements in *One Night The Moon* have been used to aid the process of story telling. There are moments when the characters communicate to each other through singing and there are also times when the characters engage in a kind of 'musical soliloquy'. These quasi-operatic qualities are used in *One Night The Moon* to reveal thematic sequences and allow the audience to consider particular characters' viewpoints.

Background

One Night The Moon is based on an incident from the life of an Aboriginal man known as 'Tracker' Riley who worked in the western area of New South Wales in the 1930s and received considerable recognition for his skills and his assistance to the police in tracking and gathering forensic evidence. His life and work were celebrated in a documentary entitled *Empire*, directed by his grandson Michael Riley and produced by Rachel Perkins, which was screened on SBS Television in 1997. Impressed by Riley's story, composer Mairead Hannan was inspired to contact writer John Romeril and they developed and submitted a treatment of a single incident from the tracker's life – the lost child drama commemorated in their eventual film – to a music theatre funding scheme established by ABC Television's Arts and Entertainment division, Opera Australia's development arm OzOpera and the production company MusicArtsDance Films[1]. Hannan and Romeril were successful in their application and work began on the project in 1998, with director Rachel Perkins coming on board at a later stage when the music and script were already being drafted. Romeril has specified that the "terms of reference" of the project funding "were to ensure that the film was a narrative driven by music" (quoted in Millard, 2001a: online). Initially it was also intended to include dance sequences in the film but budgetary restrictions prevented this from being realised.

The film's musical co-ordinator, Hannan, had experience in Irish music from her family background and subsequent performing career, and also in Cretan music as a member of the Xylouris Ensemble. Drawing on professional contacts in the Melbourne music scene, Hannan persuaded singer-songwriters Paul Kelly[2] and Kev Carmody to work on the film. Romeril has described writing the film's script as a collaborative project with the musical contributors:

> *There was a discussion, everyone looked at the original documentary and kind of had a bare bones grasp of the story as it was from life. And we sort of fished for song and musical occasions within it. And I went away and tried to write a kind of treatment I thought covered the bill of goods.* (ibid)

This description immediately marks *One Night The Moon* as an unusual project – both in Australia and an international context – since composers were given a role in influencing narrative and scriptwriting, rather than being added later in the process and employed to embroider a pre-existent narrative and dialogue progression. Indeed, the process described above represents so radical a departure from standard western feature film practice that no obvious comparator springs to mind. Perkins has asserted that the film operates in a space between the formerly prominent Hollywood musical form and the contemporary music video genre, and stated, " we approached it by pushing the boundaries of what you would normally do in a drama, with the style, the design and the camera" (soundtrack CD booklet, 2001:

3). The film's producer Kevin Lucas has also emphasised the project's originality:

> It is important to take risks and create new forms of productions and not be afraid. I think more filmmakers should be able to explore the boundaries of the medium, in particular the relationship of music to drama. (Interview on One Night The Moon DVD special features, 2001)

Musical Film Genre

The use of music within One Night The Moon can be likened to the 'musical' genre of Hollywood films. In such mainstream musicals, the narrative is often related to some area of artistic performance, thereby allowing the storyline to include a spectacular display of music and dance (see Feuer, 1982). This can be seen in such Hollywood productions as Singin' In The Rain (dir: Stanley Doonen/Gene Kelly, 1952) or, more recently, Baz Luhrmann's Red Curtain Trilogy[3]. Traditional uses of the musical genre have incorporated music as an aside to complement the visual images and story. In One Night The Moon, however, the storyline is informed by the use of music to the point where much of the dialogue is sung. As Romeril has stated:

> filmmakers have no qualms at all about using music mercilessly in supporting a soundtrack and are very aware of its potency. But to use music in a way that allows it to lead or drive or define the genre – it's a step that's rarely taken. (op cit)

The duration of the film is a brief 57 minutes and musical elements are a significant proportion of this time. Given that the soundtrack album, released in 2001, clocks in at just over 47 minutes and some tracks from the film are omitted from this CD, it is clear that musical items play a significant role in the film – and did so in its production process.

While challenging the border defining the musical genre, One Night The Moon bears only a passing resemblance to earlier 'experimental' musical films, such as Francis Ford Coppola's One From The Heart (1982). However, the resemblance to traditions of opera and musical theatre are more marked. This is most evident in that One Night The Moon relies strongly on lyrics and musical affectivity to produce its narrative and drama and that characters also engage in musical soliloquies. However, as discussed below, operatic affinities only account for certain elements in the production, others being more typically filmic.

One Night The Moon can be differentiated from other musicals by its general tone, its un-glitzy musical sequences and bleak setting. The highly stylised cinematography, added to the musical presentation of the narrative, serves to emphasise the narrative's social messages. This outcome is achieved in several ways. Considering the land is a contested concept between the characters in the film, geographic images are strikingly significant. The production company has tried to evoke both the colonial concept of the land as unforgiving and terrifying and its natural beauty. Time-lapse photography allows the audience to experience dramatic contrasts of both weather and landscape, alluding to the tribulations faced by the settler and

179

his search party. Unlike the often overly-glamorous brightness of main-stream musicals, the images in *One Night The Moon* are marked by dark tones. This is achieved by a bleach-bypassing process employed during post-production. Such a technique drains the visuals of pink tones, creating in the landscape a rugged and bleak atmosphere. Perkins suggested that the process of bleach-bypassing "heightened the style" of the film:

> it draws out the color and makes it more contrasting. I like what the bleach-bypassing does. When shot normally, the results look just too normal. We wanted some sort of overall thing that made it sit outside the norm. (in Millard, 2001b: online)

Perkins's observations highlight how the production company (especially Director of Photography Kim Batterham) was keen to employ cinematographic techniques to create a metaphorical landscape. Close-ups and lingering shots of the landscape are also a recognisable feature of *One Night The Moon*. Romeril argues that this technique helps to illustrate the tracker's view of the world and also to privilege an Aboriginal sensibility (in Millard, op cit). In this sense, the audience is constantly confronted with the land from two perspectives – that of the settler and that of the tracker. This highlights the differing social perspectives evident in the film. Using such techniques, the land takes the role of a 'character' in the film. The specifics of the land itself were also tied into the film music. After visiting the location in Hawker, South Australia, Hannan understood how the music would require re-writing, and recalls:

> When the music was written there was no location for it, so I got a different feeling for it in Hawker. It is really silent there! (in *One Night The Moon* Production Notes, 2001: 6)

Perkins played music on location during production and argues that it "gave us a real sense of the rhythm of the film in terms of the way people moved and the flow of the scene" (in Litson, 2001: 11).

Score Elements

The music track for *One Night The Moon* comprises various components, namely 'underscore' instrumental passages, musical soliloquies performed by the characters in the film, feature songs performed in the guise of a narrator, diegetic music and, finally, focal thematic music (both instrumental and sung).

As Rebecca Coyle identifies, underscore instrumental music runs "'underneath' the action of the film, providing expressive depth" (1998: 6). Instrumental underscore in *One Night The Moon* is used to bridge the main thematic musical numbers and also functions to thematically 'colour' the visual images. Such passages include the track (referred to as *Flinders Theme* on the soundtrack CD) that occurs during a scene that depicts the farmer and his wife performing basic farm duties. The music features traditional Irish instruments such as low tin whistles and uilleann pipes and works to establish the colonial Anglo–Celtic settler identity.

Other tracks function to communicate crucial narrative information. This is achieved through the use of musical soliloquies in which the audience hears the inner thoughts of particular characters, for example, in the opening song, *I don't know anything any more*, sung by Paul Kelly in role as the father. This song's lyrics reveal his character's grief at having lost a daughter and also his inner torment of knowing that his child might still be alive had his prejudice not clouded his judgement:

> Once I knew what was wrong and right
> God was good, black was never white
> Once I knew what I was living for
> I don't know anything any more

This and similar soliloquies help the audience to further understand the characters and their place in the narrative. The song opens the film with Kelly singing, accompanied by guitar, and is reprised towards the end of the film with a simple harmonic line on the mouth organ. By opening with this song, we are introduced to the character of the farmer but it is only when the song is reprised that we understand the grief and regret it projects. Soliloquies such as these help clarify character profiles and their roles in the narrative.

The film also includes compositions that function as external commentaries on the film and its themes. One such track, *Black and White*, is performed by Kev Carmody and includes the lyrics:

> You can walk with dignity be you woman child or man
> With the ancient knowledge and the wisdom from the spirit of this land

Diegetic music, or music written into the film narrative "as if it's there" (Coyle, 1998: 6-7), is also used within *One Night The Moon*. One notable scene depicts a gathering of Aborigines in a small hut as two of them perform on a banjo and harmonica. The use of diegetic music here (in a sequence not included on the soundtrack CD) is notable since it portrays indigenous people playing non-traditional instruments. The influence of Euro-Australian settlement and the subsequent dispossession of Aboriginal cultural forms, including music, are thereby evoked – albeit in passing. Diegetic music, while technically 'background' music, thus also has the power to reiterate thematic concepts and additional information.

In order to explore how meaning is created through music, it is useful to analyse one focal thematic track, *This Land is Mine*, and one focal thematic 'instrumental' track, *Moon Child*, and examine how these tracks are fundamental to the narrative process. In analysing the tracks, I will refer to the musical construction of the piece and explore the meanings they may produce. McClary and Walser (1988) describe two levels of musicological analysis, the syntactic and the semiotic, the syntactic referring to that which is objectively present in the music, and the semiotic referring to the meanings inherent in the text or the ways we may interpret sonic signs. Drawing on this duality, I will first describe the syntactic elements of the music and then refer to these elements from a semiotic perspective.

This Land is Mine, composed by Kelly and Carmody, is a focal thematic track that is pivotal to the overall themes in the movie (and the other songs also gravitate towards the sentiments that are introduced by this song). The song introduces specific characterisations of the white farmer (played by

181

Paul Kelly) and the Aboriginal tracker (played by Kelton Pell) and establishes a relationship between them based on their individual struggles. The song is performed on screen directly after the farmer/father turns the tracker away from 'his' property and subsequently the search for the missing girl. The song thereby deals with issues of race and reveals the prejudice held by the father. While they share few scenes together, the effect of the farmer on the tracker and vice versa is continually reinforced by musical and filmic images used in *One Night The Moon*. As Romeril has identified, this process was inscribed in the song from the beginning:

> *'This Land is Mine' was always going to be a duet idea. And Kevin and Paul wrote ... it together. It was a white man and a black man [who] have a discussion in a song and in a song the lines between are drawn ... In Paul's case he tends to write character. Whereas the voice in Kev's pieces is more often an abstract eye. And often more spiritual and metaphysical.* (in Millard, 2001a: online)

In the introduction to the song, a guitar and string section performs a high tremolo (rapid vibrational) pattern. This rapid movement between notes of small intervals creates tension to echo the tension on screen. Throughout the song, the strings move in a stepwise nature and use small semi-tonal intervals. Similarly, when the guitar enters after the second verse it echoes the small stepwise interval movement of the strings. Using slides and tremolo, the conjunctive movement of the strings and guitar generates an edgy mood to enhance the sequence of events in the film.

Befitting the importance of racial themes in the movie, particular instruments highlight the racial and cultural differences between the father and the tracker. Violins are used alongside Kelly's vocal and suggest his character's Anglo-Celtic heritage. Similarly, the didjeridu is used to introduce Pell's vocal, and becomes a sonic metaphor for Aboriginality as a whole. Despite the fact that the didjeridu was traditionally used only in a relatively small area of northern Australia, its sonic weight is such that audiences (whether Australian or international) tend to automatically associate it with representations of Aboriginality (and/or indigeneity) in general, as Kibby and Neuenfeldt observe:

> *The didjeridu has become the dominant symbol of Aboriginality ... It has been adopted by non-Aboriginals, not only as the primary signifier of Aboriginality, but also as an indicator of 'otherness', a signifier of a primitive spirituality and of an exotic landscape.* (1998: 67)

In *One Night The Moon*, the sound of the didjeridu is used to signify to the audience the presence of an 'other', in this case, the tracker, who represents an alternative perspective to the father. It also evokes the land itself as the physical object that is being contested between the father and the tracker. In evoking the landscape, the use of the didjeridu also calls into play the Aboriginal concept of land as instilled with spiritual presence. At the conclusion of *This Land is Mine* the didjeridu continues to drone after the other instruments have stopped playing. This sound is accompanied by the image and sound effects of two eagles circling above the characters. With the closing line of "They won't take it [ie the land] away from me", the tracker looks up to the sky to see the birds above. Kibby and Neuenfeldt argue that the didjeridu is grouped with sound effects, such as birdcalls, in order to construct it as part of the ambient sound (ibid: 74). The image of the birds, coupled with the use of the didjeridu, relates to the tracker's previous song line that "rock, water, animal, tree" are all part of his connection with the land. This image serves to connect the didjeridu with Aboriginal notions of land and spirituality. The vocals take primacy in the mix of this track, perhaps because the lyrical content is important in establishing the characters for the audience. The vocal approaches employed by the two singers are also used to indicate the differences of their characters. Kelly draws on a forced, heightened, 'head' voice, which, coupled with the use of strings, creates tension and reflects the father's anger, prejudice and emotion of losing his daughter. In contrast, Pell employs a restrained, almost whispering vocal delivery that is indicative of his character's frustration and sadness on being rejected because of his Aboriginality.

In relation to this song, it is the perspective towards the land that is being contested. While the father sings "this land is mine", the tracker responds by singing "this land is *me*" (emphasis added). Their different perceptions of the land and philosophies of ownership are accentuated by the difference in instrumentation between the strings (representing the farmer) and the didjeridu (representing the tracker). When the didjeridu is first heard, it indicates the presence of the tracker as he begins his response to the father's claim that the land is his. Along with the didjeridu, the guitar and double bass are heard and begin a steady rhythm with a strong accent on the first beat. These rhythmic accents work on a semiotic level to create a steady marching feel, indicative of the movement of the search party leaving the homestead to find the missing girl. This strong rhythmical movement may also reflect another signifier of Aboriginality. A western audience may associate a continuous, steady and repetitive rhythm with traditional Aboriginal music (ibid: 66), further accentuating the differences that are being established between the tracker and the non-Aboriginal characters.

Another focal thematic passage is the instrumental track *Moon Child*, composed by Mairead Hannan. While the track uses voices, these express wordless vocal melodies and can be regarded as instrumental elements. This track is prominent in the film because it has a distinct and recognisable tonal quality, and it is played to accompany full-screen images of the moon in the night sky. *Moon Child* recurs throughout the film and has particular links to three characters: the missing daughter (played by Memphis Kelly), the mother (Kaarin Fairfax) and the tracker. The theme is also significant because it provides a musical contrast to the scene that immediately precedes it. *Moon Child* directly follows the scene in which the mother and father sing a lullaby (*One Night the Moon*) to their daughter. The song serves to emphasise the love shared by them. Romeril initially conceived the song functionally ("as a good idea for the band to sing the kid to sleep" [in Millard, 2001a: online]). The light and simple melody of the lullaby, coupled with the sweet tonality of the mandolin accompaniment, fulfill this brief by creating a calm and happy atmosphere. Romeril also considered an irony to the song, in that "the kid's fascination with the moon had grown from her parents singing her this song and, what do you know, one night she actually does follow the moon" (ibid). The song's lyrics, written by Romeril and Kelly, inscribe this, relating that:

One night the moon came a sailing by
Called all the dreamers to come for a ride

and thereby hinting at the drama that is to unfold. The lullaby sequence works to establish a happy family image that slowly breaks down over the course of the narrative. This process begins with the disappearance of the daughter to the strains of *Moon Child*[4].

Moon Child is played alongside the visual image of the daughter as she wakes with moonlight streaming across her bed, climbs out of her bedroom window and follows the moon across the ranges, seemingly entranced by it. *Moon Child* is performed acapella by Mairead and Deirdre Hannan and contains no other instrumentation, save for a low whistle at the conclusion of the track. Two voices begin singing a 'mmmm' sound, five semi-tones apart. The higher voice continues singing one note while the lower voice proceeds to hum a melodic line with a conjunctive movement. This quickly becomes layered, with many voices singing various melodic lines that occur simultaneously and move independently of the others. This polyphonic texture creates a rich and full sound, building a breathy but smooth tonal colour. This leads into a layer of many voices singing a somewhat dissonant chordal 'ahhh'. More vocal layers are added and slide into another dissonant chord, which becomes louder and leads to a prominent 'lead voice' that takes the centre of the audio mix. This voice becomes the feature melodic line of the track intoning 'da da dum' syllables. Its melodic tonal quality is reminiscent of traditional Celtic music, with the use of slides and trills. Other voices are added to harmonise with it, culminating in the use of a low whistle, which complements the main melodic line, at the conclusion of the track.

These aspects create a haunting and eerie texture, which evokes the romantic colonial image of the 'lost child' and reflects the image of the moon 'calling' the girl towards it. The use of vocal layers, dissonant chords, slides and trills create an almost un-earthly sound, signaling the heavenly flight of the moon. The use of multi-layered vocals suggests the sound of an 'angelic choir', an image often aligned with the heavens. While this track is played, the visuals show the young girl following the moon, running across the ranges towards a rocky outcrop. However, reprises of this theme occur throughout the film, mainly whenever there is a direct close-up of the moon. This musical theme thus comes to signify the moon itself and, in doing so, the audience responds to the moon as a character in the narrative. Not only does this musical theme signal the moon, it is also linked to the characters of the mother, daughter and the tracker. It is used to communicate each character's development and how the moon itself has affected them. For the mother, the *Moon Child* theme is played at various stages throughout the film when she has flashbacks to memorable moments with her daughter. In one scene, she is looking across the ranges from the veranda and the sight of the clothesline reminds her of chasing games with the girl in the backyard.

Another scene features the mother in the kitchen reminiscing about her daughter helping her roll pastry. On both occasions the theme underscores the flashback sequences.

The other character to which this song is aligned is the Aboriginal tracker, Albert. When the moon appears in the visuals alongside Albert, the audience is reminded of his knowledge that the missing girl has followed the moon. After a confrontation at the farmhouse with the mother, in which Albert signals to her that he knows where her daughter might be, Albert returns to his campfire. *Moon Child* is played while Albert looks up at the moon through the trees. Played in this context, the theme signals that the presence of the moon weighs heavily upon the tracker. The final time *Moon Child* is heard is when Albert and the mother begin the search for the child together. After Albert explains, "Emily followed the moon, kids follow light", the full moon rears up above the rocky outcrop accompanied by the track. When heard this time, the audience is assured that a conclusion to the narrative is approaching. This is because the sonic power of *Moon Child* links the moon, the tracker, the mother and the daughter together, for each of these players relies on the others for resolution.

In looking at the two focal thematic tracks *This Land Is Mine* and *Moon Child*, we can see how music can function as effective narrative cues. However, music also has the power to affect the audience's reception of the 'other'. As the film largely explores issues of race, a dichotomy has been established within the narrative between self and other. In *One Night The Moon*, notions of otherness have been inflected by the use of music. Throughout the film, music illustrates differences in culture and perspective by drawing on colonial and (limited) Aboriginal cultural signifiers. It can be argued that both the music and visual aspects of the film have relied upon broad cultural stereotypes in order to translate issues of cultural difference. For instance, the lyrical content of the song *This Land Is Mine* communicates both metaphorically and literally a Black / White relationship to the land. The 'white' perspective of the farmer relates land as a commodity, something he "signed on the dotted line" to purchase. Whereas the 'other'/'black' perspective of the tracker refrains that "this land owns me". I have also previously remarked on how the didjeridu has been used alongside the character of the tracker to define him as the 'other' and how it has been employed in a limited capacity to communicate a kind of pan-Aboriginality. Similarly, the predominant use of specific Anglo-Celtic instrumentation and performance styles solidifies the cultural identity of the Euro-Australian settlers and positions them within a specific historical context. These perspectives highlight the filmmakers' reliance upon essentialisms in order to communicate cultural identity.

Representation

Questioning how music represents cultural formations raises many issues. One perspective of this debate could argue that the collaborative team on *One Night The Moon* have not employed more complex representations of Aboriginality and have preferred to rely on stereotypes and essentialisms perhaps to communicate specifically to a white audience. This could be taken to mean that, however stylistically imaginative, the film has not attempted to 'push the boundaries' of the representation of cultural identity. This is not to say that the film does not communicate the history of oppression and displacement of minority cultures in a western world, in fact it is *through* the coupling of music and image that *One Night The Moon* has attempted to show precisely these problematic issues. However, it must be asked if – in the homogenising practice of re-using tried and tested cultural stereotypes in film – it runs the risk of alienating a heterogeneous group and, worse, perpetuating misunderstandings of cultural identity.

Another reading of the way music has been used in this film may indicate that the filmmakers have attempted to communicate the reality of the dispossession of Aboriginal cultural practices. The music in the film is heavily embedded within western modes of musical practice with the style and instrumentation of predominantly Anglo-Celtic origin. Despite the use of the didjeridu, traditional Aboriginal music styles have not been incorporated into the music track or narrative. It raises the issue of why traditional Aboriginal music has been eschewed when Aboriginal cultural issues form major themes. John Castles terms this discourse "the traditional-contemporary problem" (1992: 25). Castles has argued that the labeling of Aboriginal music with terms such as 'traditional' and 'contemporary' "expresses a wish to deny the irreversibility of this contact" (ibid). It is problematic to classify such music in these terms because the very act of performing "traditional" music has taken on new layers of meaning since European settlement (ibid). In this sense, music in the film may serve to communicate the affects of colonisation upon Aboriginal people.

It is pertinent, in this regard, that the film was set in the 1930s, a time in Australia's history when many Aboriginal people were forced into missions and 'mixed-race' Aboriginal children were forcibly removed from their families[5]. Through such means, cultural forms such as music and language began to break down. While the subject material of the film deals with notions of power and racial inequality, *One Night The Moon* can be situated within a contemporary context of social and political issues surrounding land rights, the 'stolen generation' and current Prime Minister John Howard's refusal to say 'sorry' for past atrocities committed against indigenous Australians. That director Rachel Perkins is the daughter of the late Charles Perkins, one of the forefathers of the Aboriginal social rights movement, is not insignificant in this context. A crucial element of the film is the farmer's racist rejection of the black tracker. This aspect of the film metaphorically depicts the history of the dispossession of Aboriginal communities and invites comparison to how, in contemporary society, issues of Aboriginal rights are still fiercely contested. The Reconciliation movement, which includes the desire for the current Australian government to apologise on behalf of past governments for their treatment of Aboriginal peoples, is also highlighted within the film. The song *Unfinished Business*, sung as a duet by the mother and the tracker, at once signals the unfinished business of finding the daughter but, in a broader sense, signals the unfinished business of the Reconciliation movement (Probyn and Simpson, 2002) and the notion of difference between indigenous and non-indigenous Australians:

Unfinished business
Keeping us sleepless
Unfinished business
You and me

The ballad based musical style of a large part of the music track is dictated by the contributions of Kelly and Carmody[6]. Their positions as significant songwriters within Australia is, to an extent, deployed politically within *One Night The Moon*. Both are renowned for their public support of indigenous social rights, and their music has often dealt with such issues. The use of such artists is significant for an Australian audience, as their profiles deliver and support the political and social messages within the film.

One Night The Moon also includes musical performances that express the historical impact of colonisation on music. Aboriginal musician Ruby Hunter performs a Christian hymn *O Breathe on Me* during the funeral scene at the conclusion of the movie. The CD notes state that the song is based on "an ancient Irish melody" with lyrics by Edwin Hatch, and is sung acapella by Hunter in the character of the tracker's wife. The performance of this hymn indicates the influence of Christian missionaries on Aboriginal religious beliefs and also on musical performance. But there is no sense that Hunter's character is borrowing her song from another culture. Rather, her strong and intense performance reinvigorates it through its adoption into Aboriginal culture. Hunter sings in a low-pitched, resonant voice, at a slow and measured pace. Her vocalisation is muted to the point where the 'message' of the hymn is carried by its timbre, sonic texture and emotional weight rather than its lyrics.

As previously discussed, there is also a scene in the film where a gathering of Aboriginal people plays 'non-traditional' instruments. I have suggested that this scene might be read as evoking the manner in which colonial practices have irrevocably altered 'traditional' Aboriginal music culture. Yet the scene also suggests that culture is not a static object. The adoption of new styles into cultural forms indicates that culture is a receptive and interactive construct. Philip Hayward has identified this with regard to the Ngaro people's reassertion of their cultural identity in the Whitsunday Islands. During a discussion of contemporary Ngaro people's use of the didjeridu, Hayward raised the issue of how its use represented a local adoption of a pan-Aboriginal cultural form (rather than a revival of past practices). Unconcerned, an indigenous informant responded by stating that the instrument had now been adopted into modern Ngaro culture – a point Hayward took to illustrate that this group perceived culture "as a living, adaptive and reactive form rather than a museumified referent" (2001: 173).

Examining the use of music in *One Night The Moon*, it is apparent that the music track is not a subservient element of the narrative process. It was the conscious ambition of the filmmakers to use music as a vehicle to inform thematic sequences and dramatic highlights. The ranges of music used in the film, including instrumentals, diegetic music and focal thematic music, have all been employed in aid of communicating meaning to the audience. Especially in the second half of the film, music carries the narrative on an emotional level. As producer Kevin Lucas suggests, "what the music demands is for us to allow the space to work so that we can emotionally relate to something and not intellectualise it" (op cit, 2001). This signals how film music *can* operate on an unconscious level, influencing our reception of the events on screen.

One Night The Moon's achievement and originality resides in the extent to which narrative is brought to life by the music track and conveyed in richer, more associative ways than usual in mainstream cinema. In addition, the film exploits the manner by which music is integrally implicated with culture and social change. In this sense, the emotional content of the music is enhanced by a cultural awareness of and identification with the actual performances. Thus *One Night The Moon*, through its music content, musical style and performance, represents a complex set of referents operating on several levels.

> Thanks to Philip Hayward for his comments on an earlier draft of this chapter.

Notes

1. In 1997 Music Drama Television was initiated by head of ABC Arts & Entertainment (and musician/composer) Paul Grabowsky with Opera Australia's R&D division, OzOpera, and music and dance documentary production company MusicArtsDance (MAD Films), who wanted to develop a series of opera-films. Rather than commission artists directly, advertisements invited artists to form their own creative teams and develop ideas around the creation of a film project that had music especially commissioned for it. Aanya Whitehead of MAD Films recalls that, "The music had to be developed exactly along the lines of a script in order to drive the story. We wanted the music to completely influence the story and vice versa" (*One Night The Moon* production notes, 2001: 4). *One Night The Moon* was one of four out of 270 submissions to be produced, and the first of the series.

2. Litson observes that, "Kelly was initially involved in the project as a musician rather than an actor, but Perkins had seen him act on stage in Adelaide years ago and was keen to cast him as father. He was initially reluctant and insisted on an audition... [I]t was a bit of an embarrassing process for everyone, but he came across really well." (2001: 11).

3. Especially *Strictly Ballroom* (1992); and *Moulin Rouge* (2002).

4. The relationship of the three family characters is also strengthened by the fact that Kelly's actual wife and daughter play those characters in the film. The emotional bond between these characters is thus particularly poignant throughout the film.

5. An issue discussed in the chapter examining *Rabbit-Proof Fence*, elsewhere in this volume.

6. Carmody was taken from his parents (Irish father and Murri mother) at age ten and raised in a Christian school.

Chapter Twelve

TRANSCENDENT VOICES: Choral Music in *Paradise Road*

JUDE MAGEE

The narrative of Bruce Beresford's 1997 feature film *Paradise Road* relates the history, based loosely on fact, of a group of mostly European women (including Australian nurses), captured and held in Sumatra by Japanese soldiers after the fall of Singapore in 1942. These women relieve the seemingly unendurable brutality and stress of imprisonment by forming a 'vocal orchestra' that renders wordless arrangements of popular classics. In effect, the choral voice is able to emerge as a heroic character in the film. However the female acapella sound is only one of the musical forces contributing to the film. Popular music of the period, the Japanese anthem and a folk song, music by Edward Elgar and Gustav Holst, and original music by Australian composer Ross Edwards (written both in his own style, and in that of Elgar) are all used to evoke potent imagery while giving voice to dualities of subjugation and impotence, masculinity and femininity, exoticism and familiarity, Europe and Asia.

Paradise Road's music track clearly shows that film music can present the voice of the characters but also act as an independent heroic character in its own right. This is particularly evident in the choral music that poses several analytical questions. How is it that the choral voice is able to speak so intimately, and inspire such a potent emotional response in this film? Is it the choice of the popular classics, with their inherent associations, or the narrative role of the music that gives it strength? Is it the privileging of the music within the diegesis, or its placement in relation to image that allows the choral music to impact so strongly on the affect? To explore these questions in detail, choral cues will be analysed for their narrative impact, their musical function, the way musical sound interacts with the image, and the implications of their placement at specific points in the drama. Further, the interrelated association and affect of 'acapella', 'female', and 'popular classical' music will be examined.

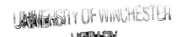

Film Background

Residual memories of Japanese treatment of Allied prisoners during World War II have lingered in the Australian psyche, as well as in English and American literature, resulting in a number of filmic representations. The first was based on Nevil Shute's novel *A Town Like Alice* (dir: Jack Lee, 1956), followed closely by *The Bridge On The River Kwai* (dir: David Lean, 1957) and *King Rat* (dir: Bryan Forbes, 1965). The first two films feature orchestral scores typical of 1950s Hollywood by Matyas Seiber and Malcolm Arnold, while *King Rat* features an early, and very restrained, John Barry score. These films make no musical reference to the Japanese at all. A Japanese perspective appeared with *Merry Christmas Mr Lawrence* (dir: Nagisa Oshima, 1982) featuring a synthesiser score by Ryuchi Sakamoto that was influenced more by popular music than traditional Japanese music but given an 'Oriental' flavour through the use of pentatonic scales and parallel fourth movement.

Since the 1980s there have been four television series dealing with the subject: the Australian production of *A Town Like Alice* (dir: David Stevens, 1981) and the BBC/ABC production of *Tenko* (dir: Pennant Roberts, 1981), both dealing with POW camps for women; the parallel story of Japanese prisoners of war in Australia in Kennedy Miller's *Cowra Breakout* (dir: Phillip Noyce and Chris Noonan, 1985), and, in 2002, the ABC production of John Doyle's *Changi* (dir: Kate Woods, 2001). Most of these productions have applied a clichéd use of the traditional Japanese scale (with flattened second and sixth notes) along with ersatz shakuhachi and shamisen sounds combined with western orchestra to evoke images of Japanese characters and situations. Only the last of these, *Changi*, features music as central to the plot, in common with *Paradise Road*.

Beresford's *Paradise Road* was released in 1997. Featuring a strong western female ensemble cast (including Glenn Close, Frances McDormand, Pauline Collins, Jennifer Ehle, Wendy Hughes and Cate Blanchett in her first full length feature role), it was inspired initially by Beresford's response to a recording from a Perth memorial concert for nurses interned in camps in Malaya during World War II:

> *Despite the technical imperfections, the effect of the music was so overwhelming, and so sublime, that I immediately became obsessed with the idea of a film telling the story of its creation.* (in Unattributed, 1997: unpaginated[1])

Beresford and producer Sue Milliken researched the story (loosely based on a version by David Giles and Martin Meader[2]) over two years, referring to published and unpublished diaries, and interviewing around twenty survivors from the Japanese camps in Australia, England, Holland and the United States.

The original 'vocal orchestra' was the creation of Norah Chambers (Royal Academy trained wife of a government engineer in Malaya) and Margaret Dryburgh (English missionary, piano teacher, organist and choir director who had served in China and Hong Kong). Chambers assisted Dryburgh in recreating from memory the scores of over thirty popular orchestral works, notating and teaching them in secret to a group of about thirty singers. The choir performed over twelve months from December 1943, until about half of the members, including Dryburgh, had died from tropical diseases or starvation. It is on record that for members of the vocal orchestra, singing was:

> the most wonderful thing that has happened in this camp ... to sit on logs or stools or tables in the crude old attap-roofed kitchen, with only one light, and then to be lifted right out of that atmosphere with this music is sheer joy. It is so easy to forget one is a prisoner. (Jeffrey, 1954: 87)

The first of a number of post war re-creations of these scores was performed in Palo Alto, California in 1982. A later recording, inspired by a Dutch survivor, *Song Of Survival* by the Malle Babbe Choir from Holland (directed by Leny van Schaik), was incorporated into the film music track[3]. Beresford required that actresses (auditioned for singing ability even though they are never heard) mime the parts[4]. In Australia, vocal orchestras inspired by the original music have been established in Sydney and Hobart (Benzie, 2002: 12). The fact that vocal orchestra members' prohibited copies of the manuscripts survived the camps, and that these scores are used 'authentically' in the music track for *Paradise Road* intensifies the emotional impact of the music and the strength of the film.

The music for the vocal orchestra, while critical to the narrative, is only one aspect of the total music score for *Paradise Road* and, before examining it in detail, it is pertinent to first discuss the various roles and functions that other music plays in the film. Music appears both within the diegesis (within the hearing of or performed by the characters) and as underscore, audible only to the audience.

Outline of Music Cues

There are four styles of diegetic music that do not use the vocal orchestra: a Noel Coward song, the Japanese National Anthem, a dance band recording, and a Japanese folk song. The narrative opens at Raffles Hotel in Singapore, with a typical dinner dance band of the era playing Noel Coward's torch song *Mad About The Boy* (1933)[5]. The song establishes the era, underscoring conversations around the ballroom involving each of the principal players, establishing their social status, occupations, relationships, and confident attitudes towards the war. In particular, the lyric of the song invites reference to Rosemary's (Jennifer Ehle) passionate love affair with her husband, and Susan (Cate Blanchett) and the other nurses' passing involvements with soldiers they may never see again. The music is interrupted by the first bombs exploding in Singapore but struggles on, before being interrupted with the news that Singapore, against all odds, has been invaded.

The next use of diegetic music is the wind-up gramophone recording (rather old and scratchy) of the Japanese National Anthem played at the initial roll call (tenko) in the women's first POW camp. It is used to establish the dominance of the invaders and the alienness of the place for the prisoners. However the fact that the period recording is played by a military band in a western arrangement speaks much for the cultural imperialism of the West preceding the era in which the film is set.

The third use of diegetic music is when a needle is dropped onto a recording of Thomas Connor singing *When You Come Home Again*, a dance band arrangement with crooning lyric of a popular American ballad style song of the period[6]. The context however is that the younger women prisoners must choose whether or not to live in relative comfort in a brothel for the Japanese officers. The irony of the choice of song is not pronounced but nevertheless evident.

The fourth, and most interesting, use of diegetic music occurs after the first performance of the vocal orchestra. In this extraordinary scene, the sadistic guard Sergeant Tomiashi, known as 'The Snake' (Clyde Kusatsu), isolates Adrienne (Glenn Close) from the rest of a working party and takes her into the forest. The terrified woman is expecting violence. What unfolds is a rendition by Snake of a traditional Japanese folk ballad, *Itsuki no Komoriuta* ('Lullaby of Itsuki'), from the Itsuki village (in the Kumamoto region of Kyushu). The song itself, popularised (particularly by geisha singer Otomaru) in Japan after the end of the War, was selected by composer Ross Edwards and director Bruce Beresford for the scene[7] but, coincidentally, was also used by the actor Kusatsu for his audition. It is a lament variously describing the woes of poor girls who were sold by their parents[8], or a song of woe by a baby nurse ill-treated by her employers. As a narrative about loss, it might be construed as Snake's subconscious fear for the dissolution of Japanese culture or that the Japanese could lose the war. The guttural, gravelly bass pitches and slides so characteristic of traditional Japanese folk music, together with the language that neither the character Adrienne nor most of the western audience understand, combine to provide a striking contrast to the high, rather airy female sound of the vocal orchestra in the film. The implication is that, while Snake is enemy, and 'superior' to the European female prisoners – Daisy opines that Japanese invaders most despised Europeans, "then prisoners, then women" – he does have a softer side. He is also a man of culture, and recognises this strength in the women (despite the song's content about women and violence). He too is able to express himself with music but only in secret, away from his peers and the other prisoners. In this way, the narrative role of the music addresses complexities of orientalist discourses by exploring representations of the 'East', relationships of power between East and West, and the limitations imposed by them (see Said, 1978). Later, the camp commander requests the vocal orchestra to perform Japanese songs but Adrienne refuses.

These examples of diegetic music help create mood, assist in establishing location and time, position the audience in relation to character, and carry a subtle interchange with the visual images, either underlining or contradicting the narrative. The underscore also plays a potent role in determining audience response, and falls into three clear categories: British concert music, Edwards's cues in the style of Elgar, and Edwards's stylistically identifiable cues.

The first utilises British concert music by Holst and Elgar. Scenes following the first bombs in Singapore, until the bombing and stranding of the women and children at sea, are accompanied by two long musical cues. The first is from the opening of *Adagio* from Elgar's *Cello Concerto in E minor, Op 85* (1919), followed by an excerpt from *Jupiter, Bringer of Jollity*, from *The Planets Suite* by Holst (1916). Both works represent high points in the English music renaissance that occurred in the late 19th and early 20th centuries. The melody of the Holst work, in particular, has become an anthem-like hymn and has been used in many contexts to arouse or represent feelings of British patriotism. The Elgar excerpt, with its subtle but rich chromatic harmonic language and persistent use of sequential repetition, is more haunting and poignant. Kenneth McLeish suggests that the Elgar work "epitomized the Edwardian imperial twilight in sound" (1985: 326), while Grout observes that Elgar's music is:

> not in the least touched by folk song nor has it any technical charac-
> teristics that seem to derive from the national musical tradition. Yet it
> "sounds English". It has been suggested that this may be due to the
> resemblance between Elgar's typical melodic line (wide leaps and a
> falling trend ...) and the intonation patterns of British speech. (Grout,
> 1960: 595)

Significantly too, Simon Rattle discusses how Elgar was able, in the *Cello Concerto*, to "express a sense of loss by recalling earlier material as if it were a memory to be lingered over" (in Hall, 1996: 2) and to convey "the feeling that the world he loved was slipping away" with contradictions in the music pointing "to the fact that all the old certainties were evaporating" (ibid: 35).

Certainly, both works represent western cultural imperialism: the strength of the British Empire, and the 'stiff upper lip' approach to adversity. It is not until the music from *Jupiter* stops abruptly, with three of the principal characters (Susan, Adrienne and Rosemary) afloat together somewhere in the Malay Straits, that there is an acknowledgement that the Empire has indeed taken a blow. The theme from the Elgar concerto is also used later in the film, as a point of cultural recognition between Adrienne and Margaret 'Daisy' Drummond (Pauline Collins) when the idea of the vocal orchestra first begins to take shape.

The second category of underscore consists of cues written by composer Ross Edwards in the style of Elgar. This music is scored for string orchestra, using the simple rhythms, the soaring violin melodies and the sweet poignant harmonies characteristic of Elgar's music. These cues are used to underscore ideas associated with the women and their clinging to 'civilisa-tion': their march to the prison camp; Rosemary's intense love for her husband; their response to the funeral for Wing, a Malay woman set on fire by Captain Tanaka (Stan Egi) after black marketeering to obtain quinine for the women; the deaths of Mrs O'Riordan (Lia Scallon) and Daisy; and the arduous journey to the final remote and more primitive camp.

The third category of underscore music is notably based on Edward's own composition style[9]. Characteristic short, intense ostinati, rhythmic gestures made up of repeated textural clusters, patterns with constant time signature changes (modeled on the unmetred repetitive sounds of insects in the bush) and idiosyncratic use of piano, clarinet and percussion with strings and brass may be found in many of his scores, particularly *The Tower of*

Remoteness (1978), *Yarrageh* (1989) and *Symphony Da Pacem Domine* (1991). In addition, his writing for shakuhachi player Riley Lee and percussionist Ian Clements, both specialists in the music of Japan, adds traditional elements of improvisation, complex metre, and characteristic timbres that identify and represent the non-European, the alien, the other.

All of the instrumental and recorded music cues, both diegetic and non-diegetic, are intimately tied to the narrative. However the music of the vocal orchestra exists as much more, becoming a central character in the unfolding of the story.

The Vocal Orchestra

The manner in which the vocal music plays a privileged role in the narrative associates the film with the structure of a musical. But while the characters sing, the choral score is not a commentary on or addition to the action: indeed it is wordless. In this form, it is an integral element of both the narrative and the diegesis.

The music of the vocal orchestra functions at different points in the film as diegetic, non-diegetic, and extra-diegetic (moving between events while the music is performed 'onscreen'). It is used diegetically in the various rehearsals and performances that provide such a strong component of the narrative structure. However it also appears outside the diegesis, in an underscore role, and extra-diegetically to highlight events occurring away from the diegesis in which the music is audible. There are only five music cues in which the choir is actually featured (not including the two short rehearsal scenes which are disrupted by the Japanese guards, and the 'warm up' for the first performance) yet the choral music exists as an undercurrent to the whole entity. In fact, the first vocal orchestra cue does not occur until halfway through the film.

The musical pieces performed by the vocal orchestra and their relationship to the narrative and diegesis are in the table overleaf.

Having detailed how the vocal orchestra cues appear in the film, in the next section I will explore the sets of affects they offer.

Vocal Orchestra: Affective Devices

In addition to describing the narrative action that any given piece of music score accompanies, it is also essential to ascertain what the music is actually doing, that is, how it is functioning structurally, and how it is creating meaning for the audience. Aaron Copland (1949) proposed five basic functions of music score as being: to create atmosphere, time and place; to develop psychological states; to accent buildup and denouement; to assist in continuity; and to provide neutral background filler. Claudia Gorbman (1987) posited seven principles of composition, mixing and editing: that music should be invisible, inaudible (that is subordinate to dialogue and visuals), that it should signify emotions, interpret and illustrate narrative events, provide continuity, indicate point of view, and establish setting and character. Her seventh, and perhaps most important, principle is that:

> *a given film score may violate any of the principles above, providing the violation is at the service of the other principles.* (Gorbman, 1987: 73)

194

Table 1: Vocal Orchestra Performed Items

Title	Composer	Narrative	Duration	Diegetic function
Largo from *Symphony No 5 in E minor, "From The New World"*	Antonin Dvorak (1841–1904)	First performance of the vocal orchestra in the camp (immediately after Adrienne's beating and imprisonment in cage).	3:15	Diegetic-some listeners in view of the vocal orchestra, others about the camp, but all able to 'hear' the singing.
Andante Cantabile from *String Quartet No 1 in D major*	Peter Ilich Tchaikovsky (1840–1893)	Rosemary leaves camp illicitly to meet her husband/shots of choir singing earnestly.	2:31	Moving between diegetic and non-diegetic at first, then purely as underscore.
Prelude Op 28 No 20 in C minor, "Funeral March"	Frederic Chopin (1810–1849)	Final phase of Susan's torture (second day) – Tanaka prepares to behead her but, on the final chord, only cuts off a lock of hair.	1:06	Non-diegetic
Bolero	Maurice Ravel (1875–1937)	Susan released. Performance to whole camp, foregrounding Commander, interpreter, doctor, Snake, guards, as willing audience.	1:57	Non-diegetic as Susan is released. Extra-diegetic – time passes. Diegetic as the camp listens to performance. Insertion of a piece of (genuine?) handwritten score.
Country Gardens	Percy Grainger (1882–1914)	End of the War. Moves between images of jubilation as the Japanese leave, and a flashback to a concert performance by the vocal orchestra in earlier days, focusing on members who have since died.	1:19	Diegetic/Extra-diegetic
Londonderry Air	Traditional	Underscores text on screen outlining the fate of the women, the vocal orchestra itself and the use of original scores in the film, then end credits. Followed by orchestral arrangement of same tune.	2:27	End credits

195

Further to this, she observes that music functions in three distinct ways: as pure musical code (with all of the inherent expectations and cultural associations of concert music); as cultural code, conforming to Hollywood practice and expectations; and to cinematic code, where placement of a music cue determines the meaning of the music. Given that it is often only heard subconsciously, music is easily able to move in and out of the diegesis, to multi-task, to mask contradictions and provide emotional contexts and thematic, dramatic, rhythmic and structural continuity.

> *Its freedom from the explicitness of language or photographic images, its useful denotative and expressive values easily comprehended by listeners raised in the nineteenth-century orchestral tradition, its mal-leability, its spatial rhythmic, and temporal values, give it a special and complex status in the narrative film experience.* (ibid: 55)

To observe how these codes are functioning in *Paradise Road*, some general observations must be made about the impact of the vocal orchestra cues. They are all performed by an acapella (unaccompanied) women's choir in four parts (soprano 1 and 2, and alto 1 and 2). They represent selections from the 'popular classics' of the late 19th and early 20th Century, and are performed without lyrics. Only six songs are used (the last for the end credits), a total of about 12 minutes of music (from total of about 40 minutes of music) – and yet the dominance of the music seems much greater, perhaps because it is so much in the foreground of the narrative.

That music activities sustained prisoners in camps such as Changi and the European camp where Messiaen's *Quartet for the End of Time* was first performed, is historical fact. But these prisoners had access to instruments, however poor. The women in the Japanese camps had no such luxury. The choice of acapella singing, though currently popular (and therefore a point of connection with the film's audience) was not an artistic choice but a necessity. Indeed, part of the attraction, the affinity that a listener has with this film, may be directly attributed to the lack of instruments. It is a symbol of the dispossession the women were suffering, and of their ability to rise above the absence of the trappings of western civilisation. Although there is an instrumental underscore, what attracts the audience's ear is the sound of acapella voices, of raw music coming 'from the heart'.

Singing is something that everyone can do at some level. It is a bodily expression beyond speech that is not mediated through a musical instru-ment. For many people, engagement in group singing makes the whole experience more intense as the visceral nature of singing is shared. The current rise of community choirs in Australia and abroad is a well-docu-mented phenomenon[10]. Geraldine Doogue, in her presentation of the tele-vised documentary *The Gift of Song* (2003)[11] found that:

> *Those who sing with others find that the experience fosters tolerance and acceptance and a sense of connection not found easily in other activities. For many, its power remains inexplicable, yet intensely rewarding, and points to something bigger than self.*

In the same documentary, community choir director Jane Rigby dis-cusses her experience:

It's a sense you have – it's partly the 'high' that singing gives you – you get a sense that you're lifted to another plane. You feel uplifted and often really quite strongly elated with that experience of group singing. And you're not quite sure where your spirit is but it soars somewhere. It fills us with a sense of hope.

Aspects of the representation of the vocal orchestra such as the conductor's role and the singers' performative and body movements are glimpsed onscreen but the music track more potently carries information about singing as an enriching activity. Singing affects the human condition at different levels: physical, intellectual, emotional, aesthetic, cultural and spiritual. On a physical level, singing stimulates the heart and lungs, activating endorphins in much the same way as sporting activity[12]. On an intellectual level, a high degree of concentration, discipline and teamwork is required, particularly for complex rhythmic and harmonic expression, as well as the conscious control of physical attributes such as breathing, and volume and tone control. At an emotional level singing permits the expression of thoughts, feelings and desires that are often beyond articulation. On a cultural level singing allows groups of people to express their idea of community through mutually meaningful activity[13]. In the actual camp (and the film), singing allowed the women to express a facet of western civilisation that was forbidden by their captors in most other arenas. Singing thus became both a symbolic and an active resistance to their imprisonment. On a spiritual level, singing has long been associated with an expression of the soul, and a means of connecting with god/s in both Christian and non-Christian traditions. In *The Gift of Song* video Reverend Gordon Bannon observes:

when we sing, when I sing, I am somehow connected in a way beyond words, to that holy other. To me, singing connects me with the deeper part of myself that I can't touch through reading, through thinking, through praying with words, even through silence. It takes me to a deeper sacred space.

In the film *Paradise Road*, as in real life, singing provides a means of escape, however temporary, from the pain of starvation, separation, deprivation and isolation. The title of the film was taken from a poem by Margaret Dryburgh, quoted in the film, in which the term 'Paradise Road' is a metaphor for release from travail, a euphemism for death. That ordinary women, finding themselves in such an extraordinary situation, could find joy and solace through singing in harmony, through the transcendent power of music, is directly connected to the six levels of activity discussed above. The episodes of singing, and the narrative associations with the singing, refer to the way in which music and shared engagement with music-making can provide sustenance and a sense of community, of solidarity. The music is represented as an enabling element, allowing the women to temporarily 'escape' their immediate situation. As such it is 'believable'.

More than just singing, though, is the recognition of the sound of the female voice – not the intensively-trained tones of opera or the highly produced technologically mediated sounds of popular music, but the recognisable timbres of ordinary women singing for enjoyment. In this form the voice is as familiar as a mother's lullaby, one that sings along with the radio or hums around the house and in the shower. It is a voice not always perfectly in tune, at times rather thin and airy. It is a personal, private voice that is identifiable from community or public and institutional singing at school, at church, in social gatherings. The screenplay emphasises that the vocal orchestra included women who had no formal musical training. Furthermore, as Tony Backhouse observes:

> *A capella choirs tend to be less formal than conventional choirs. There is no audition for some choirs. The material is generally easy to learn and sing, and singers can swap parts. They tend to learn the songs by ear and are free to sing with an untrained, 'folk' timbre.* (2003: 15)

Another point of identification that is offered by the vocal orchestra is the quality of arrangements written by the fictional Daisy Drummond (Margaret Dryburgh in real life). Working from memory, with scavenged paper and pencil, Dryburgh put together simple arrangements that an average school or community choir could perform with ease. The ranges fall comfortably into the tessitura (the reliable, unstrained part of a singing range) for untrained soprano and alto voices. The harmonies and rhythms are not complex, and relatively easy to master. Moreover, the tunes are familiar. Working in two to four parts (no doubt becoming more confident as the group increased in proficiency) the arrangements of the popular classics are simple, melodic, manageable by the amateur but, most importantly, musically convincing and effective. Dryburgh was obviously aware of the techniques for reducing a complex orchestral score to a few parts. Apart from the predominant melodies, the harmonic foundation and strong rhythmic ideas that impel the music are consistently present in her scores. In this sense, Dryburgh captured the 'essence' of the works.

In addition, the 'tunes' themselves are part of the western collective consciousness. Even though the original choral arrangements were written during World War II, the pieces and the composers are still highly popular representatives of 19th and early 20th Century classical repertoire: Dvorak's *New World Symphony* (particularly the section with the popular tune that appears in most beginner keyboard books), Ravel's *Bolero*, Chopin's 'Funeral March' *Prelude* and the evergreen *Londonderry Air* (notably sung without its 'Danny Boy' lyrics)[14]. While the tunes may be popular, the messages their cultural 'baggage' convey are far from simple because the connotations are so various, so widely spread – not just within the context of the film but for western audiences in the 20th Century. Some items evoke a cultural cringe because of their ubiquitous character. For example, Grainger's *Country Gardens*[15] (heard as the Japanese desert the prisoners–of–war camp at the end of the War) would, for many Australians of the baby-boomer generation, conjure an image of vegetable soup due to the television advertising campaign by the Edgell Soup Company in the 1950s and 1960s. This tends to diminish emotional engagement with the scenes it accompanies. Similarly, *Londonderry Air* is so common in films that its appearance supporting the final text is almost counterproductive in terms of evoking nostalgia or identification.

Anahid Kassabian (2001) posits that it is ultimately intertextuality that determines the contemporary direction of theoretical analysis of film music. Drawing on notions of perception, she argues that specific musics engage listeners differently across different cultural borders, with composers and perceivers drawing on a common heritage of meaning. Existing music used in a film brings its own history of connotation, allusion and association. It has a variety of relationships: to other music (both in and out of a film), to the film diegesis (narrative world), and to other tracks within a film. In the context of *Paradise Road*, there is a valid argument for treating the 'classical' music as 'popular' music. However, to the women in the camp, these pieces would have embodied familiarity and shared experience transcending elements of class, age, nationality and other aspects of their individual backgrounds. These works would have represented 'civilisation'.

Detailed Image/Music Cue Sequence – 'Beheading' Scene

Using one specific choir cue it is possible to examine how the music assists in creating the total narrative affect. The very short Chopin *Prelude Op. 28 No 20*, 'Funeral March' is used in the scene where Tanaka almost beheads Susan. The melody is a simple eight bar structure, using a repeated rhythm. In terms of musical code, the title alone ('Funeral March') suggests imminent death. The use of a minor key also suggests tragedy, although the modulation to the relative major in bars 3 and 4 holds out a ray of hope. The repeated, very slow two bar rhythm suggests travail. Utilising the vocal orchestra as performing media is also able to suggest the strong community support Susan is receiving from her fellow prisoners.

Table 2: Tanaka Execution Image Sequence with Music

Music section	Dramatic action	Function of the music
Bar 1	Japanese flag, symbol of conquest and domination in full glare of sun.	Segue from overnight scene, creating an atmosphere of restraint and suffering.
Bar 2	Susan's legs with spikes sticking into calves, full face suffering, falling towards sharpened spikes but pulling herself back up.	Phrase repeated as a falling sequence. Dotted rhythm represents a stumble as Susan tries not to fall.
Bar 3	Tanaka with soldiers entering compound through gate.	Melody rises. Major third as she summons the energy to save herself.
Bar 4	Prisoners watching from a distance. Adrienne close up, pan round as soldiers walk towards Susan.	Bar 3 repeated sequentially, higher this time, representing the prisoners' hope that the soldiers have come to release Susan.
Bar 5	Tanaka approaches Susan (near distance shot).	New phrase, different view. Highest note in song, but falling motif – despair.
Bar 6	Susan (head and shoulder shot) with Tanaka behind drawing sword, main characters foregrounded, gasping in shock.	Sequential, lower. Hope fades, horror grows.

Music section	Dramatic action	Function of the music
Bar 7	Tanaka lowers to Susan's neck (as if taking aim). Close up of Susan from waist up, shot of doctor's disbelief. Adrienne full screen, framed behind wooden bar. Resignation?	Reprise of opening two bars (except for first note) but with a different harmonisation.
Bar 8	Mrs Roberts – hands over face. Sword raised (hands and sword only in shot). Sun glinting on sword. Susan waits for the end. Doctor witnesses.	Perfect cadence. Final. Melody note on lower tonic.
Final chord	Full face shot as Tanaka prepares to bring sword down. He strikes with full force. Shots of women in despair – hands over faces, eyes shut, turning away, Adrienne looks to the ground.	Tonic minor chord, crescendo to very loud. Melody note on upper tonic. Chord represents shocked disbelief and terror at the act of violence. Chord also represents triumph – Tanaka's triumph over the women, even if he has only frightened them into believing that he has executed Susan.
Silence	Lock of Susan's hair falls to the ground.	Silence: Allows the fact that he never intended to behead her sink in but how he wished to torture her.

In terms of Hollywood cultural code, the music affect is held, intense, and highly emotive. The marked crescendo on the last note, leading to chopped hair (not head), exemplifies how a single chord can imply both terror and triumph in a moment. As cinematic code, the placement of the shots in sync with the music as detailed in the table above enables the director to gain maximum effect from a very simple piece of music, in particular the final use of silence (or absence of music) as the lock of hair falls to the ground. The bodily aspect of singing is aligned to the physicality of the images.

Conclusion

Paradise Road, featuring a strong women's ensemble cast, received ambivalent reviews, and there are certainly sections in the latter part of the film that lack structural cohesion. Yet the voice of the choir is able to communicate through its emotive narrative position because of its cultural associations as unaccompanied, as female and as a choral sound, and through the relationship that we as audience have with the popular classics it presents. Music can sound the voice of the characters and also act as an independent heroic character in its own right, and this necessitates it being privileged within the diegesis for maximum narrative impact. The context of the vocal arrangements as actual historical artifacts also considerably strengthens the emotional power of the music, particularly in combination with its placement with visual images.

At a time in Australian history when the treatment of 'alien' people in camps or prisons – whether asylum seekers, refugees or migrants – is a hotly debated issue, a film dealing with prisoners we can easily identify with, struggling against a culturally alien captor, has cultural resonance. In

Paradise Road, the music is integral in creating and supporting explorations of strength and weakness, conquest and suppression, familiar and alien, Oriental and Occidental, and power plays between male and female characters. The vocal orchestra ultimately symbolises survival, demonstrating how a powerfully affective appeal can be heard in the worst of circumstances. In the end, it is the music that emerges as hero, as the women travel their road to Paradise.

Thanks to: Garrick Jones for his comments on an earlier draft of this chapter, Junko Konishi for her research insights into Japanese song, and Robin Ryan and Mark Evans for additional direction on choral music.

Notes

1. Distributor's production package.
2. Giles and Meader are credited as Co-Executive Producers. Milliken recalls their introduction to the story:

   One day I was in Brisbane for a meeting at Film Queensland when two writers asked to see me. They took me down a corridor and without explanation, handed me a walkman. One of them put the earphones on my ears and said, listen... The voice I heard was Sister Vivian Bullwinkel, sole survivor of the massacre of twenty-one Australian nurses by the Japanese on Banka Island, Sumatra in February 1942. She was introducing a concert of vocal orchestra music recreated from the original scores in Perth in 1990... I knew a little of the story of the nurses, but nothing of the vocal orchestra, which I immediately saw as the way to dramatise the story. I knew that Bruce Beresford, with his love of music and his sensitivity in directing films about women, would be interested in the idea. (Milliken, 2004: unpaginated)

3. Plus soundtrack CD:*Paradise Road: Song of Survival* (1997) Malle Babbe Women's Choir (original motion picture soundtrack, includes vocal orchestra arrangements, and excerpts from Ross Edwards's score).
4. Interview with April Shelton (extra chorister/actress in *Paradise Road*) 1/8/2003 at Southern Cross University, Lismore.
5. It is, in fact, well-known Australian cabaret singer Julie Anthony, singing at the Marrickville Town Hall.
6. Originally written by H.A Donald to words by C.O Erwood during the First World War.
7. Interview by author with Ross Edwards, Sydney, 5/10/2002.
8. Junko Konishi notes:

   According to Akasaka Norio, a folklorist, there are 70 lyrics of Itsuki no komoriuta *('Komoriuta no tanjou: Itsuki no komoriuta o meguru seishin shi ['The birth of lullaby: a mental history of Itsuki no komoriuta]', 1994). The field collections by folklorists (both local and national) began around the 1930s, and the local branch of NHK radio began to broadcast a version in 1935. After the World War Two, a popular "geisha" singer, Otomaru recorded it and in the 1950s, a version arranged to popular music style (called "kayoukyoku") spread all over Japan. So, there are two types of* Itsuki no komoriuta; *1) the local one and 2) the version spread by media .... Generally it is right [that the lyrics are the sorrows of an ill-treated baby nurse]. But the lyrics of local versions are various; they consist of 1) violent words to a crying baby, 2) violent words to other girls, 3) gossip and so on.* (pc to Rebecca Coyle, 30/5/2004)

9. See Bebbington, W (1997); Hannan, M (1986); Ford, A (1993); and Stanhope, P (1994). See also 'Credo: Ross Edwards', *Sounds Australian*, Spring 1989, and Jonathon Mills's sleeve notes for *Ecstatic Dances*, 1994 (TP051).
10. According to a study by Chorus America, there are nearly 28.5 million participants

in American choirs, that is, at least one adult in each fifteen households (Unattributed, 2004: online).

11. *The Gift Of Song* from *Compass* ABC TV, produced by Kerrie Hannan, presented by Geraldine Doogue. Broadcast 25/12/2003.

12. In a study by the Department of Psychology, Royal Holloway University of London, investigating the effect of solo singing, choral singing and swimming on mood and heart rate, the findings were "that both swimming and singing made people feel more positive, more energetic, and less tense, as well as increasing their heart rate ... the fact that singing also improved mood is consistent with the role of emotional factors in music" (Evans and Valentine, 2001: online). Of further interest is their finding that "there was little difference between solo and choral singing," so there was no support in this study for the role of social factors. This is directly contradicted by the findings of the Chorus America survey.

13. "The broad appeal of choral singing is based in the unsurpassed opportunity it offers each singer to participate in an activity that involves them artistically, builds community, enhances their skills, and results in a product of great beauty. In working toward a beautiful choral sound, people contribute to an artistic product greater than themselves and forge friendships that change the course of their lives. The synergy of this musical mission infuses choral organizations and their singers with energy and purpose that result in extraordinary contributions to their communities." (Unattributed, 2004: online)

14. Including an appearance in *Changi*.

15. This work was originally provided for Grainger, who was interested in folk song, by collector Cecil Sharp as a handkerchief dance song *The Vicar of Bray*. Grainger roughly sketched the work for two whistlers and a few instruments about 1908 but then developed the piece for piano for a birthday gift for his mother in 1918. It was well received and, after publishing it, *Country Gardens* broke records, in the USA selling more than 40,000 copies. Despite his antipathy to the work, *Country Gardens* continues to generate income.

Chapter Thirteen

MUSICAL INTERTEXTUALITY IN *THE BANK*

MICHAEL HANNAN

Alan John's score for *The Bank* (dir: Robert Connolly, 2001) won best feature film score at the 2002 APRA-AGSC[1] Screen Music Awards. In contrast to many widely-distributed Australian films recently, *The Bank* features primarily 'original' music rather than existing tracks or rearrangements. In this chapter I will examine the way in which the score was composed, drawing on intertextual elements. I will focus on John's incorporation of screen composition techniques derived from Bernard Herrmann, and other composers, and the way this functions in propelling the narrative devices of the movie. Other obvious intertextual elements in John's score will also be discussed, notably his use of sacred choral textures and settings of Latin texts from the *Requiem Mass* in order to comment on the action. Some attention is given to the sound design of the film but the emphasis in the chapter is on the music scoring and its references to other musical texts.

While intertextuality is essentially a literary concept, it has been applied to 'texts' in other artforms such as music and film. In his *Image, Music, Text*, Roland Barthes argues, "The text is a tissue of quotations drawn from the innumerable centres of culture" (1977: 146). David Macey provides a basic premise for intertextuality:

> *any text is essentially a mosaic of references to or quotations from other texts; a text is not a closed system and does not exist in isolation. It is involved in a dialogue with other texts.* (2000: 203)

Accordingly, there is no single original source of meaning but meaning is accumulated and generated across texts. Also meanings derive from relationships *between* texts in a self-conscious process of allusions and oblique references. In the case of western music there is a long history of conscious use of existing texts as a foundation for new texts. The *cantus firmus*, a pre-existent melody (usually a chant or a hymn) acting as the framework upon which other musical parts are added, was the foundation of the long tradition of European polyphonic composition from the 13th to the 18th Century. The idea of sets of variations on a theme (usually a well-known piece) gained popularity from the late 16th Century onwards. Composers writing in standard musical forms, styles and genres, and using 'common practice' approaches to handling musical materials, are doing so in dialogue with the works that have been already composed in these traditions.

In a multi-artform such as film, intertextuality will apply to all the constituent arts (screenplay, casting, acting, cinematography, visual effects, lighting, sound, music etc.) both individually and in the ways they interact with each other. Furthermore, film music as a specific genre (or set of genres) draws upon musical allusions, references and signifiers to offer an intertextual element in its own right (see Kassabian, 2001: 37-60). An additional level of intertextuality is provided by the discourses that surround the work such as press releases, reviews and the additional features often available in the DVD format. *The Bank* DVD, for example, has an extra hour of special features including director's commentary, interviews with the producer, production designer, composer, sound designer, computer graphics designer, and other film texts such as deleted scenes and two short films by the director. These subsidiary texts extend the reader's interpretation of the primary text, and will be drawn upon in the following discussion of *The Bank*.

Research for this chapter was supplemented by a telephone interview conducted by the author with Alan John (26/10/03). All quotations by John, unless otherwise cited, are from this source.

The Bank Composer

Alan John studied musicology at the University of Sydney before making a career in the theatre as an actor and musical director. Since 1980 he has written original music and/or arrangements for over forty theatre productions by directors such as John Bell, Neil Armfield, Jim Sharman and Robin Nevin (Chappell, 2003: 6). Although John has concentrated on writing music for theatre and a full length opera, *The Eighth Wonder* (1995), he has also scored several screen projects including the feature films *Twelfth Night* (dir: Neil Armfield, 1987), *Travelling North* (dir: Carl Schultz, 1986), and *Looking for Alibrandi* (dir: Kate Woods, 2001) as well as projects for television. During an episode of a television drama series, *Close-Ups* (1996), John first worked with *The Bank* screenwriter and director Robert Connolly (not to be confused with film documentary maker Bob Connolly). Having worked in theatre, Connolly was interested John's theatre and dramaturgical background. Connolly also recruited a significant number of actors who are best known for their live theatre work including Mitchell Butel (who plays Stephen), Mandy McElhinney (Diane), Greg Stone (Vincent) and Sue Jones (the barrister representing the bank).

The Bank Story

The Bank critiques a broad range of unethical and unpopular practices attributed to Australian banks in recent times. The story includes issues such as the widespread closure of suburban and regional bank branches, the retrenchment of frontline banking staff, the reduction of services to clients who do not have significant income or capital, the practice of not informing clients of the risks of taking out loans, the use of deceptive tactics in order to avoid litigation, the obsession with profit, the use of insider information to inform investment decisions, and the willingness of large corporations to exploit the vulnerability of the small investor in order to create large financial gains for their shareholders. Significantly the CEO of the bank is an American expatriate (played by Anthony LaPaglia), a point that acknowledges ambivalent attitudes to US/Australian relations where ruthless US-style work practices are both derided as 'un-Australian', as well as eulogised for their apparent efficiency. These themes resonate in contemporary Australian society. The Australian attitude is summed up by the central protagonist's punchline in accounting for his devastating actions: "I just hate banks".

Connolly conceptualises the story of *The Bank* as "a tale of alchemy" (2002: DVD), with the protagonist, Jim Doyle (played by David Wenham), as "a modern-day alchemist who, instead of promising that he can turn any metal into gold, [is] promising that he can make unlimited fortunes on the stock market" (ibid). Connolly sees CentaBank's CEO, Simon O'Reily (LaPaglia), as a "Gordon Gekko for the new millennium" (ibid)[2]. Simon's greed for money and power makes him susceptible to Jim's elaborate scheme (the Bank Trading Simulation Experiment or BTSE) based on the proposition that the behaviour of the stock market can be predicted using the mathematics of chaos theory. In fact Jim has worked his way into CentaBank with the aim of destroying it in revenge for his father's suicide following bankruptcy precipitated by CentaBank's unethical practices. Using techniques of the thriller genre, the narrative is structured so that the audience is unaware of Jim's real motives and is therefore suspicious of why he should be willing to behave unethically to the point of perjury. The audience is also meant to be puzzled by Jim's reluctance to confide in his bank-officer love interest, Michelle (Sibylla Budd), although it eventually becomes clear that Jim suspects (incorrectly) that she is spying on him for Simon.

Connolly uses a subplot to represent a decent world diametrically opposed to the world of the bank and the stock market. This focuses on a couple (Wayne and Diane [Steve Rodgers and Mandy McElinney]) who lose their regionally-based boat hire business because the bank did not explain the risks of the loan they took out. They also lose their young son who drowns soon after an eviction summons is served on him in his parents' absence. In the course of their ambitious court action against the bank, Jim is recruited by Simon to give false evidence against their complaint.

Sound Design

The contrast between the city-based world of CentaBank and the lakeside world of the couple is emphasised by Sam Petty's sound design in the film. Like many of Connolly's other collaborators, Petty had experience in live theatre (including working with John in the Belvoir Theatre's production of *Emma's Nose*) and had previously worked with Connolly on the film adaptation of the play, *The Boys* (dir: Rowan Woods, 1998 for which

Connolly was producer). The sound design of *The Bank* sprang from a mutual interest by director and sound designer, as Connolly recalls:

> *We'd both been heavily influenced by Stanley Kubrick's* 2001: A Space Odyssey *which has certain very clever decisions about the sparseness of the environment in these technological spaces.* (2002: *The Bank* DVD[3])

Certainly CentaBank's mainframe computer C-LOG-PRO represents a strong reference to HAL, the spaceship computer of which the space travellers finally lose control.

Petty explains his approach to sound design in *The Bank*:

> *the challenge is really to find a way to give the corporate world a cold and soulless feel and, to go about this, we tried to remove the natural sounds from the soundtrack particularly around the world of CentaBank and the computer labs inside the building; and [we] really concentrated on low and high frequencies a fair way away from the voice which is in the middle of our hearing range.* (ibid)

Petty used "a lot of low, low throbs and hums and quite high whines often just on the edge of our hearing" to "unsettle the viewer and remain cold" (ibid).

By comparison, the sound design for scenes of the lake where the family lives is characterised by birdcalls and insect noises and sounds of lapping water. The sound design also features effects that give the impression of open spaces and sound echoing around the hills surrounding the lake. This sound quality is reinforced by the presence of warm colours for these scenes in contrast to the grey and blue washes common in the cityscapes. The techniques used for the lakeside scenes are designed to communicate a sense of naturalness, innocence and vulnerability.

Generally the sound design in *The Bank* does not compete with the music. The low rumbling and high-pitched sounds used by Petty usually underpin long stretches of dialogue without music. Indeed, their subtle presence in the audience's consciousness, and therefore their purpose in creating a mood, would be negated by the use of music. There was one particular instance, however, of a clash between sound design and music, as articulated by John:

> *there was a large sound design element from Sam Petty. I get on really well with Sam: he's one of the few sound designers who thinks musically. He's very keen to work in with my demos in terms of pitch and rhythm and all that sort of stuff, which is good; but on the other hand, for the big chaos sequence where the stock market crashes, he's put a lot of work into a particular cue that's trying to give a sort of spinning effect in the theatre. The music and the sound designer are both striving for the same effect and if you just put them together they don't work. So often there are compromises.*

The Score Development

John wrote all the music[4] used in locations associated with the CentaBank, even the few items of diegetic music: a cocktail jazz tune used as low background music in the bar where Jim and Michelle begin their affair; and a latin/jazz big band piece played live (by session musicians) at a lavish party at Simon's mansion.

The remainder of the score is orchestral (performed by Sinfonia Australis) and some cues also include a choral component (performed by Cantillation, a Sydney-based professional choir). There are no electronic music components in John's score: all electronic sounds heard in the film are part of the sound design. Films using one composer for all the music cues are rare in contemporary times since often producers are looking to increase the cross marketability of their films by including existing tracks by well-known artists. In addition many films use locations or sequences that demand the use of diegetic or extra-diegetic music covering a broad spectrum of popular and other styles.

According to John, the initial process for the development of major themes for *The Bank* was:

> [Connolly] *sent me a pretty* [-much] *finished script. And then we had a couple of meetings. He didn't really know what he wanted. He did know he wanted a substantial score and he also had some ideas for three different layers.*

John describes these intended layers and the way the project evolved:

> *In the director's mind the three strands were connected to the plot, the sub-plot (Wayne and family) and Jim's secret motivation (ultimately revealed through flashback). I think we talked generally about the strands in terms of: 1) 'thriller' plus some antique flavour to connect with the alchemy theme; 2) choral or solo vocal; and 3) some distinctive solo instrument eg Jan Garbarek style sax which could superimpose itself over both textures.*

> *For various reasons things became more integrated. The piano and percussion colours (which in my mind were connected with things magical, glittering and seductive) became more prominent and the flashback hints which were to be scattered throughout the film became confined to the end, by which time it was too late to meaningfully introduce a new colour into the score.*

Connolly and John settled on the choral element as a means to lift the music "to a mythical level" (Connolly, 2002b: DVD[5]). Connolly specifically requested a big orchestral score in the tradition of Bernard Herrmann's scores for Alfred Hitchcock's *Vertigo* (1958) and *North By Northwest* (1959). In particular he was attracted to Saul Bass's animated title sequences for those films and to the substantial pieces of music by Herrmann that accompanied them. Connolly saw these as "like an overture to introduce the film" (ibid) and asked John to produce something similar.

John elaborates on the composition of his title music:

> *It's fairly unusual today to get an overture like that. It was fairly standard in the 60s. You'd have a big sequence with interesting graphics ... [For* The Bank*] they had a very young graphic designer* [Sheldon Gardner] *who tendered for the project and he was so keen to do it, all that fractal kind of work. They thought there was good potential for quite a long title sequence. But musically I think it came out of a couple*

*of early demos, more from my point of view trying to get a feel for the
thematic language for the film. They wanted something that would tell
the audience that they were in some sort of classic thriller territory.*

John's title music cue and a number of other cues in *The Bank* are clearly
influenced by Herrmann's music. Graham Bruce believes that:

*Herrmann's extensive experience in radio scoring taught him the effec-
tiveness of widely differing and often unconventional groups of instruments in allying music with drama.* (1985: 74)

Defying the Hollywood convention of using a full symphony orchestra
Herrmann opted, for example, to use strings only (*Psycho*, 1960), to use
only low strings (*The Bride Wore Black*, dir: Francois Truffaut, 1967) or to
dispense with strings altogether (*Journey to the Centre of the Earth*, dir: Henry
Levin, 1959) (op cit: 95-115). Scores like *Citizen Kane* (dir: Orson Welles,
1941) have a dark brooding quality achieved by focusing on low brass
instruments (French horns and trombones) and low woodwind instruments
(bassoons and bass clarinets) in the orchestration. John acknowledges that
his own score's orchestration was "very much a homage to [Herrmann's]
style".

John omitted the trumpets from his orchestral line-up to achieve a dark
and sombre brass sound quality reminiscent of Herrmann, and he also
employed low woodwind and stringed instruments for a similar tone-
colouring effect. Examples include the low chords played by bassoons and
low strings while the police are searching the lake for the young boy's body;
and the same musical idea scored for clarinet, bass clarinet and low strings
at the start of the journey along the river to Simon's mansion. A low-pitched
texture of repeated French horn and trombone chords is another example
of this dark sound quality and it is associated generally with Simon. This is
heard frequently: in the title sequence (and also the end title); where Simon
and his henchmen discuss Jim's job interview; underscoring a telephone
conversation between Jim and Simon; and when the CentaBank board agrees
to Simon's plan. Finally, a variant of this motif is used after CentaBank has
collapsed.

There are other distinctively Herrmannesque elements in John's score.
Like Herrmann's music, most of John's cues use a triad-based harmonic
style including the use of added sevenths. This musical idiom locates the
music in fairly accessible territory for listeners familiar with classical music
styles. Herrmann's trademark minor chord with a major seventh used at
the beginning of both *Vertigo* and *Psycho* (Brown, 1994: 159) is also used by
John, notably at the climactic end of the court scene where, after Jim
perjures himself, Michelle storms out of the building in disgust.

In both composers' work the harmonic progressions often do not stay
within the chords defined by a particular key. Rather they progress in a
manner designed to solicit an unsettling response from the listener. Royal
S. Brown describes this quality in Herrmann's style:

*the essence of Herrmann's Hitchcock scoring lies in a kind of harmonic
ambiguity, hardly new to Western music but novel in film music,
whereby the tonal musical language familiar to Western listeners serves*

as a point of departure, only to be modified in such a way that norms are thrown off centre and expectations are held in suspense for much longer periods of time than the listening ears and feeling viscera are accustomed to. (1994: 150)

This technique is often used in conjunction with short one or two bar textural ideas that are repeated up or down a step. An example is found in Herrmann's score in the early scene in *Psycho* where Marion is contemplating stealing the money entrusted to her. This same technique is used in *The Bank* in the cue for the scene where Simon convinces the Board of CentaBank to go along with the plan that Jim has proposed. This particular cue is probably the most obviously Herrmann-influenced of John's score.

Figure 1: Two staves from 'The Board Caves In' cue (bars 11-14)

Here the melodic idea of bar 11 is repeated a minor third higher in bar 12; then the entire two-bar pattern (bars 11-12) is repeated but transposed up a semitone in bars 13 to 14.

Bruce (1985: 133-135) notes the extensive use of ostinato (a short melodic or rhythmic idea that is repeated insistently) in Herrmann's scores, providing examples from *The Man Who Knew Too Much* (dir: Alfred Hitchcock, 1956), *Psycho*, and *North By Northwest*. John also relies on ostinato in his cues for *The Bank*. The musical example quoted above supports this observation but there are more obvious examples of this technique, notably a one-bar syncopated rhythm played on timpani that is used under a number of scenes. These include: when Jim first takes the stand in the courtroom; when he gives his false testimony; when the plan to profit from the stock market collapse is put into operation (D Day); when Wayne is asking directions to Simon's house because he is planning revenge; and when Michelle is putting a microfilm into a reader and is therefore on the verge of revealing Jim's true identity (both to herself and the CentaBank spy standing behind her).

Figure 2: Timpani ostinato from 'Jim Takes the Stand'

This rhythm is first heard in the brass chords of the title music and related cues mentioned above, but thereafter it is used to create a foreboding atmosphere through the use of soft and low timpani tones.

Ostinato permeates the score and is sometimes the sole method of cue construction. For example the percussion-based cue which is heard with the voice-over recitation of the seven times tables at the very beginning of the film (and accompanies a shot of a car driving through the country side) is made of five layers of repeated tuned-percussion patterns. This cue also underscores the final shot of Jim as he walks towards his flight lounge after getting through customs undetected.

The use of repetitive techniques also indicates the influence on John of musical minimalism. John acknowledges admiration for the work of a number of composers such as John Adams, Steve Reich, Louis Andriessen and Ross Edwards whose work uses repetitive processes (in Chapple, 2003: 13). The brass chord rhythmic cue used as a background for a telephone conversation between Simon and Jim also contains repeated arpeggiated string patterns reminiscent of the musical style of Philip Glass, perhaps the most well-known minimalist concert and stage composer with screen credits such as *Koyaanisqatsi* (dir: Godfrey Reggio, 1983), *Mishima: A Life in Four Chapters* (dir: Paul Schrader, 1985), and *The Thin Blue Line* (dir: Errol Morris, 1988). John argues that Glass may have been strongly influenced by Herrmann. There are textures present in Herrmann's score for *North By Northwest* that may have influenced Glass, for example during the scene late in the film when Vandamm (James Mason) is plotting with Leonard (Martin Landau) to throw Eve Kendall (Eva Marie Saint) out of their aeroplane once it is airborne. While such influences enable a grasp of the score for *The Bank* in terms of its generic approach, John's score incorporates specific features of its own.

Thematic development

Thematic development is a strong feature of John's score for *The Bank*. John tends to use very short motifs in line with Herrmann's practice. Brown quotes Herrmann as arguing that "the short phrase is easier to follow for audiences, who listen with only half an ear" (1994: 154). Certainly short motivic ideas are more adaptable to the repetitive and transformational compositional processes common to Herrmann and John.

Many of the short-phrase motifs that recur to strengthen connections between the various narrative elements in *The Bank* are first found in the title music overture. Some of these have already been discussed above (for example the repeated brass chords and the timpani ostinato). The most striking theme in the overture is a two-bar melodic pattern heard in the first violins (bars 13-18):

Figure 3: Overture theme

Although this theme stands out, it is not reiterated in the overture once it is first stated. It does occur in a number of other cues, first, in a varied form to underscore a scene where Jim is writing mathematical formulae on the laboratory whiteboard; and second, in an even more varied form, underscoring Simon's speech to the CentaBank board of directors.

Arguably the main theme for *The Bank* is a melodic line involving a rising four-tone scale that is used in many different guises throughout the film. It is first heard at the outset of the overture:

Figure 4: Overture opening, bars 3-7

This pattern becomes the basis for the prominent riff-based texture of the overture (beginning at bar 9) and also spawns some ostinato devices used to create complex textural effects in the overture (such as at bar 13, bar 17). Variants of this theme are found in 21 of the 43 cues used in the film, mostly in scenes related to BTSE, the software that Jim has developed to predict the behaviour of the stock market. In this way, the software is given its own character as well as narrative role.

Another ostinato-based theme is also found in seven of these BTSE-related cues:

Figure 5: Bars 1-2 of 'Inkblots'

There are several motifs (short melodic themes) that recur in a few places throughout the score. One involves a step-wise contour that rises and falls and is supported by solemn chordal backing. It first appears in the scene where BTSE is given a successful trial run.

Figure 6: 'Trial Run' bars 20-22

211

This motif is used again underscoring a scene where Jim goes to a restaurant by himself and writes some mathematical calculations on the tablecloth, in a deliberate ruse to deceive the CentaBank spies. A variant of the motif is employed when Jim takes the witness stand in the courtroom. An even more disguised variant is used when Simon reminds the CentaBank board of directors that they will benefit personally from the impending collapse of the stock market. Thus this motif could be interpreted as signifying deception. Everyone at the bank believes that Jim is a genius, whereas his mathematical calculations are intended to deceive even those with mathematical skills.

Another angular motif is used just twice in the score: first, after the summons is served on the young boy, and second, just after Jim dares Simon to go ahead with the scheme on the predicted day of the stock market crash. It is played very high in pitch by violins using tremolo bowing near the bridge of the instrument (*sul ponticello*). In both cases the cue is signalling danger.

"Boogieman"

Figure 7: 'Boogieman' bars 11-13

Another motif is clearly associated with Michelle. It is used under the first meeting of Jim and Michelle and for their love scene. Its main function seems to be to indicate Michelle's attempts to uncover the mystery of Jim's identity. It underscores the scenes where Michelle is going through Jim's possessions, where Jim spots Michelle talking to one of Simon's henchmen at her desk in the bank, and finally as Michelle searches for evidence of Jim's identity in his apartment following the court scene.

"Michelle"

Figure 8: 'Michelle' bars 1-3

Several cues feature a falling semitone motif. This is an affective device used to stimulate a response across a range of emotions such as grief and fear. The falling semitone is integrated into many of the motifs already discussed but is also found alone in a number of cues and sometimes as pairs of falling semitones in sequence. It is used particularly effectively in two cues associated with Wayne at the climax of the film: when he first appears with the shotgun pointed at Simon; and when he realises that he can take ultimate revenge on Simon by destroying the phone connection to the mansion.

The Choral Music

A variety of vocal and choral cues are used to enhance the orchestral textures in *The Bank*. However, one set of cues has a major thematic role. This is John's setting of the Latin text of 'Lacrymosa' (a verse from the sequence of the traditional Latin *Requiem* Mass, the dramatic 'Dies Irae') that occurs a number of times in the film to signify grief. The text:

Lacrymosa dies illa
Qua resurget ex favilla
Judicandus homo reus
Huic ergo parce, Deus

translates as:

O this day full of tears
When from the ashes arises
Guilty man be judged
O Lord, have mercy upon him! (in Unattributed, 2004: online[6])

The use of liturgical texts in the vocal component of the score is explained by John:

Once you have a vocal or a choral element you have to have words for them to sing, so I went to the standard liturgical texts and found that in the Requiem Mass there were lots of very apt parts – so often when text is being sung behind an image there's a little coded message in there from the Latin for those few Latin scholars – they might pick up clues as to what's really going on. (2002: DVD)

Gorbman draws attention to "the standard practice of segregating song lyrics from dialogue and significant action" (1987: 20). She notes, however, that theme songs "behave somewhat like a Greek chorus, commenting on a narrative temporarily frozen into spectacle" (ibid). John's use of Latin texts suggests that the competition for attention between lyric and image is removed for most viewers, although further signifiers are there for those able to decipher them. Latin text signifies religious ritual and other-world-liness, and the use of choristers to provide lyrics offers a connection with speakers drawing upon obscure discourses. The use of Latin texts parallels some of the other mysterious signifiers in the film, such as: the use of un-subtitled dialogue in Japanese between Jim and his mathematical collaborator, Toshio (Kazuhiro Muroyama); and the use of chaos theory mathematics. These elements heighten the generic conventions of the thriller in *The Bank*, and build the anticipation and surprise in the film climax.

John has structured his 'Lacrymosa' song melody in a style that has resonances of the English baroque composer Henry Purcell. In particular, the descending chromatic bass-line around which the song is composed, is clearly a reference to Purcell's aria 'When I am Laid in Earth' from his opera *Dido and Aeneas* (1689). This reference brings another intertextual level into the frame.

The 'Lacrymosa' cue is introduced for the grim shot of the police scouring the marshes for the young boy's body.

"Murky Waters"

Figure 9: 'Murky Waters' motif

An instrumental version of the tune then underscores the scene where Jim and Michelle travel by boat to the party at Simon's mansion. The watery location refers back to the search scene where the vocal cue is initially used. The song next appears, again instrumentally, to accompany the scene where, in a flashback, the young Jim Doyle gets off the bus on his way home from school. Soon after that, the vocal version is of the song is used to highlight young Jim's discovery of his father's body hanging in the barn. It is used again after the demise of CentaBank to accompany a series of aftermath shots including Wayne returning home from his confrontation with Simon. The 'Lacrymosa' cue is also added to the main title music to construct the end title music. Thus the main use of the various versions of 'Lacrymosa' is to indicate the human tragedy of death, in this case death that could have been avoided if the bank had been fairer and more sympathetic towards its clients.

As indicated above, other texts from the *Requiem* Mass are set in cues backed by orchestral textures. These texts usually provide an obvious commentary on the narrative. The first instance, however, links the phrase, "In paradisum" ("In paradise") enigmatically with a shot of Jim flying in CentaBank's Lear jet through the clouds on his way to his interview with its executives. Less obscure is the use of a verse of the 'Libera Me' (from the 'Absolution of the Dead'): "Tremens factus sum ego, et timeo, dum discussio venerit" ("I am seized with trembling and I am afraid until the day of reckoning shall arrive"). This comments on the scene where Jim goes to a restaurant alone and writes his bogus formulae on the tablecloth knowing that it will be discovered by Simon's henchmen. It suggests that Jim's revenge on the bank is not too far off.

Then follows a series of settings of verses from the 'Dies Irae'. A fractal computer graphics sequence is scored with a driving minimalist chordal texture. On a cut to a shot of Jim working in the laboratory, the orchestral texture thins out and the choir enters with "Quidquid latet, apparebit: Nil inultum remanebit" ("All that is hidden shall appear, nothing will remain unavenged"). The verse "Quando judex est venturis, Cuncta stricte discussurus" ("When the judge shall come to weigh everything strictly") adds to the feeling of impending disaster. It is used to accompany the shots of the installation of the new computer system needed to run the stockmarket prediction software. The verse fragment "Nil inultum remanebit" ("Nothing will remain unavenged") accompanies a shot of Michelle in Jim's hometown library where she is just about to discover his true identity.

For the stock market crash where the camera whirls round in dizzying circles over frenetic traders, the chorus sings from the Offertory part of the Mass text: "Libera eas de ore leonis, ne absorbeat eas tartarus, ne cadant in obscurum" ("Deliver them from the lion's mouth, lest the jaws of Hell swallow them, lest they fall into everlasting darkness"). At that point the screen goes black for an uncomfortable length of time before it cuts to the next scene of chaos in the bank's computer laboratory.

The use of these texts from the Latin *Requiem* Mass, mostly referring to the Day of Judgement, effectively dramatise the connection between the Christian God's revenge on sinners and Jim's revenge on CentaBank, its executives and shareholders. The use of the Latin language also provides a connection to the medieval and renaissance texts of alchemy, many of which were written in Latin. It is worth noting that there has been a long tradition of classical music composers writing settings of the *Requiem* Mass texts. This is mainly to do with the fact that the *Requiem* Mass may be sung on most days of the liturgical calendar (for funerals and anniversaries of deaths, for example) and therefore is more likely to be performed regularly than those Mass texts that can only be celebrated on one specific day of the liturgical calendar. Prominent composers who have written *Requiem* Mass settings including Wolfgang Amadeus Mozart (1791), Hector Berlioz (1837), Giuseppi Verdi (1974), and Gabriel Fauré (1887). The existence of these settings provides another intertextual dimension to the new setting offered by John.

Although mostly modern in approach, John's Latin text settings show a strong affinity for pre-Renaissance and Renaissance styles of four-part vocal writing ranging from strictly homorhythmic textures ('Libera eas') to hocket-like constructions (the introduction to the first 'Lacrymosa' cue; and 'Quid quid latet') to rhythmical independent parts ('Quando judex'). This latter cue is reminiscent of the late medieval motet where the parts often contained different texts sung in texturally contrasting rhythms. John's musicology background is clearly evident in these dramatic and evocative choral inventions.

Conclusion

Although this chapter has concentrated on intertextual elements in the music of *The Bank*, there are also a number of intertextual elements in other components of the film, some of which have been mentioned above. Director Robert Connolly sees *The Bank* in the thriller tradition of Hitchcock's *North By Northwest*, a movie that, like *The Bank*, depends on the disguised identity of a major character (Eve Kendall) as well as strong comedic elements in the dialogue. *The Bank* also has an animated titles segment that is a reference to Saul Bass's titles sequences for a number of Hitchcock's movies, but is clearly a specific homage to the swirling imagery used for the titles of Hitchcock's *Vertigo*. Sheldon Gardner's computer graphics for the title sequence and a number of other animated sequences in *The Bank* draw on the Mandelbrot Set imagery as published in Gleick (1987: colour plates between 114 and 115) and on the symbols and formulae used in fractal mathematics. One of the clues that Michelle uses to discover Jim's identity is a copy of Charles Dickens's novel *A Tale of Two Cities* (1859) that has Jim's real name (Paul) written in it. This novel has a main character (Darnay) whose identity, like Jim's, is disguised. As already discussed, the technological ambience of *The Bank* draws on *2001: A Space Odyssey*, particularly in the sound design and the reference to the spaceship computer (HAL). Like HAL, CentaBank's computer C-LOG-PRO carries out the task it has been programmed to do regardless of the wishes of the humans who are relying on it to do what they want. There is a conscious reference in *The Bank* to the mysterious tradition of alchemy, represented by the bogus mathematics that Jim uses to convince CentaBank that he is able to predict the stock market.

The Bank has a clear anti-corporatised bank political stance and, although it is primarily a tale of revenge, may also be considered a reference to the Robin Hood and/or Ned Kelly stories. In destroying the bank, Jim redistributes money to a number of worthy people including to Wayne and Diane, the young couple who have been deceived by CentaBank and lost their son as a result of the bank's actions to foreclose on them.

The music for *The Bank* interfaces effectively with the general intertextual agenda of the film. Alan John has composed an overture that clearly references the tradition of Herrmann's overtures for Hitchcock films such as *North By Northwest*, *Vertigo* and *Psycho*. In his orchestral writing, John also adopts references to Herrmann's musical language including actual chords, styles of chord progressions, orchestral colorations, and techniques of short motivic transformation and development.

By far the most distinctive musical element in the score of *The Bank* is the use of vocal and choral parts in combination with orchestra. The vocal elements were included in the score to reinforce the intended parallel of Connolly's modern-day tale of revenge with the medieval and renaissance practices of alchemy. Although John's vocal and choral writing is modern in style it contains significant aspects of older styles of music from the medieval, Renaissance and baroque periods and suggests an historical connection with alchemy. The choice of Latin language for the texts supports this connection. Many alchemical texts, written in Latin, used allegory to obfuscate the practical processes being discussed (Roberts, 1994: 66). There was a parallel tendency in late medieval and Renaissance polyphony to obscure the meaning of the text through non-vertical alignment of word syllables. John has used these polyphonic setting techniques in a number of his cues. John also adds another level of meaning to the film by his choice of texts from the *Requiem* Mass. In particular the use of the doomsday text 'Dies Irae' provides a potent biblical analogy of Jim's revenge on CentaBank. By these means, the music and sound design for *The Bank* operate through a series of allusions and oblique references, thereby supporting the complexity of the central protagonist's purpose and machinations. It is possible that the film and its sound track offer an alternative solution to the ethos of greed and corruption represented by CentaBank, namely, the use of imagination, wit and humanism to execute revenge.

Notes

1. Australian Performing Rights Association and Australian Guild of Screen Composers.

2. A reference to the figure played by Michael Douglas in *Wall Street* (dir: Oliver Stone, 1987).

3. Unattributed (2002) 'Special Features: Extras: The Bank Production' (including 3. Sound Design: Interview with Sam Petty (Sound Designer) and Robert Connolly, 4. Original Music: Interview with the Alan John (composer) and Robert Connolly), *The Bank* (DVD).

4. Detailed analysis of score elements enabled through provision of unpublished music score (2001) by Alan John.

5. See details in footnote 3 above.

6. All translations of Latin *Requiem* Mass used in this chapter taken from this source.

Chapter Fourteen

CARL VINE'S SCORE IN
beDevil

CATHERINE SUMMERHAYES AND ROGER HILLMAN

The film *beDevil* (dir: Tracey Moffatt, 1993) brought together indigenous Australian director Tracey Moffatt, producer Tony Buckley, and composer Carl Vine. While not a commercial success, the film is highly distinctive beyond the cultural blend emerging even from this sketchy outline of its creative team. *beDevil* comprises three ghost stories[1], and is minimal in its resources and budget but not its range of styles and fantasy. These three stories are drawn from Moffatt's Irish Australian and Aboriginal backgrounds. They are stories of hauntings and all closely refer to the nostalgia and distorted temporal experiences that are so often the narrative markers of ghost-theme films. The second story, 'Choo Choo Choo Choo', combines stylistic elements of an artfilm and surrealism with, in Moffatt's own words, "fake documentary" (in Conomos and Caputo, 1993: 28) incorporating 'to camera' interviews with various characters and the hesitant camerawork of amateur live recording. *beDevil's* surrealism extends from the hyperreal landscapes of this second story to the broad gender and cultural mix of the third story 'Lovin' the Spin I'm In'. Actors and characters are drawn from indigenous Australia as well as from Greek and Chinese Australia. Luke Roberts plays a Frida Kahlo figure with unflappable dignity, the cross-dressing pointing to a different kind of bedevilment and haunting[2].

Thematically the film explores both gender and multiculturalism via the unusual perspective of the supernatural. Inspired by the four Japanese ghost stories of *Kwaidon* (dir: Masaki Kobayoshi, 1964), Moffatt negotiates highly ambitious territory without a single grand statement, simply evoking and suggesting connections between seen and unseen worlds, and between disparate elements of culture – Anglo-Australian, indigenous Australian, American, Asian, Mediterranean-Australian. An exception is the occasional, explicit visual representation of ghosts such as the blind girl walking along the railway line at the end of the second story 'Choo Choo Choo Choo'; otherwise the effects of haunting are largely registered with those susceptible to them, in a far from Gothic manner. (In this second story, for example, a couple of brief appearances of props, like an arm appearing round a corner or a self-propelled wig, create humour rather than suspense.) This film is much closer in mood to the supernatural world of indigenous Australia's Dreamtime in which living is also dreaming. The subliminal, fleeting sounds and images of *beDevil*'s three ghost stories and the weaving of the supernatural into everyday life evoke the timelessness of those stories of totemic ancestors that are fundamental to Aboriginal cosmology[3].

The same composer, Carl Vine, was commissioned for the original music in *White Fellas Dreaming: A Century of Australian Cinema* (dir: George Miller, 1996) for the worldwide series on national cinema movements. Of most relevance to this commission was undoubtedly Vine's score for *beDevil* but his distinctive career to date is worth summarising briefly, not least because he currently combines composing with being Artistic Director of Musica Viva. The sheer range of his output made him an ideal choice for scoring this film. The strongly rhythmical, gestural nature of his work has been applied to dance, film and the theatre[4]. As well as co-founding the contemporary music ensemble Flederman, with an emphasis on new Australian music, he has been resident composer with the Sydney Dance Company (1978), the London Contemporary Dance Theatre (1979), the New South Wales State Conservatorium (1985), the Australian Chamber Orchestra (1987) and the University of Western Australia (1989). Predating *beDevil*, Vine's dance scores were deemed "too dependent on visual elements to transfer well to the concert hall" (Noone and Parker, 1989: 104). Precisely these qualities made him the perfect choice for *beDevil*, an assignment he conceived in the following terms:

> *I wanted to find a truly unique sound for this film. It looks like no other Australian feature I've seen and I wanted the music to accentuate the extraordinary qualities in the script. In the under-scoring I've tried to draw together the complex webs of interaction between the characters, but when the music is in the foreground I wanted people to think that this was something they'd never heard before in an Australian film.* (*beDevil* Production Notes: undated, unpaginated)[5]

Vine's application of these aims was to exploit the 'surreal' elements in his music and to negotiate that approach with the director's brief:

> *I liked the way the film needed a dream feel ... and a relationship between surrealism and reality. At first Tracey wanted it to sound like a James Bond movie, and the opening credits still have that 1960s jazz flavour. But that wasn't right for the whole film. In the end I used a large body of live string players, plus various weird electronic sounds, and the interplay between them, to represent different layers of reality.* (*beDevil* Press Kit, 1993: unpaginated)[6]

Our approach in this chapter will be to interweave the Moffatt and Vine contributions to the film in a fashion comparable to the score's relationship to the visuals. Beyond a general analysis of the sound track and of the role of music within it, we will focus our discussion on the film's narrative as it is told via this audio channel rather than through the visual. Far beyond this chapter and this volume, such an approach still does not have sufficient currency within Film Studies. But a text of such richness demands it. The Moffatt/Vine team may so far be a one-off collaboration, without particular commercial success, but it does emerge as an achievement that rewards closer listening and analysis.

Narrative Outline

What kind of film score might do justice to the complexity of Moffatt's film, a complexity nonetheless rendered with great simplicity? For a start, Vine makes no attempt at cultural appropriation, with a total absence of token didjeridus or any gestures towards 'ethnographic' sounds as exoticism. Nor does it bristle with tritones to evoke western rendering of ancient musical bedevilment. At the same time it is a score that makes a virtue of severe budgetary constraints, roughly $15,000 for the whole commission, performance and recording of the score, as the composer recalls[7]. It is a score that is prominent in the film's dramatic balance, and one with a wide expressive range. The director herself felt: "The sound is really ... half the movie in *beDevil*" (in Conomos and Caputo, 1993: 28). This single feature invokes comparison to the sound design of David Lynch and a handful of other directors but the prominence of the music score within the sound far exceeds Lynch's usual balance between these two major sonic strands – broadly music and sounds (excluding dialogue)[8]. In 1993 the score received the Australian Guild of Screen Composers Award for Best Music for a Feature Film, while the film was also deemed to have Best Soundtrack at the 1993 SITGES International Film Festival (Spain). Producer Tony Buckley also acknowledges its achievement: "*beDevil* was a particular challenge. Carl did a superb job" (in Summerhayes, 2001: 316). Part of the 'particular challenge' for the spatial aspect of music was no doubt matching the border hopping of Moffatt's visual and cultural conception:

> I look at spaces differently because I have a background in both cultures. But I don't think you can call the stories particularly white or Aboriginal... I merely reflect what I see in Australian society. For me, Australian society is now a very mixed society, very multicultural – a hybrid society. (in Conomos and Caputo, 1993: 28)

Moffatt's interwoven narrative of contemporary Australian society is neatly summarised in Glen Masato Mimura's synopsis of *beDevil*:

> The first story, 'Mr. Chuck', recounts the arrival of suburban development to an island after the Second World War. Narrated in the present by an incarcerated Aboriginal man and a white woman residing in one of the island's subdivisions, the film reconstructs their reminiscences of the ghost of an American GI who drove his tank into a local swamp. The second story, 'Choo Choo Choo Choo', revolves around a ghost train that has, in the present, become a lucrative legend for the local tourist industry. In contrast, a less commercial retelling of the region's history, and its supernatural past, is given by a middle-aged Aboriginal woman, visiting her home of earlier years. The last story, 'Lovin' the Spin I'm In', takes place in a sleepy coastal town that some enterprising businessmen are seeking to convert into a gambling casino. Toward this effort, a local landlord is trying to evict his tenants, including a Torres Strait Islander woman whose son had died, with his lover, in a

mysterious fire. The landlord's son, however, discovers that his father's warehouse is haunted by the lovers' ghosts, which leads to a surprising conclusion. (Mimura, 2003: 111)

Mimura compresses the bones of the plot, hints at the elements the author will pursue, and restricts himself to themes while evoking their visual realisation. But sound is absent. And in this film, even before looking at/listening for music, sound plays a crucial role in themes and in interaction with visuals. The ghost train of part 2 is characterised by its childlike rendition as a sound: "Choo Choo Choo Choo – you can hear it, but you can't see it!" Part 1 includes a flashback to the Aboriginal boy Rick (played by Ben Kennedy) being thrashed by his stepfather (Ric MacClure), a form of violence still more disturbing because we hear it without seeing violent acts in the film's image track. Rather we establish our own images suggested by the noises we hear. These noises include the sharp bark of a dog, which introduces the shadowy figure of Rick's stepfather. The overall sound design for this beating is created from sharp metallic clangs and the muffled, low rumblings of a distorted voice – slowed down to sound part human, part 'wild beast'. There is only one distinct sound of a blow, although the shattering, breaking glass window might well be the result of young Rick been thrown against it. All the sounds in this sequence are suggestive rather than explicit. The violence, in other words, lingers as a ghost with the same degree of materiality and insubstantiality blended in the figure of the blind girl. So this is a film where sound clearly has an important role, and one where retelling the story through sound, rather than sight and themes, is likely to yield a texture and a richness of detail that might give a different slant to our interpretation of the overall narrative. Moffatt's use of sound and music in all three stories reveals a narrative layer that indeed embodies these stories with ghostly meanings and fears. If we ignore this narrative layer in the sound track, then we do so at the expense of the story's substance.

This role of narrative underpinning alone places more dramatic weight on this musical score than on most, for sound – whether ambient or musical (as explored below) – acts here to haunt. And it also confounds standard divisions between diegetic and non-diegetic, as well as between sound effects and music. We are used to conventions whereby we the audience hear offscreen, unsourced music which the screen characters clearly can't hear, and – outside ghost stories and the like – we mostly expect sound effects to be matched to a clear visual source, action or event. But at the end of its second ghost story in particular, *beDevil* merges the experience of onscreen characters with the audience's viewing experience. In this short closing sequence, we are also in the vulnerable situation of hearing but not seeing the ghost train. What we in the audience hear combines sound effects with a musical rendering of sound effects which finally explodes the story's driving, urging suspense into a fleeting glimpse of a little blind white girl tapping her way down the old railway line. In another of Moffatt's wry comments on racial relations, this 'white girl' was played by a blond Aboriginal girl named Karen Saunders.

Our own often ghostly existence as a cinema audience (phantom-like, disbelief suspended) is challenged in a rather different way to what we normally confront. The link created here between onscreen figures and cinema audience implies, we feel, some negotiation of a political level innate in the subject matter. *beDevil's* unfinished, hesitant, almost broken narratives evoke relations between indigenous and non-indigenous Australians. At this level, the film also uses numerous 'to camera' addresses that confront the audience not only with their content and style (for example Rick's memories of abuse or Ruby's presentation of 'bush cuisine' at the site of a modern-day midden). These direct gazes into or just past the camera also recall Paul Willemen's analysis of what he calls "the fourth look" in cinema – the imagined 'look' at the viewer, via the camera, by the people whose images appear on screen (Willemen, 1994: 107). Willemen developed his idea of a 'fourth look' in cinema drawing on Laura Mulvey's seminal description of cinema's three looks: "that of the camera as it records the pro-filmic event, that of the audience as it watches the final product, and that of the characters at each other within the screen illusion" (Mulvey, 1989: 25). In *beDevil*, characters address the camera in all but the third story – they speak their stories directly to the camera and audience. Their voices demand our attention as they look at us, and interestingly, these addresses occur in the absence of music. These characters are thereby situated in our world, the real world, and not in the ghostly world denoted (and connoted) by Vine's music.

The monkeys of legend see no evil, hear no evil and speak no evil, an association evoked by the playful, childlike gestures of those people waving at the 'film people' and lining the streets of Charleville – the town and surrounding desert landscapes feature in the story 'Choo Choo Choo Choo'. In relation to issues of domestic violence and possibly of the Stolen Generations, 'evil' does emerge via one of these channels, confronting us the audience with the choice of damming up the intrusion, or else extending our insights to the other channels. The particularly bourgeois woman (Diana Davidson) on Bribie Island has a heart: she is distressed that an amorphous "we" knew exactly what was going on from what "we" heard, even if at that stage they didn't "speak" it. And so the complex issue of the dispossession and forced assimilation of indigenous Australians during the 20th Century is noted via inference in this film, together with non-indigenous Australians' relative ignorance of this issue until the 1990s.

Stories Told by Music

Let's re-tell the story then, focusing this time on the music. The opening titles of the film appear dramatically over the swirling silhouettes of dancers from the Bangarra Dance Company. They dance with a strong sense of theatricality to frenetic music, scored for synthesiser and featuring jagged cross rhythms. The 'real' beginning after about 1'40" switches briefly to ambient sound with a traveling shot across a marsh, and then chords combining extreme string registers accompany visuals of the swamp, ahead of a xylophone. The choice of instrument itself hints at more exotic and mysterious elements beneath the surface. This counterpoint between the two styles is later extended by an echoing gong effect. At the end of this introduction, a young Aboriginal boy is pulled into the muddy water, whereupon the music climaxes, the screen darkens, and then the first ghost story, whose ending has just been foretold, is recounted in full.

'Mr Chuck' tells the grim story from "that island", as it is called by the central character, an Aboriginal man called Rick (Jack Charles). The motif which accompanies wide, aerial traveling shots of the island where the GI found a watery grave in World War II, is rendered by lush music ascending the scale in the bland style of a tourist advertisement, with muted conga drums later indicating how domesticated any exotic elements have become in this setting. Restless music accompanies the young Rick's appearance; pizzicato strings, with piano and strings over the woman's narration, inter-cut with the young Aboriginal boy. A mock stinger chord signals her blinding by a flash of light/insight. The music continues to render the dramatic mood of the sequence, becoming agitated (in the manner of its opening instrumentation and rhythm) when the boy steals chocolates, and using tense strings to accompany his slashing of the cinema deckchairs. The ghostly apparition of the GI is underpinned by chords, competing with slowed down voices and the sound of barrels rolling, which mark the boy's beating. This is reinforced by the sight of blood flowing through the drainpipe and the sound of the child's muffled sobs.

A new musical style appears as the camera withdraws from the island resort. The music gathers momentum via tonal changes in the piano sounds and an ascending motif is played on high-pitched strings, contrasting with emphatic timpani beats at the other end of the register. This music lifts us up into a magic carpet ride of sweeping aerial views onto 'safe' suburban scenes of sun, surf and sand, the terrain of the 'white' Anglo-Celtic population of Bribie Island, despite this being the setting for this ghost story. Against this urgent yet sinuous stream of music we also hear another set of sounds. These sounds are again muffled and even more confusing than those heard during and after the young Rick's beating. This sequence must be played over and over to make some sense of the sonic world of the film at this stage in its storytelling. Although this need for repeated audition may indicate a failure in cinematic practice (perhaps it doesn't 'work'), it can rather be considered as yet another layer in this film's complex layering of narratives, not least its political narrative: the difficulty an Aboriginal point of view has in being heard. We do hear the sounds, but as to what they are... well, perhaps they rather indicate that we need to be careful, to listen closely, to listen again before we can judge. Against this 'safe', consumer conscious music, we hear the sounds of a fight. A bucket is knocked over, men swear and grunt at each other. We have just come out of an 'interview' with the older Rick who is clearly in a place of detention, and the clumsy sounds of desperation and institutionalised violence thread their way through the urgent textures of pianos and strings and ascending motifs of the music associated with 'that island'. Embedded within this music are the muffled shouts and blows of men fighting and the sound of metal buckets being knocked over. This particularly complex audiovisual sequence, we believe, illustrates both Moffatt's and Vine's coherent use of sound, music and vision to tell more than one story at the same time.

The opening shots of the second ghost story signal an abrupt change of scene to a freestanding house amidst a desert landscape. There is less obvious music in this section of the film; some sound effects blend into musical effects (such as the train sound), yielding a kind of musique concrète. After the title 'Choo Choo Choo Choo' is established, the Aboriginal women on the back of a truck sing along to a ghetto blaster playing Herbie Laughton's country music song *Ghan to the Alice* (1999), as sung by Aboriginal actor Auriel Andrews (who also plays the older Ruby in this second story). This one song is the sole example of pre-existing music in the music track. It again points to the intermeshing of cultural styles that Moffatt uses to challenge racial stereotypes, with its 'country music' style so much liked, written and played by contemporary Aboriginal people. But the characteristic, recurring sound of this second story is made up of synthesised fragments of sounds suggesting the presence of ghostly trains, absent visually, yet whistling, chugging, shunting and screeching on the soundtrack. These sounds are interspersed with fleeting visuals that, in places, feature braille characters filling the screen. This combination evokes the blind girl walking down the tracks, her presence 'visible' at the end of the sequence. The ghostly whistling over riffs of the train-type sounds is also accompanied by insistent percussion instruments, their unreality very different to that of the consciously romantic music when the camera roves across the stars. Both the visual and sonic editing of this story create a sense of intercutting between real and dream scenes, the latter including the train of the title's legend. The sense of this house then being a liminal outpost of 'civilisation' is enhanced by the outlook across endless expanses of surreal, even hyperreal, colours and artificial termite mounds. Moffatt's visual imaginings in this sequence present to us a disturbing meld of fantastic Dreamtime and *Wizard of Oz* landscapes. A lively track concludes the music for 'Choo Choo Choo Choo', where the dominating experience is of melodic stasis: a thread of synthesised high-pitched whistling floats eerily above a deeper rhythm of synthesised 'pan pipes' in a very low register. Through these sounds and music, rather than from fleeting visual images, we follow the ghostly train as it chugs inexorably out across the desert.

The title of *beDevil's* third and last ghost story alludes to the Johnny Mercer/Harold Arlen evergreen *That Old Black Magic* (1942); "lovin' the spin I'm in" comes from the song's lyrics and serves as a self-reflective gesture by the filmmaker. The song's title is clearly linked to that of the entire film. This final story explores bedevilment through love. 'Spin' as in 'spinning around' also becomes a central motif in this section, both with the swirling dancers and with the final, circling image of the getaway car simply rotating on the spot, like the fire of a Catherine-wheel fixed on its axis. We have already seen another Catherine-wheel at the end of the second story, where the hurtling, sparkling circle is watched intently by a child by the side of a lonely desert railway. This spinning movement also mirrors that of the film's overall narrative. Far from exorcising the ghost of the drowned GI in 'Mr Chuck', this last ghost story only offers a further variation on the lingering presence of ghosts from the past, as characters from the story's narrative 'present' are removed into the shadowy world of the narrative's past in which the ghosts continue to fight, dance and love. The music highlights this movement of visual 'spin' with a dramatic passage that first appears at the end of the first story and returns here at the end, providing a linking device across the three stories in this otherwise highly varied score.

'Lovin' the Spin I'm In' begins with smoky, dynamic images of dancers, recalling the opening sequence of the first story. But this time, the music that accompanies them is upbeat and furiously restless. A dialogue between real estate brokers, conducted without music, is counterpointed against the Torres Strait Islander mother Emelda (Debai Baira) and her brooding on the somewhat cryptic events of twelve years ago, involving her son's unhappy love affair. New tones are struck here, with a clarinet, slides across adjacent notes in the celeste and strings, and then highly percussive effects mixed in for the stylised female dancer. This part also features the measured, sad crooning of Emelda, and the raucous singing of the party crowd in the old warehouse. Snatches of a different music again underscore Dimitri (Lex Marinos) over-hearing a monologue by the Frida Kahlo figure, with pizzicato strings as if accompanying Sylvester the Cat in celebrated animation style, plus slides in the strings (two effects which recur when this character later mysteriously departs). This combination of pizzicato and sliding strings then is blended with the low sound of Imelda's mourning. As Dimitri escapes from the party and the warehouse, the broadest string sound of the score alternates with piano/celeste riffs, and many sound motifs (including bird calls) are fused as Dimitri shakes his head and sheds his confusion at enjoying the company of the people whom he is evicting the next day.

Dimitri's 14-year-old son Spiro (Riccardo Natoli) has been 'witnessing' a reenactment of the past in his present, and as he (and we, positioned by his viewpoint) muse on the red light emitting from behind the charmed door of the ramshackle warehouse, the music conveys passion and anger. While the red light links visually with the young boy's blood mixed with the down-pipe water in the first story, 'Mr Chuck', the storyline here is at its most punctuated and associative. The music carries considerable weight in lending dramatic cohesion, its suggestiveness often clarifying a particular mood or crystallising connections. Highly agitated when the ghostly couple (the ill-fated lovers) appears to Dimitri's son, the score returns to what seems to be its home territory for the lovers' red-lit ballet, choreographed alongside the rollerblade gymnastics of Dimitri's son. A sudden end to the visuals is echoed by an abrupt cadence in the music, just ahead of the opening rhythms which sound over the end titles, and before we are returned to the second story's Chinese Australian guide, Bob Malley (Cecil Parkee), of the Charleville museum, who embodies the cultural mix of the film.

This account of the film via a focus on its music is more detailed than the synopsis first considered but it also tells a rather different story. While it is self-evident that a film score of any quality interacts with the visual material, the converse is all too frequently overlooked, and visuals are treated in unwarranted isolation if a score as elaborate as the one for this film is present. Sound theorist, Michel Chion, has gone as far as to claim for films in general that "there is no soundtrack" (1994: 5), by which he means there is no acoustic entity that is distinct from the images with which it interacts. Vine's score by turns dramatises, projects, and in places virtually creates the narrative, with a range of moods and effects that function to integrate an ambitious and often elusive narrative. Just as Moffatt's narrative exposes fault lines in the laconic and rational aspects of iconic white Australia on screen, the sheer weighting allowed Vine's score is at odds with that allowed many Australian films, beyond those permeated by pre-existing elements such as *Strictly Ballroom* (dir: Baz Luhrmann, 1992) or *The Dish* (dir: Rob Sitch, 2000).

There are many stories within stories at issue in the tidy encapsulation of the three confronting narratives of *beDevil*. The film touches on many different kinds of 'looking' at both people and various social problems. In 'Mr Chuck', for example, the blond children silently watch shadows behind a frosted window and listen helplessly to the young Rick sobbing after his beating; the woman behind the clear glass windows and doors of her middle-class suburban home beats soundlessly on this glass to attract the attention of the departing camera and points to an old photograph – it is as if she knows that words alone cannot ever bear enough of the load of witnessing tragedy. These two sequences are part of a repeated pattern of performative motifs. Visually, these are motifs of eyes watching (replicated in Imelda's line, "I see you watching me boy... it doesn't matter"): eyes that stare confrontingly, glance quickly, turn away and back again – eyes that see much more than the audience does. These visual motifs are matched with a quite different kind of motif in the sound track constituted by a bewildering array of music and soundscapes. Yet there is nevertheless a pattern in what we hear throughout this film. Whilst eyes, both the audience's and the screen characters', are limited by the mechanics of vision, Vine's music travels across a broad palette of synthesised and acoustic instruments, using contrasting dynamic effects which pull the viewer into a realisation that all three ghost stories are concerned with issues of violence and race.

Vine's music performs for the audience a spatial awareness of complex situations. For example, at the beginning of 'Lovin' the Spin I'm In', simple percussive rhythms patter quietly underneath atonal sliding sounds as we glimpse waving fields of green sugarcane and hear the sound of laughter and singing. By the end of this story, these sounds and rhythms develop into a jarring, jagged mass of contrapuntal music that evokes the confused desperation of dreamed tragedies. Much more clearly than the visual images of roller-bladers and a spinning car, the sounds and mood of Vine's closing music for this story gather together all the discordant and sweetly disturbing sounds that permeate the film's three ghost stories. The visual motif, watching, is only accessible through vision. The sonic motif is one of unrestrained, ever-present passion, both sorrowful and playful. The sound track of this film vibrates through the listener's body and resonates with the limitless sense of sounds and hearing over which we have no control.

Conclusion

beDevil may unfortunately well prove a rarity with regard to the degree of flexibility accorded the score by the director. Vine's appreciation of this lack of intervention by Moffatt is supported by comments of production designer Stephen Curtis: "She allows people a lot of room to make a creative contribution" (in *beDevil* Press Kit, op cit). Mimura raises the issue of "what is at stake in this struggle between black Australian memory and leisure industry capitalism? ...nothing less than the myth-image of Australian national culture" (Mimura, 2003: 115). But the myth-image of Australian music is also at stake, both in terms of markers of national identity – never easy for Australian film (witness the use of the Albinoni *Adagio* at the key dramatic moment of *Gallipoli* [dir: Peter Weir, 1981]) – and in terms of music's place within the Australian film industry as well as the global film industry when it draws on 'Australian' components. *beDevil* presents to an audience an outstanding narrative partnership between what we see and what we hear, and neither aspect is a conventional representation of 'black Australian memory'. In making *beDevil*, Moffatt had enough courage and respect for a composer's ability to allow her film to develop as a rare work: a true amalgam of sight, sound and music.

Notes

1. For an excellent discussion of this genre, see Lim, B (2001).
2. Tony Buckley claims: "Luke Roberts has always played Frida Kahlo, always... he lives it. It's a 'life role'" (in Summerhayes, 2001: 317). Summerhayes's interview with Buckley conducted 30/11/99.
3. For a discussion of what the terms 'Dreamtime' and 'Dreaming' refer to in Australian Aboriginal culture, see Morton, J (2000).
4. Vine met Moffat while working on *The Master Builder* at the Belvoir Street Theatre in 1991.
5. Ronin Films Production notes (undated), courtesy of Andrew Pike. Some of the biographical material here is drawn from the Australian Music Centre website at http://www.amcoz.com.au.
6. In *beDevil* press kit, available in AFTRS library, Sydney, 1993.
7. We are grateful to Carl Vine for agreeing to an interview with Roger Hillman, and for allowing access to his copy of the score, which is not publicly available. While he corrected some false assumptions of the interviewer, interpretative aspects of this chapter are the sole responsibility of the authors, and do not necessarily reflect the composer's own view.
8. The sound design of *beDevil* is worthy of examination elsewhere. Acclaimed sound designer Frank Lipson observed how much "fun" he had working on the film due to the "creative room" offered to him by Moffat as well as producers Tony Buckley and Carol Hughes who were "committed to giving us time to experiment" (*beDevil* press kit, Sydney, 1993: unpaginated). Sound effects were electronically distorted and manipulated to give them surreal qualities, for example, the choo choo train sound was built from a combination of tiger's roar, an F1-11 aeroplane and various metallic sounds.

Chapter Fifteen

THE COMPOSER AS ALCHEMIST: An Overview of Australian Feature Film Scores 1994-2004

MICHAEL ATHERTON

When music first accompanied film it was performed live to image by an improvising composer/performer. Typically a pianist or organist filled the bill – anticipating sequences, interpreting emotions, adding a psychological dimension to the pictures. In a metaphoric sense, this was and still is a form of alchemy[1] needed to create the 'invisible character'[2] in the film. In the last decade the composer as alchemist not only writes original music but also conceives and produces a score that is a seamless and distinctive component of the composite soundtrack (Neumeyer and Buhler, 2001). And the composer as collaborator is often called on to blend genres and styles – for example, songs, world music, orchestral music and electronic textures.

This chapter accepts the various roles and functions of film music as described in literature from the last three decades (see Gorbman, C [1987]; Prendergast, R.M [1992]; Brown, R.S [1994]; Lack, R [1997]; Coyle, R [1998]; Donnelly, K [2001]; Kassabian, A [2001]). In relation to the last decade, I argue that the composer is also a filmmaker caught up in an evolving aesthetic shaped by multiple approaches to creating the music. This chapter considers collaborative processes, interactions with directors and uses of technology as a way of mapping a variety of approaches and trends in scoring the feature film. I examine film scores from various perspectives, namely: classical legacies, hybrids and compilations, popular voices, musical offerings, and innovation. My study draws primarily on the experiences of leading Australian film composers[3], using material largely from personal interviews conducted in 2003-2004[4], to provide an overview of the last decade. All quotations from composers, unless otherwise cited, are from interviews conducted by the author.

228

Collaboration

Current practice offers a range of possibilities for creating and/or compiling a music score. At one extreme there are scores that rely on classical music – or interpretations of classic works – to be cut and pasted by music producers/composers, an approach that began with the piano/organ players accompanying films. At the other extreme, there are films that blur the boundaries between sound and music, each having an equal role in interpreting and manipulating the emotion of a film.

Composers emphasise that creating film music is a complex collaborative process, which involves working in multiple roles – composing, orchestrating, music preparation and music editing. Composers have idiosyncratic working methods. Nerida Tyson-Chew, for example, a predominantly orchestral composer and conductor of her own film music, keeps to a specific time frame:

Week One – I ask myself how many minutes I need to write … work out the budget … break the film into threads. Where are the big moments? Where are the intimate moments?

Week Two – I write 2 to 3 minutes a day, orchestrating as I go, working through the film and to a deadline. My approach means planning first, composing second.

Week Three – I preview with the director … play themes on the piano over the telephone. [To] give the orchestral effect I will do a mock up using Digital Performer and a sampling library.

Others such as Burkhard Dallwitz suggest early involvement in the film production process:

Sometimes you get involved when the film is in its early state, and sometimes at the final cut stage … I sometimes start with a melody idea or just some sounds. (in Walker, 1999: online)

David Bridie closely connects film music and sounds with the musicians who will record them:

I create a palette of sounds and think of particular musicians playing the music. I view the whole film and think of say six to eight key scenes that stand out for me, and I compose a whole bunch of things, sometimes using a theme and variation approach.

The use of the temporary ('temp') track by the director is a major issue for film composers. A temp is a shortcut as well as a tool for understanding. It gives the editor and director something to cut to or discuss with the composer. Temps are mostly used early in postproduction to present rough assemblies to producers. Some composers never want to hear temps because they are a constraint that can pollute their own creativity. Martin Armiger sees the use of temporary tracks as problematic:

The professional of course works around them but there is much ambivalence. I watch the film without 'temp' tracks, then sit at the piano for three to four days. I test chords, textures and melodies and check things again against pictures to see if they work, to see what needs to be developed.

229

The Influence of Digital Technologies

The increasing use of electronic sound in film is linked to rapid developments in technology in the 1990s that have influenced the way a composer works. There is also a greater appreciation of sound design *per se*. Sound is as important an experience as the music or the images (Lack, 1997: 288; Buhler, 2001: 52). Sound effects and atmospheres, 'foley' design and the sound of the dialogue, and composition are more finely integrated into the aural dimension (de Vilder).

The development of music technology has made the job of a film composer easier in the last decade. Orchestral samples not only substitute live performance, but the dedicated orchestral composer will use them as a mock-up to prepare directors for the final result. However, this does not preclude the composer still using the more traditional approach to playing the score on the piano for the director, describing aspects of the full orchestration (Dallwitz in Walker, op cit). But it's now a common expectation of producers, directors and music editors to want the mock-up, much like record companies expect a well-realised demo.

New technology has had another significant effect on scoring. Art Phillips says:

> It has enabled the composer to find a logical tempo to match the visuals, providing ... space to think imaginatively without being impeded by mathematical calculations. (in Hallett, 1991: online)

With computers and non-linear editing, a composer can see five different versions of the film, whereas once reels had to be changed and physically spliced. Tyson-Chew says, "While the computer has helped me to get faster, it's also a tool for the other collaborators, and one that is often waiting for me to catch up!"

Grid based composer software has provided more options and flexibility for composers. Nearly every project finishes up in a Protools format or similar. This has negated the risk of quality loss in analogue transfer. The composer delivers what is heard in the final mix (Armiger). A composer or editor can take a cue and cut it around and use it anywhere. This has become a more organic way of doing things, grabbing, looping and filtering (Bridie). This technology has turned the home studio into a powerful site for composition and engineering. Bridie suggests that it alleviates some of the nervousness between composer and director if one can show 16 tracks on a computer monitor. The director can see as well as hear the geography of the music. There are no surprises when the composer can visually illustrate a gesture using different colours. It can show a director where, for example, brass enters or how the strings work together (ibid). In this way the composer can make any necessary changes in the MIDI studio environment and avoid the anxiety of significant last minute changes on the sound stage, as the orchestra sits, budget-meter ticking, waiting to record.

However, if technology helps the director to preview orchestral music before it is finally recorded, it also has the potential to alter the craft of film composition – and not necessarily to good effect. Keyboard patches can sound seductive to directors in a MIDI environment but can often flatten the final score. While a synthesiser score can of course be powerfully effective – for example Vangelis's score for *Blade Runner* (dir: Ridley Scott, 1982) – it can also be a tool of expediency for a composer with limited technique (Gordon). A chosen pre-set or sound effect might sound great on home studio speakers but it can "sound pathetic in the cinema" (Armiger). There's a trend in movie scoring at the moment in which beds of sustained string sounds come from the lush samples used in the preview or temp tracks. Tyson-Chew observes:

> It has to be kept in mind when dealing with samplers that one keystroke on a string patch may sound like 12-16 violins, so a 4-part chord in the top register may sound like 48 violins, and the budget may only allow for 8. Live strings need movement both for the sound of the music and for the musicians' intelligence. It is important to keep things moving, not only to hold the musicians' interest, but also to give the music shape and growth.

Chris Neal ponders whether music technology, while helping the conception and demonstration of a score, has a negative influence by encouraging filmmakers to devalue music. The question is a loaded one, and may only yield an answer retrospectively, in longer-term analysis of this important transitional period for music technology.

Multiple Approaches

An evolving aesthetic for film composition is also shaped by multiple approaches used for creating and/or realising the music. Every film project is essentially a *tabula rasa* for the professional composer, for which any kind of musical genre or style might be relevant, depending upon what is required and the budget to achieve it (Bell, 1994). However, in overviewing the last decade some themes emerge.

(i) Classical legacies

Many Australian composers, if given the opportunity, aspire to projects involving orchestral music. Like their 1970s and 1980s counterparts, for example, Brian May and Bruce Smeaton, some contemporary composers such as Christopher Gordon, Nerida Tyson-Chew, Alan John, Sharon Calcraft and Nigel Westlake are committed to an orchestral approach. For them, an orchestra allows the composer to be "subliminal, effective and emotional" (Tyson-Chew)[5]. In a sense they emulate and build on a Hollywood-influenced aesthetic grounded in classical compositional techniques. Composer Guy Gross feels passionately about the value of classical music for film:

> I believe it's because classical music is simply more expressive and can contain great empathy, sorrow, depth, you name it ... all the range of emotions. Perhaps the contemporary music of today will become the classical music of tomorrow but I don't think so. I'm a huge fan of closely following dialogue, action, camera moves, etc. (in Florianz, undated: online)

Gordon goes further: "Certain musical events press emotional buttons". He cites Richard Wagner as a model for seeking the psychological element, resulting in his uses of harmonic clusters, and consonance and dissonance.

Before composing for the telemovie *Moby Dick* (dir: Franc Roddam, 1998), Gordon looked at all the characters in relation to the main character Ahab. He viewed all the characters as aspects of Ahab's psyche and created a detailed score. Whenever Ahab was 'centre-stage' he used the key of Bminor and its dominant Fsharp. But when the action changed he would "go off into lots of keys, returning abruptly whenever the attention returned to Ahab".

Tyson-Chew composed the score for *Hotel Sorrento* (dir: Richard Franklin, 1995). It was her first feature film, for which she composed, orchestrated and conducted a music score that combines a commitment to a classical aesthetic with a respect for the orchestral musicians with whom she works:

> In Hotel Sorrento *violas and second violins would often interchange and therefore sometimes violas would be above the second violins. I think this also helps to keep the music full of life and prevents things from becoming a bit dull – especially for cues under dialogue or voice-over.*

For the film *Under the Lighthouse Dancing* (dir: Graeme Rattigan, 1997) Tyson-Chew produced another memorable score, although the film did not attract strong box office figures. The striking imagery of its Rottnest Island location is matched by richly textured and lengthy orchestral music cues. In the psychological thriller, *Visitors* (dir: Richard Franklin, 2002), Tyson-Chew combines her neoclassical aesthetic with the benefits of new technology. Electronically processed string colours ("pre-recorded weird sounds of creepy strings" according to Tyson-Chew) are combined with written cues for musicians. This layering approach is common in contemporary film scoring where the approach is often dictated by budget.

(ii) Hybrids and compilations

The creatively compiled score is another prominent approach used in Australian feature films over the last decade. This score typically includes original music supporting pre-existing musical repertoire – that may itself be arranged – and requires the composer to be a supreme alchemist to create a workable flow for the film as a whole.

The compositional aesthetic is often tempered by having to work in and around existing classical repertoire chosen by the director. Such was the case for *Babe* (dir: Chris Noonan, 1995). In contending with music by Camille Saint-Saëns, Léo Delibes, Edvard Grieg and Gabriel Fauré, film composer Nigel Westlake created transitions using lively dance rhythms, helping keep up the pace between dialogue and action. The film's theme comes from Saint-Saëns's *The Carnival of the Animals* (from *Symphony No 3 in C* [1886]). The music is heard throughout the film in a number of arrangements – for example, as a lullaby and an Irish jig. This is an exuberant and engaging music score for a fairytale-like film, one that resonates with the Hollywood cartoon animation. Westlake uses the full resources of the orchestra with plenty of layers and a brightness achieved through featured combinations of instruments such as piccolo, xylophone, celeste and string pizzicatos. Repetition in the musical segments is an important structural device in the film, one that a young audience would particularly relate to. There are musical interludes 'sung by' a chorus of mice. There are also elements of intertextuality, as when the protagonist Babe sees the implements of butchering, the fate of most pigs, and the music is momentarily reminiscent of Bernard Herrmann's music for *Psycho* (dir: Alfred Hitchcock, 1960) (Graydanus, 2003).

In *Shine* (dir: Scott Hicks, 1996) composer David Hirschfelder accepted the challenge of providing a score that "makes emotional comment" that is "unobtrusive and evocative" (Hallett, 1996: 26). Hirschfelder had to integrate his own music with the idiosyncratic piano playing of David Helfgott, the subject of the film, playing music by Ludwig van Beethoven, Robert Schumann, Franz Liszt, Frédéric Chopin and Sergei Rachmaninoff (see Magowan, 1998).

A more recent hybrid score is *The Truman Show* (dir: Peter Weir, 1998) for which postproduction was completed in Australia and an Australian composer, Burkhard von Dallwitz, was engaged. Director Weir's approach to the film incorporated a meld of composers (including David Hirschfelder) and styles. Dallwitz provided most of the original music[6] for which he used synthesisers, strings, piano and percussion with some vocal colours. This was integrated with Weir's choices of existing works by Philip Glass, Chopin, Wojciech Kilar, and the song *Twentieth Century Boy* (1973) by Marc Bolan.

Weir often pushes for a hybrid musical approach to suit specific needs. For *Master and Commander: The Far Side of the World* (dir: Peter Weir, 2003)[7] he invited three different Australian composers to join the project: Iva Davies, Christopher Gordon and Richard Tognetti. This is an unusual collaboration between three leaders in their own fields: Davies comes from a popular music background as instigator of Icehouse but is a classically trained oboist with experience in writing for dance and film. Tognetti is the inspirational leader and virtuoso violinist in the Australian Chamber Orchestra. And Gordon is an orchestral film composer with an Imax film *The Story of Sydney* (dir: Bruce Beresford, 2001) and a major television feature, *Moby Dick*, to his credit. Davies was engaged initially to supply an electronic element, and Tognetti worked on set in Mexico teaching Russell Crowe to play the violin. Weir added Gordon, when he heard the composition called *The Ghost of Time*, a piece based on one of Davies' Icehouse themes, written for the Millennium Eve celebrations at the Sydney Opera House. Weir was impressed by this music and wanted the trio to explore it in Los Angeles, so engaged the trio as his "personal palette" (Gordon, in Dalkin, 2003: online).

Tognetti developed the source music, comprising folk music and classical arrangements played on solo violin and in duet with the cello; Davies drew on his experience with synthesisers to provide an electronic soundscape; and Gordon worked on most of the orchestration. Gordon describes the process:

> *I don't recall a single cue in which we all composed the piece equally. Iva worked on the sounds of the ship, the Surprise, and also the tempo changes. Peter wanted drums as a call to battle. Iva developed these sections and we used Taiko drums. Iva did MIDI realisations and I would compose the orchestral material. These would be passed onto a hired assistant who would realise the cues electronically with samples. We then presented them to Peter Weir. Often he would surprise us by asking*

for melody where we had not thought of it. In one case Iva and Richard wrote a counter-melody and worked it up on the synthesizers. A new draft was produced, and I produced a new orchestral version. We realised we were Peter's paintbrush, he would try things out. Of course, as professionals, we would often get cues right first go. (in Dalkin, ibid)

Weir had two main requirements for the music. To emphasise that the ship was on a journey to the unknown, suggesting a lonely space voyage, electronic sounds were used to reinforce other-worldliness. The other requirement related to the harsh lives of the men on the *Surprise*. All they knew was war and preparing for or engaging in it. The film begins and ends with a battle. Clearly, Weir was working away from the convention of the sea adventure and the swashbuckling stereotype. The result is a largely textural and hybrid music track. Gordon recalls:

When Iva gave Peter The Ghost of Time *album he pointed out the latter part of* Endless Ocean *as a possible style or texture for some of the film. We were quite surprised when we found that Peter had placed the beginning of the piece into a couple of spots in the film. It is a growing single sustained note that is eventually joined by another.* Endless Ocean *plays this three times before breaking loose. Peter liked the tension and even the irritation that this relentless crescendo brought to the scenes. I re-scored it to fit the picture but it is essentially the introduction to* Endless Ocean *... as it turns out, a great choice of title!* (ibid)

One of the unifying devices in the film is in the use of three inversions of a major seventh chord, which the composer called the 'ghost' chord, referring to its original in *The Ghost of Time*. Another motivic element is heard in the drumming with a couple of rhythmic cells being repeated[8].

Davies acknowledges Weir's musical concept as something that became an organic process: "Weir was putting things in front of us ... that had elements he liked." For example, one recurring element in the score is the use of large Japanese taiko drums. The taut skins of these instruments lend themselves to sharply defined sonorities, and are used in the film to enhance the battle scenes and became a signature call to action.

The whole idea of a ship of that period going off into totally uncharted territory was a bit like setting off for Mars. I guess he wanted to submerge everybody in the idea that these people were in danger and they didn't know quite what they were going to run into. In that sense, rather than do the obvious Hollywood thing [the score] is quite minimal and futuristic in a peculiar way. (Davies in http://www.christopher-gordon.net/master.html)

In addition to original music from Davies and Gordon, the film also includes folk music and incorporates existing recordings of classical music and arrangements for violin and cello by Richard Tognetti. Weir goes against Hollywood convention by using a hybrid score, looking for contrasts, and avoiding thematic construction. The combination of contemporary drum rhythms, electronic sounds and foreboding strings is achieved through a unique collaborative approach, one that is in sharp contrast with the expected through-composed seafaring score.

(iii) Popular voices

The 1990s saw a new wave of film composers (Baker, 1992) with popular music or rock and roll backgrounds, notably Phil Judd, John Clifford White, David Hirschfelder, Martin Armiger, David Bridie, Ricky Fataar, Chris Neal and Art Phillips, all of whom work in a range of genres and styles (Whiteoak and Scott-Maxwell, 2003: 164).

Judd, formerly from the band Split Enz, moved into film composition with his music for the black comedy *Death in Brunswick* (dir: John Ruane, 1991)[9]. This film's story centres on an Anglo-Australian leading character. The setting is a Greek nightclub in an inner city suburb with a large ethnic population. Most of the supporting characters are of Greek and Turkish origin. The music is simple but melodic and catchy, and is redolent of multicultural Melbourne. Judd includes specifically Greek compositions by bouzouki player Peter Volaris, and hired a multicultural ensemble of session musicians to perform his score.

The band Not Drowning, Waving led by David Bridie[10] worked as a collective on several feature films including *Proof* (dir: Jocelyn Moorhouse, 1991), in which orchestral strings are added to percussion, piano and guitar. The textures are light and allow dialogue to be highlighted in the film to augment the blind protagonist's flashbacks to early childhood. Bridie subsequently became a film composer in his own right. His craft has developed out of a range of skills that includes song-writing and intercultural collaboration epitomised in the *sui generis* album *Tabaran* (1991). Bridie's thorough exploitation of music technology is realised in scores for *In a Savage Land* (dir: Bill Bennett, 1999) and *Tempted* (dir: Bill Bennett, 2001). The latter film is set in the swamp country of New Orleans. Bridie did location recordings of crickets, frogs and a range of soundscapes. He mixes music and natural sounds instinctively, even using recordings of cars driving over a creaky bridge to sample and create loops. Bridie believes that early involvement in the film project and going on location makes his contribution more germane to the project, the location helping him to become more engaged emotionally. This was the case for his score for *In a Savage Land* set in the Trobriand Islands, Papua New Guinea (discussed elsewhere in this volume). Bridie went on location to record, and then created a multi-layered score that won the 1999 AFI Best Original Score award.

Bridie also writes orchestral music according to the needs of a film and its budget, as in *The Man who Sued God* (dir: Mark Joffe, 2001). While he appreciates an orchestra's capacity for creating a big sound, he is also an advocate for being more experimental, and cautions against the credo that the orchestra is the only way to create successful film music. His capacity to blend music and sound to create specific timbres and textures suggest a different aesthetic to that of his neo-classically oriented colleagues.

The seamless blending of music and sound seems particularly valued by composers coming from a popular music background, to the point that in some films it becomes an identifiable aesthetic. *Romper Stomper* (dir: Geoffrey Wright, 1992) exemplifies the meld of high volume music, in particular punk or skinhead songs, and industrial noise that contributes to the confrontational power of this film. Clifford White's approach to the music is antithetical to neoclassicism, suiting the director's vision for this style conveyed in the original spotting session (see Miller, 1998). This type of music and sound meld is also emphasised in the work of director, composer and musician Philip Brophy (see Samartzis, 1998).

Other well-regarded voices amongst Australian film composers[11] draw on jazz and improvisation backgrounds for their work. David Hirschfelder created the score for *Better Than Sex* (dir: Jonathan Teplitzky, 2000)[12]. Hirschfelder composed for an ensemble of violin, drums, guitar, double bass, vibraphone, piano and Hammond organ. The score is a combination of original music, standards, and items by The Cruel Sea and Kylie Minogue. Hirschfelder exploits his multiple skills as music director, keyboard performer and composer to create subtle underscore for the dialogue and the humour in *Better Than Sex*.

(iv) Musical offerings

A notable development in the 1990s Australian feature film is the incorporation of popular songs and dance in a way that suggests the Hollywood musical. The compilation approach is dynamically realised in *Strictly Ballroom* (dir: Baz Luhrmann, 1992), *The Adventures of Priscilla, Queen of the Desert* (dir: Stephan Elliott, 1994), *Muriel's Wedding* (dir: PJ Hogan, 1994) and *Moulin Rouge* (dir: Baz Luhrmann, 2001).

These musical offerings also use existing recordings as well as original composition in the music track. In some cases the songs function as the narrative itself. Such films require a composer with experience as a musical performer/producer/director. For the *Strictly Ballroom* score, David Hirschfelder developed dance elements while also celebrating cultural diversity through music[13].

Hirschfelder describes his experience as having to create a score that was a "seamless marriage" between the diegetic dance music and the underscore:

> I was getting to utilise all of my hats as a producer of popular music, as an arranger and blend that into underscore ... The Blue Danube was used as the 'heroic call' of the Ballroom world. Time After Time was chosen by Luhrmann as a feature song that would connect with the audience, and connect the film with modern culture instantly ... We structured it as a theatre piece. (Hirschfelder in Gordon, 1992: 4-5)

Hirschfelder substituted the Zubin Mehta *Blue Danube* recording chosen by Luhrmann with a computer generated version in order to fit the dance timings required and also because the rights to the original were too expensive.

Other musical offerings such as *The Adventures of Priscilla, Queen of the Desert* and *Muriel's Wedding* draw on conventions of musical comedy where songs carry the narrative through performance in the film (Lumby, 1998). Peter Best's skills as a songwriter are exploited in *Muriel's Wedding* where he created a score to support a collection of ABBA songs, including a fully orchestrated instrumental version of the 1976 hit, *Dancing Queen* (Berardinelli, 1995). Best also composed the scores for *Dad and Dave: On Our Selection* (dir: George Whaley, 1995) and *Doing Time for Patsy Cline* (dir: Chris Kennedy, 1997). Having worked in commercials production, Best developed versatile popular music compositional skills, and demonstrates a strong sense of how a sequence of songs can work as a unifying device. In *Doing Time for Patsy Cline* he explores Nashville and Australian country music approaches.

The use of the off-camera singing voice as a narrator is central to the narrative of *The Tracker* (dir: Rolf de Heer, 2002) with music by Graham Tardif and lyrics by de Heer[14]. This is an allegorical film dealing with race relations (especially between Aboriginal people and European settlers) and reconciliation in the 1920s. The story takes place in the spectacular Flinders Ranges. Like the medieval morality play, the characters do not have proper names but are identified by their role and function in the narrative: Tracker (David Gulpilil), Fanatic (Gary Sweet), Follower (Damon Gameau) and Veteran (Grant Page). De Heer conveys the story through a combination of music, movement and painting, reflecting multiple modes used by indigenous storytellers. Graphic violence is depicted in images painted by Peter Coad, while the song-based sound track conveys the actions behind the images.

Another film narrated through song but operating with film musical references is *One Night the Moon* (dir: Rachel Perkins, 2001). The score is by Paul Kelly, Kevin Carmody and Mairead Hannan and resembles a singer-songwriter musical with country and western resonances (as discussed by Kate Winchester elsewhere in this volume).

(v) Innovation

Australian film composers are also innovators and given to experimenting with different approaches to film composition. These styles are not merely designed as expedient means to produce original music scored elements with limited budgets but also reflect a set of aesthetic techniques.

Some composers have developed distinctive voices, for example Cezary Skubiszewski[15] who argued, "I started doing film music to surprise myself, to push myself. I wanted to break the rules, stretch myself, and get extra energy and inspiration." He lists influences including Penderecki, and, "being a big fan of French films, I'm caught up in the way they create a *cool* atmosphere." Skubiszewski's first feature film score was for *Lillian's Story* (dir: Jerzy Domaradzki, 1995) in which he claims to bring:

> a delicate dimension to the film, contributing to it without overpowering it. There are three main themes. The opening theme uses a chord progression as a melodic device, moving it along every two bars.

There are subtle voicings of muted strings contributing in the words of the composer to a "sad sound". A piano theme appears as a simple statement in rondo form, only to be developed by using cello and shifting the melody by semitones. The orchestral music includes a choir singing chords off the beat, following an example from Penderecki, and creating clusters in 16-part harmony. This provides tension in a courthouse scene, in particular when the topic of child abuse is addressed. Simple rhythmic elements are assigned to percussive writing for basses and cellos. The music is often sparse yet so poignant, especially under Lillian's opening soliloquy where the high voices bring us closer to Lillian's emotional state.

The Sound of One Hand Clapping (dir: Richard Flanagan, 1998) is a film about migration and the building of a dam in Tasmania. Skubiszewski's music reflects on and combines various cultural influences in Australia in a bold approach. He focuses on Gypsy musical heritage as a unifying device, using a hammered dulcimer, in this case an Iranian santur, common to the music of the Middle East, southern and central Europe. The score locates time, place and ethnicity in the writing. An orchestra supports Irish uillean pipes – not dissimilar in colour to the Macedonian gaida. Gypsy-influenced clarinet and violin styles as well as Spanish castanets and hand-clapping are included. Other instruments in the score include vocals, bodhran, cajon and a sampled music box. A significant innovation here is the combination of quartertones played by the santur set against the orchestra in equal temperament. This is not simply world music per se. Skubiszewski is making an aesthetic statement about film composition that is Australian, multicultural and of our time. He frequently features solo instruments such as Spanish guitar or accordion, or, in the case of *The Sound of One Hand Clapping*, the bright steely timbre of the santur. In *Two Hands* (1999) he contrasts what he describes as "twisted Morricone type guitars with big jazzy brass, playing around with conventional voicings so that the music is never fully serious".

Humour is also noticeable, as in *La Spagnola* (dir: Brendan Maher, 2001) with a score combining colours and rhythms that suggest the cross-cultural experience of life in Australia. Vibrant combinations of brass, guitars, accordion, castanets and orchestral strings constitute much of the sound palette. A sex scene in this film is underscored by music that might be heard at a bullfight. The instrumentation includes trumpets, tuba, soprano saxophone and snare drum. Innovation, versatility and humour are also evident in Skubiszewski's score for *The Rage in Placid Lake* (dir: Tony McNamara, 2003). Here he combines bossa nova with hip-hop to capture the upbeat and youthful feel of the film. Peer appreciation of Skubiszewski's techniques is evident in the number of awards he has achieved since 1995[16].

Conclusion

The strength of the feature film composer in Australia includes the capacity to use multiple and diverse approaches, including Hollywood orchestral influences, cross-cultural music and new technologies. It is notable that when Hollywood-based directors such as Peter Weir work with Australian composers they also require these sorts of approaches, which questions whether Australian composers have developed specific profiles along these lines. Certainly this chapter suggests that a new type of film culture is emerging in Australia, one that is "moving away from large-scale systems" (Neal). Overall, fewer personnel are required in shooting and post production. Copyright libraries continue to have a prominent status in the realisation of the score, as filmmakers shift towards a blurring of sound and music. Furthermore, in a period of severely limited budgets for original music components (as distinct from budgets for royalty payments for existing musics) the film composer has to be protean to survive.

Training and development of the film composer for such a role presents a problem: what is the ideal training and development for the film composer, as musicians with different sets of skills come onto the scene, especially those who rely on technology to produce a music closer to sound effects? Furthermore, training and development (see Atherton, 2003) is required, not just for aspiring composers but also for other personnel in the filmmaking team, in order for a full exploration of the composer's role in future film productions. Given the evolving aesthetic described in this study, the composer's alchemy will change commensurately in another decade.

Notes

1. Alchemy is a "power or process of transmuting" (Delbridge, A et al (eds) 1997: 85).

2. Art Phillips in 'The invisible character', a talk given at the Australian Guild of Screen Composers/ Australian Film Institute Seminar, Chauvel Cinema, Paddington, NSW, 29/7/1992.

3. I am concerned with Australian composers and their work on feature films that may or may not have been produced and directed in Australia or deal with Australian locations.

4. Interviews conducted by the author with:
    - Armiger, Martin (2003) Kings Cross, 21/12, and further discussions via telephone, 24/12.
    - Bridie, David (2003) via telephone, 22/12.
    - de Vilder, Yantra (2003) via email, 23/10, and further discussions via telephone, 25/10.
    - Gordon, Christopher (2003) Rozelle, 9/11, and further discussions via telephone, 12/11.
    - Gross, Guy (2003) via email, 16/10.
    - Hirschfelder, David (2003) in 'On the Couch' hosted by Michael Atherton for Australian Guild of Screen Composers, 20/5.
    - Neal, Chris (2003) via email, 24/10.
    - Skubiszewski, Cezary (2003) via telephone, 21/11 and via email, 22/12.
    - Tyson-Chew, Nerida (2004) Darlinghurst, 11/1, and further discussions via telephone, 15/1.

5. Nerida Tyson-Chew is a multi-award winning composer who commenced her career as a concert pianist before studying film composition in Los Angeles.

6. Dallwitz won a Golden Globe Award for his work.

7. *Master and Commander: The Far Side of the World* received 9 nominations at the 76th Annual Academy Awards, 2004, including Best Picture. Russell Boyd won an Oscar for Cinematography; Richard King for Sound Editing.

8. This working process is unusual for Gordon who usually looks at the structure of the film right down to tonality as would a symphonist.

9. *Death In Brunswick* (1991) Best Original Score, APRA Awards 1991. Another film – *The Big Steal* (1990) Best Original Score, AFI 1990.

10. Bridie's background is detailed in Hayward (1998). He currently works as a musician, producer, songwriter and composer.

11. Other composers with a popular music background deserving mention are Chris Neal (*Turtle Beach* dir: Stephen Wallace, 1992), Ricky Fataar (*Spotswood* dir: Mark Joffe, 1992) and Paul Grabowsky (*Last Days of Chez Nous* dir: Gillian Armstrong, 1992).

12. *Better than Sex* was voted best feature film score by the Australian Guild of Screen Composers in 2000.

13. For a detailed discussion of the film, refer to Coyle (2003) Chapter 4:' "Soundbites of Cultures": Hearing Multicultural Australia in *Strictly Ballroom's* Music', pp135–213.

14. Graham Tardif worked as a sound editor before moving into film composition.

15. Skubiszewski was born in Warsaw, Poland. He migrated to Australia in 1974 and has played in and composed for a number of rock, jazz and classical groups.

16. Skubiszewski has achieved a string of successes with such films as:
     Lillian's Story (1995) – Best music, Asia Pacific Film Festival 1997
     The Sound of One Hand Clapping (1998) – Best Soundtrack, APRA 1998
     Two Hands (1999) – Best Film Score APRA 2000
     Bootmen (2000) – Best Original Music Score, AFI 2001
     La Spagnola (2001) – Best Original Music Score, AFI 2001
     After the Deluge (2003) – Best Soundtrack, APRA/AGSC Screen Awards.

ABOUT THE AUTHORS

Michael Atherton is professor of music and research director in the College of Arts, Education and Social Sciences within the University of Western Sydney. His composition and intercultural collaborative work has resulted in feature film, documentary, choral, and music theatre scores. Email m.atherton@uws.edu.au

Rebecca Coyle edited *Screen Scores: Studies in Contemporary Australian Film Music* (Allen and Unwin/AFTRS, 1998) and completed a Cultural Studies PhD in film music. She is Course Coordinator of the Media Program at Southern Cross University, Lismore. Email rcoyle@scu.edu.au

Mark Evans lectures in the Department of Contemporary Music Studies, Macquarie University, Sydney, and is co-editor of *Perfect Beat: The Pacific Journal of Research into Contemporary Music and Popular Culture*. His doctoral thesis examined secularisation in contemporary Christian music. Recent film music publications include chapters on spatiality in the Matrix movies trilogy. Email mark.evans@mq.edu.au

Michael Hannan is a composer, musicologist, and music critic. He is the author of *The Australian Guide to Careers in Music* (UNSW Press, 2003) and coordinates the Contemporary Music program at Southern Cross University in Lismore. Email mhannan@scu.edu.au

Philip Hayward is professor of Contemporary Music Studies at Macquarie University, Sydney and has written and edited several books including, most recently, *Off The Planet: Music, Sound and Science Fiction Cinema* (John Libbey/Perfect Beat Publications, 2004). Email phayward@pip2.hmn.mq.edu.au

Anna Hickey-Moody, at Monash University, Melbourne, is a writer, dancer and teacher, and has published writings on contemporary Australian and youth performing arts. She is completing her PhD titled 'Unimaginable Bodies: intellectual disability, performance and becoming'. Email motionloss@yahoo.com.au or anna.hickeymoody@education.monash.edu.au

Roger Hillman is currently Head of Film Studies and Convenor of German Studies at the Australian National University, Canberra. Publications in the areas of film and music include a collaboration with Deborah Crisp, and the forthcoming monograph *Unsettling Scores: German Film, Music, Ideology* (Indiana University Press, 2005). Email Roger.Hillman@anu.edu.au

Shane Homan teaches media and cultural studies at the University of Newcastle, Australia. He is author of *The Mayor's A Square: Live Music and Law and Order in Sydney* (Local Consumption Publications, 2003) and several published writings on the Australian music industry and cultural policy. He is a former chair of the Australia-New Zealand branch of the International Association for the Study of Popular Music. Email Shane.Homan@newcastle.edu.au

Melissa Iocco lectures in Gender Studies at the University of Tasmania and is completing a PhD on perverse masculinities and contemporary film. Her published work examines intersections between psychoanalysis, gender and cultural studies. Email melissa.iocco@utas.edu.au

Bruce Johnson is an established jazz musician based in the School of English, University of New South Wales, Sydney. He has written on popular music,

cultural politics and Australian studies in *The Oxford Companion to Australian Jazz* (Oxford UP, 1987) and *The Inaudible Music* (Currency Press, 2000) examining jazz, gender and Australian modernity. He is active in arts administration, research and policy formation, including the establishment of the government funded Australian Jazz Archives. Email B.Johnson@unsw.edu.au

Marjorie Kibby is a senior lecturer in Cultural Studies at the University of Newcastle, Australia. Her research and teaching interests focus on the representations of cultural groups, practices and artifacts in the media, including the use of the didjeridu as a symbol in film, music and on the Internet. Email marj.kibby@newcastle.edu.au

Jude Magee lives and works in Lismore, Northern New South Wales. She has taught musicianship and music theory at Southern Cross University, Lismore, as well as several high schools, and directs a regularly performing acapella group, Isabella a Capella. Her Honours thesis explored industry practices and processes in Australian film music production, and her PhD research is on the various functions of the *Paradise Road* film music. Email mageejessup@dodo.com.au

Tony Mitchell is a senior lecturer in Cultural Studies at UTS. He is the author of *Popular Music and Local Identity* (Leicester UP, 1996), the editor of *Global Noise: Rap and Hip Hop Outside the USA* (Wesleyan UP, 2001) and *Liminal Sounds and Images: Transnational Chinese Popular Music* (2004, forthcoming) as well as four recent articles about the films of Clara Law. Email tony.mitchell@uts.edu.au

Helen O'Shea recently completed a doctoral thesis at Victoria University of Technology, Melbourne, on 'Foreign Bodies in the River of Sound: Identity and Irish Traditional Music'. She has taught Australian Studies and Gender Studies at Victorian universities and has played Irish traditional music in Australia and Ireland since the 1970s. Email hoshea@bigpond.net.au

Gaye Poole currently lectures in the Department of Theatre Studies, University of Waikato, New Zealand. She has stage credits as an actor in numerous productions for stage and television. She has taught theatre and film studies in Australian universities and in Europe, and completed an MA (Hons) at the University of New South Wales. Her publications include *Reel Meals, Set Meals: Food in Film and Theatre* (Currency, 1999). Email gpoole@waikato.ac.nz

Jon Stratton is professor of Cultural Studies at Curtin University of Technology, Perth, and has published widely including, most recently, *Race Daze: Australia in Identity Crisis* (Pluto Australia, 1998) and *Coming Out Jewish: Constructing Ambivalent Identities* (Routledge, 2000). He is currently completing a number of essays on popular music in Australia. Email J.Stratton@curtin.edu.au

Catherine Summerhayes's doctoral thesis, 'Film As Cultural Performance' and subsequent monograph includes close analyses of *beDevil* (dir: Tracey Moffatt, 1993) and David MacDougall's documentary *Link-Up Diary* (1988). Her most recent research area is intertextuality in the context of documentary film. Her thesis for her Bachelor of Letters degree at Australian National University, Canberra, examined film, fiction and anthropology. Email Catherine.Summerhayes@anu.edu.au

Kate Winchester completed an Honours degree in 2003 combining Anthropology and Contemporary Music studies at Macquarie University, Sydney. As a musician, she has performed in Australia and Europe. Email winchester_kate@hotmail.com

242

BIBLIOGRAPHY

Allen, R (1999) 'Psychoanalytic Film Theory' in Miller, T and Stam, R (eds) *A Companion to Film Theory*, Oxford: Blackwell

Altman, R (ed) (1992) *Sound Theory/Sound Practice*, New York/London: Routledge

– – – (1999) "Nickelodeons and Popular Song' in Brophy, P (ed)

Anderson, B (1991) *Imagined Communities*, London: Verso

Andriote, J (2001) *Hot Stuff: A Brief History of Disco*, New York: Harper Entertainment

Atherton, M (2003) 'Educating the Screen Composer in Australia', *Sounds Australian* n61

Backhouse, T (2003) '*A capella* singing' in Whiteoak, J and Scott-Maxwell, A (eds)

Baker, G.A (1992) 'See me, Hear me', *The Bulletin*, 13/10

Bandt, R (2001) *Hearing Australian Identity: Sites as Acoustic Spaces, An Audible Polyphony*, Melbourne: The Australian Centre, The University of Melbourne, http://www.soundesign.unimelb.edu.au/site/NationPaper/NationPaper.html

Barker, C (2000) *Cultural Studies: Theory and Practice*, London, etc: Sage

Barrett, R (2000) 'NSW releases findings of police misconduct inquiry', *PM* archive, ABC Radio 18/10, http://www.abc.net.au/pm/s201131.htm

Barthes, R (1973) 'The New Citroën' in his *Mythologies*, London: Paladin

– – – (1977) *Image, Music Text*, Glasgow: Fontana

Bebbington, W (ed) (1997) *The Oxford Companion to Australian Music*, Oxford: Oxford University Press

Belfrage, J (1994) *The Great Australian Silence: Inside Acoustic Space*, Melbourne: The Australian Centre, The University of Melbourne, http://www.soundesign.unimelb.edu.au/site/papers/AusSilence.html

Bell, D (1994) *Getting the Best for Your Score: A Filmmakers' Guide to Music Scoring*, Los Angeles: UCLA Press

Bendrups, D (2003) ' 'Latin' music and dance since 1970' in Whiteoak, J and Scott-Maxwell, A (eds)

Bennett, B (1999) 'my instinction: kiss or kill?' in Caputo, R and Burton, G (eds) *Second Take: Australian filmmakers talk*, Sydney: Allen and Unwin

Benzie, T (2002) 'In Fine Voice', *The Lamp* (Magazine of the NSW Nurses' Association) v59n7, August

Berardinelli, J (1995) 'Review of *Muriel's Wedding*', http://www.rottentomatoes.com/click/movie-1065621

Bertrand, I (2003) 'New Histories of the Kelly Gang: Gregor Jordan's *Ned Kelly*', *Senses of Cinema* n26, http://www.sensesofcinema.com.contents/03/26/ned_kelly.html

Blunt, B (2001) *Blunt: A Biased History of Australian Rock*, Melbourne: Prowling Tiger Press

Bordwell, D and Thompson, K (1985) 'Fundamental aesthetics of sound: Sound in the Cinema' in Weis, E and Belton, J (eds)

243

Bowlby, J (1980) *Attachment and Loss* (2nd edn), London: Hogarth

Branston, G (2000) *Cinema and Cultural Modernity*, Buckingham (UK)/Philadelphia (USA): Open University Press

Brewster, B and Broughton, F (2000) *Last Night a DJ Saved My Life: The History of the Disc Jockey*, New York: Grove Press

Bridie, D (1999) 'By way of explanation', *In a Savage Land* CD booklet, EMI

Brophy, P (ed) (1999) *Cinesonic: The World of Sound in Film*, Sydney: Australian Film, Television and Radio School

Brown, R.S (1994) *Overtones and Undertones: Reading Film Music*, Los Angeles: UCLA Press

Bruce, G (1985) *Bernard Herrmann: Film Music and Narrative*, Ann Arbor (USA): UMI Research Press

Burch, N (1985) 'On the Structural Use Of Sound' in Weis, E and Belton, J (eds)

Bush, N (2003) 'Mick Harvey', http://mana.com.au/mana_composers/composers_harvey.htm

Butler, J (1990) *Gender Trouble: Feminism and the Subversion of Identity*, New York: Routledge

Butterss, P (1998) 'When being a man is all you've got: masculinity in *Romper Stomper*, *Idiot Box*, *Blackrock* and *The Boys*', *Metro* n117

– – – (2001) 'Becoming a Man in Australian Film in the Early 1990s: *The Big Steal*, *Death in Brunswick*, *Strictly Ballroom* and *The Heartbreak Kid*' in Craven, I (ed)

Cairns, D and Richards, S (1988) *Writing Ireland: Colonialism, Nationalism and Culture*, Manchester: Manchester University Press

Caputo, R (2003) 'Very Sound: Phillip Brophy', *Metro* n136

Carrington, K (1998) *Who killed Leigh Leigh? A story of shame and mateship in an Australian town*, Sydney: Random House

Castles, J (1992) '*Tjungaringanyi*: Aboriginal rock' in Hayward, P (ed) *From Pop to Punk to Postmodernism*, Allen and Unwin

– – – (1998) '*Tjungaringanyi*: Aboriginal Rock (1971-1991)' in Hayward, P (ed) *Sound Alliances: Indigenous Peoples, Cultural Politics and Popular Music in the Pacific*, London: Cassell

Castles, S (2003) 'In the Nick of Time', *The Bulletin* v121n28, http://bulletin.ninemsn.com.au/bulletin/eddesk.nsf/0/

Castles, S et al (1988) *Mistaken Identity: Multiculturalism and the Demise of Nationalism in Australia*, Sydney: Pluto Press

Chapple, P (2003) *The Eighth Wonder* [Study Kit], Sydney: Australian Music Centre

Chion, M (1994) *Audio-Vision: Sound on Screen* (trans Gorbman, C) (2nd edn), New York: Columbia University Press

– – – (1999) *The Voice in Cinema* (trans Gorbman, C), New York: Columbia University Press

Chorus America (2001) *About Choral Singing*, http://chorusamerica.org/about_choralsinging.shtml

Clover, C (1992) *Men, Women, and Chain Saws: Gender in the Modern Horror Film*, Princeton (USA): Princeton University Press

Connell, R.W (1995) *Masculinities*, Sydney: Allen and Unwin

Conomos, J and Caputo, R (1993) 'Tracey Moffatt interviewed by John Conomos and Raffaele Caputo', *Cinema Papers* v93

Copland, A (1957) *What To Listen For In Music*, London: Penguin Books

Cordaiy, H (2001) '*Lantana*: a Story of Men and Women: An Interview With Ray Lawrence', *Metro* n129/130, Spring

– – – (2002) '*Walking on Water*: an interview with Tony Ayres', *Metro* n133

Coyle, R (ed) (1998) *Screen Scores: Studies in Contemporary Australian Film Music*, Sydney: Allen and Unwin/Australian Film, Television and Radio School

– – – (1998) 'Introduction: Tuning Up' in Coyle, R (ed)

244

– – – (2001) 'Speaking 'Strine': Locating 'Australia' in Film Voice and Speech' in Brophy, P (ed)

– – – (2003) 'Scoring Australia. Film Music and Australian Identities in *Young Einstein*, *Strictly Ballroom* and *The Adventures of Priscilla, Queen of the Desert*', unpublished PhD thesis, Sydney: Macquarie University

Crane, J.L (1994) *Terror and Everyday Life: Singular Moments in the History of the Horror Film*, Thousand Oaks (USA): Sage Publications

Craven, I (ed) *Australian Cinema in the 1990s*, London: Frank Cass Publishers

Creed, B (1993) *The Monstrous Feminine: Film, Feminism, Psychoanalysis*, London: Routledge

Creswell, T and Fabinyi, M (2000) *The Real Thing: Adventures in Australian Rock and Roll*, Sydney: Random House

Crowdy, D and Hayward, P (2001) 'Questions of Origin: George Telek and David Bridie's collaborative recordings', *Kulele* n3

Dalkin, G (2003) 'Interview with Christopher Gordon', http://www.christophergordon.net/master.html

Danbury, H (1996) *Bereavement Counselling Effectiveness*, Aldershot/Brookfield (USA): Avebury

Daniel, A (1994) 'Values' in Bambrick, S (ed) *The Cambridge Encyclopedia of Australia*, Cambridge: Cambridge University Press

Delbridge, A et al (eds) (1997) *The Macquarie Dictionary* (3rd edn), Sydney: Macquarie University Library

– – – (2001) *The Macquarie Dictionary* (Revised 3rd edn), Sydney: Macquarie University Library

Deleuze, G and Guattari, F (1983) *Anti-Oedipus: Capitalism and Schizophrenia*, Minneapolis: University of Minnesota Press

Deleuze, G and Guattari, F (1994) *What is Philosophy* (trans Tomlinson, H and Burchell, G), New York: Columbia University Press

Dermody, S and Jacka, E (1988) *The Screening of Australia: Vol II: Anatomy of a National Cinema*, Sydney: Currency

Dickinson, K (ed) *Movie Music: The Film Reader*, London/New York: Routledge

Dicks, B.L (2002) 'Steve Kilbey and Brett Leigh Dicks talk about everything', http://church.tristesse.com/intrview/9706bld.htm

Doanne, M (1985) 'The Voice in the Cinema: The Articulation of Body and Space' in Weis, E and Belton, J (eds)

Donnelly, K.J (2001) *Film Music: Critical Approaches*, Edinburgh: Edinburgh University Press

Drewe, R (1991) *Our Sunshine*, Melbourne: Penguin Books

Easton, D (1998) 'The role of sound in *To have and to hold*', Sydney: unpublished 'Screen Soundtracks' undergraduate seminar paper, Sydney: Macquarie University

Elder, B (2001) 'Now listen...', *The Sydney Morning Herald*, 15-16/9

– – – (2002) 'Interview With Phillip Noyce', *Sydney Morning Herald*, 16/2

Eng, D (1999) 'Melancholia/Postcoloniality: Loss in *The Floating Life* [sic]', *Qui Parle* v11n2

Enker, D (1994) 'Australia and the Australians', in Murray, S (ed) *Australian Cinema*, Sydney: Allen and Unwin with Australian Film Commission

Enright, N (1994) *A Property of the Clan*, Sydney: Currency Press

Evans, C and Valentine, E (2001) *Do Singing And Swimming Make You Feel Better?* , http://www.pc.rhul.ac.uk/schools/Liz/singing.html

Evans, M (2004) 'Mapping The Matrix: Virtual Spatiality and the Realm of the Perceptual' in Hayward, P (ed)

Ferres, K (2001) '*Idiot Box*: Television, Urban Myths and Ethical Scenarios' in Craven, I (ed)

Feuer, J (1982) *The Hollywood Musical*, Bloomington (USA): Indiana University Press

Flaus, J (2001) 'Be nice or be gone', *Metro* n129/130

Flinn, C (1992) *Strains of Utopia: Gender, Nostalgia and Hollywood Film Music*, Princeton (USA): Princeton University Press

– – – (2000) 'Sound, Woman and the Bomb: Dismembering the "great whatisit" in *Kiss Me Deadly*', *Screening the Past* n10, June, http://www.latrobe.edu.au/screeningthepast/classics/rr0600/cfrr10b.htm

Florianz, M (undated) 'There are 88 notes, I put them in a certain order', http://www.fodonline.com/interview_guygross.html

Ford, A (1993) *Composer to Composer*, Sydney: Allen and Unwin

Freeland, C.A (2000) *The Naked and the Undead: Evil and the Appeal of Horror*, Boulder (USA): Westview Press

French, L (2000) 'Romance, Fantasy, and Female Sexuality in *feeling sexy*', *Metro* n123

Frith, S (1990) 'Rock and Sexuality' in Frith, S and Goodwin, A (eds) *On Record: Rock, Pop and the Written Word*, New York: Pantheon Books

– – – (1996) 'Music and identity' in Hall, S and du Gay, P (eds) *Questions of Cultural Identity*, London: Sage

– – – (2003) 'Music and Everyday Life' in Clayton, M; Trevor Herbert, T and Middleton, R (eds) *The Cultural Study of Music: A Critical Introduction*, London: Routledge

Fung, A (1998) Review of *Floating Life*, http://www.ncf.carleton.ca

Gabriel, P (nd) *Discussing Rabbit-Proof Fence*, http://petergabriel.com/rpf

Ganley, T (2003) 'What's All This Talk About Whiteness?', *Dialogue*, v1n2

Garwood, I (2003) 'Must you remember this? Orchestrating the "standard" pop song in *Sleepless in Seattle*' in Dickinson, K (ed)

Gee, M (1999) 'The Mick Harvey Interview – *To have and to hold*', *Imagazine*, http://www.thei.aust.com/isite/mick1.html

Gibson, R (1983) 'Camera Natura: Landscapes in Australian Film', *Framework* n22-23

– – – (1994) 'Formative Landscapes' in Murray, S (ed) *Australian Cinema*, Sydney: Allen and Unwin

Gleick, J (1987) *Chaos: Making a New Science*, New York: Penguin

Goldsmith, B (2001) 'All Quiet on the Western Front? Suburban Reverberations in recent Australian Cinema' in Craven, I (ed)

Gorbman, C (1985) *Unheard Melodies: Narrative Film Music*, London: BFI Publishing/Indiana University Press

Gordon, C (1992) 'Interview with David Hirschfelder: *Strictly Ballroom*', *APRA newsletter* n6, Winter

Greydanus, S (2003) 'Review of *Babe*', http://www.decentfilms.com/reviews/babe.html

Grossberg, L (2003) 'Cinema, Postmodernity and Authenticity' in Dickinson, K (ed)

Grout, D.J (1960) *A History of Music and Musical Style*, London: J M Dent & Sons

Groves, T (2003) 'Dogs in Space', *Senses of Cinema* n29, Nov-Dec, http://www.sensesofcinema.com/contents/01/15/cteq/dogs_in_space.html

Guiffre, E (2001) ' "... with a gun-totin' trigger-happy tranny named Kinky Renee ...": Identity, Australianness and contemporary popular music', Sydney: unpublished Honours thesis, University of New South Wales

Gunew, S (1994) *Framing Marginality: Multicultural Literary Studies*, Melbourne: Melbourne University Press

Hage, G (1998) *White Nation: Fantasies of White Supremacy in a Multicultural Society*, Sydney: Pluto Press

Hall, M (1996) *Leaving Home: A Conducted Tour Of Twentieth-Century Music With Simon Rattle*, London: Faber and Faber

Hall, S (1985) *Critical Business: The New Australian Cinema in Review*, Adelaide: Rigby

– – – (1990) 'Cultural identity and diaspora' in Rutherford, J (ed) *Identity: Community, Culture, Difference*, London: Lawrence and Wishart

Hallett, B (1991) 'Ingenuity helps film composer hit the right chord', *The Australian* n8347, 25/6, http://www.theaustralian.news.com.au

– – – (1996) 'River deep, mountain high', *The Australian* (Weekend Review) 24-25/8, http://www.theaustralian.news.com.au

Hannan, M (1986) 'Ross Edwards: A Unique Sound World', *APRA Newsletter*, March

Harcourt, T (2002) 'Trade through time', Australian Trade Commission web site, http://www.austrade.gov.au/corporate/layout/0,,0_S1-1_CORPXID0029-2_-3_PWB1 845403-4_-5_-6_-7_,00.html

Harley, R (1998) 'Creating a Sonic Character: Non-Diegetic Sound in the *Mad Max* Trilogy' in Coyle, R (ed)

Haslam, D (2001) *Adventures on the Wheels of Steel*, London: Fourth Estate

Hayden, D (1995) *The Power of Place: Urban Landscapes as Public History*, Cambridge(USA)/London: MIT Press

Hayward, P (1996) 'Music at the Borders: Not Drowning, Waving and their engagement with Papua New Guinean Culture (1986-1994)', Sydney: unpublished PhD thesis Macquarie University

– – – (1997) *Music at the Borders: Not Drowning, Waving and their engagement with Papua New Guinean Culture (1986-1996)*, Sydney: John Libbey and Co

– – – (2001) *Tide Lines: Music, Tourism and Cultural Transition in the Whitsunday Islands*, Lismore (Australia): Music Archive for the Pacific Press

– – – (ed) (2004) *Off The Planet: Music, Sound and Science Fiction Cinema*, Sydney: John Libbey/Perfect Beat Publications

Hayward, S (1997) *Key Concepts in Cinema Studies*, New York: Routledge

– – – (2000) *Cinema Studies: the key concepts* (2nd edn), London/New York: Routledge

Hewson, J (2002) 'A Moving Picture of Hope', *Australian Financial Review*, 12/4

Homan, S (2003) *The Mayor's A Square: Live Music and Law and Order in Sydney*, Sydney: Local Consumption Publications

Hopkins, J (1994) 'A Mapping of Cinematic Places: Icons, Ideology, and the Power of (Mis)representation' in Aitken, S.C and Zonn, L.E (eds) *Place, Power, Situation & Spectacle: A Geography of Film*, Maryland (USA): Rowman and Littlefield

Howson, P and Moore, D (2002) 'A Rabbit-Proof Fence Full of Holes', *The Australian*, 11/3, http://www.bennelong.com.au/papers/Articles/howson-moore.html

Hughes D'eath, T (2002) 'Which Rabbit-Proof Fence? Empathy, Assimilation, Hollywood', *Australian Humanities Review*, September, http://www.lib.latrobe.edu.au/AHR/archive/Issue-September-2002/hughesdaeth.html

Hughes, R (1988) *The Fatal Shore*, London: Pan Books

Human Rights and Equal Opportunity Commission (1997) *Bringing Them Home: Report of the National Inquiry into the Separation of Aboriginal and Torres Strait Islander Children from their Families*, Canberra: Commonwealth of Australia

Iveson, K (1997) 'Partying, Politics and Getting Paid – hip hop and national identity in Australia,' *Overland* n147

Jamrozik, A; Boland, C and Urquhart, R (1995) *Social Change and Cultural Transformation in Australia*, Cambridge: Cambridge University Press

Jeffrey, B (1954) *White Coolies*, Sydney/Melbourne: Angus & Robertson

Jennings, L (2003) 'Tap Dogs Rebooted', *Guardian Unlimited Online*, 8/8, http://www.guardian.co.uk/arts/reviews/story/0,11712,1014356,00.html

Johnson, B and Poole, G (1998) 'Sound and Author/Auteurship: Music in the Films of Peter Weir' in Coyle, R (ed)

Johnson, C (2004) 'Hip Hop Revolution', http://www.geocities.com/SunsetStrip/Balcony/5541/art.html

Joyce, S (1996) 'Brave New Sonic Worlds', *Metro* n108

Karlin, F and Wright, R (1989) *On the Track. A Guide to Contemporary Film Scoring*, New York: Schirmer

Kassabian, A (2001) *Hearing Film: Tracking Identifications in Contemporary Hollywood Film Music*, New York/London: Routledge

Keech, A (2001) 'A review of *The Truman Show*', http://www.shef.ac.uk/~cm1jwb/trumancd.html

Keil, C and Feld, S (1994) *Music Grooves: Essays and Dialogues*, Chicago: University of Chicago Press

Khoo, O (2004) 'The Sacrificial Asian in Australian Film', *Real Time* 59, February–March

Khoo, S, et al (2002) *Second Generation Australians*, Canberra: Australian Centre for Population Research and the Department of Immigration and Multicultural and Indigenous Affairs

Kibby, M and Neuenfeldt, K (1997) 'Sound, Cinema and Aboriginality' in Coyle, R (ed)

Kozloff, S (2000) *Overhearing Film Dialogue*, Berkeley (USA): University of California Press

Kress, G (1988) 'Communication and Culture' in Kress, G (ed) *Communication and Culture: An Introduction*, Sydney: University of New South Wales Press

Kristeva, J (1980) *Desire in Language: A Semiotic Approach to Literature and Art*, Roudiez L.S (ed) (trans Gora, T; Jardine, A and Roudiez L. S), New York: Columbia University Press

– – – (1995) *New Maladies of the Soul* (trans Gumerman, R), New York: Columbia University Press

Kubler-Ross, E (1984) *Living with Death and Dying*, New York: Collier Books

Lacan, J (1977) *The Four Fundamental Concepts of Psychoanalysis* (trans Sheridan, A), London: The Hogarth Press

Lack, R (1997) *Twenty Four Frames Under: A Buried History of Film Music*, London: Quartet Books

Lanza, J (1995) *Elevator Music*, London: Quartet

Law, C (1996) 'Director's Statement', Pardo Film Festival, http://www.pardo.ch/1996/festival96/floatingreg.html

– – – (2001) 'An Interview with Clara Law', http://www.palace.net.au/goddess/clara.htm

Leonard, R (2000) '*Bootmen* review', Australian Catholic Bishops Conference web site, http://www.catholic.org.au/film/2000/bootmen.html

Leydon, R (2004) 'Hooked on Aetherophonics: *The Day the Earth Stood Still*', in Hayward, P (ed)

Lim, B (2001) 'Spectral Times: The Ghost Film As Historical Allegory', *positions: east asia cultures critique* v9n2

Litson, J (2001) 'A father facing the tracks of his fears', *The Australian*, 'The Arts' section, 1/6

Lumby, C (1998) 'Music and Camp: Popular Music Performance in *Priscilla* and *Muriel's Wedding*' in Coyle, R (ed)

Ma, L (2001) 'Reconciliation between Generations and Cultures: Clara Law's Film *Floating Life*', in Ommundsen, W (ed) *Bastard Moon: Essays on Chinese-Australian Writing*, *Otherland Literary Journal* n7, July

Macey, D (2000) *The Penguin Dictionary of Critical Theory*, London: Penguin

Magee, J (1996) 'From Fine Cut To Mix: An Exploration of Processes and Issues in Australian Film Score Composition', unpublished Honours thesis, Lismore: Southern Cross University

Magowan, F (1998) '*Shine*: Musical Narratives and Narrative Scores' in Coyle, R (ed)

Malone, P (1996) 'A *De Profundis* Film' in De Heer, R (ed) *Bad Boy Bubby*, Sydney: Currency Press

Manne, R (2002) 'The Colour of Prejudice', *Sydney Morning Herald*, 23/2, http://smh.com.au/news/2002/23/spectrum/spectrum1.html

– – – (2003) 'A Long Trek to the Truth', *Washington Post*, 2/2

Marchetta, M (1992) *Looking for Alibrandi*, Melbourne: Puffin Books

Margetts, J (1997) '*Blackrock* – the Steven Vidler Interview', *Izine*, http://www.thei.aust.com/film97/vidler.html

Marriott, E (2003) 'Hard-core addiction', *Sydney Morning Herald*, Spectrum 22-23/11

Maxwell, I (2001) 'Hip Hop Down Under Comin' Up' in Mitchell, T (ed) *Global Noise: Rap and Hip-Hop Outside the USA*, Middletown (USA): Wesleyan University Press

McClary, S and Walser, R (1990) 'Start Making Sense! Musicology Wrestles with Rock', in Frith, S and Goodwin, A (eds) *On Record: Rock, Pop and the Written Word*, London: Routledge

McFarlane, B (1983) *Words and Images: Australian Novels into Film*, Melbourne: Heinemann

McFarlane, B; Mayer, G and Bertrand, I (eds) (1999) *The Oxford Companion to Australian Film*, Melbourne: Oxford University Press

McKissock, M and McKissock, D (1995) *Coping With Grief* (3rd edn), Sydney: ABC Books

McLeish, K (1985) *The Penguin Companion To The Arts In The Twentieth Century*, Harmondsworth: Penguin Books

Megalogenis, G (2003) *Faultlines: Race, Work and the Politics of Changing Australia*, Melbourne: Scribe Publications

Metcalfe, A (1994) 'Crisis in Newcastle? Restructuring industry and rewriting the past', Sydney: unpublished paper School of Sociology, University of New South Wales

Millard, K (2001) 'An Interview with Clara Law', *Senses of Cinema*, http://www.sensesof-cinema.com/contents/01/13/law.html

– – – (2001a) '*One Night The Moon*: Interview with John Romeril', *Senses of Cinema* n17, Nov-Dec, http://www.sensesofcinema.com/contents

– – – (2001b) '*One Night The Moon*: Interview with Rachel Perkins', *Senses of Cinema* n17, Nov-Dec, http://www.sensesofcinema.com/contents

Miller, T (1997) 'The Violence of Sound: *Romper Stomper*' in Coyle, R (ed)

Milliken, S (2004) *Longford Lyell Lecture 2004:* If it was easy they'd have girls doing it – *A Life in Australian Film*, Canberra: ScreenSound Australia/National Screen and Sound Archive [Monograph no. 5]

Mills, J (2003) 'Watchdog: Truth and *The Rabbit-Proof Fence*', *Real Time* n48, http://www.realtimearts.net/rt48/mills.htm

Mimura, G.M (2003) 'Black Memories: Allegorizing the Colonial Encounter in Tracey Moffatt's *beDevil* (1993)', *Quarterly Review of Film and Television* v20n2, April–June

Mitchell, T (1996) *Popular Music and Local Identity: Rock, Pop, and Rap in Europe and Oceania*, London: Leicester University Press

– – – (1998) 'Italo-Australian Cinematic Soundscapes' in Coyle, R (ed)

– – – (2000) 'Boxing the 'Roo: Clara Law's *Floating Life* and Transnational Hong Kong–Australian Identities', *UTS Review* v6n2, November

– – – (2001) 'Clara Law's *Farewell China* – A Melodrama of Chinese Migration', *Hybridity* v1n2

– – – (2003a) 'Clara Law's *Floating Life* and Hong-Kong Australian "flexible citizenship"', *Ethnic and Racial Studies* v26n2, March

– – – (2003b) 'Migration, Memory, and Transitional Identities in Clara Law's *Autumn Moon*', *Cultural Studies Review* v9n1, May

Morris, M (1980) 'Personal Relationships and Sexuality', in Murray, S (ed) *The New Australian Cinema*, Melbourne: Nelson

Mortimer, L (1999) 'Masculinity', in McFarlane, B; Mayer, G and Bertrand, I (eds)

Morton, J (2000) 'Aboriginal Religion Today', *The Oxford Companion to Aboriginal Art and Culture*, Oxford/New York: Oxford University Press

Mulvey, L (1975) 'Visual pleasure and narrative cinema', *Screen* v16n3

– – – (1989) *Visual and Other Pleasures*, Bloomington (USA): Indiana University Press

Naldrett, P (2002) 'Another PostGenesis Spectacle', *Music-Critic*, http://www.music-critic.com

Napthali, D (1999) 'Music' in McFarlane, B; Mayer, G & Bertrand, I (eds)

Neumeyer, D and Buhler, J (2001) 'Analytical and Interpretive Approaches to Film Music (1) Analysing the Music', in Donnelly, K.J (ed)

Noone, M and Parker, R (eds) (1989) *Anthology of Australian Music on Disc – Handbook*, Canberra: Canberra School of Music

Noyce, P (2002) 'Interview with Michael Gurr of Radio National's *The Nightclub*', http://www.abc.net.au/arts/film/stories/s488231.htm

– – – (nd) 'Interview with David Edwards', *The Blurb* n15, http://www.the-blurb.com.au/Issue15/PhilNoyce.htm

O'Farrell, P (2000) *The Irish in Australia*, Sydney: University of New South Wales Press

O'Regan, T (1996) *Australian National Cinema*, London: Routledge

Overstreet, J (2002) *Peter Gabriel – Long Walk Home* [Music From the Film *Rabbit-Proof Fence* Looking Closer], http://promontoryartists.org/lookingcloser/music/longwalk-home.htm

Parkes, C.M (1986) *Bereavement: Studies of Grief in Adult Life*, London/New York: Tavistock Publications

Pettman, D (2000) 'The floating life of fallen angels: unsettled communities and Hong Kong cinema', *Postcolonial Studies* v3n1

Phillips, R (2001) 'Confused and Cold-hearted', *World Socialist Web Site*, 30/4, http://www.wsws.org/articles/2001/apr2001/godd-a30.shtml

Prendergast, R.M (1992) *Film Music: A Neglected Art* (2nd edn), New York: Norton

Probyn, F and Simpson, C (2002) 'This Land is Mine/This Land is Me: Reconciling Harmonies in One Night The Moon', *Senses of Cinema* n19, http://www.sensesof-cinema.com/contents

Raphael, B (1984) *Anatomy of Bereavement: a handbook for the caring professions*, London: Hutchinson

Rarebird (1999) 'Michael Hutchence Review', http://home.att.net/~rare-bird9/hutch.html

Rayner, J (2000) 'Western Australia: Australian Western – Moral Landscapes in Australian Film', *Australian Studies* v15n1, Summer

Read, M (1991/2001) *From The Inside: The Confessions of Mark Brandon Read*, London: Blake Publishing [ex-Kilmore (Australia): Floradale]

Riley, V (1992) 'Death Rockers of the world unite! Melbourne 1978-80 – punk rock or no punk rock' in Hayward, P (ed) *From Pop to Punk to Posmodernism: Popular Music and Australian Culture from the 1960s to the 1990s*, Sydney: Allen and Unwin

Roberts, G (1994) *The Mirror of Alchemy: Alchemical Ideas and Images in Manuscripts and Books*, London: The British Library

Roche, M (2000) 'Exploiting the exotic: a Cinematic Journey into Darkness – *In a Savage Land*', *Metro* n121/122

Rowe, D (2001) 'Defining Moments and Refining Myths in the Making of Place Identity: the Newcastle Knights and the Australian Rugby League Grand Final', *Australian Geographical Studies* v39 n1, March

Roxburgh, M (1997) 'Clara Law's *Floating Life* and Australian Identity', *Metro* n110

Sadie, S (ed) (2001) *The New Grove Dictionary of Music and Musicians* v18 (2nd edn), London: Macmillan

Said, E (1978) *Orientalism*, London: Penguin

Samartzis, P (1998) 'Avant-garde Meets Mainstream: The Film Scores of Philip Brophy' in Coyle, R (ed)

Savage, J (1992) *England's Dreaming: Anarchy, Sex Pistols, Punk Rock, and Beyond*, New York: St Martin's Press

Schafer, M (1977) *The Tuning of the World*, Toronto: McClelland and Stewart

Scheer, E (1998) 'Deadly visions: at home in the abyss', *Real Time* n26 (OnScreen), Aug-Sept

Schnieder, S. J (ed) (2001) "Introduction: Psychoanalysis in/and/of the Horror Film", *Senses of Cinema* n15, http://www.sensesofcinema.com/contents/01/15/hor-ror_psych.html

Shand, A (2004) 'Monsters Inc: How Melbourne Became No. 1 With A Bullet', *The Bulletin*, 24/2

Shapiro, M.J (2001) 'Sounds of Nationhood Millennium', *Journal of International Studies* v30n3

Shaviro, S (1993) *The Cinematic Body*, Minnesota (USA): University of Minneapolis Press

Shepherd, J and Wicke, P (1997) *Music and Cultural Theory*, Cambridge: Polity Press

Siemienowicz, R (1999) 'Globalisation and Home Values in New Australian Cinema', *Journal of Australian Studies*, December

Silverman, K (1988) *The Acoustic Mirror: The Female Voice in Psychoanalysis and Cinema*, Bloomington (USA): University of Indiana Press

Simmons, G (2003) 'The Other Side of the Rabbit-Proof Fence', *Australian Screen Education* n31, Autumn

Simpson, C (2000) 'Imagined Geographies: Women's Negotiation of Space in Contemporary Australian Cinema, 1988-98', unpublished PhD thesis, Perth: Murdoch University

Skeoch, A (2003) 'Rabbit-Proof Fence Listening Earth', http://www.listeningearth.com.au/pages/secondary/RPF.html

Smith, A.M.A et al (2003) 'Sex in Australia', Special issue of *Australian and New Zealand Journal of Public Health* v27n2

Smith, G (2001) 'Celtic Australia: bush bands, Irish music and the nation', *Perfect Beat* v5n2, January

Smith, J (1998) *The Sounds of Commerce: Marketing Popular Film Music*, New York: Columbia University Press

– – – (2001) 'Popular Songs and Comic Allusion in Contemporary Cinema' in Wojcik, P and Knight, A (eds) *Soundtrack Available: Essays on Film and Popular Music*, Durham/London: Duke University Press

Stanhope, P (1994) 'The Music of Ross Edwards: Aspects of Ritual', unpublished MA (Hons) thesis, Woollongong: University of Wollongong

Stevenson, D (1998) *Agendas in Place: Urban and Cultural Planning for Cities and Regions*, Rockhampton (Australia): Central Queensland University

Stewart, A (2003) 'Scoring the Soundtrack for Master & Commander – The Far Side of the World', *AudioTechnology* n30

St George, N (nd) *Heavy Entertainment Radio Segment*, http://petergabriel.com/rpf/

Stilwell, R.J (2002) 'Music in Films: A Critical Review of Literature, 1980-1996', *The Journal of Film Music* v1n1

Storm Roberts, J (1999) *The Latin Tinge. The Impact of Latin American Music on the United States* (2nd edn), New York/Oxford: Oxford University Press

Stratton, D (1998) 'Review of *Floating Life*', http://www.theaustralian.com.au/arts/film/

Stratton, J (1998) *Race Daze: Australia in Identity Crisis*, Sydney: Pluto Press

– – – (1999) 'Multiculturalism and the Whitening Machine, or How Australians Become White' in Hage, G and Couch, R (eds) *The Future of Australian Multiculturalism: Reflections on the Twentieth Anniversary of Jean Martin's The Migrant Presence*, Sydney: Research Institute for Humanities and Social Sciences, University of Sydney

– – – (2003) 'Whiter Rock: The "Australian Sound" and the Beat Boom', *Continuum: Journal of Media and Cultural Studies* v17n3

– – – (2004a) 'Pub Rock and the Ballad Tradition in Australian Popular Music', *Perfect Beat: The Pacific Journal of Research into Contemporary Music and Popular Culture* v7n1, January

– – – (2004b) 'Borderline Anxieties: Whitening the Irish and Keeping Out Asylum Seekers' in Moreton-Robinson, A (ed) *Whitening Race: Essays in Social and Cultural Criticism*, Canberra: Aboriginal Studies Press

Summerhayes, C (2001) 'Film as Cultural Performance', unpublished PhD thesis, Canberra: Australian National University

Summers, A (1975) *Damned Whores and God's Police: The Colonization of Women in Australia*, Melbourne: Penguin

251

Tagg, P (1984) 'Understanding Musical 'Time Sense' – Concepts, Sketches and Consequences' in *Tvarspel-Festskrift for Jan Ling (50 Ar)*, Goteburg: Skrifter fran Musikvetenskapliga Institutionen

Tagg, P and Clarida, B (2003) *Ten Little Title Tunes: Towards a Musicology of the Mass Media*, New York/Montreal: The Mass Media Music Scholars' Press

Tan, B (2000) 'Moving Out', http://bonza.rmit.edu.au/essays/1998/multicultural/Moving_Out.html

Taylor, T (1997) *Global Pop: World Music, World Markets*, New York: Routledge

Terrill, R (2000) *The Australians: The Way We Live Now*, Sydney: Doubleday

Thompson, P (2001) 'Review of *The Goddess of 1967*', http://Sunday.ninemsn.com.au/Sunday/film_reviews/article_796.asp, 22/4

Tsiolkas, C (1995) *Loaded*, Sydney: Vintage

Tyson-Chew, N (2003) 'Beyond the Music: A Film Composer's Challenges', *Sounds Australian* n61

Unattributed (1997) *Paradise Road* Production Information, Roadshow Film Distributors (Australia)

– – – (1998) 'In a Savage Land' (press kit), Sydney: Beyond Films

– – – (2001) 'Review of Chopper soundtrack CD', http://www.palace.net.au/chopper/soundtrack.html

– – – (2002) 'Peter Gabriel *Long Walk Home*' (Virgin/Real World), http://www.bbc.co.uk/music/easy/reviews/gabriel_longwalkhome.html

– – – (2004) 'General Latin Mass Lyrics', http://requiemonline.tripod.com/lyrics/latin-lyrics.htm

Urban, A (1993) 'Serious Stuff', *The Australian Magazine*, 20-21/3

van Leeuwen, T (1999) *Speech, Music, Sound*, Basingstoke (UK): Macmillan

Villella, F.A (2001) 'Materialism and Spiritualism in *The Goddess of 1967*', *Senses of Cinema* n13, http://www.sensesofcinema.com/contents/01/13/goddess.html

Walker, R (1999) 'Burkhard Dallwitz', *Australian Musician* n17, Autumn, http://www.australianmusic.asn.au/mag/autumn99/burkhard.html

Walsh, M (1995) 'Running up the Scores' *Time* v146n11, 11/9

– – – (2003), 'Year of the Piss Take', *Real Time* n58, December/January

Ward, R (1958) *The Australian Legend*, Melbourne: Oxford University Press

Wark, M (1994) *Virtual Geography: Living With Global Media Events*, Bloomington (USA): University of Indiana Press

Weis, E (1999) 'Eavesdropping: An Aural Analogue of Voyeurism' in Brophy, P (ed)

Weis, E and Belton, J (eds) (1985) *Film Sound: Theory and Practice*, New York: Columbia University Press

White, H (1998) *The Keeper's Recital: Music and Cultural History in Ireland, 1770-1970*, Cork: Cork University Press

Whiteoak, J and Scott-Maxwell, A (eds) (2003) *Currency Companion to Music and Dance in Australia*, Sydney: Currency

– – – (2003) 'Composing Music' in Whiteoak, J and Scott-Maxwell, A (eds)

Willemen, P, (1994) *Looks and Frictions: Essays in cultural studies and film theory*, Bloomington (USA): Indiana University Press/BFI Publishing

Williams, L (1996) 'When the Woman Looks' in Grant, B.K (ed) *The Dread of Difference: Gender and the Horror Film*, Austin (USA): University of Texas Press

Wilson, W (1994) *Sexuality in the land of Oz: Searching for Safer Sex in the Movies*, Lanham/New York/London: University Press of America

Windschuttle, K (2003) 'Rabbit-Proof Fence: a "true story"?', *New Criterion* v21n7, March

Yue, A (2000) 'Asian Australian Cinema, Asian-Australian Modernity' in Gilbert, H et al, *Diaspora: Negotiating Asian-Australia*, Brisbane: University of Queensland Press

Zion, L (2004) 'I'm with Muriel', *Weekend Australian*, 18-19/9

Index